W9-BVS-867

CHRISTIAN SOCIAL TEACHINGS

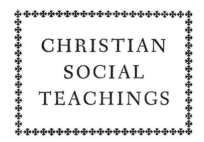

CHRISTIAN SOCIAL TEACHINGS

A READER IN

CHRISTIAN SOCIAL ETHICS

FROM THE BIBLE

TO THE PRESENT

•

COMPILED AND EDITED BY

GEORGE W. FORELL

RELIGION CENTER
ST. MARY, KENOSHA

Soc
671

AUGSBURG PUBLISHING HOUSE
MINNEAPOLIS, MINNESOTA

F

CHRISTIAN SOCIAL TEACHINGS

Copyright © 1966 by George W. Forell

First Augsburg Edition, 1971

A Doubleday Anchor Original, 1966

Library of Congress Catalog Card No. 66-21010

International Standard Book No. 0-8066-1126-X

All rights reserved. No part of this book may be used or reproduced in any manner whatsoever without written permission except in the case of brief quotations in critical articles and reviews. For information address Augsburg Publishing House, 426 South Fifth Street, Minneapolis, Minnesota 55415.

Manufactured in the United States of America

For Madeleine and Mary

The author is grateful to the following for the use of the selections listed below:

The Clarendon Press, Oxford, for material from *On Consideration* by Bernard of Clairvaux, translated by George Lewis. Used by permission.

Fortress Press for material from *Pia Desideria* by Philip Jacob Spener, translated by T. G. Tappert. Used by permission.

Harper & Row, Publishers, for material from *Meister Eckhart—A Modern Translation.* Copyright 1941 by Harper & Row, Publishers; *An Interpretation of Christian Ethics* by Reinhold Niebuhr. Copyright 1935–1956 by Harper & Brothers, *On Religion: Speeches to Its Cultured Despisers* by Friedrich Schleiermacher, translated by John Oman. All used by permission.

Harvard University Press and the Loeb Classical Library for material from "The Epistle of Barnabas," XVIII–XXI, Kirsopp Lake, translator, *The Apostolic Fathers,* Vol. I; "Clement: The Rich Man's Salvation," G. W. Butterworth, translator, *Clement of Alexandria:* Reprinted with the permission of Harvard University Press, the Loeb Classical Library, and William Heinemann, London.

The Macmillan Company for material from *A Theology for the Social Gospel* by Walter Rauschenbusch. Reprinted with permission of The Macmillan Company from *A Theology for the Social Gospel* by Walter Rauschenbusch. Copyright 1917, The Macmillan Company, Renewed 1945 by Pauline E. Rauschenbusch; for material from *Ethics* by Dietrich Bonhoeffer, edited by Eberhard Bethge. Reprinted with permission of The Macmillan Company from *Ethics* by Dietrich Bonhoeffer. Copyright © 1955, The Macmillan Company; for material from *Letters and Papers from Prison* by Dietrich Bonhoeffer, edited by Eberhard Bethge. Reprinted with permission of The Macmillan Company from *Letters and Papers from Prison* by Dietrich Bonhoeffer. Copyright 1953, The Macmillan Company. Both used also with the permission of SCM Press, London.

The Mennonite Quarterly Review for "The Schleitheim Confession of Faith," translated by John C. Wenger, from the issue of October 1945, Vol. XIX, No. 4. Used by permission.

Dr. Reinhold Niebuhr for material from "Justice and Love," which appeared originally in *Christianity and Society,* Fall

1950; from "Christian Faith and Natural Law," which appeared originally in *Theology*, February 1940; from "The Hydrogen Bomb," which appeared originally in *Christianity and Society*, 1950. All used with permission of Dr. Niebuhr.

Oxford University Press for material from *Love, Power, and Justice* by Paul Tillich. Copyright 1954 by Oxford University Press, Inc. Reprinted by permission.

SCM Press and Doubleday & Company, Inc., for material from "The Christian Community and the Civil Community," taken from *Against the Stream: Shorter Post-War Writings 1946–52* by Karl Barth, London: SCM Press (1954). Used by permission.

Wm. B. Eerdmans Publishing Co. for material from *Institutes of the Christian Religion* by John Calvin, translated by Henry Beveridge. Used by permission.

PREFACE

The most persistent and disturbing problem confronting the Christian community since its birth in Palestine two thousand years ago to the very present has been and continues to be its relationship to the surrounding world. How are Christians to deal with the existing social order? How are they to react to it or act upon it? Whether the Christian community was a small minority threatened with extinction by the overwhelming power of a pagan world or whether it was the dominant social force which could shape and direct its environment according to its own desires, the relationship of Christianity to society remained a central and inescapable concern. Thus Christian thought had always to deal with the relationship of the Christian community and the individual Christian with the social and political environment.

While the problem persisted the solutions suggested by various Christian thinkers have been quite different. From the beginning the Old Testament pattern of a chosen people in a Gentile world was formally adopted by the Church, but the fact of the ethnic and cultural diversity of the Christian community made this traditional approach somewhat unreal. Old Testament images were used but in view of the new context received quite different meanings.

Actually three basic patterns of social teaching emerged in the course of history which were elaborated in various ways throughout the entire history of the Christian Church. They could be called the separation pattern, the domination pattern and the integration pattern.

The separation pattern is characterized by the effort to reduce any involvement of the Christian community with the non-Christian world to the barest minimum. If possible, actual geographic withdrawal is practiced in order to avoid any contamination by the things of this world. This option was viable only as long as Christians were a very small group. Afterwards it was possible only for certain small segments within Christendom who practiced withdrawal either as a particularly rigorous form of Christianity or symbolically on behalf of the entire Christian Church. Rural life lent itself to this solution most easily. The more complex and interrelated society became, the more difficult it was to withdraw successfully from the world until in our time the symbolic suicide became the only effective way of withdrawal and of implementing the separation pattern. This, however, was an action so profoundly counter to the injunction against self-destruction that it was not a real alternative except for the most profoundly alienated members of the Christian community. Thus the separation pattern, though one of the most persistent solutions to the problem of the relationship between Church and Culture, has been obsolescent as a result of the interdependence of man in modern society.

The second approach, the domination pattern, has also a long and distinguished history. As soon as the Christian community achieved a position of power, as soon as rulers associated themselves with the Church, an effort was made to use the power of those rulers to enforce a Christian pattern upon all of society, and eventually to outlaw all unbelievers and heretics. This domination pattern was responsible for the development of the great Christian societies dominated by one spirit which permeated every aspect of life. The Christian world-view influenced politics as well as economics, literature as well as architecture; in short the entire culture became an expression of this faith.

The price for this achievement was the suppression or even persecution of dissenters and the isolation of the Christian community from all non-Christian societies. Christendom built an ideological wall around itself and avoided contact with those outside the wall. If followers of another religion, as for example the Jews, were tolerated in Christian lands they were enclosed in ghettos in order to reduce all possible contacts with the Christian world to the absolute minimum. There were lists of forbidden books, and libraries had locked sections where the volumes containing the proscribed ideas were safely sheltered from the eyes of all but the most reliable.

This pattern was more or less successfully maintained into the nineteenth century, when it began to crumble until it became totally obsolete in the twentieth century, except for some few countries whose effort to maintain such a pattern doomed them to become backwaters of history. It was the increasing contacts between Christians and members of other religions or no formal religion at all which undermined the domination pattern.

The integration pattern is a result of the realization that the Christian Faith has to live, if it is to survive, in vital contact with a non-Christian world. This form of relationship, which sometimes has been described as "dialogical," does not imply the abandonment of Christian ideas and convictions, but rather their development and articulation in correlation with the ever-changing spirit of the age. Christian social teachings are now not heteronomously forced upon society but the evolving structures of society are carefully studied and Christian social teachings formulated on the basis of such investigations. This means, however, that Christian social teachings are no longer considered to be absolute and final principles, but rather in the process of development to make the Christian life an instrument of divine reconciliation in a constantly changing society. Whether this integration can be accomplished successfully without abandoning Christianity in the process is the ethical problem of our time. In the solution of this problem the efforts of the past presented in this volume may be of some help.

Obviously not all of them will prove equally suggestive and constructive in the contemporary discussion, but all of them reveal the permanency of the problem which the relationship to the surrounding world has always constituted for the Christian community and the seriousness with which this question has been addressed in the past.

The selections range from the universally accessible writings of the Bible to some obscure Pietist documents here made available for the first time in the English language. The selections are generally substantial rather than mere fragments. They should illustrate the flow and diversity of Christian thought through the centuries and encourage the student of Christian social ethics to see the problems of the day in the context of their historical development.

In the preparation of this book the editor has been assisted by the conscientious help of many people, especially Miss Meredith Medler and Miss Sheila Bauer and the staff of the library of the University of Iowa.

George W. Forell

CONTENTS

INTRODUCTION

Franklin H. Littell

History has often been written as chronicle. Attention is directed to dramatic events in the lives of great men: popes and emperors, bishops and princes. In recent years, however, scholars have devoted increasing attention to factors affecting the common folk. Less time is spent on genealogical charts than formerly, and more upon the control of disease, the development of food supplies, the shifting patterns of social and political controls. Moreover, although decisive moments are recognized and identified, the principle of continuity is stressed. Whatever the unusual incidents which lent an atmosphere of romance and adventure to the lives of rulers, up until very recently (and only excepting very privileged nations even today) the life of the ordinary human being has been a short and almost unrelieved round of struggle for bare existence.

With the development in some areas of economies capable of feeding and housing and providing medical care and even culture for the masses of mankind, with the appearance of leisure and its problems outside the ruling classes of old, and especially with the development of popular sovereignty, teachings which were once mere sermons or bare admonitions to those who held power become explosive instruments. Utopias, the dreamworlds of the frustrated and powerless, become programs of popular revolution. Even within the former ethnic religions (Hinduism, Buddhism, Islam), reform movements have appeared in the last half century to compete in the world forum for the personal commitment of ordinary human beings all over the world.

Church History has often been written as the history of ideas and concepts. During the centuries when decisions within the movement were restricted to lords temporal and spiritual, and intelligent discussion was practically limited to the small number of literate teachers and theologians, this idealistic bent went largely unchallenged. Today, however, large numbers of those who carry the world's work are perfectly capable of carrying on their own "dialogue with the past" without let or hindrance. And in the nature of things their attention is drawn to those materials in the history of the Christian movement which are relevant to their own daily life, problems, and decisions.

The intellectual discipline of believing men remains, of course, very important. But books of Christian sources will not again soon be devoted primarily to those items of interest to a small intellectual class. With the coming of a literate people (a *Laos tou Theou*), concerned for their general priesthood (Protestant) or lay apostolate (Catholic), the moral and ethical and social disciplines of a faithful community press forward for study and debate. Political justice, peace, civil rights, family law, natural liberties, and a host of other "worldly" problems now concern the ordinary member of the Church and the common citizen of the republic—and not just those set aside to teach, or those entrusted with the authority of government.

The great value of Professor Forell's selection and edition of sources lies in the fact that they are aimed not primarily at service to the specialist, although they will be useful at that level, but to any serious student of the dialogue between the Church and the world. Items which were once virtually unknown outside limited circles, and reached the larger constituencies of Church and commonwealth only in translated and abridged form, can now become part of the informed discussions which create a wise public opinion.

This volume is presented, therefore, not only as a comprehensive and professionally highly competent panorama of basic Christian social teachings, of great use to university and seminary students and professors, but as a handbook and reference tool for all who think about these issues with the intention to avoid shipwreck in the shallows of mere contemporaneity.

FRANKLIN H. LITTELL

I OLD TESTAMENT INFLUENCES

The ethics of the Old Testament is the ethics of a chosen people. "Selective service" is the task of this people. It must lead mankind in the conquest of nature by history, and it does so by obeying the Law. "The Law often demands this struggle of man against both external nature and undisciplined human nature, and in this struggle morality emerges."[1] By obeying the Law man is enabled to conquer nature. But for the Jew this obedience is social. As Professor S. W. Baron has expressed it, "Individual righteousness has so little direct bearing on the advent of the Messiah that according to one version he may come in a generation consisting exclusively of sinners. To this day orthodox Jewish ethics has remained in its essence national rather than individual, and this accounts, incidently, for the otherwise incomprehensible legal theorem of the common responsibility of all Jews for the deeds of each."[2] The ethical life is lived by obeying God who has revealed his Law. While other nations worship nature and its creative and destructive powers, Israel is called to worship the God who acted in history by calling his people out of Egypt. This distinction is sharply drawn in Deuteronomy 4:19,20: "And beware lest you lift up your eyes to heaven, and when you see the sun and the moon and the stars, all the host of heaven, you be drawn away and worship them and serve them, things which the Lord your God has allotted to all the peoples under the whole heaven. But the Lord has taken you, and brought you forth out of the iron furnace, out of Egypt, to be a people of his own possession, as at this day."

The insistence that God is revealed in history, not nature, makes the Jews and their social ethical teachings utterly unacceptable to those who worship nature—be it the stars or earth, blood or race. It must be kept in mind while reading their laws as recorded in the Old Testament. Only if an event in history, namely the Exodus, could have ultimate significance for a nation and the world is it possible to understand why certain Jews could later believe that an event like the Cross could be decisive. Thus the significance of Jewish thought for Christianity is not that Christians inherited a number of individual doctrines or particular moral commandments from the Jews. Rather, they learned that not nature but history is decisive. It is not the abstractions of ethical monotheism which Jews and Christians have in common, but the obedience that comes from knowing the God of Abraham and Isaac and Jacob who led Israel out of Egypt and who acts in history.

SELECTION 1
Exodus 20:21–23:33

The following sections from the book of Exodus constitute a summary of the Old Testament Law which later became determinative for much of the social teaching of the Christian Church. In chapter 20:1–17 are the so-called Ten Commandments. It is significant that law is presented here in the context of God's merciful redemption of Israel "out of the land of Egypt, out of the house of bondage" (20:2). God's grace and justice, the gospel and the law, are seen as complementary to each other. It is the God who has demonstrated his steadfast love who gives the law, and obedience to the law is seen as response to this steadfast love. Exodus 20:21–23:33 is known as "The Book of the Covenant." It reveals much of the social situation of the time and deals in detail with social problems from slavery and capital punishment to witchcraft, hospitality, and the regulations of festivals. It illustrates graphically the social character of Old Testament Ethics.

And the people stood afar off, while Moses drew near to the thick cloud where God was. And the Lord said to Moses, "Thus you shall say to the people of Israel: 'You have seen for yourselves that I have talked with you from heaven. You shall not make gods of silver to be with me, nor shall you make for yourselves gods of gold. An altar of earth you shall make for me and sacrifice on it your burnt offerings and your peace offerings, your sheep and your oxen; in every place where I cause my name to be remembered I will come to you and bless you. And if you make me an altar of stone, you shall not build it of hewn stones; for if you wield your tool upon it you profane it. And you shall not go up by steps to my altar, that your nakedness be not exposed on it.'

"Now these are the ordinances which you shall set before them. When you buy a Hebrew slave, he shall serve six years, and in the seventh he shall go out free, for nothing. If he comes in single, he shall go out single; if he comes in married, then his wife shall go out with him. If his master gives him a wife and she bears him sons or daughters, the wife and her children shall be her master's and he shall go out alone. But if the slave plainly says, 'I love my master, my wife, and my children; I will not go out free,' then his master shall bring him to God, and he shall bring him to the door or the doorpost; and his master shall bore his ear through with an awl; and he shall serve him for life.

"When a man sells his daughter as a slave, she shall not go out as the male slaves do. If she does not please her master, who has designated her for himself, then he shall let her be redeemed; he shall have no right to sell her to a foreign people, since he has dealt faithlessly with her. If he designates her for his son, he shall deal with her as with a daughter. If he takes another wife to himself, he shall not diminish her food, her clothing, or her marital rights. And if he does not do these three things for her, she shall go out for nothing, without payment of money.

"Whoever strikes a man so that he dies shall be put to death. But if he did not lie in wait for him, but God let him fall into his hand, then I will appoint for you a place to which he may flee. But if a man willfully attacks another to kill him treacherously, you shall take him from my altar, that he may die.

"Whoever strikes his father or his mother shall be put to death.

"Whoever steals a man, whether he sells him or is found in possession of him, shall be put to death.

"Whoever curses his father or his mother shall be put to death.

"When men quarrel and one strikes the other with a stone or with his fist and the man does not die but keeps his bed, then if the man rises again and walks abroad with his staff, he that struck him shall be clear; only he shall pay for the loss of his time, and shall have him thoroughly healed.

"When a man strikes his slave, male or female, with a rod and the slave dies under his hand, he shall be punished. But if the slave survives a day or two, he is not to be punished; for the slave is his money.

"When men strive together, and hurt a woman with child, so that there is a miscarriage, and yet no harm follows, the one who hurt her shall be fined, according as the woman's husband shall lay upon him; and he shall pay as the judges determine. If any harm follows, then you shall give life for life, eye for eye, tooth for tooth, hand for hand, foot for foot, burn for burn, wound for wound, stripe for stripe.

"When a man strikes the eye of his slave, male or female, and destroys it, he shall let the slave go free for the eye's sake. If he knocks out the tooth of his slave, male or female, he shall let the slave go free for the tooth's sake.

"When an ox gores a man or a woman to death, the ox shall be stoned, and its flesh shall not be eaten; but the owner of the ox shall be clear. But if the ox has been accustomed to gore in the past, and its owner has been warned but has not kept it in, and it kills a man or a woman, the ox shall be stoned, and its owner also shall be put to death. If a ransom is laid on him, then he shall give for the redemption of his life whatever is laid upon him. If it gores a man's son or daughter, he shall be dealt with according to this same rule. If the ox gores a slave, male or female, the owner shall give to their master thirty shekels of silver, and the ox shall be stoned.

"When a man leaves a pit open, or when a man digs a pit and does not cover it, and an ox or an ass falls into it, the owner of the pit shall make it good; he shall give money to its owner and the dead beast shall be his.

"When one man's ox hurts another's, so that it dies, then they shall sell the live ox and divide the price of it; and the dead beast also they shall divide. Or if it is known that the ox has been accustomed to gore in the past, and its owner has not kept it in, he shall pay ox for ox, and the dead beast shall be his.

"If a man steals an ox or a sheep, and kills it or sells it, he shall pay five oxen for an ox, and four sheep for a sheep. He shall make restitution; if he has nothing, then he shall be sold for his theft. If the stolen beast is found alive in his possession, whether it is an ox or an ass or a sheep, he shall pay double.

"If a thief is found breaking in, and is struck so that he dies, there shall be no bloodguilt for him; but if the sun has risen upon him, there shall be bloodguilt for him.

"When a man causes a field or vineyard to be grazed over, or lets his beast loose and it feeds in another man's field, he shall make restitution from the best in his own field and in his own vineyard.

"When fire breaks out and catches in thorns so that the stacked grain or the standing grain or the field is consumed, he that kindled the fire shall make full restitution.

"If a man delivers to his neighbor money or goods to keep, and it is stolen out of the man's house, then, if the thief is found, he shall pay double. If the thief is not found, the owner of the house shall come near to God, to show whether or not he has put his hand to his neighbor's goods.

"For every breach of trust, whether it is for ox, for ass, for sheep, for clothing, or for any kind of lost thing, of which one says, 'This is it,' the case of both parties shall come before God; he whom God shall condemn shall pay double to his neighbor.

"If a man delivers to his neighbor an ass or an ox or a sheep or any beast to keep, and it dies or is hurt or is driven away, without any one seeing it, an oath by the LORD shall be between them both to see whether he has not put his hand to his neighbor's property; and the owner shall accept the oath, and he shall not make restitution. But if it is stolen from him, he shall make restitution to the owner. If it is torn by beasts, let him bring it as evidence; he shall not make restitution for what has been torn.

"If a man borrows anything of his neighbor, and it is hurt or dies, the owner not being with it, he shall make full restitution. If the owner was with it, he shall not make restitution; if it was hired, it came for its hire.

"If a man seduces a virgin who is not betrothed, and lies with her, he shall give the marriage present for her, and make her his wife. If her father utterly refuses to give her to him, he shall pay money equivalent to the marriage present for virgins.

"You shall not permit a sorceress to live.

"Whoever lies with a beast shall be put to death.

"Whoever sacrifices to any god, save to the LORD only, shall be utterly destroyed.

"You shall not wrong a stranger or oppress him, for you were strangers in the land of Egypt. You shall not afflict any widow or orphan. If you do afflict them, and they cry out to me, I will surely hear their cry; and my wrath will burn, and I will kill you with the sword, and your wives shall become widows and your children fatherless.

"If you lend money to any of my people with you who is poor, you shall not be to him as a creditor, and you shall not exact interest from him. If ever you take your neighbor's garment in pledge, you shall restore it to him before the sun goes down; for that is his only covering, it is his mantle for his body; in what else shall he sleep? And if he cries to me, I will hear, for I am compassionate.

"You shall not revile God, nor curse a ruler of your people.

"You shall not delay to offer from the fulness of your harvest and from the outflow of your presses.

"The first-born of your sons you shall give to me. You shall do likewise with your oxen and with your sheep: seven days it shall be with its dam; on the eighth day you shall give it to me.

"You shall be men consecrated to me; therefore you shall not eat any flesh that is torn by beasts in the field; you shall cast it to the dogs.

"You shall not utter a false report. You shall not join hands with a wicked man, to be a malicious witness. You shall not follow a multitude to do evil; nor shall you bear witness in a suit, turning aside after a multitude, so as to pervert justice; nor shall you be partial to a poor man in his suit.

"If you meet your enemy's ox or his ass going astray, you shall bring it back to him. If you see the ass of one who hates you lying under its burden, you shall refrain from leaving him with it, you shall help him to lift it up.

"You shall not pervert the justice due to your poor in his suit. Keep far from a false charge, and do not slay the innocent and righteous, for I will not acquit the wicked. And you shall take no bribe, for a bribe blinds the officials, and subverts the cause of those who are in the right.

"You shall not oppress a stranger; you know the heart of a stranger, for you were strangers in the land of Egypt.

"For six years you shall sow your land and gather in its yield; but the seventh year you shall let it rest and lie fallow, that the poor of your people may eat; and what they leave the wild beasts may eat. You shall do likewise with your vineyard, and with your olive orchard.

"Six days you shall do your work, but on the seventh day you shall rest; that your ox and your ass may have rest, and the son of your bondmaid, and the alien, may be refreshed. Take heed to all that I have said to you; and make no mention of the names of other gods, nor let such be heard out of your mouth."

SELECTION 2
Amos 6, 7, 8, 9:1–7

Amos is the oldest of the prophetic books in the Old Testament. A shepherd from Tekoa near Jerusalem, Amos flourished in the first half of the eighth century B.C. The selection here given reveals the passion for social justice of this prophet. Unwilling to accept the self-congratulations of the Israelites, he proclaims the devastating word of the Lord: "'Are you not like the Ethiopians to me, O people of Israel?' says the Lord. 'Did I not bring up Israel from the land of Egypt, and the Philistines from Caphtor and the Syrians from Kir?'" (9:7). God is the Lord of all men who has selected Israel to serve, not to indulge herself.

Therefore, "Israel shall surely go into exile away from its land" (7:17).

Amos' words, being part of the Bible of the Christian Church, have repeatedly awakened men at other times to their social responsibility.

"Woe to those who are at ease in Zion, and to those who feel secure on the mountain of Samaria, the notable men of the first of the nations, to whom the house of Israel come! Pass over to Calneh, and see; and thence go to Hamath the great; then go down to Gath of the Philistines. Are they better than these kingdoms? Or is their territory greater than your territory, O you who put far away the evil day, and bring near the seat of violence?

"Woe to those who lie upon beds of ivory, and stretch themselves upon their couches, and eat lambs from the flock, and calves from the midst of the stall; who sing idle songs to the sound of the harp, and like David invent for themselves instruments of music; who drink wine in bowls, and anoint themselves with the finest oils, but are not grieved over the ruin of Joseph! Therefore they shall now be the first of those to go into exile, and the revelry of those who stretch themselves shall pass away."

The Lord GOD has sworn by himself (says the LORD, the God of hosts); "I abhor the pride of Jacob, and hate his strongholds; and I will deliver up the city and all that is in it. . . ."

Hear this, you who trample upon the needy, and bring the poor of the land to an end, saying, "When will the new moon be over, that we may sell grain? And the sabbath, that we may offer wheat for sale, that we may make the ephah small and the shekel great, and deal deceitfully with false balances, that we may buy the poor for silver and the needy for a pair of sandals, and sell the refuse of the wheat?"

The LORD has sworn by the pride of Jacob: "Surely I will never forget any of their deeds. Shall not the land tremble on this account, and every one mourn who dwells in it, and all of it rise like the Nile, and be tossed about and sink again, like the Nile of Egypt?"

"And on that day," says the Lord GOD, "I will make the sun

go down at noon, and darken the earth in broad daylight. I will turn your feasts into mourning, and all your songs into lamentation; I will bring sackcloth upon all loins, and baldness on every head; I will make it like the mourning for an only son, and the end of it like a bitter day. . . .

"Though they dig into Sheol, from there shall my hand take them; though they climb up to heaven, from there I will bring them down. Though they hide themselves on the top of Carmel, from there I will search out and take them; and though they hide from my sight at the bottom of the sea, there I will command the serpent, and it shall bite them. And though they go into captivity before their enemies, there I will command the sword, and it shall slay them; and I will set my eyes upon them for evil and not for good."

The Lord, GOD of hosts, he who touches the earth and it melts, and all who dwell in it mourn, and all of it rises like the Nile, and sinks again, like the Nile of Egypt; who builds his upper chambers in the heavens, and founds his vault upon the earth; who calls for the waters of the sea, and pours them out upon the surface of the earth—the LORD is his name.

"Are you not like the Ethiopians to me, O people of Israel?" says the LORD. "Did I not bring up Israel from the land of Egypt, and the Philistines from Caphtor and the Syrians from Kir?"

SELECTION 3
Isaiah 10 and 11

The vision of God as the Lord of history is nowhere more overwhelming than in the book of Isaiah. The two chapters here reproduced show the prophetic repudiation of injustice, the assertion of the sovereignty of God, who uses Assyria as the rod of his anger, and the great vision of a messianic reign when "the wolf shall dwell with the lamb." All three aspects of the prophetic message have influenced Christian social thought.

Woe to those who decree iniquitous decrees, and the writers who keep writing oppression, to turn aside the needy from justice and to rob the poor of my people of their right, that widows may be their spoil, and that they may make the fatherless their prey! What will you do on the day of punishment, in the storm which will come from afar? To whom will you flee for help, and where will you leave your wealth? Nothing remains but to crouch among the prisoners or fall among the slain. For all this his anger is not turned away and his hand is stretched out still.

Ah, Assyria, the rod of my anger, the staff of my fury! Against a godless nation I send him, and against the people of my wrath I command him, to take spoil and seize plunder, and to tread them down like the mire of the streets. But he does not so intend, and his mind does not so think; but it is in his mind to destroy; and to cut off nations not a few; for he says: "Are not my commanders all kings? Is not Calno like Carchemish? Is not Hamath like Arpad? Is not Samaria like Damascus? As my hand has reached to the kingdoms of the idols whose graven images were greater than those of Jerusalem and Samaria, shall I not do to Jerusalem and her idols as I have done to Samaria and her images?"

Shall the ax vaunt itself over him who hews with it, or the saw magnify itself against him who wields it? As if a rod should wield him who lifts it, or as if a staff should lift him who is not wood! Therefore the Lord, the LORD of hosts, will send wasting sickness among his stout warriors, and under his glory a burning will be kindled, like the burning of fire. The light of Israel will become a fire, and his Holy One a flame; and it will burn and devour his thorns and briers in one day. The glory of his forest and of his fruitful land the LORD will destroy, both soul and body, and it will be as when a sick man wastes away. The remnant of the trees of his forest will be so few that a child can write them down.

In that day the remnant of Israel and the survivors of the house of Jacob will no more lean upon him that smote them, but will lean upon the LORD, the Holy One of Israel, in truth. A remnant will return, the remnant of Jacob, to the mighty God. For though your people Israel be as the sand of the sea, only a remnant of them will return. Destruction is decreed, overflowing with righteousness. For the Lord, the LORD of hosts, will make a full end, as decreed, in the midst of all the earth.

Therefore thus says the Lord, the LORD of hosts: "O my people, who dwell in Zion, be not afraid of the Assyrians when they smite with the rod and lift up their staff against you as the Egyptians did. For in a very little while my indignation will come to an end, and my anger will be directed to their destruction. And the LORD of hosts will wield against them a scourge, as when he smote Midian at the rock of Oreb; and his rod will be over the sea, and he will lift it as he did in Egypt. And in that day his burden will depart from your shoulder, and his yoke will be destroyed from your neck."

There shall come forth a shoot from the stump of Jesse, and a branch shall grow out of his roots. And the Spirit of the LORD shall rest upon him, the spirit of wisdom and understanding, the spirit of counsel and might, the spirit of knowledge and the fear of the LORD. And his delight shall be in the fear of the LORD.

He shall not judge by what his eyes see, or decide by what his ears hear; but with righteousness he shall judge the poor, and decide with equity for the meek of the earth; and he shall smite the earth with the rod of his mouth, and with the breath of his lips he shall slay the wicked. Righteousness shall be the girdle of his waist, and faithfulness the girdle of his loins.

The wolf shall dwell with the lamb, and the leopard shall lie down with the kid, and the calf and the lion and the fatling together, and a little child shall lead them. The cow and the bear shall feed; their young shall lie down together; and the lion shall eat straw like the ox. The suckling child shall play over the hole of the asp, and the weaned child shall put his hand on the adder's den. They shall not hurt or destroy in all my holy mountain; for the earth shall be full of the knowledge of the LORD as the waters cover the sea.

In that day the root of Jesse shall stand as an ensign to the peoples; him shall the nations seek, and his dwellings shall be glorious.

In that day the Lord will extend his hand yet a second time to recover the remnant which is left of his people, from Assyria, from Egypt, from Pathros, from Ethiopia, from Elam, from Shinar, from Hamath, and from the coastlands of the sea. He will raise an ensign for the nations, and will assemble the outcasts of Israel, and gather the dispersed of Judah from the four corners of the earth. The jealousy of Ephraim shall depart, and those who harass Judah shall be cut off; Ephraim shall not be jealous of Judah, and Judah shall not harass Ephraim. But they shall swoop down upon the shoulder of the Philistines in the west, and together they shall plunder the people of the east. They shall put forth their hand against Edom and Moab, and the Ammonites shall obey them. And the LORD will utterly destroy the tongue of the sea of Egypt; and will wave his hand over the River with his scorching wind, and smite it into seven channels that men may cross dryshod. And there will be a highway from Assyria for the remnant which is left of his people, as there was for Israel when they came up from the land of Egypt.

II NEW TESTAMENT INFLUENCES

The message of the New Testament has been summarized in Mark 1:15: "The time is fulfilled, and the kingdom of God is at hand; repent and believe in the gospel." The whole of New Testament ethics is implicit in this proclamation. It is the ethics resulting from repentance and faith in the light of the realization that the *kairos* has come, the time is fulfilled, the kingdom of God is at hand.

In continuity with the Old Testament, the New Testament does not present ethical principles but calls man to respond to the action of God. The same God who once led Israel out of Egypt has "in these last days . . . spoken to us by a Son, whom he appointed the heir of all things" (Heb. 1:2). In order to understand the ethical teachings of the New Testament (*Didache*), they must be seen as the description of the result of the proclamation of the redemptive act of God in the life, death, and resurrection of Jesus, the Christ (*Kerygma*).

To men who have lived in the darkness of sin, which expresses itself dramatically in personal as well as social disorder and conflict, comes the light of the world. "What causes wars, and what causes fightings among you?" asks the author of James, and he answers, "Is it not your passions that are at war in your members? You desire and do not have; so you kill. And you covet and cannot obtain; so you fight and wage war" (James 4:1 f.). Into this darkness caused by human sin shines the light and it creates a new society dialectically related to the world, opposing and permeating it simultaneously like leaven or salt. Christians, as a colony of heaven, have a double function. They support the law and the order of God wherever it is found and regardless of whoever happens to administer these structures (cf. Romans 13 or I Peter 2:11 ff.). Yet they are also free from the alien law that slavishly subjects men. Through the power of God the Holy Spirit they are freed to serve mankind to the glory of God the Father. As the author of Titus exhorts: "Remind them [the Christians] to be submissive to rulers and authorities, to be obedient, to be ready for any honest work, to speak evil of no one, to avoid quarreling, to be gentle, and to show perfect courtesy toward all men. For we ourselves were once foolish, disobedient, led astray, slaves to various passions and pleasures, passing our days in malice and envy, hated by men and hating one another; but when the goodness and loving kindness (*philanthropia*) of God our Savior appeared, he saved us, not because of deeds done by us in righteousness, but in virtue of his own mercy, by the washing of regeneration and renewal in the Holy Spirit, which he poured out upon us richly through Jesus Christ our Savior, so that we might be justified by his grace and become heirs in hope of eternal life" (Titus 3:1–7). Men who are alienated from God and therefore from themselves and their fellow men are ethically paralyzed; they are regenerated and renewed in the Holy Spirit. But as Paul writes to the Galatians, "If you are led by the Spirit you are not under the law" (Gal. 5:18). Though supporting the law and bound by it because of the power of sin—in themselves and in others—Christians are free from the law if led by the Spirit. For the old man there is the law which maintains a minimum of order in society. But the people of God have received the *agape* of God poured into their hearts through the Holy Spirit which has been given to them (cf. Rom. 5:5). They are taught by God (*theodidaktoi*) so that Paul can write to the Thessalonians, "Concerning love of the brethren you have no need to have any one write to you, for you yourselves have been taught by God to love one another" (I Thess. 4:9). It is this *agape* as the ground of the life of the Christian in the world which is so eloquently described in I Corinthians 13. It is this same *agape* which undergirds the life of the people of God in I John.

This love, made possible through the grace of God the

Holy Spirit accepted in faith, inspires all later articulations of the Christian ethic.

SELECTION 1
Matthew 5–7

The so-called "Sermon on the Mount" here given is the best-known source of Christian ethics. It states that, "They who, conscious of their poverty, wait weeping and hungering for salvation, are identical with those who are merciful, pure of heart, and peace-makers."[3] Christ's people are the salt of the earth and the light of the world, thus responsible for the well-being of the entire created order and not only for their own religious community. They are called to be perfect even as their heavenly Father is perfect. It is in this context that the Golden Rule appears, and in this context only it assumes an absolute meaning far beyond the similarly worded prudential counsel occurring in some form in the sacred writings of all major religions.

Seeing the crowds, he went up on the mountain, and when he sat down his disciples came to him. And he opened his mouth and taught them, saying:

"Blessed are the poor in spirit, for theirs is the kingdom of heaven.

"Blessed are those who mourn, for they shall be comforted.

"Blessed are the meek, for they shall inherit the earth.

"Blessed are those who hunger and thirst for righteousness, for they shall be satisfied.

"Blessed are the merciful, for they shall obtain mercy.

"Blessed are the pure in heart, for they shall see God.

"Blessed are the peacemakers, for they shall be called sons of God.

"Blessed are those who are persecuted for righteousness' sake, for theirs is the kingdom of heaven.

"Blessed are you when men revile you and persecute you and utter all kinds of evil against you falsely on my account. Rejoice and be glad, for your reward is great in heaven, for so men persecuted the prophets who were before you.

"You are the salt of the earth; but if salt has lost its taste, how shall its saltness be restored? It is no longer good for anything except to be thrown out and trodden under foot by men.

"You are the light of the world. A city set on a hill cannot be hid. Nor do men light a lamp and put it under a bushel, but on a stand, and it gives light to all in the house. Let your light so shine before men, that they may see your good works and give glory to your Father who is in heaven.

"Think not that I have come to abolish the law and the prophets; I have come not to abolish them but to fulfil them. For truly, I say to you, till heaven and earth pass away, not an iota, not a dot, will pass from the law until all is accomplished. Whoever then relaxes one of the least of these commandments and teaches men so, shall be called least in the kingdom of heaven; but he who does them and teaches them shall be called great in the kingdom of heaven. For I tell you, unless your righteousness exceeds that of the scribes and Pharisees, you will never enter the kingdom of heaven.

"You have heard that it was said to the men of old, 'You shall not kill; and whoever kills shall be liable to judgment.' But I say to you that every one who is angry with his brother shall be liable to judgment; whoever insults his brother shall be liable to the council, and whoever says, 'You fool!' shall be liable to the hell of fire. So if you are offering your gift at the altar, and there remember that your brother has something against you, leave your gift there before the altar and go; first be reconciled to your brother, and then come and offer your gift. Make friends quickly with your accuser, while you are going with him to court, lest your accuser hand you over to the judge, and the judge to the guard, and you be put in prison; truly, I say to you, you will never get out till you have paid the last penny.

"You have heard that it was said, 'You shall not commit adultery.' But I say to you that every one who looks at a woman lustfully has already committed adultery with her in his heart. If your right eye causes you to sin, pluck it out and throw it away; it is better that you lose one of your members than that your whole body be thrown into hell. And if your right hand causes you to sin, cut it off and throw it away; it is better that you lose one of your members than that your whole body go into hell.

"It was also said, 'Whoever divorces his wife, let him give her a certificate of divorce.' But I say to you that every one who divorces his wife, except on the ground of unchastity, makes her an adulteress; and whoever marries a divorced woman commits adultery.

"Again you have heard that it was said to the men of old, 'You shall not swear falsely, but shall perform to the Lord what you have sworn.' But I say to you, Do not swear at all, either by heaven, for it is the throne of God, or by the earth, for it is his footstool, or by Jerusalem, for it is the city of the great King. And do not swear by your head, for you cannot make one hair white or black. Let what you say be simply 'Yes' or 'No'; anything more than this comes from evil.

"You have heard that it was said, 'An eye for an eye and a tooth for a tooth.' But I say to you, Do not resist one who is evil. But if any one strikes you on the right cheek, turn to him the other also; and if any one would sue you and take your coat, let him have your cloak as well; and if any one forces you to go one mile, go with him two miles. Give to him who begs from you, and do not refuse him who would borrow from you.

"You have heard that it was said, 'You shall love your neighbor and hate your enemy.' But I say to you, Love your enemies and pray for those who persecute you, so that you may be sons of your Father who is in heaven; for he makes his sun rise on the evil and on the good, and sends rain on the just and on the unjust. For if you love those who love you, what reward have you? Do not even the tax collectors do the same? And if you salute only your brethren, what more are you doing than others? Do not even the Gentiles do the same? You, therefore, must be perfect, as your heavenly Father is perfect.

"Beware of practicing your piety before men in order to be seen by them; for then you will have no reward from your Father who is in heaven.

"Thus, when you give alms, sound no trumpet before you, as the hypocrites do in the synagogues and in the streets, that they may be praised by men. Truly, I say to you, they have their reward. But when you give alms, do not let your left hand know what your right hand is doing, so that your alms may be in secret; and your Father who sees in secret will reward you.

"And when you pray, you must not be like the hypocrites; for they love to stand and pray in the synagogues and at the street corners, that they may be seen by men. Truly, I say to you, they have their reward. But when you pray, go into your room and shut the door and pray to your Father who is in secret; and your Father who sees in secret will reward you.

"And in praying do not heap up empty phrases as the Gentiles do; for they think that they will be heard for their many words. Do not be like them, for your Father knows what you need before you ask him. Pray then like this: Our Father who art in heaven, Hallowed be thy name. Thy kingdom come, Thy will be done, On earth as it is in heaven. Give us this day our daily bread; And forgive us our debts, As we also have forgiven our debtors; And lead us not into temptation, But deliver us from evil.

For if you forgive men their trespasses, your heavenly Father also will forgive you; but if you do not forgive men their trespasses, neither will your Father forgive your trespasses.

"And when you fast, do not look dismal, like the hypocrites, for they disfigure their faces that their fasting may be seen by men. Truly, I say to you, they have their reward. But when you fast, anoint your head and wash your face, that your fasting may not be seen by men but by your Father who is in secret; and your Father who sees in secret will reward you.

"Do not lay up for yourselves treasures on earth, where moth and rust consume and where thieves break in and steal, but lay up for yourselves treasures in heaven, where neither moth nor rust consumes and where thieves do not break in and steal. For where your treasure is, there will your heart be also.

"The eye is the lamp of the body. So, if your eye is sound, your whole body will be full of light; but if your eye is not sound, your whole body will be full of darkness. If then the light in you is darkness, how great is the darkness!

"No one can serve two masters; for either he will hate the one and love the other, or he will be devoted to the one and despise the other. You cannot serve God and mammon.

"Therefore I tell you, do not be anxious about your life, what you shall eat or what you shall drink, nor about your body, what you shall put on. Is not life more than food, and the body more than clothing? Look at the birds of the air: they neither sow nor reap nor gather into barns, and yet your heavenly Father feeds them. Are you not of more value than they? And which of you by being anxious can add one cubit to his span of life? And why are you anxious about clothing? Consider the lilies of the field, how they grow; they neither toil nor spin; yet I tell you, even Solomon in all his glory was not arrayed like one of these. But if God so clothes the grass of the field, which today is alive and tomorrow is thrown into the oven, will he not much more clothe you, O men of little faith? Therefore do not be anxious, saying, 'What shall we eat?' or 'What shall we drink?' or 'What shall we wear?' For the Gentiles seek all these things; and your heavenly Father knows that you need them all. But seek first his kingdom and his righteousness, and all these things shall be yours as well.

"Therefore do not be anxious about tomorrow, for tomorrow will be anxious for itself. Let the day's own trouble be sufficient for the day.

"Judge not, that you be not judged. For with the judgment you pronounce you will be judged, and the measure you give will be the measure you get. Why do you see the speck that is in your brother's eye, but do not notice the log that is in your own eye? Or how can you say to your brother, 'Let me take the speck out of your eye,' when there is the log in your own eye? You hypocrite, first take the log out of your own eye, and then you will see clearly to take the speck out of your brother's eye.

"Do not give dogs what is holy; and do not throw your pearls before swine, lest they trample them underfoot and turn to attack you.

"Ask, and it will be given you; seek and you will find; knock, and it will be opened to you. For every one who asks receives, and he who seeks finds, and to him who knocks it will be opened. Or what man of you, if his son asks him for a loaf, will give him a stone? Or if he asks for a fish, will give him a serpent? If you then, who are evil, know how to give good gifts to your children, how much more will your Father who is in heaven give good things to those who ask him? So whatever you wish that men would do to you, do so to them; for this is the law and the prophets.

"Enter by the narrow gate; for the gate is wide and the way is easy, that leads to destruction, and those who enter by it are many. For the gate is narrow and the way is hard, that leads to life, and those who find it are few.

"Beware of false prophets, who come to you in sheep's clothing but inwardly are ravenous wolves. You will know them by their fruits. Are grapes gathered from thorns, or figs from thistles? So, every sound tree bears good fruit, but the bad tree bears evil fruit. A sound tree cannot bear evil fruit, nor can a bad tree bear good fruit. Every tree that does not bear good fruit is cut down and thrown into the fire. Thus you will know them by their fruits.

"Not every one who says to me, 'Lord, Lord,' shall enter the kingdom of heaven, but he who does the will of my Father who is in heaven. On that day many will say to me, 'Lord, Lord, did we not prophesy in your name, and cast out demons in your name, and do many mighty works in your name?' And then will I declare to them, 'I never knew you; depart from me, you evildoers.'

"Every one then who hears these words of mine and does them will be like a wise man who built his house upon the rock; and the rain fell, and the floods came, and the winds blew and beat upon that house, but it did not fall, because it had been founded on the rock. And every one who hears these words of mine and does not do them will be like a foolish man who built his house upon the sand; and the rain fell, and the floods came, and the winds blew and beat against that house, and it fell; and great was the fall of it."

And when Jesus finished these sayings, the crowds were astonished at his teaching, for he taught them as one who had authority, and not as their scribes.

SELECTION 2
Matthew 25:31–46

The Parable of the Last Judgment restates in graphic terms, "You will know them by their fruits" (Matthew 7:20).

That man serves God by serving the neighbor is part of the Old Testament tradition. According to Isaiah 58:6, 7, the Lord says, "Is not this the fast that I choose: to loose the bonds of wickedness, to undo the thongs of the yoke, to let the oppressed go free, and to break every yoke? Is it not to share your bread with the hungry, and bring the homeless poor into your house; when you see the naked, to cover him, and not to hide yourself from your own flesh?" What is new is that the Christian is told that he meets the Christ himself in the hungry and thirsty, in the stranger and the naked, in the sick and the imprisoned.

"When the Son of man comes in his glory, and all the angels with him, then he will sit on his glorious throne. Before him will be gathered all the nations, and he will separate them one from another as a shepherd separates the sheep from the goats, and he will place the sheep at his right hand, but the goats at the left. Then the King will say to those at his right hand, 'Come, O blessed of my Father, inherit the kingdom prepared for you from the foundation of the world; for I was hungry and you gave me food, I was thirsty and you gave me drink, I was a stranger and you welcomed me, I was naked and you clothed me, I was sick and you visited me, I was in prison and you came to me.' Then the righteous will answer him, 'Lord, when did we see thee hungry and feed thee, or thirsty and give thee drink? And when did we see thee a stranger and welcome thee, or naked and clothe thee? And when did we see thee sick or in prison and visit thee?' And the King will answer them, 'Truly, I say to you, as you did it to one of the least of these my brethren, you did it to me.'

Then he will say to those at his left hand, 'Depart from me, you cursed, into the eternal fire prepared for the devil and his angels; for I was hungry and you gave me no food, I was thirsty and you gave me no drink, I was a stranger and you did not welcome me, naked and you did not clothe me, sick and in prison and you did not visit me.' Then they also will answer, 'Lord, when did we see thee hungry or thirsty or a stranger or naked or sick or in prison, and did not minister to thee?' Then he will answer them, 'Truly, I say to you, as you did it not to one of the least of these, you did it not to me.' And they will go away into eternal punishment, but the righteous into eternal life."

SELECTION 3
Romans 13, *Ephesians* 5 and 6:1–20

These selections from the Pauline epistles show the dialectic relationship of the Christian to the world whose rulers are accepted as agents of God but which nevertheless is seen under the domination of the evil powers which must be opposed. Love (*agape*), is described as the fulfillment of the law. The selection from Ephesians gives some very practical illustrations of the manner in which this love is at work in the world.

Romans 13 Let every person be subject to the governing authorities. For there is no authority except from God, and those that exist have been instituted by God. Therefore he who resists the authorities resists what God has appointed, and those who resist will incur judgment. For rulers are not a terror to good conduct, but to bad. Would you have no fear of him who is in authority? Then do what is good, and you will receive his approval, for he is God's servant for your good. But if you do wrong, be afraid, for he does not bear the sword in vain; he is the servant of God to execute his wrath on the wrongdoer. Therefore one must be subject, not only to avoid God's wrath but also for the sake of conscience. For the same reason you also pay taxes, for the authorities are ministers of God, attending to this very thing. Pay all of them their dues, taxes to whom taxes are due, revenue to whom revenue is due, respect to whom respect is due, honor to whom honor is due.

Owe no one anything, except to love one another; for he who loves his neighbor has fulfilled the law. The commandments, "You shall not commit adultery, You shall not kill, You shall not steal, You shall not covet," and any other commandment, are summed up in this sentence, "You shall love your neighbor as yourself." Love does no wrong to a neighbor; therefore love is the fulfilling of the law.

Besides this you know what hour it is, how it is full time now for you to wake from sleep. For salvation is nearer to us now than when we first believed; the night is far gone, the day is at hand. Let us then cast off the works of darkness and put on the armor of light; let us conduct ourselves becomingly as in the day, not in reveling and drunkenness, not in debauchery and licentiousness, not in quarreling and jealousy. But put on the Lord Jesus Christ, and make no provision for the flesh, to gratify its desires.

Ephesians 5 and 6:1–20 Therefore be imitators of God, as beloved children. And walk in love, as Christ loved us and gave himself up for us, a fragrant offering and sacrifice to God.

But immorality and all impurity or covetousness must not even be named among you, as is fitting among saints. Let there be no filthiness, nor silly talk, nor levity, which are not fitting; but instead let there be thanksgiving. Be sure of this, that no immoral or impure man, or one who is covetous (that is, an idolator), has any inheritance in the kingdom of Christ and of God. Let no one deceive you with empty words, for it is because of these things that the wrath of God comes upon the sons of disobedience. Therefore do not associate with them, for once you were darkness, but now you are light in the Lord; walk as children of light (for the fruit of light is found in all that is good and right and true), and try to learn what is pleasing to the Lord. Take no part in the unfruitful works of darkness, but instead expose them. For it is a shame even to speak of the things that they do in secret; but when anything is exposed by the light it becomes visible, for anything that becomes visible is light. Therefore it is said, "Awake, O sleeper, and arise from the dead, and Christ shall give you light."

Look carefully then how you walk, not as unwise men but as wise, making the most of the time, because the days are evil. Therefore do not be foolish, but understand what the will of the Lord is. And do not get drunk with wine, for that is debauchery; but be filled with the Spirit, addressing one another in psalms and hymns and spiritual songs, singing and making melody to the Lord with all your heart, always and for everything giving thanks in the name of our Lord Jesus Christ to God the Father.

Be subject to one another out of reverence for Christ. Wives, be subject to your husbands, as to the Lord. For the husband is the head of the wife as Christ is the head of the church, his body, and is himself its Savior. As the church is subject to Christ, so let wives also be subject in everything to their husbands. Husbands, love your wives, as Christ loved the church and gave himself up for her, that he might sanctify her, having cleansed her by the washing of water with the word, that the church might be presented before him in splendor, without spot or wrinkle or any such thing, that she might be holy and without blemish. Even so husbands should love their wives as their own bodies. He who loves his wife loves himself. For no man ever hates his own flesh, but nourishes and cherishes it, as Christ does the church, because we are members of his body. "For this reason a man shall leave his father and mother and be joined to his wife, and the two shall become one." This is a great mystery, and I take it to mean Christ and the church; however, let each one of you love his wife as himself, and let the wife see that she respects her husband.

Children, obey your parents in the Lord, for this is right. "Honor your father and mother" (this is the first commandment with a promise), "that it may be well with you and that you may live long on the earth." Fathers, do not provoke your children to anger, but bring them up in the discipline and instruction of the Lord.

Slaves, be obedient to those who are your earthly masters, with fear and trembling, in singleness of heart, as to Christ; not in the way of eyeservice, as men-pleasers, but as servants of Christ, doing the will of God from the heart, rendering service with a good will as to the Lord and not to men, knowing that whatever good any one does, he will receive the same again from the Lord, whether he is a slave or free. Masters, do the same to them, and forbear threatening, knowing that he who is both their Master and yours is in heaven, and that there is no partiality with him.

Finally, be strong in the Lord and in the strength of his might. Put on the whole armor of God, that you may be able to stand against the wiles of the devil. For we are not contending against flesh and blood, but against the principalities, against the powers, against the world rulers of this present darkness, against the spiritual hosts of wickedness in the heavenly places. Therefore take the whole armor of God, that you may be able to withstand in the evil day, and having done all, to stand. Stand therefore, having girded your loins with truth, and having put on the breastplate of righteousness, and having shod your feet with the equipment of the gospel of peace; above all taking the shield of faith, with which you can quench all the flaming darts of the evil one. And take the helmet of salvation, and the sword of the Spirit, which is the word of God. Pray at all times in the Spirit, with all prayer and supplication. To that end keep alert with all perseverance, making supplication for all the saints, and also for me, that utterance may be given me in opening my mouth boldly to proclaim the mystery of the gospel, for which I am an ambassador in chains; that I may declare it boldly, as I ought to speak.

SELECTION 4
I Peter 2:9–3:22

The author develops the duties of the Christians in the world as a people whose citizenship is in heaven. He calls them to follow the example of Christ, who now rules the universe.

But you are a chosen race, a royal priesthood, a holy nation, God's own people, that you may declare the wonderful deeds of him who called you out of darkness into his marvelous light. Once you were no people but now you are God's people; once you had not received mercy but now you have received mercy.

Beloved, I beseech you as aliens and exiles to abstain from the passions of the flesh that wage war against your soul. Maintain good conduct among the Gentiles, so that in case they speak against you as wrongdoers, they may see your good deeds and glorify God on the day of visitation.

Be subject for the Lord's sake to every human institution, whether it be to the emperor as supreme, or to governors as sent by him to punish those who do wrong and to praise those who do right. For it is God's will that by doing right you should put to silence the ignorance of foolish men. Live as free men, yet without using your freedom as a pretext for evil; but live as servants of God. Honor all men. Love the brotherhood. Fear God. Honor the emperor.

Servants, be submissive to your masters with all respect, not only to the kind and gentle but also to the overbearing. For one is approved if, mindful of God, he endures pain while suffering unjustly. For what credit is it, if when you do wrong and are beaten for it you take it patiently? But if when you do right and suffer for it you take it patiently, you have God's approval. For to this you have been called, because Christ also suffered for you, leaving you an example, that you should follow in his steps. He committed no sin; no guile was found on his lips. When he was reviled, he did not revile in return; when he suffered, he did not threaten; but he trusted to him who judges justly. He himself bore our sins in his body on the tree, that we might die to sin and live to righteousness. By his wounds you have been healed. For you were straying like sheep, but have now returned to the Shepherd and Guardian of your souls.

Likewise you wives, be submissive to your husbands, so that some, though they do not obey the word, may be won without a word by the behavior of their wives, when they see your reverent and chaste behavior. Let not yours be the outward adorning with braiding of hair, decoration of gold, and wearing of robes, but let it be the hidden person of the heart with the imperishable jewel of a gentle and quiet spirit, which in God's sight is very precious. So once the holy women who hoped in God used to adorn themselves and were submissive to their husbands, as Sarah obeyed Abraham, calling him lord. And you are now her children if you do right and let nothing terrify you.

Likewise you husbands, live considerately with your wives, bestowing honor on the woman as the weaker sex, since you are joint heirs of the grace of life, in order that your prayers may not be hindered.

Finally, all of you, have unity of spirit, sympathy, love of the brethren, a tender heart and a humble mind. Do not return evil for evil or reviling for reviling; but on the contrary bless, for to this you have been called, that you may obtain a blessing. For

"He that would love life
and see good days,
let him keep his tongue from evil
and his lips from speaking guile;
let him turn away from evil and do right;
let him seek peace and pursue it.
For the eyes of the Lord are upon the righteous,
and his ears are open to their prayer.
But the face of the Lord is against those that do evil."

Now who is there to harm you if you are zealous for what is right? But even if you do suffer for righteousness' sake, you will be blessed. Have no fear of them, nor be troubled, but in your hearts reverence Christ as Lord. Always be prepared to make a defense to any one who calls you to account for the hope that is in you, yet do it with gentleness and reverence; and keep your conscience clear, so that, when you are abused, those who revile your good behavior in Christ may be put to shame.

SELECTION 5
I John 3:1–18, 4:1–21

Nowhere is the source of the Christian life in the love of God more colorfully expressed than in this letter, which claims that he who does not love his brother cannot love God.

See what love the Father has given us, that we should be called children of God; and so we are. The reason why the world does not know us is that it did not know him. Beloved, we are God's children now; it does not yet appear what we shall be, but we know that when he appears we shall be like him, for we shall see him as he is. And every one who thus hopes in him purifies himself as he is pure.

Every one who commits sin is guilty of lawlessness; sin is lawlessness. You know that he appeared to take away sins, and in him there is no sin. No one who abides in him sins; no one who sins has either seen him or known him. Little children, let no one deceive you. He who does right is righteous, as he is righteous. He who commits sin is of the devil; for the devil has sinned from the beginning. The reason the Son of God appeared was to destroy the works of the devil. No one born of God commits sin; for God's nature abides in him, and he cannot sin because he is born of God. By this it may be seen who are the children of God, and who are the children of the devil: whoever does not do right is not of God, nor he who does not love his brother.

For this is the message which you have heard from the beginning, that we should love one another, and not be like Cain who was of the evil one and murdered his brother. And why did he murder him? Because his own deeds were evil and his brother's righteous. Do not wonder, brethren, that the world hates you. We know that we have passed out of death into life, because we love the brethren. He who does not love remains in death. Any one who hates his brother is a murderer, and you know that no murderer has eternal life abiding in him. By this we know love, that he laid down his life for us; and we ought to lay down our lives for the brethren. But if any one has the world's goods and sees his brother in need, yet closes his heart against him, how does God's love abide in him? Little children, let us not love in word or speech but in deed and in truth.

✧ ✧ ✧ ✧

Beloved, let us love one another; for love is of God, and he who loves is born of God and knows God. He who does not love does not know God; for God is love. In this the love of God was made manifest among us, that God sent his only Son into the world, so that we might live through him. In this is love, not that we loved God but that he loved us and sent his Son to be the expiation for our sins. Beloved, if God so loved us, we also ought to love one another. No man has ever seen God; if we love one another, God abides in us and his love is perfected in us.

By this we know that we abide in him and he in us, because he has given us of his own Spirit. And we have seen and testify that the Father has sent his Son as the Savior of the world. Whoever confesses that Jesus is the Son of God, God abides in him, and he in God. So we know and believe the love God has for us. God is love, and he who abides in love abides in God, and God abides in him. In this is love perfected with us, that we may have confidence for the day of judgment, because as he is so are we in this world. There is no fear in love, but perfect love casts out fear. For fear has to do with punishment, and he who fears is not perfected in love. We love, because he first loved us. If any one says, "I love God," and hates his brother, he is a liar; for he who does not love his brother whom he has seen, cannot love God whom he has not seen. And this commandment we have from him, that he who loves God should love his brother also.

SELECTION 6
Revelation 13

While the Book of Revelation is not easy to understand, the thirteenth chapter here given is the counterpart to Romans 13. There is a limit to the acceptance of the authority of the rulers of this world. The saints will endure. This book, in spite of its ambiguity, has been for Christians a source of power to resist the demonic pretensions of human authorities all through the history of the Christian Church.

And I saw a beast rising out of the sea, with ten horns and seven heads, with ten diadems upon its horns and a blasphemous name upon its heads. And the beast that I saw was like a leopard, its feet were like a bear's, and its mouth was like a lion's mouth. And to it the dragon gave his power and his throne and great authority. One of its heads seemed to have a mortal wound, but its mortal wound was healed, and the whole earth followed the beast with wonder. Men worshiped the dragon, for he had given his authority to the beast, and they worshiped the beast, saying, "Who is like the beast, and who can fight against it?"

And the beast was given a mouth uttering haughty and blasphemous words, and it was allowed to exercise authority for forty-two months; it opened its mouth to utter blasphemies against God, blaspheming his name and his dwelling, that is, those who dwell in heaven. Also it was allowed to make war on the saints and to conquer them. And authority was given it over every tribe and people and tongue and nation, and all who dwell on earth will worship it, every one whose name has not been written before the foundation of the world in the book of life of the Lamb that was slain. If any one has an ear, let him hear:

> If any one is to be taken captive,
>   to captivity he goes;
> if any one slays with the sword,
>   with the sword must he be slain.

Here is a call for the endurance and faith of the saints.

Then I saw another beast which rose out of the earth; it had two horns like a lamb and it spoke like a dragon. It exercises all the authority of the first beast in its presence, and makes the earth and its inhabitants worship the first beast, whose mortal wound was healed. It works great signs, even making fire come down from heaven to earth in the sight of men; and by the signs which it is allowed to work in the presence of the beast, it deceives those who dwell on earth, bidding them make an image for the beast which was wounded by the sword and yet lived; and it was allowed to give breath to the image of the beast so that the image of the beast should even speak, and to cause those who will not worship the image of the beast to be slain. Also it causes all, both small and great, both rich and poor, both free and slave, to be marked on the right hand or the forehead, so that no one can buy or sell unless he has the mark, that is, the name of the beast or the number of its name. This calls for wisdom: let him who has understanding reckon the number of the beast, for it is a human number, its number is six hundred and sixty-six.

III EARLY CHRISTIAN FATHERS

The ethical teachings of the early Christian Fathers receive their special character from the fact that they are written by Gentiles living in a pagan world. No longer can the Torah of the Old Testament be assumed. The society in which they write is the hellenistic society of the Roman Empire. Thus whether these writings are called specifically apologies or not, they serve an apologetic purpose. Moral exhortations concerning infanticide become necessary which in the context of a Jewish environment would seem redundant. The Epistle of Barnabas states, "Thou shalt not procure abortion, thou shalt not commit infanticide."

Slavery is a basic and inescapable reality, and Christians are exhorted to obey their masters as a "type of God in modesty and fear," and if they happen to be masters themselves they are told, "thou shalt not command in bitterness thy slave or handmaid who hope on the same God."

Magic and all sorts of witchcraft are practiced avidly everywhere in their environment but strictly condemned by these writers. But above all, a pervasive spirit of moral relativism prevails everywhere, which these early Christian Fathers see as blasphemy against God. Justin writes, "In the beginning [God] made the race of men endowed with intelligence, able to choose the truth and the right, so that all men are without excuse before God, for they were made with the powers of reason and observation. Anyone who does not believe that God cares for these things either manages to profess that he does not exist, or makes out that he exists but approves of evil or remains [unaffected] like a stone, and that virtue and vice are not realities, but that men consider things good or bad by opinion alone; this is the height of impiety and injustice."[4]

In the background of all their writings is the confident expectation of the impending day of judgment—"The day is at hand when all things shall perish with the Evil one."[5] The hope of the coming of the Lord is the clue to their ethical teachings in regard to both society and the individual. It explains their radical individual ethical demands as well as their conservatism in regard to social institutions.

SELECTION I

The Epistle of Barnabas XVIII, XIX, XX, XXI

This is an anonymous document of the end of the first or beginning of the second century considered canonical (part of the Bible) in some circles which states with particular clarity a familiar theme: the ethics of the "two ways," the distinction of the children of light and the children of darkness.

Now let us pass on to another lesson and teaching. There are two Ways of teaching and power, one of Light and one of Darkness. And there is a great difference between the two Ways. For over the one are set light-bringing angels of God, but over the other angels of Satan. And the one is Lord from eternity and to eternity, and the other is the ruler of the present time of iniquity.

The Way of Light is this: if any man desire to journey to the appointed place, let him be zealous in his works. Therefore the knowledge given to us of this kind that we may walk in it is as follows:—Thou shalt love thy maker, thou shalt fear thy Creator, thou shalt glorify Him who redeemed thee from death, thou shalt be simple in heart, and rich in spirit; thou shalt not join thyself to those who walk in the way of death, thou shalt hate all that is not pleasing to God, thou shalt hate all hypocrisy; thou shalt not desert the commandments of the Lord. Thou shalt not exalt thyself, but shalt be humble-minded in all things; thou shalt not take glory to thyself. Thou shalt form no evil plan against thy neighbour, thou shalt not let thy soul be froward. Thou shalt not commit fornication, thou shalt not commit adultery, thou shalt not commit sodomy. Thou shalt not let the word of God depart from thee among the impurity of any men. Thou shalt not respect persons in the reproving of transgression. Thou shalt be meek, thou shalt be quiet, thou shalt fear the words which thou hast heard. Thou shalt not bear malice against thy brother. Thou shalt not be in two minds whether it shall be or not. "Thou shalt not take the name of the Lord in vain." Thou shalt love thy neighbour more than thy own life. Thou shalt not procure abortion, thou shalt not commit infanticide. Thou shalt not withhold thy hand from thy son or from thy daughter, but shall teach them the fear of God from their youth up. Thou shalt not covet thy neighbour's goods, thou shalt not be avaricious. Thou shalt not be joined in soul with the haughty but shalt converse with humble and righteous men. Thou shalt receive the trials that befall thee as good, knowing that nothing happens without God. Thou shalt not be double-minded or talkative. Thou shalt obey thy masters as a type of God in modesty and fear; thou shalt not command in bitterness thy slave or handmaid who hope on the same God, lest they cease to fear the God who is over you both; for he came not to call men with respect of persons, but those whom the Spirit prepared. Thou shalt share all things with thy neighbour and shalt not say that they are thy own property; for if you are sharers in that which is incorruptible, how much more in that which is corruptible? Thou shalt not be forward to speak, for the mouth is a snare of death. So far as thou canst, thou shalt keep thy soul pure. Be not one who stretches out the hands to take, and shuts them when it comes to giving. Thou shalt love "as the apple of thine eye" all who speak to thee the word of the Lord. Thou shalt remember the day of judgment day and night, and thou shalt seek each day the society of the saints, either labouring by speech, and going out to exhort, and striving to save souls by the word, or working with thine hands for the ransom of thy sins. Thou shalt not hesitate to give, and when thou givest thou shalt not grumble, but thou shalt know who is the good paymaster of the reward. "Thou shalt keep the precepts" which thou hast received, "adding nothing and taking nothing away." Thou shalt utterly hate evil. "Thou shalt give righteous judgment." Thou shalt not cause quarrels, but shalt bring together and reconcile those that strive. Thou shalt confess thy sins. Thou shalt not betake thyself to prayer with an evil conscience. This is the Way of Light.

But the Way of the Black One is crooked and full of cursing, for it is the way of death eternal with punishment, and in it are the things that destroy their soul: idolatry, frowardness, arrogance of power, hypocrisy, double-heartedness, adultery, murder, robbery, pride, transgression, fraud, malice, self-sufficiency, enchantments, magic, covetousness, the lack of the fear of God; persecutors of the good, haters of the truth, lovers of lies, knowing not the reward of righteousness, who "cleave not to the good," nor to righteous judgment, who attend not to the cause of the widow and orphan, spending wakeful nights not in the fear of God, but in the pursuit of vice, from whom meekness and patience are far and distant, "loving vanity, seeking rewards," without pity for the poor, working not for him who is oppressed with toil, prone to evil speaking, without knowledge of their Maker, murderers of children, corrupters of God's creation, turning away the needy, oppressing the afflicted, advocates of the rich, unjust judges of the poor, altogether sinful.

It is good therefore that he who has learned the ordinances of the Lord as many as have been written should walk in them. For he who does these things shall be glorified in the kingdom of God, and he who chooses the others shall perish with his works. For this reason there is a resurrection, for this reason there is a recompense. I beseech those who are in high positions, if you will receive any counsel of my goodwill, have among yourselves those to whom you may do good; fail not. The day is at hand when all things shall perish with the Evil one; "The Lord and his reward is at hand." I beseech you again and again be good lawgivers to each other, remain faithful counsellors of each other, remove from yourselves all hypocrisy.

SELECTION 2

The First Apology of Justin, the Martyr 13–17, 27–29

Written by a Gentile native of Palestine who flourished in the middle of the second century and died as a martyr, this work is a particularly successful example of the literary form of "Apology" which attempts to defend the Christian faith and convert the pagan opponent simultaneously. The selections chosen illustrate the conflict with the pagan environment.

. . . We warn you in advance to be careful, lest the demons whom we have attacked should deceive you and prevent your completely grasping and understanding what we say. For they struggle to have you as their slaves and servants, and now by manifestations in dreams, now by magic tricks, they get hold of all who do not struggle to their utmost for their own salvation—as we do who, after being persuaded by the Word, renounced them and now follow the only unbegotten God through his Son. Those who once rejoiced in fornication now delight in continence alone; those who made use of magic arts have dedicated themselves to the good and unbegotten God; we who once took most pleasure in the means of increasing our wealth and property now bring what we have into a common fund and share with everyone in need; we who hated and killed one another and would not associate with men of different tribes because of [their different] customs, now after the manifestation of Christ live together and pray for our enemies and try to persuade those who unjustly hate us, so that they, living according to the fair commands of Christ, may share with us the good hope of receiving the same things [that we will] from God, the master of all. So that this may not seem to be sophistry, I think fit before giving our demonstration to recall a few of the teachings which have come from Christ himself. It is for you then, as mighty emperors, to examine whether we have been taught and do teach these things truly. His sayings were short and concise, for he was no sophist, but his word was the power of God.

About continence he said this: "Whoever looks on a woman to lust after her has already committed adultery in his heart before God." And: "If your right eye offends you, cut it out; it is better for you to enter into the Kingdom of Heaven with one eye than with two to be sent into eternal fire." And: "Whoever marries a woman who has been put away from another man commits adultery." And: "There are some who were made eunuchs by men, and some who were born eunuchs, and some who have made themselves eunuchs for the Kingdom of Heaven's sake; only not all [are able to] receive this."

And so those who make second marriages according to human law are sinners in the sight of our Teacher, and those who look on a woman to lust after her. For he condemns not only the man who commits the act of adultery, but the man who desires to commit adultery, since not only our actions but our thoughts are manifest to God. Many men and women now in their sixties and seventies who have been disciples of Christ from childhood have preserved their purity; and I am proud that I could point to such people in every nation. Then what shall we say of the uncounted multitude of those who have turned away from incontinence and learned these things? For Christ did not call the righteous or the temperate to repentance, but the ungodly and incontinent and unrighteous. So he said: "I have not come to call the righteous but sinners to repentance." For the Heavenly Father wishes the repentance of a sinner rather than his punishment.

This is what he taught on affection for all men: "If you love those who love you, what new thing do you do? for even the harlots do this. But I say to you, Pray for your enemies and love those who hate you and bless those who curse you and pray for those who treat you despitefully."

That we should share with those in need and do nothing for [our] glory he said these things: "Give to everyone who asks and turn not away him who wishes to borrow. For if you lend to those from whom you hope to receive, what new thing do you do? Even the publicans do this. But as for you, do not lay up treasures for yourselves on earth, where moth and rust corrupt and thieves break in, but lay up for yourselves treasures in heaven, where neither moth nor rust corrupts. For what will it profit a man, if he should gain the whole world, but lose his own soul? Or what will he give in exchange for it? Lay up treasures therefore in the heavens, where neither moth nor rust corrupts." And: "Be kind and merciful, as your Father is kind and merciful, and makes his sun to rise on sinners and righteous and wicked. Do not worry as to what you will eat or what you will wear. Are you not better than the birds and the beasts? and God feeds them. So do not worry as to what you will eat or what you will wear, for your Heavenly Father knows that you need these things. But seek the Kingdom of Heaven, and all these things will be added to you. For where his treasure is, there is the mind of man." And: "Do not do these things to be seen of men, for otherwise you have no reward with your Father who is in heaven."

About being long-suffering and servants to all and free from anger, this is what he said: "To him that smites you on one cheek turn the other also, and to him that takes away your cloak do not deny your tunic either. Whoever is angry is worthy of the fire. And whoever compels you to go one mile, follow him for two. Let your good works shine before men, that they as they see may wonder at your Father who is in heaven."

For we ought not to quarrel; he has not wished us to imitate the wicked, but rather by our patience and meekness to draw all men from shame and evil desires. This we can show in the case of many who were once on your side but have turned from the ways of violence and tyranny, overcome by observing the consistent lives of their neighbors, or noting the strange patience of their injured acquaintances, or experiencing the way they did business with them.

About not swearing at all, but always speaking the truth, this is what he commanded: "Swear not at all, but let your yea be yea and your nay nay. What is more than these is from the evil one."

That God only should be worshiped he showed us when he said: "The greatest commandment is: Thou shalt worship the Lord thy God and him only shalt thou serve with all thy heart and all thy strength, the Lord who made thee." And: "When one came to him and said, Good Teacher, he answered and said, There is none good, except only God who made all things."

Those who are found not living as he taught should know that they are not really Christians, even if his teachings are on their lips, for he said that not those who merely profess but those who also do the works will be saved . . .

More even than others we try to pay the taxes and assessments to those whom you appoint, as we have been taught by him. For once in his time some came to him and asked whether it were right to pay taxes to Caesar. And he answered, "Tell me, whose image is on the coin." They said, "Caesar's." And he answered them again, "Then give what is Caesar's to Caesar and what is God's to God." So we worship God only, but in other matters we gladly serve you, recognizing you as emperors and rulers of men, and praying that along with your imperial power you may also be found to have a sound mind. If you pay no attention to our prayers and our frank statements about everything, it will not injure us, since we believe, or rather are firmly convinced, that every man will suffer in eternal fire in accordance with the quality of his actions, and similarly will be required to give account for the abilities which he has received from God, as Christ told us when he said, "To whom God has given more, from him more will be required. . . ."

✧ ✧ ✧ ✧

That we may avoid all injustice and impiety, we have been taught that to expose the newly born is the work of wicked men—first of all because we observe that almost all [foundlings], boys as well as girls, are brought up for prostitution. As the ancients are said to have raised herds of oxen or goats or sheep or horses in their pastures, so now [you raise children] just for shameful purposes, and so in every nation a crowd of females and hermaphrodites and doers of unspeakable deeds are exposed as public prostitutes. You even collect pay and levies and taxes from these, whom you ought to exterminate from your civilized world. And anyone who makes use of them may in addition to [the guilt of] godless, impious, and intemperate intercourse, by chance be consorting with his own child or relative or brother. Some even prostitute their own children and wives, and others are admittedly mutilated for purposes of sodomy, and treat this as part of the mysteries of the mother of the gods—while beside each of those whom you think of as gods a serpent is depicted as a great symbol and mystery. You charge against us the actions that you commit openly and treat with honor, as if the divine light were overthrown and withdrawn—which of course does no harm to us, who refuse to do any of these things, but rather injures those who do them and then bring false witness [against us].

Among us the chief of the evil demons is called the serpent

and Satan and the devil, as you can learn by examining our writings. Christ has foretold that he will be cast into fire with his host and the men who follow him, [all] to be punished for endless ages. God delays doing this for the sake of the human race, for he foreknows that there are some yet to be saved by repentance, even perhaps some not yet born. In the beginning he made the race of men endowed with intelligence, able to choose the truth and do right, so that all men are without excuse before God, for they were made with the powers of reason and observation. Anyone who does not believe that God cares for these things either manages to profess that he does not exist, or makes out that he exists but approves of evil or remains [unaffected] like a stone, and that virtue and vice are not realities, but that men consider things good or bad by opinion alone; this is the height of impiety and injustice.

SELECTION 3
Irenaeus Against Heresies, Chap. XXIV

Bishop of Lyon in the latter half of the second century, Irenaeus is one of the most important early Christian theologians, particularly because of his biblically oriented theology developed in conflict with gnosticism. His claim that the entire universe is God's is illustrated in our selection where the "kingdoms of this world" are claimed for God.

As therefore the devil lied at the beginning, so did he also in the end, when he said, "All these are delivered unto me, and to whomsoever I will I give them." For it is not he who has appointed the kingdoms of this world, but God; for "the heart of the king is in the hand of God." And the Word also says by Solomon, "By me kings do reign, and princes administer justice. By me chiefs are raised up, and by me kings rule the earth." Paul the apostle also says upon this same subject: "Be ye subject to all the higher powers; for there is no power but of God: now those which are have been ordained of God." And again, in reference to them he says, "For he beareth not the sword in vain; for he is the minister of God, the avenger for wrath to him who does evil." Now, that he spake these words, not in regard to angelical powers, nor of invisible rulers—as some venture to expound the passage—but of those of actual human authorities, [he shows when] he says, "For this cause pay ye tribute also: for they are God's ministers, doing service for this very thing." This also the Lord confirmed, when He did not do what He was tempted to by the devil; but He gave directions that tribute should be paid to the tax-gatherers for Himself and Peter; because "they are the ministers of God, serving for this very thing."

For since man, by departing from God, reached such a pitch of fury as even to look upon his brother as his enemy, and engaged without fear in every kind of restless conduct, and murder, and avarice; God imposed upon mankind the fear of man, as they did not acknowledge the fear of God, in order that, being subjected to the authority of men, and kept under restraint by their laws, they might attain to some degree of justice, and exercise mutual forbearance through dread of the sword suspended full in their view, as the apostle says: "For he beareth not the sword in vain; for he is the minister of God, the avenger for the wrath upon him who does evil." And for this reason too, magistrates themselves, having laws as a clothing of righteousness whenever they act in a just and legitimate manner, shall not be called in question for their conduct, nor be liable to punishment. But whatsoever they do to the subversion of justice, iniquitously, and impiously, and illegally, and tyrannically, in these things shall they also perish; for the just judgment of God comes equally upon all, and in no case is defective. Earthly rule, therefore, has been appointed by God for the benefit of nations, and not by the devil, who is never at rest at all, nay, who does not love to see even nations conducting themselves after a quiet manner, so that under the fear of human rule, men may not eat each other up like fishes; but that, by means of the establishment of laws, they may keep down an excess of wickedness among the nations . . .

IV TERTULLIAN

Tertullian, born about 160 in Carthage, North Africa, the son of a pagan centurion attached to the Roman proconsul of the region, is one of the most colorful Christian writers of the early church. Trained as a lawyer, he became after his conversion (ca. 195) an eloquent defender of the Christian faith. His idiosyncratic legal and military vocabulary and style helped shape the theological language of Western Christendom. Thus, his influence reaches into the present although his own theological development led him eventually away from mainstream Christianity into the moral perfectionism and apocalyptic speculations of Montanism (ca. 203). Some of his later writings are therefore full of bitter attacks against the "moral laxity" of the catholic church and even the remission of sins granted by the bishop of Rome. He died after 220, apparently by then at odds even with the Montanists.

Tertullian is an outstanding representative of an extreme, yet recurring Christian attitude towards society, that of complete and disdainful separation from the "world." He is the paradigm of the "Christ against Culture" pattern (H. R. Niebuhr). Because of the colorful expression which he gave this attitude in his writings, he has been the favorite Christian author of those critics who would like to identify all of Christianity with this particular expression of it (e.g. Edward Gibbon, *The Decline and Fall of the Roman Empire*).

Yet this attitude was by no means normative and must be seen in the context of writers like Irenaeus (see above) and Clement of Alexandria (see below) who were far more accepting of the culture of their time. Nevertheless, the shape of the total impact of Christian social teaching upon culture would be incomprehensible without a knowledge of the Christian enemies of secular culture like Tertullian.

SELECTION I
The Apology, Chap. 39–45

A book which dates from the time before Tertullian became involved in Montanism, *The Apology* is a slashing attack against the illegal treatment of Christians before the Roman courts. In the following selection he presents the positive side of the Christian life:

We are a body knit together as such by a common religious profession, by unity of discipline, and by the bond of a common hope. We meet together as an assembly and congregation, that, offering up prayer to God as with united force, we may wrestle with him in our supplications. This violence God delights in. We pray, too, for the emperors, for their ministers and for all in authority, for the welfare of the world, for the prevalence of peace, for the delay of the final consummation. We assemble to read our sacred writings, if any peculiarity of the times makes either forewarning or reminiscence needful. However it be in that respect with the sacred words, we nourish our faith, we animate our hope, we make our confidence more steadfast; and no less by inculcations of God's precepts we confirm good habits. In the same place also exhortations are made, rebukes and sacred censures are administered. For with a great gravity is the work of judging carried on among us, as befits those who feel assured that they are in the sight of God; and you have the most notable example of judgment to come when any one has sinned so grievously as to require his severance from us in prayer, and the meeting, and all sacred intercourse . . . But it is mainly the deeds of a love so noble that lead many to put a brand upon us. See, they say, how they love one another, for themselves are animated by mutual hatred; how they are ready even to die for one another, for they themselves will sooner put to death. And they are wroth with us, too, because we call each other brethren; for no other reason, as I think, than because among themselves names of consanguinity are assumed in mere pretence of affection. But we are your brethren as well, by the law of our common mother nature, though you are hardly men, because brothers so unkind. At the same time, how much more fittingly they are called and counted brothers who have been led to the knowledge of God as their common Father, who have drunk in one spirit of holiness, who from the same womb of a common ignorance have agonized into the same light of truth! But on this very account, perhaps, we are regarded as having less claim to be held true brothers, that no tragedy makes a noise about our brotherhood, or that the family possessions, which generally destroy brotherhood among you, create fraternal bonds among us. One in mind and soul, we do not hesitate to share our earthly goods with one another. All things are common among us but our wives. We give up our community where it is practiced alone by others, who not only take possession of the wives of their friends, but most tolerantly also accommodate their friends with theirs, following the example, I believe, of those wise men of ancient times, the Greek Socrates and the Roman Cato, who shared with their friends the wives whom they had married, it seems for the sake of progeny both to themselves and to others; whether in this acting against their partners' wishes, I am not able to say. Why should they have any care over their chastity, when their husbands so readily bestowed it away? O noble example of Attic wisdom, of Roman gravity!—the philosopher and the censor playing pimps! What wonder if that great love of Christians towards one another is desecrated by you! For you abuse also our humble feasts, on the ground that they are extravagant as well as infamously wicked. To us, it seems, applies the saying of Diogenes: "The people of Megara feast as though they were going to die on the morrow; they build as though they were never to die!" But one sees more readily the mote in another's eye than the beam in his own. Why, the very air is soured with the eructations of so many tribes, and curiae, and decuriae; the Salii cannot have their feast without going into debt; you must get the accountants to tell you what the tenths of Hercules and the sacrificial banquets cost; the choicest cook is appointed for the Apaturia, the Dionysia, the Attic mysteries; the smoke from the banquet of Serapis will call out the firemen. Yet about the modest supper-room of the Christians alone a great ado is made. Our feast explains itself by its name. The Greeks call it love. Whatever it costs, our outlay in the name of piety is gain, since with the good things of the feast we benefit the needy; not as it is with you, do parasites aspire to the glory of satisfying their licentious propensities, selling themselves for a belly-feast to all disgraceful treatment,—but as it is with God himself, a peculiar respect is shown to the lowly. If the object of our feast be good, in the light of that consider its further regulations. As it is an act of religious service, it permits no vileness or immodesty. The participants, before reclining, taste first of prayer to God. As much is eaten as satisfies the cravings of hunger; as much is drunk as befits the chaste. They say it is enough, as those who remember that even during the night they have to worship God; they talk as those who know that the Lord is one of their auditors. After manual ablution, and the bringing in of lights, each is asked to stand forth and sing, as he can, a hymn to God, either one from the holy Scriptures or one of his own composing,—a proof of the measure of our drinking. As the feast commenced with prayer, so with prayer it is closed. We go from it, not like troops of mischief-doers, nor bands of roamers, nor to break out into licentious acts, but to have as much care of our modesty and chastity as if we had been at a school of virtue rather than a banquet. Give the meeting of the Christians its due, and hold it unlawful, if it is like assemblies of the illicit sort: by all means let it be condemned, if any complaint can be validly laid against it, such as lies against secret factions. But who has ever suffered harm from our assemblies? We are in our meetings just what we are when separated from each other; we are as a community what we are as individuals; we injure nobody, we trouble nobody. When the upright, when the virtuous meet together, when the pious, when the pure assemble in congregation, you ought not to call that a faction, but a curia—a sacred meeting.

. . . But we are called to account as harm-doers on another ground, and are accused of being useless in the affairs of life. How in all the world can that be the case with people who are living among you, eating the same food, wearing the same attire, having the same habits, under the same necessities of existence? We are not Indian Brahmins or Gymnosophists, who dwell in woods and exile themselves from ordinary human life. We do not forget the debt of gratitude we owe to God our Lord and Creator; we reject no creature of His hands, though certainly we exercise restraint upon ourselves, lest of any gift of His we make an immoderate or sinful use. So we sojourn with you in the world, abjuring neither forum, nor shambles, nor bath, nor booth, nor workshop, nor inn, nor weekly market, nor any other places of commerce. We sail with you, and fight with you, and till the ground with you; and in like manner we unite with you in your traffickings—even in the various arts we make public property of our works for your benefit. How it is we seem useless in your ordinary business, living with you and by you as we do, I am not able to understand. But if I do not frequent your religious ceremonies, I am still on the sacred day a man. I do not at the Saturnalia bathe myself at dawn, that I may not lose both day and night; yet I bathe at a decent and healthful hour, which preserves me both in heat and blood. I can be rigid and pallid like you after ablution when I am dead. I do not recline in public at the feast of Bacchus, after the manner of the beast-fighters at their final banquet. Yet of your resources I partake, *wherever* I may chance to eat. I do not buy a crown for my head. What matters it to you how I use them, if nevertheless the flowers are purchased? I think it more agreeable to have them free and loose, waving all about. Even if they are woven into a crown, we smell the crown with our nostrils: let those look to it who scent the perfume with their hair. We do not go to your spectacles; yet the articles that are sold there, if I need them, I will obtain more readily at their proper places. We certainly buy no frankincense. If the Arabias complain of this, let the Sabaeans be well assured that their more precious and costly merchandise is expended as largely in the burying of Christians as in the fumigating of the gods. At any rate, you say, the temple revenues are every day falling off: how few now throw in a contribution! In truth, we are not able to give alms both to your human and your heavenly mendicants; nor do we think that we are required to give any but to those who ask for it. Let Jupiter then hold out his hand and get, for our compassion spends more in the streets than yours does in the temples. But your other taxes will acknowledge a debt of gratitude to Christians; for in the faithfulness which keeps us from fraud upon a brother, we make conscience of paying all their dues: so that, by ascertaining how much is lost by fraud and falsehood in the census declarations—the calculation may easily be made—it would be seen that the ground of complaint in one department of revenue is compensated by the advantages which others derive.

I will confess, however, without hesitation, that there are some who in a sense may complain of Christians that they are a sterile race: as, for instance, pimps, and panders, and bath-suppliers; assassins, and poisoners, and sorcerers; soothsayers, too, diviners, and astrologers. But it is a noble fruit of Christians, that they have no fruits for such as these. And yet, whatever loss your interests suffer from the religion we profess, the protection you have from us makes amply up for it. What value do you set on persons, I do not here urge who deliver you from demons, I do not urge who for your sakes present prayers before the throne of the true God, for perhaps you have no belief in that—but from whom you can have nothing to fear?

Yes, and no one considers what the loss is to the common weal,—a loss as great as it is real, no one estimates the injury entailed upon the state, when, men of virtue as we are, we are put to death in such numbers, when so many of the truly good suffer the last penalty. And here we call your own acts to witness, you who are daily presiding at the trials of prisoners, and passing sentence upon crimes. Well, in your long lists of those accused of many and various atrocities, has any assassin, any cutpurse, any man guilty of sacrilege, or seduction, or stealing bathers' clothes, his name entered as being a Christian too? Or when Christians are brought before you on the mere ground of their name, is there ever found among them an ill-doer of the sort? It is always with your folk the prison is steaming, the mines are sighing, the wild beasts are fed: it is from you the exhibitors of gladiatorial shows always get their herds of criminals to feed up for the occasion. You find no Christian there, except simply as being such; or if one is there as something else, a Christian he is no longer.

We, then, alone are without crime. Is there aught wonderful in that, if it be a very necessity with us? For a necessity indeed it is. Taught of God himself what goodness is, we have both a perfect knowledge of it as revealed to us by a perfect Master; and faithfully we do his will, as enjoined on us by a Judge we dare not despise. But your ideas of virtue you have got from mere human opinion; on human authority, too, its obligation rests: hence your system of practical morality is deficient, both in the fulness and authority requisite to produce a life of real virtue. Man's wisdom to point out what is good, is no greater than his authority to exact the keeping of it; the one is as easily deceived as the other is despised. And so, which is the ampler rule, to say, "Thou shalt not kill," or to teach, "Be not even angry?" Which is more perfect, to forbid adultery, or to restrain from even a single lustful look? Which indicates the higher intelligence, interdicting evil-doing, or evil-speaking? Which is more thorough, not allowing an injury, or not even suffering an injury done to you to be repaid? Though withal you know that these very laws also of yours, which seem to lead to virtue, have been borrowed from the law of God as the ancient model . . . But what is the real authority of human laws, when it is in man's power both to evade them, by generally managing to hide himself out of sight in his crimes, and to despise them sometimes, if inclination or necessity leads him to offend? Think of these things, too, in the light of the brevity of any punishment you can inflict—never to last longer than till death. On this ground Epicurus makes light of all suffering and pain, maintaining that if it is small, it is contemptible; and if it is great, it is not long-continued. No doubt about it, we, who receive our awards under the judgment of an all-seeing God, and who look forward to eternal punishment from him for sin,—we alone make real effort to attain a blameless life, under the influence of our ampler knowledge, and the impossibility of concealment, and the greatness of the threatened torment, not merely long-enduring, but everlasting, fearing him, whom he too should fear who the fearing Judges, fearing God, I mean, and not the proconsul.

SELECTION 2

On Pagan Shows, Chap. 24–30

This selection from Tertullian's denunciation of the popular Roman shows is an excellent example of his total rejection of the "ways of the world."

In how many other ways shall we yet further show that nothing which is peculiar to the shows has God's approval, or without that approval is becoming in God's servants? If we have succeeded in making it plain that they were instituted entirely for the devil's sake, and have been got up entirely with the devil's things (for all that is not God's, or is not pleasing in His eyes, belongs to His wicked rival), this simply means that in them you have that pomp of the devil which in the "seal" of our faith we abjure. But we should have no connection with the things which we abjure, whether in deed or word, whether by looking on them or looking forward to them. But do we not abjure and rescind that baptismal pledge, when we cease to bear its testimony? Does it then remain for us to apply to the heathens themselves? Let them tell us, then, whether it is right in Christians to frequent the show. Why, the rejection of these amusements is the chief sign to them that a man has adopted the Christian faith. If any one, then, puts away the faith's distinctive badge, he is plainly guilty of denying it. What hope can you possibly retain in regard to a man who does that? When you go over to the enemy's camp, you throw down your arms, desert the standards and the oath of allegiance to your chief: you cast in your lot for life or death with your new friends.

Seated where there is nothing of God, will one be thinking of his Maker? Will there be peace in his soul when there is eager strife there for a charioteer? Wrought up into a frenzied excitement, will he learn to be modest? Nay, in the whole thing he will meet with no greater temptation than that gay attiring of the men and women. The very intermingling of emotions, the very agreements and disagreements with each other in the bestowment of their favours, where you have such close communion, blow up the sparks of passion. And then there is scarce any other object in going to the show, but to see and to be seen.

When a tragic actor is declaiming, will one be giving thought to prophetic appeals? Amid the measures of the effeminate player, will he call up to himself a psalm? And when the athletes are hard at struggle, will he be ready to proclaim that there must be no striking again? And with his eye fixed on the bites of bears, and the sponge-nets of the net-fighters, can he be moved by compassion? May God avert from His people any such passionate eagerness after a cruel enjoyment! For how monstrous it is to go from God's church to the devil's—from the sky to the stye, as they say; to raise your hands to God, and then to weary them in the applause of an actor; out of the mouth, from which you uttered Amen over the Holy Thing, to give witness in a gladiator's favour; to cry "for ever" to any one else but God and Christ!

Why may not those who go into the temptations of the show become accessible also to evil spirits? We have the case of the woman—the Lord Himself is witness—who went to the theatre, and came back possessed. In the out-casting, accordingly, when the unclean creature was upbraided with having dared to attack a believer, he firmly replied, "And in truth I did it most righteously, for I found her in my domain." Another case, too, is well known, in which a woman had been hearing a tragedian, and on the very night she saw in her sleep a linen cloth—the actor's name being mentioned at the same time with strong disapproval—and five days after that woman was no more. How many other undoubted proofs we have had in the case of persons who, by keeping company with the devil in the shows, have fallen from the Lord! For no one can serve two masters. What fellowship has light with darkness, life with death?

We ought to detest these heathen meetings and assemblies, if on no other account than that there God's name is blasphemed—that there the cry "To the lions!" is daily raised against us—that from thence persecuting decrees are wont to emanate, and temptations are sent forth. What will you do if you are caught in that heaving tide of impious judgments? Not that there any harm is likely to come to you from men: nobody knows that you are a Christian; but think how it fares with you in heaven. For at the very time the devil is working havoc in the church, do you doubt that the angels are looking down from above, and marking every man, who speaks and who listens to the blaspheming word, who lends his tongue and who lends his ears to the service of Satan against God? Shall you not then shun those tiers where the enemies of Christ assemble, that seat of all that is pestilential, and the very superincumbent atmosphere all impure with wicked cries? Grant that you have there things that are pleasant, things both agreeable and innocent in themselves; even some things that are excellent. Nobody dilutes poison with gall and hellebore: the accursed thing is put into condiments well seasoned and of sweetest taste. So, too, the devil puts into the deadly draught which he prepares, things of God most pleasant and most acceptable. Everything there, then, that is either brave, or noble, or loud-sounding, or melodious, or exquisite in taste, hold it but as the honey drop of a poisoned cake; nor make so much of your taste for its pleasures, as of the danger you run from its attractions.

With such dainties as these let the devil's guests be feasted. The places and the times, the inviter too, are theirs. Our banquets, our nuptial joys, are yet to come. We cannot sit down in fellowship with them, as neither can they with us. Things in this matter go by their turns. Now they have gladness and we are troubled. "The World," says Jesus, "shall rejoice; ye shall be sorrowful." Let us mourn, then, while the heathen are merry, that in the day of their sorrow we may rejoice; lest, sharing now in their gladness, we share then also in their grief.

V THE ALEXANDRIAN SCHOOL

The two outstanding exponents of the theology of the Alexandrian catechetical school, the first Christian university, where Clement of Alexandria (ca. 150–ca. 215) who became its leader about 200 and Origen (185–254) who gave it its greatest influence.

Clement was the author of the first book which could be described as an exposition of Christian ethics, *The Instructor* (*Paidagogos*). Basing his thought on a biblical faith, he uses the Greek philosophical tradition of the time eclectically to support the superiority of the Christian way of life. By doing it somewhat superficially, emphasizing manners almost as much as morals, Clement illustrates a permanent temptation to Christian ethical teachers, a legalistic concern with formal observance of the law as over against its dynamic intention. Thus he writes in detail about proper eating habits: "From all slavish habits and excess we must abstain and touch what is set before us in a decorous way; keeping the hand and couch and chin free from stains. . . . We must guard against speaking anything while eating: for the voice becomes disagreeable and inarticulate when it is confined by full jaws. . . ."[6] Similarly he comments on proper clothing and shoes, cosmetic jewelry, and hairstyles. His comments about hair are typical: "Let the head of men be shaven, unless it has curly hair. But let the chin have the hair. But let not twisted locks hang far down from the head, gliding into womanish ringlets. For an ample beard suffices for men."[7] Yet at the same time the book will contain advice like this: ". . . you are not prohibited from conducting affairs in the world decorously according to God. Let not him who sells or buys aught name two prices for what he buys or sells; but stating the net price, and studying to speak the truth, if he get not his price, he gets the truth, and is rich in the possession of rectitude."[8]

Another book by the same author, *The Rich Man's Salvation,* is a fascinating attempt to come to terms with the problems of a Christian community which now has also the wealthy and cultured among its members. It represents an elaborate interpretation of the meaning of Mark 10:17–31, stating that it is not wealth itself but the love of wealth which separates men from God. If wealth is used in God's service it appears an asset rather than a liability. It is by means of his allegorical interpretation of "wealth" as "wealth of passions" that Clement is enabled to adjust Mark's report to the conditions of an affluent society. In doing so he set a pattern which has been used repeatedly in the history of Christian social ethics.

Origen, though theologically more significant than Clement, did not deal in any one surviving book specifically with ethics. In his reply to Celsus, however, he propounds certain social-ethical notions which are significant for the attitude of the Christian church to political life in the time before Constantine.

SELECTION I
Clement: *The Instructor,* Book I, Chap. XIII

In this selection Clement shows his dependence upon the philosophical ideas of his time in the presentation of his ethics. This utilization of Greek philosophical methodology and terminology became a consistent pattern in the articulation of Christian ethics up to the present.

Everything that is contrary to right reason is sin. Accordingly, therefore, the philosophers think fit to define the most generic passions thus: lust, as desire disobedient to reason; fear, as weakness disobedient to reason; pleasure, as an elation of the spirit disobedient to reason. If, then, disobedience in reference to reason is the generating cause of sin, how shall we escape the conclusion, that obedience to reason—the Word—which we call faith, will of necessity be the efficacious cause of duty? For virtue itself is a state of the soul rendered harmonious by reason in respect to the whole life. Nay, to crown all, philosophy itself is pronounced to be the cultivation of right reason; so that, necessarily, whatever is done through error of reason is transgression, and is rightly called (*Hamartema*) sin. Since, then, the first man sinned and disobeyed God, it is said, "And man became like to the beasts:" being rightly regarded as irrational, he is likened to the beasts. Whence Wisdom says: "The horse for covering; the libidinous and the adulterer is become like to an irrational beast." Wherefore also it is added: "He neighs, whoever may be sitting on him." The man, it is meant, no longer speaks; for he who transgresses against reason is no longer rational, but an irrational animal, given up to lusts by which he is ridden (as a horse by his rider).

But that which is done right, in obedience to reason, the followers of the Stoics call *Prosekon* and *Kathekon,* that is, incumbent and fitting. What is fitting is incumbent. And obedience is founded on commands. And these being, as they are, the same as counsels—having truth for their aim, train up to the ultimate goal of aspiration, which is conceived of as the *end* (*Telos*). And the end of piety is eternal rest in God. And the beginning of eternity is our end. The right operation of piety perfects duty by works; whence, according to just reasoning, duties consist in actions, not in sayings. And Christian conduct is the operation of the rational soul in accordance with a correct judgment and aspiration after the truth, which attains its destined end through the body, the soul's consort and ally. Virtue is a will in conformity to God and Christ in life, rightly adjusted to life everlasting. For the life of Christians, in which we are now trained, is a system of reasonable actions—that is, of those things taught by the Word—an unfailing energy which we have called faith. The system is the commandments of the Lord, which, being divine statutes and spiritual counsels, have been written for ourselves, being adapted for ourselves and our neighbours. Moreover, they turn back on us, as the ball rebounds on him that throws it by the repercussion. Whence also duties are essential for divine discipline, as being enjoined by God, and furnished for our salvation. And since, of those things which are necessary, some relate only to life here, and others, which relate to the blessed life yonder, wing us for flight hence; so, in an analogous manner, of duties, some are ordained with reference to life, others for the blessed life. The commandments issued with respect to natural life are published to the multitude; but those that are suited for living well, and from which eternal life springs, we have to consider, as in a sketch, as we read them out of the Scriptures.

SELECTION 2
Clement: *The Rich Man's Salvation*

Here Clement's use of allegory is shown in its application to a problem of social ethics:

. . . This is written in the gospel according to Mark, and in all the other accepted gospels the passage as a whole shows the same general sense, though perhaps here and there a little of the wording changes. And as we are clearly aware that the Saviour teaches His people nothing in a merely human way, but everything by a divine and mystical wisdom, we must not understand His words literally, but with due inquiry and intelligence we must search out and master their hidden meaning. (Mark 10: 17–31)

✧ ✧ ✧ ✧

What then was it that impelled him to flight, and made him desert his teacher, his supplication, his hope, his life, his previous labours? "Sell what belongs to thee." And what is this? It is not what some hastily take it to be, a command to fling away the substance that belongs to him and to part with his riches, but to banish from the soul its opinions about riches, its attachment to them, its excessive desire, its morbid excitement over them, its anxious cares, the thorns of our earthly existence which choke the seed of the true life. For it is no great or enviable thing to be simply without riches, apart from the purpose of obtaining life. Why, if this were so, those men who have nothing at all, but are destitute and beg for their daily bread, who lie along the roads in abject poverty, would, though "ignorant" of

God and "God's righteousness," be most blessed and beloved of God and the only possessors of eternal life, by the sole fact of their being utterly without ways and means of livelihood and in want of the smallest necessities. Nor again is it a new thing to renounce wealth and give it freely to the poor, or to one's fatherland, which many have done before the Saviour's coming, some to obtain leisure for letters and for dead wisdom, others for empty fame and vainglory—such men as Anaxagoras, Democritus and Crates.

What then is it that He enjoins as new and peculiar to God and alone life-giving, which did not save men of former days? If the "new creation," the Son of God, reveals and teaches something unique, then His command does not refer to the visible act, the very thing that others have done, but to something else greater, more divine and more perfect, which is signified through this; namely, to strip the soul itself and the will of their lurking passions and utterly to root out and cast away all alien thoughts from the mind. For this is a lesson peculiar to the believer and a doctrine worthy of the Saviour. The men of former days, indeed, in their contempt for outward things, parted with and sacrificed their possessions, but as for the passions of the soul, I think they even intensified them. For they became supercilious, boastful, conceited and disdainful of the rest of mankind, as if they themselves had wrought something superhuman. How then could the Saviour have recommended to those who were to live forever things that would be harmful and injurious for the life He promises? And there is this other point. It is possible for a man, after having unburdened himself of his property, to be none the less continually absorbed and occupied in the desire and longing for it. He has given up the use of wealth, but now being in difficulties and at the same time yearning after what he threw away, he endures a double annoyance, the absence of means of support and the presence of regret. For when a man lacks the necessities of life he cannot possibly fail to be broken in spirit and to neglect the higher things, as he strives to procure these necessities by any means and from any source.

And how much more useful is the opposite condition, when by possessing a sufficiency a man is himself in no distress about money-making and also helps those he ought? For what sharing would be left among men, if nobody had anything? And how could this doctrine be found other than plainly contradictory to and at war with many other noble doctrines of the Lord? "Make to yourselves friends from the mammon of unrighteousness, that when it shall fail they may receive you into the eternal habitations." "Acquire treasures in heaven, where neither moth nor rust doth consume, nor thieves break through." How could we feed the hungry and give drink to the thirsty, cover the naked and entertain the homeless, with regard to which deeds He threatens fire and the outer darkness to those who have not done them, if each of us were himself already in want of all these things? But further, the Lord Himself is a guest with Zacchaeus and Levi and Matthew, wealthy men and tax-gatherers, and He does not bid them give up their riches. On the contrary, having enjoined the just and set aside the unjust employment of them, He proclaims, "Today is salvation come to this house." It is on this stipulation,—that He commands them to be shared, to give drink to the thirsty and bread to the hungry, to receive the homeless, to clothe the naked. And if it is not possible to satisfy these needs except with riches, and He were bidding us stand aloof from riches, what else would the Lord be doing than exhorting us to give and also not to give the same things, to feed and not to feed, to receive and to shut out, to share and not to share? But this would be the height of unreason.

We must not then fling away the riches that are of benefit to our neighbours as well as ourselves. For they are called possessions because they are things possessed, and wealth because they are to be welcomed and because they have been prepared by God for the welfare of men. Indeed, they lie at hand and are put at our disposal as a sort of material and as instruments to be well used by those who know. An instrument, if you use it with artistic skill, is a thing of art; but if you are lacking in skill, it reaps the benefit of your unmusical nature, though not itself responsible. Wealth too is an instrument of the same kind. You can use it rightly; it ministers to righteousness. But if one uses it wrongly, it is found to be a minister of wrong. For its nature is to minister, not to rule. We must not therefore put the responsibility on that which, having in itself neither good nor evil, is not responsible, but on that which has the power of using things either well or badly, as a result of choice; for this is responsible just for that reason. And this is the mind of man, which has in itself both free judgment and full liberty to deal with what is given to it. So let a man do away, not with his possessions, but rather with the passions of his soul, which do not consent to the better use of what he has; in order that, by becoming noble and good, he may be able to use these possessions also in a noble manner. "Saying good-bye to all we have," and "selling all we have," must therefore be understood in this way, as spoken with reference to the soul's passions.

SELECTION 3
Origen: *Against Celsus*, Book VIII

In this impressive defense of the Christian Faith against an intelligent and knowledgeable pagan Origen describes here the basis for the Christian approach to political and social responsibility:

In the next place, Celsus urges us "to help the king with all our might, and to labour with him in the maintenance of justice, to fight for him; and if he requires it, to fight under him, or lead an army along with him." To this our answer is, that we do, when occasion requires, give help to kings, and that, so to say, a divine help, "putting on the whole armour of God." And this we do in obedience to the injunction of the apostle, "I exhort, therefore, that first of all, supplications, prayers, intercessions, and giving of thanks, be made for all men, for kings, and for all that are in authority;" and the more any one excels in piety, the more effective help does he render to kings, even more than is given by soldiers, who go forth to fight and slay as many of the enemy as they can. And to those enemies of our faith who require us to bear arms for the commonwealth, and to slay men, we can reply: "Do not those who are priests at certain shrines, and those who attend on certain gods, as you account them, keep their hands free from blood, that they may with hands unstained and free from human blood offer the appointed sacrifices to your gods; and even when war is upon you, you never enlist the priests in the army. If that, then, is a laudable custom, how much more so, that while others are engaged in battle, these too should engage as the priests and ministers of God, keeping their hands pure, and wrestling in prayers to God on behalf of those who are fighting in a righteous cause, and for the king who reigns righteously, that whatever is opposed to those who act righteously may be destroyed!" And as we by our prayers vanquish all demons who stir up war, and lead to the violation of oaths, and disturb the peace, we in this way are much more helpful to the kings than those who go into the field to fight for them. And we do take our part in public affairs, when along with righteous prayers we join self-denying exercises and meditations, which teach us to despise pleasures, and not to be led away by them. And none fight better for the king than we do. We do not indeed fight under him, although he require it; but we fight on his behalf, forming a special army—an army of piety—by offering our prayers to God.

And if Celsus would have us to lead armies in defence of our country, let him know that we do this too, and that not for the purpose of being seen by men, or of vainglory. For "in secret," and in our own hearts, there are prayers which ascend as from priests in behalf of our fellow-citizens. And Christians are benefactors of their country more than others. For they train up citizens, and inculcate piety to the Supreme Being; and they promote those whose lives in the smallest cities have been good and worthy, to a divine and heavenly city, to whom it may be said, "Thou hast been faithful in the smallest city, come into a great one," where "God standeth in the assembly of the gods, and judgeth the gods in the midst;" and He reckons thee among them, if thou no more "die as a man, or fall as one of the princes."

Celsus also urges us to "take office in the government of the country, if that is required for the maintenance of the laws and the support of religion." But we recognise in each state the existence of another national organization, founded by the Word of God, and we exhort those who are mighty in word and of blameless life to rule over churches. Those who are ambitious of ruling we reject; but we constrain those who, through excess of modesty, are not easily induced to take a public charge in the church of God. And those who rule over us well are under the constraining influence of the great King, whom we believe to be the Son of God, God the Word. And if those who govern in the church, and are called rulers of the divine nation—that is, the church—rule well, they rule in accordance with the divine commands, and never suffer themselves to be led astray by worldly policy. And it is not for the purpose of escaping public duties that Christians decline public offices, but that they may reserve themselves for a diviner and more necessary service in the church of God—for the salvation of men. And this service is at once necessary and right. They take charge of all—of those that are within, that they may day by day lead better lives, and of those that are without, that they may come to abound in holy words and in deeds of piety; and that, while thus worshipping God truly, and training up as many as they can in the same way, they may be filled with the word of God and the law of God, and thus be united with the supreme God through His Son the Word, wisdom, truth, and righteousness, who unites to God all who are resolved to conform their lives in all things to the law of God.

VI CHRYSOSTOM

John of Constantinople (354–407) called since the sixth century Chrysostom (gold-mouth) because of his eloquent use of the Greek language, lived after the Christian Church had become the ruling religion of the Roman Empire. Priest in Antioch and since 398 bishop of Constantinople, he became deeply involved in the political controversies of his time. Because of his efforts to assert the independence of the Church from the emperor and his open criticism of the moral laxity at the court he was eventually deposed and expelled. He died in exile. Chrysostom illustrates the ethical teaching of the Christian Church shortly after it had come to power and the new problems which its close association with the empire produced.

SELECTION I

Concerning the Statutes, Homily XII, 9 ff.

When God formed man, he implanted within him from the beginning a natural law. And what then was this natural law? He gave utterance to conscience within us; and made the knowledge of good things, and of those which are the contrary, to be self-taught. For we have no need to learn that fornication is an evil thing, and that chastity is a good thing, but we know this from the first. And that you may learn that we know this from the first, the Lawgiver, when He afterwards gave laws, and said, "Thou shalt not kill," did not add, "since murder is an evil thing," but simply said, "Thou shalt not kill;" for He merely prohibited the sin, without teaching. How was it then when He said, "Thou shalt not kill," that He did not add, "because murder is a wicked thing." The reason was, that conscience had taught this beforehand; and He speaks thus, as to those who know and understand the point. Wherefore when He speaks to us of another commandment, not known to us by the dictate of conscience, He not only prohibits, but adds the reason. When, for instance, He gave commandment respecting the Sabbath; "On the seventh day thou shalt do no work;" He subjoined also the reason for this cessation. What was this? "Because on the seventh day God rested from all His works which He had begun to make." And again; "Because thou wert a servant in the land of Egypt." For what purpose then I ask did He add a reason respecting the Sabbath, but did no such thing in regard to murder? Because this commandment was not one of the leading ones. It was not one of those which were accurately defined of our conscience, but a kind of partial and temporary one; and for this reason it was abolished afterwards. But those which are necessary and uphold our life, are the following; "Thou shalt not kill; Thou shalt not commit adultery; Thou shalt not steal." On this account then He adds no reason in this case, nor enters into any instruction on the matter, but is content with the bare prohibition.

✧ ✧ ✧ ✧

But it may be objected, that the Gentile allows nothing of this sort. Come then, let us discuss this point, and as we have done with respect to the creation, having carried on the warfare against these objectors not only by the help of the Scriptures, but of reason, so also let us now do with respect to conscience. For Paul too, when he was engaged in controversy with such persons, entered upon this head. What then is it that they urge? They say, that there is no self-evident law seated in our consciences; and that God hath not implanted this in our nature. But if so, whence is it, I ask, that legislators have written those laws which are among them concerning marriages, concerning murders, concerning wills, concerning trusts, concerning abstinence from encroachments on one another, and a thousand other things? For the men now living may perchance have learned them from their elders; and they from those who were before them, and these again from those beyond? But from whom did those learn who were the originators and first enactors of laws among them? Is it not evident that it was from conscience? For they cannot say, that they held communication with Moses; or that they heard the prophets. How could it be so when they were Gentiles? But it is evident that from the very law which God placed in man when He formed him from the beginning, laws were laid down, and arts discovered, and all other things. For the arts too were thus established, their originators having come to the knowledge of them in a self-taught manner.

So also came there to be courts of justice, and so were penalties defined, as Paul accordingly observes. For since many of the Gentiles were ready to controvert this, and to say, "How will God judge mankind who lived before Moses? He did not send a lawgiver; He did not introduce a law; He commissioned no prophet, nor apostle, nor evangelist; how then can He call these to account?" Since Paul therefore wished to prove that they possessed a self-taught law; and that they knew clearly what they ought to do; hear how he speaks; "For when the Gentiles who have not the law, do by nature the things contained in the law, these having not the law, are a law unto themselves; which shew the work of the law written in their hearts." But how without letters? "Their conscience also bearing witness, and their thoughts the meanwhile accusing, or else excusing one another. In the day when God shall judge the secrets of men by Jesus Christ according to my gospel." And again; "As many as have sinned without law, shall perish without law; and as many as have sinned in the law, shall be judged by the law." What means, "They shall perish without law?" The law not accusing them, but their thoughts, and their conscience; for if they had not a law of conscience, it were not necessary that they should perish through having done amiss. For how should it be so if they sinned without a law? but when he says, "without a law," he does not assert that they had no law, but that they had no written law, though they had the law of nature. And again; "But glory, honour, and peace, to every man that worketh good, to the Jew first, and also to the Gentile."

But these things he spake in reference to the early times, before the coming of Christ; and the Gentile he names here is not an idolater, but one who worshipped God only; unfettered by the necessity of Judaical observances, (I mean Sabbaths, and circumcision, and divers purifications,) yet exhibiting all manner of wisdom and piety. And again, discoursing of such a worshipper, he observes, "Wrath and indignation, tribulation and anguish, upon every soul of man that doeth evil, of the Jew first, and also of the Gentile." Again he here calls by the name of Greek one who was free from the observance of Judaic customs. If, then, he had not heard the law, nor conversed with the Jews, how could there be wrath, indignation and tribulation against him for working evil? The reason is, that he possessed a conscience inwardly admonishing him, and teaching him, and instructing him in all things. Whence is this manifest? From the way in which he punished others when they did amiss; from the way in which he set up the tribunals of justice. With the view of making this more plain, Paul spoke of those who were living in wickedness. "Who, knowing the ordinance of God, that they which commit such things are worthy of death, not only do the same, but also consent with them that practise them." "But from whence," says some one, "did they know, that it is the will of God, that those who live in iniquity should be punished with death?" From whence? Why, from the way in which they judged others who sinned. For if thou deemest not murder to be a wicked thing, when thou hast gotten a murderer at thy bar, thou shouldest not punish him. So if thou deemest it not an evil thing to commit adultery, when the adulterer has fallen into thy hands, release him from punishment! But if thou recordest laws, and prescribest punishments, and art a severe judge of the sins of others; what defence canst thou make, in matters wherein thou thyself doest amiss, by saying that thou art ignorant what things ought to be done? For suppose that thou and another person have alike been guilty of adultery. On what account dost thou punish him, and deem thyself worthy of forgiveness? Since if thou didst not know adultery to be wickedness, it were not right to punish it in another. But if thou punishest, and thinkest to escape the punishment thyself, how is it agreeable to reason that the same offences should not pay the same penalty?

This indeed is the very thing which Paul rebukes, when he says, "And thinkest thou this, O man, that judgest them which do such things, and doest the same, that thou shalt escape the judgment of God?" It is not, it cannot be possible; for from the very sentence, he means, which thou pronouncest upon another, from this sentence God will then judge thee. For surely thou art not just, and God unjust! But if thou overlookest not another suffering wrong, how shall God overlook? And if thou correctest the sins of others, how will not God correct thee? And though He may not bring the punishment upon thee instantly, be not confident on that account, but fear the more. So also Paul bade thee, saying, "Despisest thou the riches of His goodness, and forbearance, and longsuffering, not knowing that the goodness of God leadeth thee to repentance?" For therefore, saith he, doth he bear with thee, not that thou mayest become worse, but that thou mayest repent. But if thou wilt not, this longsuffering becomes a cause of thy greater punishment; continuing, as thou dost, impenitent. This, however, is the very thing he means, when he says, "But after thy hardness and impenitent heart treasurest up to thyself wrath against the day of wrath, and revelation of the righteous judgment of God Who will render to every man according to his deeds." Since, therefore, He rendereth to every man according to his works; for this reason He both implanted within us a natural law, and afterwards gave us a written one, in order that He might demand an account of sins, and that He might crown those who act rightly. Let us then order our conduct with the utmost care, and as those who have soon to encounter a fearful tribunal; knowing that we shall enjoy no pardon, if after a natural as well as written law, and so much teaching and continual admonition, we neglect our own salvation.

SELECTION 2
Homilies on Matthew, XIX

Chrysostom interprets the petition of the Lord's Prayer "Thy will be done in earth as it is in heaven" as a call to the transformation of the world, namely, "make the earth a heaven."

Behold a most excellent train of thought! in that He bade us indeed long for the things to come, and hasten towards that sojourn; and, till that may be, even while we abide here, so long to be earnest in showing forth the same conversation as those above. For ye must long, saith He, for heaven, and the things in heaven; however, even before heaven, He hath bidden us make the earth a heaven and do and say all things, even while we are continuing in it, as having our conversation there; insomuch that these too should be objects of our prayer to the Lord. For there is nothing to hinder our reaching the perfection of the powers above, because we inhabit the earth; but it is possible even while abiding here, to do all, as though already placed on high. What He saith therefore is this: "As there all things are done without hindrance, and the angels are not partly obedient and partly disobedient, but in all things yield and obey (for He saith, 'Mighty in strength, performing His word'); so vouchsafe that we men may not do Thy will by halves, but perform all things as Thou willest."

Seest thou how He hath taught us also to be modest, by making it clear that virtue is not of our endeavors only, but also of the grace above? And again, He hath enjoined each one of us, who pray, to take upon himself the care of the whole world. For He did not at all say, "Thy will be done" *in me*, or *in us*, but everywhere on the earth; so that error may be destroyed, and truth implanted, and all wickedness cast out, and virtue return, and no difference in this respect be henceforth between heaven and earth.

SELECTION 3
Eutropius and the Vanity of Riches

Since the reign of Emperor Constantine the right of the Christian Church to give asylum to refugees had been acknowledged. Emperor Theodosius had confirmed it by law in 392 (*Codex Theodos.* 9, 44). Chrysostom was an ardent defender of this right of the Church. It had been subverted by one of the strangest and most powerful of Chrysostom's contemporaries, the Consul Eutropius. A eunuch and slave, he had risen in an unbelievable career to become the most trusted counselor of the feeble Emperor Arcadius. Thus he was the actual ruler of the Eastern Empire. He had much to do with the election of Chrysostom, who, however, opposed him because of his greed and corruption and his efforts to curtail the rights of the Church. Thus Chrysostom could later say, "Was I not continually telling thee that wealth was a runaway? But you would not heed me. Did I not tell thee that it was an unthankful servant? But you would not be persuaded. . . . Did I not say to thee when you continually rebuked me for speaking the truth, 'I love thee better than they do who flatter thee?'"

Nevertheless, Eutropius had succeeded in having the Emperor sign an edict which abolished the Church's right to grant asylum to people accused of high-treason (*Codex Theodos.* 9, 45, 1 and 9, 45, 3).

Ironically after his downfall it was Eutropius who fled to the Church to find asylum under the protection of Chrysostom. It was this situation which gave Chrysostom the opportunity to deliver the following homily which gives a clue to Chrysostom's own resistance to the court which eventually caused his exile and death.

. . . A few days ago the Church was besieged: an army came, and fire issued from their eyes, yet it did not scorch the olive tree; swords were unsheathed, yet no one received a wound; the imperial gates were in distress, but the Church was in security. And yet the tide of war flowed hither; for here the refugee was sought, and we withstood them, not fearing their rage. And wherefore prithee? because we held as a sure pledge the saying "Thou art Peter, and upon this rock I will build my Church: and the gates of hell shall not prevail against it." And when I say the Church I mean not only a place but also a plan of life: I mean not the walls of the Church but the laws of the Church. When thou takest refuge in a Church, do not seek shelter merely in the place but in the spirit of the place. For the Church is not wall and roof but faith and life.

Do not tell me that the man having been surrendered was surrendered by the Church: if he had not abandoned the Church he would not have been surrendered. Do not say that he fled here for refuge and then was given up: the Church did not abandon him but he abandoned the Church. He was not surrendered from within the Church but outside its walls. Wherefore did he forsake the Church? Didst thou desire to save thyself? Thou shouldst have held fast to the altar. There were no walls here, but there was the guarding providence of God. Wast thou a sinner? God does not reject thee: for "He came not to call the righteous but sinners to repentance." The harlot was saved when she clung to His feet. Have ye heard the passage read to-day? Now I say these things that thou mayest not hesitate to take refuge in the Church. Abide with the Church, and the Church does not hand thee over to the enemy: but if thou fliest from the Church, the Church is not the cause of thy capture. For if thou art inside the fold the wolf does not enter: but if thou goest outside, thou art liable to be the wild beast's prey: yet this is not the fault of the fold, but of thy own pusillanimity. The Church hath no feet. Talk not to me of walls and arms: for walls wax old with time, but the Church has no old age. Walls are shattered by barbarians, but over the Church even demons do not prevail. And that my words are no mere vaunt there is the evidence of facts. How many have assailed the Church, and yet the assailants have perished while the Church herself has soared beyond the sky?

VII AUGUSTINE

Aurelius Augustinus, born November 13, 354, in Thagaste, North Africa, became eventually the most influential theologian of Western Christendom. His thought is seminal for Roman Catholics as well as the descendants of the Lutheran and Calvinist reformation. Especially in the area of social philosophy Augustine's influence is determinative for the West. It is expressed classically in his *City of God* though other works are also of great importance for the understanding of his social ethics. He lived seventy-six years in an age of vast social and political upheaval, reflected and addressed in all his writings, and died August 28, 430, as Bishop of Hippo while the Vandals were besieging the city. His contributions to Christian social thought are: The insistence on the goodness of creation, the understanding of all mankind as infected by original sin and the stress on the pervasiveness of sin which this implies, the analysis of history as a conflict between the two cities, and a view of justice and love which is profoundly influenced by Augustine's platonic heritage. His view of the use of force in "just" war and the defense of the "true" Church against the heretics dominated Christian thought until our time.

SELECTION 1

Enchiridion, Chap. 9–11

Undergirding all of Augustine's thought is his belief in the goodness of the Creator and thus the essential goodness of creation. Evil is a deficiency and has no independent being. It is also significant that such faith does not necessarily imply scientific knowledge, nor is this to be expected.

When, then, the question is asked what we are to believe in

regard to religion, it is not necessary to probe into the nature of things, as was done by those whom the Greeks call *physici;* nor need we be in alarm lest the Christian should be ignorant of the force and number of the elements,—the motion, and order, and eclipses of the heavenly bodies; the form of the heavens; the species and the natures of animals, plants, stones, fountains, rivers, mountains; about chronology and distances; the signs of coming storms; and a thousand other things which those philosophers either have found out, or think they have found out. For even these men themselves, endowed though they are with so much genius, burning with zeal, abounding in leisure, tracking some things by the aid of human conjecture, searching into others with the aids of history and experience, have not found out all things; and even their boasted discoveries are oftener mere guesses than certain knowledge. It is enough for the Christian to believe that the only cause of all created things, whether heavenly or earthly, whether visible or invisible, is the goodness of the Creator, the one true God; and that nothing exists but Himself that does not derive its existence from Him; and that He is the Trinity—to wit, the Father, and the Son begotten of the Father, and the Holy Spirit proceeding from the same Father, but one and the same Spirit of Father and Son.

By the Trinity, thus supremely and equally and unchangeably good, all things were created; and these are not supremely and equally and unchangeably good, but yet they are good, even taken separately. Taken as a whole, however, they are very good, because their *ensemble* constitutes the universe in all its wonderful order and beauty.

And in the universe, even that which is called evil, when it is regulated and put in its own place, only enhances our admiration of the good; for we enjoy and value the good more when we compare it with the evil. For the Almighty God, who, as even the heathen acknowledge, has supreme power over all things, being Himself supremely good, would never permit the existence of anything evil among His works, if He were not so omnipotent and good that He can bring good even out of evil. For what is that which we call evil but the absence of good? In the bodies of animals, disease and wounds mean nothing but the absence of health; for when a cure is effected, that does not mean that the evils which were present—namely, the diseases and wounds—go away from the body and dwell elsewhere: they altogether cease to exist; for the wound or disease is not a substance, but a defect in the fleshly substance,—the flesh itself being a substance, and therefore something good, of which those evils—that is, privations of the good which we call health—are accidents. Just in the same way, what are called vices in the soul are nothing but privations of natural good. And when they are cured, they are not transferred elsewhere: when they cease to exist in the healthy soul, they cannot exist anywhere else.

SELECTION 2
Enchiridion, Chap. 23–26

While God is the cause of all good, all evil—personal as well as social—is the result of the revolt against God of angels and men.

As it is right that we should know the causes of good and evil, so much of them at least as will suffice for the way that leads us to the kingdom, where there will be life without the shadow of death, truth without any alloy of error, and happiness unbroken by any sorrow, I have discussed these subjects with the brevity which my limited space demanded. And I think there cannot now be any doubt, that the only cause of any good that we enjoy is the goodness of God, and that the only cause of evil is the falling away from the unchangeable good of a being made good but unchangeable, first in the case of an angel, and afterwards in the case of man.

This is the first evil that befell the intelligent creation—that is, its first privation of good. Following upon this crept in, and now even in opposition to man's will, *ignorance* of duty, and *lust* after what is hurtful: and these brought in their train *error* and *suffering,* which, when they are felt to be imminent, produce that shrinking of the mind which is called *fear*. Further, when the mind attains the objects of its desire, however hurtful or empty they may be, error prevents it from perceiving their true nature, or its perceptions are overborne by a diseased appetite, and so it is puffed up with a *foolish joy*. From these fountains of evil, which spring out of defect rather than superfluity, flows every form of misery that besets a rational nature.

And yet such a nature, in the midst of all its evils, could not lose the craving after happiness. Now the evils I have mentioned are common to all who for their wickedness have been justly condemned by God, whether they be men or angels. But there is one form of punishment peculiar to man—the death of the body. God had threatened him with this punishment of death if he should sin, leaving him indeed to the freedom of his own will, but yet commanding his obedience under pain of death; and He placed him amid the happiness of Eden, as it were in a protected nook of life, with the intention that, if he preserved his righteousness, he should thence ascend to a better place.

Thence after his sin, he was driven into exile, and by his sin the whole race of which he was the root was corrupted in him, and thereby subjected to the penalty of death. And so it happens that all descended from him, and from the woman who had led him into sin, and was condemned at the same time with him,—being the offspring of carnal lust on which the same punishment of disobedience was visited,—were tainted with the original sin, and were by it drawn through divers errors and sufferings into that last and endless punishment which they suffer in common with the fallen angels, their corrupters and masters, and the partakers of their doom. And thus "by one man sin entered into the world, and death by sin; and so death passed upon all men, for that all have sinned." By "the world" the apostle, of course, means in this place the whole human race.

SELECTION 3
City of God v, 13 and 15

Many pagans served virtue and their country well, but they did it for the love of praise. For such virtues they receive not eternal life but the praise of men.

Nevertheless, they who restrain baser lusts, not by the power of the Holy Spirit obtained by the faith of piety, or by the love of intelligible beauty, but by desire of human praise, or, at all events, restrain them better by the love of such praise, are not indeed yet holy, but only less base. Even Tully was not able to conceal this fact; for, in the same books which he wrote, *De Republica,* when speaking concerning the education of a chief of the state, who ought, he says, to be nourished on glory, goes on to say that their ancestors did many wonderful and illustrious things through desire of glory. So far, therefore, from resisting this vice, they even thought that it ought to be excited and kindled up, supposing that that would be beneficial to the republic. But not even in his books on philosophy does Tully dissimulate this poisonous opinion, for he there avows it more clearly than day. For when he is speaking of those studies which are to be pursued with a view to the true good, and not with the vainglorious desire of human praise, he introduces the following universal and general statement:

> "Honor nourishes the arts, and all are stimulated to the prosecution of studies by glory; and those pursuits are always neglected which are generally discredited."

✧ ✧ ✧ ✧

Now, therefore, with regard to those to whom God did not purpose to give eternal life with His holy angels in His own celestial city, to the society of which that true piety which does not render the service of religion, which the Greeks call *Latreia,* to any save the true God conducts, if He had also withheld from them the terrestrial glory of that most excellent empire, a reward would not have been rendered to their good arts,—that is, their virtues,—by which they sought to attain so great glory. For as to those who seem to do some good that they may receive glory from men, the Lord also says, "Verily I say unto you, they have received their reward." So also these despised their own private affairs for the sake of the republic, and for its treasury resisted avarice, consulted for the good of their country with a spirit of freedom, addicted neither to what their laws pronounced to be crime nor to lust. By all these acts, as by the true way, they pressed forward to honors, power, and glory; they were honored among almost all nations; they imposed the laws of their empire upon many nations; and at this day, both in literature and history, they are glorious among almost all nations.

There is no reason why they should complain against the justice of the supreme and true God,—"they have received their reward."

SELECTION 4

City of God XIV, 28; XIX, 17

Augustine's description of the two cities and the reason for the discord between them:

Accordingly, two cities have been formed by two loves: the earthly by the love of self, even to the contempt of God; the heavenly by the love of God, even to the contempt of self. The former, in a word, glories in itself, the latter in the Lord. For the one seeks glory from men; but the greatest glory of the other is God, the witness of conscience. The one lifts up its head in its own glory; the other says to its God, "Thou art my glory, and the lifter up of mine head." In the one, the princes and the nations it subdues are ruled by the love of ruling; in the other, the princes and the subjects serve one another in love, the latter obeying, while the former take thought for all. The one delights in its own strength, represented in the persons of its rulers; the other says to its God, "I will love Thee, O Lord, my strength." And therefore the wise men of the one city, living according to man, have sought for profit to their own bodies or souls, or both, and those who have known God "glorified Him not as God, neither were thankful, but became vain in their imaginations, and their foolish heart was darkened; professing themselves to be wise,"—that is, glorying in their own wisdom, and being possessed by pride,—"they became fools, and changed the glory of the incorruptible God into an image made like to corruptible man, and to birds, and four-footed beasts, and creeping things." For they were either leaders or followers of the people in adoring images, "and worshipped and served the creature more than the Creator, who is blessed for ever." But in the other city there is no human wisdom, but only godliness, which offers due worship to the true God, and looks for its reward in the society of the saints, of holy angels as well as holy men, "that God may be all in all."

✧ ✧ ✧ ✧

But the families which do not live by faith seek their peace in the earthly advantages of this life; while the families which live by faith look for those eternal blessings which are promised, and use as pilgrims such advantages of time and of earth as do not fascinate and divert them from God, but rather aid them to endure with greater ease, and to keep down the number of those burdens of the corruptible body which weigh upon the soul. Thus the things necessary for this mortal life are used by both kinds of men and families alike, but each has its own peculiar and widely different aim in using them. The earthly city, which does not live by faith, seeks an earthly peace, and the end it proposes, in the well-ordered concord of civic obedience and rule, is the combination of men's wills to attain the things which are helpful to this life. The heavenly city, or rather the part of it which sojourns on earth and lives by faith, makes use of this peace only because it must, until this mortal condition which necessitates it shall pass away. Consequently, so long as it lives like a captive and a stranger in the earthly city, though it has already received the promise of redemption, and the gift of the Spirit as the earnest of it, it makes no scruple to obey the laws of the earthly city, whereby the things necessary for the maintenance of this mortal life are administered; and thus, as this life is common to both cities; so there is a harmony between them in regard to what belongs to it. But, as the earthly city has had some philosophers whose doctrine is condemned by the divine teaching, and who, being deceived either by their own conjectures or by demons, supposed that many gods must be invited to take an interest in human affairs, and assigned to each a separate function and a separate department,—to one the body, to another the soul; and in the body itself, to one the head, to another the neck, and each of the other members to one of the gods; and in like manner, in the soul, to one god the natural capacity was assigned, to another education, to another anger, to another lust; and so the various affairs of life were assigned,—cattle to one, corn to another, wine to another, oil to another, the woods to another, money to another, navigation to another, wars and victories to another, marriages to another, births and fecundity to another, and other things to other gods: and as the celestial city, on the other hand, knew that one God only was to be worshipped, and that to Him alone was due that service which the Greeks call *Latreia,* and which can be given only to a god, it has come to pass that the two cities could not have common laws of religion, and that the heavenly city has been compelled in this matter to dissent, and to become obnoxious to those who think differently, and to stand the brunt of their anger and hatred and persecutions, except in so far as the minds of their enemies have been alarmed by the multitude of the Christians and quelled by the manifest protection of God accorded to them. This heavenly city, then, while it sojourns on earth, calls citizens out of all nations, and gathers together a society of pilgrims of all languages, not scrupling about diversities in the manners, laws, and institutions whereby earthly peace is secured and maintained, but recognizing that, however various these are, they all tend to one and the same end of earthly peace. It therefore is so far from rescinding and abolishing these diversities, that it even preserves and adopts them, so long only as no hindrance to the worship of the one supreme and true God is thus introduced. Even the heavenly city, therefore, while in its state of pilgrimage, avails itself of the peace of earth, and, so far as it can without injuring faith and godliness, desires and maintains a common agreement among men regarding the acquisition of the necessaries of life, and makes this earthly peace bear upon the peace of heaven; for this alone can be truly called and esteemed the peace of the reasonable creatures, consisting as it does in the perfectly ordered and harmonious enjoyment of God and of one another in God. When we shall have reached that peace, this mortal life shall give place to one that is eternal, and our body shall be no more this animal body which by its corruption weighs down the soul, but a spiritual body feeling no want, and in all its members subjected to the will. In its pilgrim state the heavenly city possesses this peace by faith; and by this faith it lives righteously when it refers to the attainment of that peace every good action towards God and man; for the life of the city is a social life.

SELECTION 5
Of the Morals of the Catholic Church, Chap. XV, XXIV, 44, XXVI, and XXVII

Virtue is the perfect love of God; all other virtues are dependent and derivative. The proper love of self and of the neighbor is derived from it.

As to virtue leading us to a happy life, I hold virtue to be nothing else than perfect love of God. For the fourfold division of virtue I regard as taken from four forms of love. For these four virtues (would that all felt their influence in their minds as they have their names in their mouths!), I should have no hesitation in defining them: that temperance is love giving itself entirely to that which is loved; fortitude is love readily bearing all things for the sake of the loved object; justice is love serving only the loved object, and therefore ruling rightly; prudence is love distinguishing with sagacity between what hinders it and what helps it. The object of this love is not anything, but only God, the chief good, the highest wisdom, the perfect harmony. So we may express the definition thus: that temperance is love keeping itself entire and incorrupt for God; fortitude is love bearing everything readily for the sake of God; justice is love serving God only, and therefore ruling well all else, as subject to man; prudence is love making a right distinction between what helps it towards God and what might hinder it.

✧ ✧ ✧ ✧

What of justice that pertains to God? As the Lord says, "Ye cannot serve two masters," and the apostle denounces those who serve the creature rather than the Creator, was it not said before in the Old Testament, "Thou shalt worship the Lord thy God, and Him only shalt thou serve?" I need say no more on this, for these books are full of such passages. The lover, then, whom we are describing, will get from justice this rule of life, that he must with perfect readiness serve the God whom he loves, the highest good, the highest wisdom, the highest peace; and as regards all other things, must either rule them as subject to himself, or treat them with a view to their subjection. This rule of life, is, as we have shown, confirmed by the authority of both Testaments.

✧ ✧ ✧ ✧

To proceed to what remains. It may be thought that there is nothing here about man himself, the lover. But to think this, shows a want of clear perception. For it is impossible for one who loves God not to love himself. For he alone has a proper love for himself who aims diligently at the attainment of the chief and true good; and if this is nothing else but God, as has been shown, what is to prevent one who loves God from loving himself? And then, among men should there be no bond of mutual love? Yea, verily; so that we can think of no surer step towards the love of God than the love of man to man.

Let the Lord then supply us with the other precept in answer to the question about the precepts of life; for He was not satisfied with one as knowing that God is one thing and man another, and that the difference is nothing less than that between the Creator and the thing created in the likeness of its Creator. He says then that the second precept is, "Thou shalt love thy neighbor as thyself." Now you love yourself suitably when you love God better than yourself. What, then, you aim at in yourself you must aim at in your neighbor, namely, that he may love God with a perfect affection. For you do not love him as yourself, unless you try to draw him to that good which you are yourself pursuing. For this is the one good which has room for all to pursue it along with thee. From this precept proceed the duties of human society, in which it is hard to keep from error. But the first thing to aim at is, that we should be benevolent, that is, that we cherish no malice and no evil design against another. For man is the nearest neighbor of man.

Hear also what Paul says: "The love of our neighbor," he says, "worketh no ill." The testimonies here made use of are very short, but, if I mistake not, they are to the point, and sufficient for the purpose. And every one knows how many and how weighty are the words to be found everywhere in these books on the love of our neighbor. But as a man may sin against another in two ways, either by injuring him or by not helping him when it is in his power, and as it is for these things which no loving man would do that men are called wicked, all that is required is, I think, proved by these words, "The love of our neighbor worketh no ill." And if we cannot attain to good unless we first desist from working evil, our love of our neighbor is a sort of cradle of our love to God, so that, as it is said, "the love of our neighbor worketh no ill," we may rise from this to these other words, "We know that all things issue in good to them that love God."

But there is a sense in which these either rise together to fullness and perfection, or, while the love of God is first in beginning, the love of our neighbor is first in coming to perfection. For perhaps divine love takes hold on us more rapidly at the outset, but we reach perfection more easily in lower things. However that may be, the main point is this, that no one should think that while he despises his neighbor he will come to happiness and to the God whom he loves. And would that it were as easy to seek the good of our neighbor, or to avoid hurting him, as it is for one well trained and kind-hearted to love his neighbor! These things require more than mere good-will, and can be done only by a high degree of thoughtfulness and prudence, which belongs only to those to whom it is given by God, the source of all good. On this topic—which is one, I think, of great difficulty—I will try to say a few words such as my plan admits of, resting all my hope in Him whose gifts these are.

Man, then, as viewed by his fellowman, is a rational soul with a mortal and earthly body in its service. Therefore he who loves his neighbor does good partly to the man's body, and partly to his soul. What benefits the body is called medicine; what benefits the soul, discipline. Medicine here includes everything that either preserves or restores bodily health. It includes, therefore, not only what belongs to the art of medical men, properly so called, but also food and drink, clothing and shelter, and every means of covering and protection to guard our bodies against injuries and mishaps from without as well as from within. For hunger and thirst, and cold and heat, and all violence from without, produce loss of that health which is the point to be considered.

Hence those who seasonably and wisely supply all the things

required for warding off these evils and distresses are called compassionate, although they may have been so wise that no painful feeling disturbed their mind in the exercise of compassion. No doubt the word compassionate implies suffering in the heart of the man who feels for the sorrow of another. And it is equally true that a wise man ought to be free from all painful emotion when he assists the needy, when he gives food to the hungry and water to the thirsty, when he clothes the naked, when he takes the stranger into his house, when he sets free the oppressed, when, lastly, he extends his charity to the dead in giving them burial. Still the epithet compassionate is a proper one, although he acts with tranquility of mind, not from the stimulus of painful feeling, but from motives of benevolence. There is no harm in the word compassionate when there is no passion in the case.

Fools, again, who avoid the exercise of compassion as a vice, because they are not sufficiently moved by a sense of duty without feeling also distressful emotion, are frozen into hard insensibility, which is very different from the calm of a rational serenity. God, on the other hand, is properly called compassionate; and the sense in which He is so will be understood by those whom piety and diligence have made fit to understand. There is a danger lest, in using the words of the learned, we harden the souls of the unlearned by leading them away from compassion instead of softening them with the desire of a charitable disposition. As compassion, then, requires us to ward off these distresses from others, so harmlessness forbids the infliction of them.

SELECTION 6

Letter CLXXXIX (to Count Boniface, A.D. 418) *Letter* CLXXIII (to Donatus, a Presbyter of the Donatist Party, A.D. 416)

Augustine's discussion of love and justice (*City of God*, XIX, 12) roots all justice ultimately in love, but he does not hesitate in later years to advocate the use of force by the state and even on behalf of the unity of the Church, especially in the controversy with the Donatists. This attitude had fateful consequences for Christian ethics.

Letter to Count Boniface (Count Boniface was Governor of the Roman province of Africa under Placidia, who for twenty-five years ruled the Empire in the name of his son Valentinian. It was Boniface who, in order to strengthen his position, invited the vandals to Africa and lived to regret it):

Think, then, of this first of all, when you are arming for the battle, that even your bodily strength is a gift of God; for, considering this, you will not employ the gift of God against God. For, when faith is pledged, it is to be kept even with the enemy against whom the war is waged, how much more with the friend for whom the battle is fought! Peace should be the object of your desire; war should be waged only as a necessity, and waged only that God may by it deliver men from the necessity and preserve them in peace. For peace is not sought in order to the kindling of war, but war is waged in order that peace may be obtained. Therefore, even in waging war, cherish the spirit of a peacemaker, that, by conquering those whom you attack, you may lead them back to the advantages of peace; for our Lord says: "Blessed are the peacemakers; for they shall be called the children of God." If, however, peace among men be so sweet as procuring temporal safety, how much sweeter is that peace with God which procures for men the eternal felicity of the angels! Let necessity, therefore, and not your will, slay the enemy who fights against you. As violence is used towards him who rebels and resists, so mercy is due to the vanquished or the captive, especially in the case in which future troubling of the peace is not to be feared.

✧ ✧ ✧ ✧

Letter to Donatus (Donatus was a presbyter of the Donatist Party, which threatened the unity of the church by its claim that the validity of the sacraments depended upon the worthiness of the administering priest. It was in this controversy that Augustine advocated forced conversion):

If you could see the sorrow of my heart and my concern for your salvation, you would perhaps take pity on your own soul, doing that which is pleasing to God, by giving heed to the word which is not ours but His; and would no longer give to His Scripture only a place in your memory, while shutting it out from your heart. You are angry because you are being drawn to salvation, although you have drawn so many of our fellow Christians to destruction. For what did we order beyond this, that you should be arrested, brought before the authorities, and guarded, in order to prevent you from perishing? As to your having sustained bodily injury, you have yourself to blame for this, as you would not use the horse which was immediately brought to you, and then dashed yourself violently to the ground; for, as you well know, your companion, who was brought along with you, arrived uninjured, not having done any harm to himself as you did.

You think, however, that even what we have done to you should not have been done, because, in your opinion, no man should be compelled to that which is good. Mark, therefore, the words of the apostle: "If a man desire the office of a bishop, he desireth a good work," and yet, in order to make the office of a bishop be accepted by many men, they are seized against their will, subjected to importunate persuasion, shut up and detained in custody, and made to suffer so many things which they dislike, until a willingness to undertake the good work is found in them. How much more, then, is it fitting that you should be drawn forcibly away from a pernicious error, in which you are enemies to your own souls, and brought to acquaint yourselves with the truth, or to choose it when known, not only in order to your holding in a safe and advantageous way the honour belonging to your office, but also in order to preserve you from perishing miserably! You say that God has given us free will, and that therefore no man should be compelled even to good. Why, then, are those whom I have above referred to compelled to that which is good? Take heed, therefore, to something which you do not wish to consider. The aim towards which a good will compassionately devotes its efforts is to secure that a bad will be rightly directed. For who does not know that a man is not condemned on any other ground than because his bad will deserved it, and that no man is saved who has not a good will? Nevertheless, it does not follow from this that those who are loved should be cruelly left to yield themselves with impurity to their bad will; but in so far as power is given, they ought to be both prevented from evil and compelled to good. . . .

Mark also what follows:—"If I have not charity, it profiteth me nothing." To that charity you are called; by that charity you are prevented from perishing: and yet you think, forsooth, that to throw yourself headlong to destruction, by your own act, will profit you in some measure, although, even if you suffered death at the hands of another, while you remain an enemy to charity it would profit you nothing. Nay, more, being in a state of exclusion from the Church, and severed from the body of unity and the bond of charity, you would be punished with eternal misery even though you were burned alive for Christ's name; for this is the apostle's declaration, "Though I give my body to be burned, and have not charity, it profiteth me nothing." Bring your mind back, therefore, to rational reflection and sober thought; consider carefully whether it is to error and to impiety that you are being called, and, if you still think so, submit patiently to any hardship for the truth's sake. If, however, the fact rather be that you are living in error and in impiety, and that in the Church to which you are called truth and piety are found, because there is Christian unity and the love (*caritas*) of the Holy Spirit, why do you labour any longer to be an enemy to yourself? . . .

I hear that you have remarked and often quote the fact recorded in the gospels, that the seventy disciples went back from the Lord, and that they had been left to their own choice in this wicked and impious desertion, and that to the twelve who alone remained the Lord said, "Will ye also go away?" But you have neglected to remark, that at that time the Church was only beginning to burst into life from the recently planted seed, and that there was not yet fulfilled in her the prophecy: "All kings shall fall down before Him; yea, all nations shall serve Him;" and it is in proportion to the more enlarged accomplishment of this prophecy that the Church wields greater power, so that she may not only invite, but even compel men to embrace what is good. This our Lord intended then to illustrate, for although He had great power, He chose rather to manifest His humility. This also He taught, with sufficient plainness, in the parable of the Feast, in which the master of the house, after He had sent a message to the invited guests, and they had refused to come, said to his servants: "Go out quickly into the streets and lanes of the city, and bring in hither the poor, and the maimed, and the halt, and the blind. And the servant said, Lord, it is done as thou hast commanded, and yet there is room. And the Lord said unto the servant, Go out into the highways and hedges, and compel them to come in that my house may be filled." Mark, now, how it was said in regard to those who came first, "bring them in;" it was not said, "compel them to come in,"—by which was signified the incipient condition of the Church, when it was only growing towards the position in which it would have strength to compel men to come in. Accordingly, because it was right that when the Church had been strengthened, both in power and in extent, men should be compelled to come in to the feast of everlasting salvation, it was afterwards added in the parable, "The servant said, Lord, it is done as thou hast commanded, and yet there is room. And the Lord said unto the servants, Go out into the highways and hedges, and compel them to come in." Wherefore, if you were walking peaceably, absent from this feast of everlasting salvation and of the holy unity of the Church, we should find you, as it were, in the "highways;" but since, by multiplied injuries and cruelties, which you perpetrate on our people, you are, as it were, full of thorns and roughness, we find you as it were in the "hedges," and we compel you to come in. The sheep which is compelled is driven whither it would not wish to go, but after it has entered, it feeds of its own accord in the pastures to which it was brought. Wherefore restrain your perverse and rebellious spirit, that in the true Church of Christ you may find the feast of salvation.

VIII MONASTICISM

The deep involvement of the Church with the prevailing culture, which resulted from the adoption of Christianity as the official religion of the Empire, produced the monastic protest. It is a controlled version of the so-called "Christ against Culture" pattern since monasticism does not separate itself from the Church but bears witness to its rejection of many values of the prevailing culture within the Church.

Thus the involvement of monasticism with society and culture is, indeed, ambiguous. On the one hand it represents a denial of many values highly prized by culture, e.g., private property and sex. On the other hand, it is the main force in the preservation of Christian culture through the Dark Ages of the collapsing Empire. The monks preserve Western culture by transmitting it to the barbarians. The monks are the teachers of the West at least until the Reformation and it is no accident that many of the Reformers came out of the monastery (e.g., Luther). Because of the key position of monks and friars as the teachers of Christendom the teachings of monasticism became of crucial importance for Christian social thought.

SELECTION I
The Sayings of the Fathers

In the fifth century sayings of the hermits who lived in the Egyptian wilderness were being circulated. While they often were not very profound and were overly moralistic they do reflect the spirit of simplicity which characterized these early hermits and contributed to their influence on the times. This selection consists of sayings on charity.

Abba Antony said: "Now I do not fear God, but I love him: for love casteth out fear."

✧ ✧ ✧ ✧

He also said: "From our neighbour are life and death. If we do good to our neighbour, we do good to God: if we cause our neighbour to stumble, we sin against Christ."

✧ ✧ ✧ ✧

Once when Abba John was going up from Scete with other monks, their guide missed his way in the night. The brothers said to Abba John: "What are we to do, Abba, to prevent ourselves dying in the desert, now that this brother has missed the way?" The old man said: "If we say anything to him, he will be grieved. Look, I will pretend I am worn out, and say I cannot walk, and will lie here until daybreak." And they did so. The others said: "We will not go on, but will stay with you here." They stayed there until daybreak, so that they should not abuse the monk who had wrongly guided them.

✧ ✧ ✧ ✧

Abba Paphnutius is said to have drunk wine seldom. But once on a journey he happened upon a meeting-place of robbers, while they were drinking. The chief of the robber band recognized him and knew that he would not drink wine. He saw that he was tired out. So he filled a cup with wine, held a naked sword in his other hand, and said: "If you do not drink, I will kill you." The old man knew that the robber chieftain was trying to obey the commandment of God: and in his desire to help him, he took the cup and drank.

Then the robber chieftain did penance before him, and said: "Forgive me, Abba, that I grieved you." And the old man said to him: "I believe that because of this cup my God will have mercy upon you in this world and the next." And the robber chieftain answered: "And I believe in God that henceforward I shall harm no one." And the old man won over the whole band of robbers, because for God's sake he let himself fall into their power.

✧ ✧ ✧ ✧

Two monks were in Cellia. One of them was an old man, and asked the younger: "Let us stay together, my brother." The other said: "I am a sinner, and cannot stay with you, Abba." But he begged him: "Yes, we can stay together." The old man had a clean heart, and the younger did not want him to know that he sometimes fell to lust. The monk then said: "Let me go away for a week, and we will talk about it again." At the end of the week the old man came back, and the younger, wishing to test him, said: "I succumbed to a great temptation during this week, Abba. When I had gone to a village on an errand, I lay with a woman." The old man said: "Are you penitent?" And the brother said: "Yes." The old man said: "I will carry half the burden of the sin with you." Then the brother said: "Now I know that we can stay together." And they remained together till death parted them.

✧ ✧ ✧ ✧

A brother asked an old man: "There are two monks: one stays quietly in his cell, fasting for six days at a time, and laying many austerities upon himself: and the other ministers to the sick. Which of them is more acceptable to God?" The old man answered: "If the brother, who fasts six days, even hung himself up by his nostrils, he could never be the equal of him who ministers to the sick."

✧ ✧ ✧ ✧

An old man was asked: "How is it that some struggle away at their religious life, but do not receive grace like the old fathers?" The old man said: "Because then charity ruled, and each one drew his neighbour upward. Now charity is growing cold, and each of us draws his neighbour downward, and so we do not deserve grace."

✧ ✧ ✧ ✧

Two old men lived together for many years without a quarrel. One said to the other: "Let us have one quarrel with each other, as is the way of men." And the other answered: "I do not know how a quarrel happens." And the first said: "Look, I put a tile between us, and I say, That's mine. Then you say, No, it's mine. That is how you begin a quarrel."

So they put a tile between them, and one of them said: "That's mine." And the other said: "No; it's mine." And he answered: "Yes, it is yours. Take it away." And they went away unable to argue with each other.

✧ ✧ ✧ ✧

A brother asked an old man: "If I see a monk of whom I have heard as guilty of a sin, I cannot persuade my soul to bring him in." And the old man said: "If you do good to a good brother, it is little to him. To the other, give twofold, for it is he who is sick."

SELECTION 2
The Rule of Saint Benedict

Benedict of Nursia, who died in 543, founded a monastery at Monte Cassino in Italy and devised a rule for monastic life which was widely adopted. From this we select his discourse on humility:

The first degree of humility is a prompt and ready obedience. This is fitting for them who love Christ above all else. By reason of the holy duty they have undertaken, or for fear of hell, or for eternal glory, they make no more delay to comply, the very instant anything is appointed them, than if God himself had given the command. Of these the Lord said: "At the very sound of my voice he hath obeyed me." And again he declared to them that teach: "He that heareth you, heareth me."

They who are of this temper abandon all, even to their very will; instantly clear their hands and leave unfinished what they had begun; so that the command is carried out in the moment it is uttered. Master and disciple are lent wings by the fear of God and the longing for eternal life, and so the command is obeyed in a flash.

It is for the sake of obedience that they enter into the narrow way of which the Lord said: "Narrow is the way that leadeth unto life." The "narrowness" of the way is opposite to the broad way suggested by self-will and desire and pleasure: and they follow it by delighting to dwell in a community, to be subject to their abbot, and to follow the judgment of another. Such men live up to the practice of our Lord, who tells us: "I came not to do mine own will, but the will of him that sent me."

This obedience will be pleasing to God and man, when it is performed with no fear, no delay, no coldness, no complaint, no reply. The obedience we pay to superiors is paid to God: for he tells us: "He that heareth you, heareth me." And it is to be done with willing heart, "because God loveth a cheerful giver." When the disciple obeys unwillingly, with a grudge in heart or mouth, though he does the thing, yet he is so far from being pleasing to God, who sees reluctance in the heart, that he acquires no merit, but only incurs the penalty of those that murmur, till he has made a due atonement.

✧ ✧ ✧ ✧

Brethren, the Scripture asserts that "everyone that exalteth himself shall be humbled, and he that humbleth himself shall be exalted." It shows us thereby that all exaltation is in some measure the pride which the prophet tells us he took care to shun: "O Lord, my heart is not exalted, nor mine eyes lifted up: I have not aspired to great things, nor wonders above myself." And his reason for it is: because (says he): "If I had not thought humbly of myself but had exalted my soul, thou wouldst have driven away my soul like an infant weaned from the breast of its mother."

Therefore, brethren, if we want to attain true humility, and come quickly to the top of that heavenly ascent to which we can only mount by lowliness in this present life, we must ascend by good works, and erect the mystical ladder of Jacob, where angels ascending and descending appeared to him. That ascent and descent means that we go downward when we exalt ourselves, and rise when we are humbled. The ladder represents our life in this world, which our Lord erects to heaven when our heart is humbled. And the sides of the ladder represent our soul and body, sides between which God has placed several rungs of humility and discipline, whereby we are to ascend if we would answer his call.

The first degree, then, of humility is, to have the fear of God ever before our eyes: never to forget what is his due, and always to remember his commands: to revolve in the mind how hell burns those who have contemned God, and how God has prepared eternal life for them that fear him: to preserve ourselves from the sins and vices of thought, of the tongue, the eyes, hands, feet, self-will and fleshly desires. Man ought to think that God always looks down from heaven upon him, and that all he does lies open to his sight, is daily told him by the angels. The prophet shows this truth, when he describes God as present in our thoughts, "searching the heart and reins"; and, "Our Lord knows the thoughts of men"; and again, "Thou hast understood my thoughts a great way off": and, "The thought of man shall confess to thee." That he may ever watch the perverseness of his thoughts, let the right-minded brother continually repeat in the language of his heart: "Then I shall be without blemish before him, if I keep myself from mine iniquity."

As for our own will, we are forbidden to pursue it by these words of the Scripture: "Turn away from thine own will": and we are required to ask of God in prayer, that his will may be done in us. We have reason to be convinced that we ought not to be guided by our own will, when we take account of what the Scripture tells us: "There are ways which to men appear to be right, whose endings nevertheless plunge us into the very depth of hell." And again, when we reflect fearfully upon the character given to the negligent: "They are corrupt and become abominable in their own pleasures."

As regards our sensual desires, we must remember that God is ever present; as the prophet says to the Lord: "All my desire lies open before thee." So unlawful desires are to be carefully avoided, because death lurks behind the door at the very entrance to pleasure: whence the Scripture forbids us to "pursue our lusts."

If then the eyes of the Lord observe both the good and the wicked, and God looks down from heaven upon the sons of men, to see if there be any that understand or seek after God; and again, if night and day our guardian angels give an account of what we do to the Lord; we must, every moment, be on our guard, lest God, at any time, should surprise us, as the Psalmist terms it, "leaning towards evil and rendered unprofitable"; and sparing us in this life (because he is good and waits for our becoming better) should reproach us in the next: "These things didst thou do, and I kept silence."

The second degree of humility is, if anyone, not wedded to his own will, finds no pleasure in the compassing of his desires; but fulfils with his practice the word of our Lord: "I came not to do mine own will, but the will of him that sent me." The Scripture also says: "Pleasure hath its penalty, but need winneth a crown."

The third degree of humility is, when anyone submits himself with obedience to his superior for the sake of the love of God, after the example of the Lord, of whom the apostle says: "He was made obedient even unto death."

The fourth degree of humility is, when anyone, in the practice of obedience, meets with hardships, contradictions, or affronts, and yet bears them all with a quiet conscience and with patience, and continues to persevere. The Scripture says: "He who perseveres to the end, the same shall be saved," and again: "Let your heart be strengthened, and wait for our Lord." And to show that the faithful servant ought to suffer every trial for God, the Scripture speaks in the person of those that suffer: "For thy sake we are killed all the day long: we are accounted as sheep for the slaughter." And afterwards, in full assurance of their reward, they say with happiness, "But in all these things we are conquerors through him that loved us." In another place the Scripture tells us: "Thou, O God, hast proved us: thou hast tried us with fire, as silver is tried. Thou hast led us into the snare, and loaded us with afflictions." And to show that we ought to live under a superior, it goes on, "Thou hast set men over our heads."

So these sufferers live up to the command of God, bearing injuries and adversity with patience. But more: Struck on one cheek they offer the other. They give away their coat to him that takes away their cloak. Forced to walk one mile, they go two. They bear with false brethren, like Paul the apostle. They bless them that curse them.

The fifth degree of humility is, humbly to confess to the abbot every unlawful thought as it arises in the heart, and the hidden sins we have committed. The Scripture advises this, saying: "Reveal your way to God and hope in him": and again:

"Confess to God because he is good: for his mercy endureth for ever." And in the prophet: "I have made known my sin to thee, and have not covered my iniquities. I have said, I will declare to God my own iniquities against myself: and thou hast forgiven the wickedness of my heart."

The sixth degree of humility is, if a monk be content with anything though never so vile and contemptible; and to think himself inadequate, and unworthy to succeed in whatever he is commanded to do; saying with the prophet: "I was brought to nothing and knew nothing. I am become like a brute beast before thee, yet I am always with thee."

The seventh degree of humility is, when one does not merely call oneself the least and most abject of all mankind, but believes it, with sincerity of heart: humbling oneself and saying with the prophet: "I am a worm and no man: a scorn of men, and the outcast of the people." "I have been exalted, humbled, and confounded." And again: "It is good for me that thou hast humbled me, that I may learn to keep thy commandments."

The eighth degree of humility is, when a monk does nothing but what is countenanced by the constitutions of the monastery, or the example of the elders.

The ninth degree of humility is, when a monk controls his tongue and keeps silence till a question be asked. For the Scripture teaches that "in much talk you will not avoid sinning"; and "the talkative man shall live out his life hap-hazardly."

The tenth degree of humility is, not easily to lay hold on occasions of laughing. For it is written: "He who laughs loud is a fool."

The eleventh degree of humility is, when a monk discourses with moderation and composure, mixing humility with gravity; speaking few words, but home, and to the purpose; not raising the voice. "The wise man is known because he speaks little."

The twelfth degree of humility is, when the monk's inward humility appears outwardly in his comportment. And wherever he be, in the divine office, in the oratory, in the monastery, in the garden, on a journey, in the fields—wherever he is sitting, walking or standing, he is to look down with bowed head conscious of his guilt, imagining himself ready to be called to give account at the dread judgment: repeating in his heart what the publican in the Gospel said with eyes downcast: "Lord, I am not worthy, sinner that I am, to lift up my eyes to heaven"; and with the prophet "I am bowed down and humbled on every side."

After he has climbed all these degrees of humility, the monk will quickly arrive at the top, the charity that is perfect and casts out all fear. And then, the virtues which first he practised with anxiety, shall begin to be easy for him, almost natural, being grown habitual. He will no more be afraid of hell, but will advance by the love of Christ, by good habits, and by taking pleasure in goodness. Our Lord, by the Holy Spirit, will deign to show this in the servant who has been cleansed from sin.

✧ ✧ ✧ ✧

The vice of possessing property is particularly to be banished from the monastery. No one may presume to give or receive anything without the abbot's leave, or to possess anything whatever, not even book or tablets or pen. The monks' bodies and their wills are not at their own disposal. They must look to all their needs to be supplied by the common father of the monastery. No one may have anything which the abbot does not give or permit. "Everything shall be in common" as the Scripture says: "nor shall they presume to call anything their own." And if anyone be found inclined to this especial vice, he shall be told of it once and twice: and if he do not make amends he shall be liable to punishment.

SELECTION 3
The Rule of St. Francis

St. Francis of Assisi, one of the most popular religious figures of all times, did not prepare this Rule of the Franciscans. The growth of the Order demanded more specific regulations than the simple biblical exhortations he had suggested. The following selections are from the third Rule sanctioned in 1223 by Pope Honorius III.

1. This is the Rule and way of life of the brothers minor; to observe the holy Gospel of our Lord Jesus Christ, living in obedi-

ence, without personal possessions, and in chastity. Brother Francis promises obedience and reverence to our Lord Pope Honorius, and to his canonical successors, and to the Roman Church. And the other brothers shall be bound to obey brother Francis and his successors. . . .

3. The clerical brothers shall perform the divine service according to the order of the holy Roman Church; excepting the psalter, of which they may have extracts. But the lay brothers shall say twenty-four Paternosters at Matins, five at Lauds, seven each at Prime, Terce, Sext and None, twelve at Vespers, seven at the Completorium; and they shall pray for the dead. And they shall fast from the feast of All Saints to the Nativity of the Lord; but as to the holy season of Lent, which begins after the Epiphany of the Lord and continues forty days, a season the Lord consecrated by his holy fast—those who fast during this time shall be blessed of the Lord, and those who do not wish to fast shall not be bound to do so; but otherwise they shall fast until the Resurrection of the Lord. At other times the brothers shall not be bound to fast save on the sixth day (Friday); but when there is a compelling reason the brothers shall not be bound to observe a physical fast. But I advise, warn and exhort my brothers in the Lord Jesus Christ, that, when they go into the world, they shall not quarrel, nor contend with words, nor judge others. But let them be gentle, peaceable, modest, merciful and humble, with honourable conversation towards all, as is fitting. They ought not to ride, save when necessity or infirmity clearly compels them to do so. Into whatsoever house they enter let them first say, 'Peace be to this house.' And according to the holy Gospel it is lawful for them to partake of all dishes placed before them.

4. I strictly command all the brothers never to receive coin or money either directly or through an intermediary. The ministers and guardians alone shall make provision, through spiritual friends, for the needs of the infirm and for other brothers who need clothing, according to the locality, season or cold climate, at their discretion. . . .

5. Those brothers, to whom God has given the ability to work, shall work faithfully and devotedly and in such a way that, avoiding idleness, the enemy of the soul, they do not quench

the spirit of holy prayer and devotion, to which other and temporal activities should be subordinate. As the wages of their labour they may receive corporal necessities for themselves and their brothers but not coin nor money, and this with humility, as is fitting for servants of God, and followers of holy poverty.

6. The brothers shall possess nothing, neither a house, nor a place, nor anything. But, as pilgrims and strangers in this world, serving God in poverty and humility, they shall confidently seek alms, and not be ashamed, for the Lord made Himself poor in this world for us. This is the highest degree of that sublime poverty, which has made you, my dearly beloved brethren, heirs and kings of the Kingdom of Heaven; which has made you poor in goods but exalted in virtues. Let this be 'your portion,' which leads you to 'the land of the living' [Ps. cxlii. 5]. If you cleave wholly to this, beloved, you will wish to have for ever in Heaven nothing save the name of Our Lord Jesus Christ. Wherever the brethren are, and shall meet together, they shall shew themselves as members of one family; each shall with confidence unfold his needs to his brother. A mother loves and cherishes her son in the flesh; how much more eagerly should a man love and cherish his brother in the Spirit? And if any of them fall sick the other brothers are bound to minister to him as they themselves would wish to be ministered to.

7. But if any of the brethren shall commit mortal sin at the prompting of the adversary; in the case of those sins concerning which it has been laid down that recourse must be had to the provincial ministers, the aforesaid brethren must have recourse to them without delay. Those ministers, if they are priests, shall with mercy enjoin penance: if they are not priests they shall cause it to be enjoined through others, who are priests of the order, as it seems to them most expedient in the sight of God. They must beware lest they become angry and disturbed on account of the sin of any brother; for anger and indignation hinder love in ourselves and others.

IX MYSTICISM

Mysticism is a universal religious phenomenon. It is an intuition of the presence of the Divine, an awareness of God or the ultimate reality which undergirds all being. It occurs generally when priestly religion has become lifeless and routine. Since the mystic may stress contemplation exclusively and emphasize the unreality of the world of sense some mysticism is not particularly interested in the world and its troubles. It ignores evil and disdains efforts at improvement. This, however, is not the general rule and especially in the history of Christianity mystically oriented individuals have contributed substantially to the social teachings of the Church. The two representatives here included, Bernard of Clairvaux and Meister Eckhart, are significant not only for the depth of their mystical devotion and insight but also for the relevance of their ethical teaching.

Bernard of Clairvaux was born in 1090 at Fontaines near Dijon, the descendant of a noble family. In 1112 he entered the monastery of Citeaux and became in 1115 the first abbot of Clairvaux. From there Bernard decisively influenced the life of his age. He contributed significantly to the acceptance of Pope Innocent II (1130–1143) over Anacletus II (1130–1138). With his sermons he promoted the Second Crusade whose failure was a crushing blow for him. He died in 1153. His influence on Western Christendom was not limited to Roman Catholics; the Reformation churches esteemed him highly and their mystics particularly were influenced by his thought. The following selections are from his letters and from the book *On Consideration,* written in the years from 1149–1152 for the benefit of Pope Eugenius III who had once been a monk at Clairvaux.

SELECTION I

A Letter to Louis, King of France. A.D. 1142

A typical letter of Bernard to a king calling him to repentance.

God knows how great has been my affection for you from the time I first knew you, and how ardently I have wished for your honour; you too know with what toil and anxiety I throughout the past year strove together with your other faithful servants to obtain peace for you. But I am afraid that our labour in your cause has been fruitless. For you evidently are kicking with too much haste and fickleness against the good and wholesome advice you had received; and I hear that you are hurrying, under I know now what counsel of the devil, to those former evils, which you were but now bewailing, and properly bewailing, that you had been guilty of committing, and this while those wounds are still fresh. For from whom except from the devil can I say that this counsel proceeds which makes us add fires to fires and slaughter to slaughter? which causes the cry of the poor, the groanings of the captives, and the blood of the slain, to strike a second time the ears of the *Father of the fatherless, and the Judge of widows?* (Ps. lxviii, 5.) Doubtless that old victimiser (*hostis*, enemy) of our race, is pleased with these victims (*hostiis*), for he is *a murderer from the beginning* (S. John viii. 44). And do not take occasion from Count Theobald to pile up excuses for your sins; it is useless; for he says he is prepared, and in every way he begs, to come to the terms arranged between you when peace was made, and he is willing to make satisfaction in all points, according to the decision of all who love your name, *i.e.*, those who acted as mediators between you; so that if he can be convicted of any wrong, and he is confident he cannot, he will not hesitate to make immediate amends to your honour.

But you neither entertain proposals for peace, nor keep to your agreements, nor listen to good advice; but by some judgment of God you so turn everything round that you consider disgrace honour and honour disgrace. You fear for what is safe, and neglect what should be feared, and you incur the rebuke which Joab is recorded to have given to the holy and glorious King David, *Thou lovest thine enemies and hatest thy friends* (2 Sam. xix. 6). For it is not your honour but their own advantage which they seek, who are instigating you to renew your former evil-doing against an innocent person. Nay, it is not so much their own advantage as the will of the devil, in order that they may have (which God forbid) the power of the king as an effectual worker of their hot-headed purpose, which they know that they cannot accomplish by their own strength. They are enemies to your crown, and manifest disturbers of the kingdom.

But whatever it may please you to do in a matter which concerns your crown, your soul, and your kingdom, we sons of the Church cannot wholly keep silence about the injuries done to our mother, and the way in which she is despised and trodden under foot; for we perceive that these evils, besides those which we lament piteously have already fallen upon her, are again partly inflicted afresh and partly threatened. We will certainly make a stand, and fight even to death, if need be, for our mother with the weapons allowed us, not with shield and sword, but with prayers and lamentations to God. And I for my part recollect that, besides the daily prayers, which I call my Lord to witness, I humbly poured forth for your peace and salvation and for your kingdom, I also pleaded your cause by messengers and letters to the Apostolic See (I confess it), even to the damage of my own conscience, and (which I ought not to deny) to the anger of the supreme Pontiff himself against me. Now, I tell you, that provoked by your constant outrages, which you do not cease to renew daily, I begin to repent of my former folly, which made me more indulgent to your youth than I ought to have been. For the future, to the best of my little power, I will not hold back the truth.

I will not conceal the fact that you are doing all you can to again enter into alliance and fellowship with the ex-communicated, that you are keeping company (so I am told) with robbers and freebooters for the murder of men, the burning of houses, the destruction of churches, and the dispersion of the poor, according to the saying of the Psalmist, *When thou sawest a thief then thou consentedst unto him, and hast been partaker with adulterers* (Ps. 1. 18), as though you had not enough power of your own to work mischief. I will not hold back the fact that that unlawful and accursed oath foolishly taken by you against the Church of Bourges (through which so many and so great misfortunes have already deservedly followed) is still, notwithstanding all this, uncorrected by you; that you do not allow a pastor to be set over the sheep of Christ at Chalons; and moreover that you have the audacity to throw open Episcopal houses for the use of your brother and his archers and crossbowmen, against law and justice, and so expose the property of the Church to be squandered in nefarious uses of this kind. I tell you plainly that if you proceed in this way the wrong will not be unavenged, and, therefore, my lord king, I warn you as a friend and advise you as a faithful servant to desist quickly from this wickedness, so that if [God] is now preparing His hand to strike, you may, like the King of Nineveh, prevent Him with penitence and humility. I speak severely, because I fear severe things for you; but remember that the Wise Man says, *Better are the wounds of a friend than the fraudulent kisses of an enemy* (Prov. xxvii. 6).

SELECTION 2
A Letter to Pope Eugenius, A.D. 1146

Bernard addresses Pope Eugenius and urges him to go to the assistance of the Eastern Church. It is an interesting comment on Bernard's understanding of the "two swords."

It is no light news which we have heard; it is very sad and grievous. And to whom is it sad? To whom is it not? The children of wrath alone do not see God's wrath, they do not mourn with those that mourn, but they rejoice and exult in the worst evils. Besides, the sorrow is common, because the cause is common to all. You have done well in praising the most righteous zeal of our Gallican Church, and in strengthening it by the authority of your letter. I must say that we must not in such a general and grievous matter act without zeal, much less timidly. I have read in some wise man or other: "He is not a brave man whose courage does not rise in the midst of difficulties" (Seneca, ep. 22 to Lucillus). But I say that one who is faithful may be trusted even more in disaster. The waters have come in even unto the soul of Christ, the apple of His eye has been touched. In this, the second Passion of Christ, both the swords must be drawn which He allowed on the first occasion. And who should draw them but you? Both swords of Peter must be unsheathed as often as necessary, the one at his command, the other by his hand. And, indeed, of the one of which it seemed that he ought not to make use it was said: *Put up thy sword into its sheath.* Therefore that, too, was his, but not to be drawn by his own hand.

I think that now is the time, when necessity bids both be drawn in defence of the Eastern Church. You must not fall below the zeal of him whose place you occupy. What shall we say of one who holds the primacy and shrinks from its ministry? There is the voice of One crying, "I go to Jerusalem to be again crucified" (*Hegesippus de Excid.* lib. iii. c. 2). Though some be lukewarm, some deaf to those words, yet the successor of Peter may not neglect them. He himself will say, *Though all shall be offended yet will not I* (S. Matt. xxvi. 33). Nor will he be deterred by the losses of the former army, but will do his best to repair them. Is not man bound to do his duty, because God does what He pleases? I, for my part, as a faithful Christian, will hope for better things in place of such misfortunes, and will think it all joy that we are falling into divers temptations (S. Jas. i. 2). Truly we have eaten the bread of affliction, and have drunk of the wine of sorrow. Why, O friend of the Bridegroom, are you cast down, as though it were not that the kind and wise Bridegroom has, according to His custom, kept the good wine until now? Who knows if God will return and forgive, and leave a blessing behind Him? (Joel ii. 14). And certainly the Wisdom that is above is wont so to work, so to determine; I speak to a wise man. When has great good ever come to men which has not been preceded by great evil? For, to speak of nothing else, did not the death of the Saviour precede the supreme and unparalleled gift of our salvation?

Do thou, then, O friend of the Bridegroom, prove thyself a friend in His need. If thou lovest, as thou oughtest, Christ with all thy heart, with all thy soul, and with all thy strength, with that triple love of which thy predecessor was asked (S. John xxi. 15–17), then thou wilt withhold nothing, thou wilt leave nothing undone in this danger of His bride; but thou wilt devote to Her whatever strength thou hast, whatever zeal, whatever watchfulness, whatever authority, whatever power. A great danger demands a great effort. The foundation is shaken, and we must put forth all our strength as though the building were now ready to fall. And these things I have said to you with full trust in you, as well as loyalty.

I suppose you have heard the news that at the assembly at Chartres, by some strange caprice, I was chosen as general and leader of the expedition. Be assured that this was not of my seeking, and was and is against my will; and that, as I gauge my strength, it is altogether beyond my powers. Who am I that I should have charge of a camp and go out before the faces of armed men? Is there anything more inconsistent with my profession, even if I had the necessary strength and skill? But it is not my place to teach you wisdom; you know all these things. Only I implore you, by that love which you specially owe me, give me not over to the will of man, but, as is peculiarly incumbent on you, seek for counsel from God, and endeavour that His will may be done on earth as it is in heaven.

SELECTION 3
A Letter to Henry, Archbishop of Mainz, A.D. 1146

In this letter Bernard expresses the more "liberal" attitude towards the Jews as over against those who would convert them by force.

. . . There are three things in him most worthy of blame: his usurpation of the right to preach, his contempt of the authority of the Bishop, and finally his inciting to murder. What new power is this? Do you suppose yourself greater than our father Abraham (Gen. xxii.), who laid down his sword at the bidding of him at whose command he had taken it up? Are you greater than the Prince of the Apostles who inquired of the Lord, *Lord, shall we strike with the sword?* (S. Luke, xxii. 49). If you were instructed in all the wisdom of the Egyptians, that is the wisdom of this world which is foolishness towards God (I Cor. iii. 19), and you reply to the question of Peter in a different manner than He did who said to Peter: Put up again thy sword into its sheath, for he who takes the sword shall perish by the sword (S. Matt. xxvi. 52). Does not the Church triumph a hundred times better over the Jews in convincing them every day of their error and in converting them to the faith, than if it were to exterminate them once for all by the edge of the sword? Does the Church universal from the rising of the sun even to its setting put up to God to no purpose that universal petition on behalf of the unbelieving Jews that our Lord God would take away the veil from their hearts and enable them to pass out of darkness into the light of truth? It would seem useless and vain to pray for them if she had not hope that though now without faith they will one day believe. But she understands with a pious insight that the Lord who renders good for evil and love for hatred has a purpose of grace towards them. Where is then that which is spoken. *See that thou slay them not* (Ps. lix. 11). Or this: *When the fulness of the Gentiles shall have come in then shall all Israel be saved* (Rom. xi. 25, 26). Or this: *The Lord doth build up Jerusalem and will gather together the outcasts of Israel?* (Ps. cxlvii. 2). Are you not the man who will make the Prophets liars and will render empty and useless all the treasures of the piety and mercy of Jesus Christ? Your doctrine is not yours, but that of your father who sent you. It is not surprising if you are as your master: *for he was a murderer from the beginning, a liar and the father of falsehood* (S. John viii. 44). O frightful knowledge; O infernal wisdom contrary to the Prophets, hostile to the Apostles, a subversion of piety and grace! O unclean heresy, sacrilegious deceiver, filled with the spirit of falsehood, which hath conceived sorrow and brought forth ungodliness (Ps. vii. 15). I would wish, but fear, to say more. In conclusion, to sum up briefly all that I think upon these matters: the man is great in his own eyes, full of the spirit of arrogance. His words and his actions reveal that he is striving to make a name for himself among the great of the earth, but he has not the means to succeed in his object. Farewell.

SELECTION 4
On Consideration, Book III, Chap. III–IV

Bernard was a teacher of kings and popes. In his little book *On Consideration* he tries to guide Pope Eugenius III, who had once been a monk at Clairvaux. In this selection Bernard asserts that the rulers of the Church exist to benefit the people.

And I suppose I must certainly not pass over the first thing that occurs to me. You are at the head of affairs, without a rival. Why are you thus placed? The question, I tell you, requires consideration. Is it that you may become great through those beneath you? By no means, but that you may make them great. They have chosen you chief, but for their own sake, not for yours. If it is not so, can you reckon yourself above the very persons for whose favours you are a candidate? Listen to the Lord's words, 'They who have authority over them are called benefactors.' That, however, relates to them that are without. What has it to do with us? You are falsely so called if you aim not so much at being a benefactor as at ruling your benefactor. A man shows a poor spirit when he seeks not the welfare of those beneath him, but to make his own profit out of them. Such conduct is specially discreditable in a commander-in-chief. How beautifully did the Master of the Gentiles express his opinion that parents ought to lay up for the children, not children for the parents. He several times says, and it is a glorious saying, 'Not that I seek a gift, but fruit.' But now let us pass on, lest some one find my lingering here an indication of avarice in you; though how far you are removed from that vice I testified in a former book.

. . . There is something else—if it be something else, for it might perhaps be said to be part of the same subject—and let your consideration give good heed to it. He does not appear to be far from the truth who thought that what I am about to speak of should be classed as a variety of avarice. For myself, I would not deny either that it is a kind of avarice, or that it looks like avarice. At all events if you aim at perfection you should shun not only things bad in themselves, but things that have the appearance of evil. In the one case you have regard to your conscience, in the other to your reputation. A particular line of conduct under different circumstances may be lawful; nevertheless, if it does not look well, deem it unlawful. In a word, ask your ancestors, and they will answer, 'Abstain from every appearance of evil.' Let the Lord's servant by all means imitate his Lord, for He Himself says, 'If any man serve me, let him follow me.' And concerning Him you know it is said, 'The Lord hath reigned, he hath put on beauteous apparel, he hath clothed himself with strength.' Be you also strong in faith, beauteous in glory, and you have shown yourself an imitator of God. Your strength is the confidence of a faithful conscience, your beauty is the splendour of a good character. So then, I beseech you, be clothed with strength, for your strength is the joy of the Lord. Moreover, He delights in your fair beauty no less, as it were, than in His own likeness. Put on your glorious vestments; be clothed with the two robes wherewith the virtuous woman was wont to clothe her household. Let there not be in your conscience a trace of a weak and feeble faith: let there not be in your reputation the blemish of a bad appearance. You will then wear the two robes, and the Bridegroom will rejoice over your soul which He has betrothed to Himself; your God will joy over you. Are you wondering what my drift is, and do you not yet perceive my meaning? I will not keep you in suspense any longer. I refer to the murmuring and complaining of the Churches. They cry aloud that they are being mutilated and dismembered. There are none, or very few, which are not either already smarting under the scourge, or dreading its approach. Do you ask how that is? Abbots are exempted from their bishops, bishops from archbishops, archbishops from patriarchs or primates. Does this look well? I should be surprised if any justification could be found for such doings. The constant practice shows that you have authority, but possibly not so keen a sense of justice. You do this because you have the power, but whether you have the right is open to question. You are where you are that you may uphold the gradations of honour and dignity, secure to every one his proper rank, and not grudge any one his due; as one of your predecessors says, 'Honour to whom honour.'

Meister Eckhart was born in Hochheim, Thuringia, Germany in 1260 of a noble family. He joined the Dominicans at Erfurt. He studied in Paris and in 1302 received the degree of Magister which explains his name "Meister Eckhart." He served his order in many important administrative positions. Eventually he was accused of heresy, which he denied, and some of his more esoteric mystical teachings were condemned in the Bull *In Agro Dominico* (1329) by Pope John XXII. He died sometime between 1327 and 1329. As one of the great medieval Christian mystics Eckhart demonstrates the profound interrelation between faith and works, contemplation and action.

SELECTION 5
The Talks of Instruction, Nos. 2, 4, 5, 7, 18

These are taken from *The Talks of Instruction* and show his typical association of prayer and work and the claim that being comes before doing.

The strongest prayer, one well-nigh almighty in what it can effect, and the most exalted work a man can do proceed from a pure heart. The more pure it is, the more powerful, and the more exalted, useful, laudable and perfect is its prayer and work. A pure heart is capable of anything.

What is a pure heart?

A pure heart is one that is unencumbered, unworried, uncommitted, and which does not want its own way about anything but which, rather, is submerged in the loving will of God, having denied self. Let a job be ever so inconsiderable, it will be raised in effectiveness and dimension by a pure heart.

We ought so to pray that every member and faculty, eyes, ears, mouth, heart, and the senses shall be directed to this end and never to cease prayer until we attain unity with him to whom our prayers and attention are directed, namely, God.

✧ ✧ ✧ ✧

Know that no man in this life ever gave up so much that he could not find something else to let go. Few people, knowing what this means, can stand it long, [and yet] it is an honest requital, a just exchange. To the extent that you eliminate self from your activities, God comes into them—but not more and no less. Begin with that, and let it cost you your uttermost. In this way, and no other, is true peace to be found.

People ought not to consider so much what they are to do as what they *are;* let them but *be* good and their ways and deeds will shine brightly. If you are just, your actions will be just too. Do not think that saintliness comes from occupation; it depends rather on what one is. The kind of work we do does not make us holy but we may make it holy. However "sacred" a calling may be, as it is a calling, it has no power to sanctify; but rather as we *are* and have the divine being within, we bless each task we do, be it eating, or sleeping, or watching, or any other. Whatever they do, who have not much of [God's] nature, they work in vain.

Thus take care that your emphasis is laid on *being* good and not on the number or kind of thing to be done. Emphasize rather the fundamentals on which your work depends.

✧ ✧ ✧ ✧

This is the basis on which human nature and spirit are wholly good, and from which our human actions receive their worth; a mind completely devoted to God. Direct your study to this end, that God shall be great in you, so that in all your comings and goings your zeal and fervor are toward him. In fact, the more you do so, the better your behavior will be, whatever your work. Hold fast to God and he will add every good thing. Seek God and you shall find him and all good with him. Indeed, with such an attitude, you might step on a stone and it would be a more pious act than to receive the body of our Lord, thinking of yourself, and it would distract your soul far less. To the man who cleaves to God, God cleaves and adds virtue. Thus, what you have sought before, now seeks you; what once you pursued, now pursues you; what once you fled, now flees you. Everything comes to him who truly comes to God, bringing all divinity with it, while all that is strange and alien flies away.

✧ ✧ ✧ ✧

There are many people who are not hindered by the things they handle, since those things leave no lasting impression on their minds. It is a stage easily reached if one desires to reach it, for no creature may find a place in a heart full of God. Still we should not be satisfied, for we shall profit by assuming that things are as we are, that they are what we see and hear, however strange and unfamiliar. Then and not until then shall we be on the right road—a road to which there is no end—on which one may grow without stopping, profiting more and more by making true progress.

In all his work, and on every occasion, a man should make clear use of his reason and have a conscious insight into himself and his spirituality and distinguish God to the highest possible degree in everything. One should be, as our Lord said, "Like people always on the watch, expecting their Lord." Expectant people are watchful, always looking for him they expect, always ready to find him in whatever comes along; however strange it may be, they always think he might be in it. This is what awareness of the Lord is to be like and it requires diligence that taxes a man's senses and powers to the utmost, if he is to achieve it and to take God evenly in all things—if he is to find God as much in one thing as in another.

In this regard, one kind of work does indeed differ from another but if one takes the same attitude toward each of his various occupations, then they will be all alike to him. Thus being on the right track and God meaning this to him, he will shine, as clear in worldly things as heavenly. To be sure, one must not of himself behave intemperately or as being worldly, but whatever happens to him from without, whatever he sees or hears, let him refer it to God. The man to whom God is ever present, and who controls and uses his mind to the highest degree—that man alone knows what peace is and he has the Kingdom of Heaven within him.

To be right, a person must do one of two things: either he must learn to have God in his work and hold fast to him there, or he must give up his work altogether. Since, however, man cannot live without activities that are both human and various, we must learn to keep God in everything we do, and whatever the job or place, keep on with him, letting nothing stand in our way. Therefore, when the beginner has to do with other people, let him first commit himself strongly to God and establish God firmly in his own heart, uniting his senses and thought, his will and powers with God, so that nothing else can enter his mind.

✧ ✧ ✧ ✧

You shall not be concerned about the style of your food and clothing, thus laying too much stress on them, but rather accustom your heart and mind to be exalted above such things, so that nothing may move you to pleasure or to love except God alone. Let your thoughts be above all else.

Why?

Because only a feeble spirit could be moved by the garments of appearance; the inner man should govern the outer, and only this will do for you. But if it happens that you are well off, in your heart be tranquil about it—if you can be just as glad and willing for the opposite condition. So let it be with food, friends, kindred, or anything else that God gives or takes away.

So I hold this to be best, that a man should give himself over to God and let God throw on him what he will, offenses, work, or suffering, and that then he takes them gladly and thankfully, allowing God to put such things upon him even if he does not choose them for himself. To learn from God gladly in all things, and to follow after him only, is to be on the right track. In this frame of mind, a man may enjoy his honor or comfort—if he is just as glad to take hardship and disgrace when they come along. Thus, they may eat with perfect right and good conscience who are as ready and glad to fast.

Probably this is the reason why God spares his friends so many and such great wounds—which his incomparable honor would not otherwise permit: many and great are the blessings to be found in suffering. And while it would not suit God, nor would he wish to withhold any good thing, yet sometimes he does withhold these things, being content with his just good will; and again, he skips no degree of suffering because of the benefits inherent in it. Therefore, you should be content as long as God is, and inwardly so responsive to his will as not to be concerned with ways and works. Avoid especially any singularity in clothes, food, or speech, such as the use of high-flown language, for example, or eccentric mannerisms, which help not at all.

Still, you should know that not all singularity is forbidden. On many occasions, among many people, you will have to be singular. There are times when distinctive people cannot avoid standing out in many ways, for spiritually a man must conform to our Lord Jesus Christ in all things so that men may see his divine form, the reflection of him at work. In all you do, keep in yourself as perfect a likeness of him as possible. You are to sow and he is to reap. Work devotedly, with wholehearted conviction, and thus train your mind and heart so that you may represent him at all time.

SELECTION 6
from *The Sermons*

This is an excerpt from one of Meister Eckhart's sermons revealing his unique approach to ethical teaching.

. . . You may, however, say: Alas, good man, if, to be prepared for God, one needs a heart freed from ideas and activities which are natural to the agents of the soul, how about those deeds of love which are wholly external, such as teaching and comforting those who are in need? Are these to be denied? Are we to forgo the deeds that occupied St. Paul on behalf of the people, so much that he was like a father to them? Shall we be denied the [divine] goodness because we do virtuous deeds?

Let us see how this question is to be answered. The one [contemplation] is good. The other [deeds of virtue] is necessary. Mary was praised for having chosen the better part but Martha's life was useful, for she waited on Christ and his disciples. St. Thomas [Aquinas] says that the active life is better than the contemplative, for in it one pours out the love he has received in contemplation. Yet it is all one; for what we plant in the soil of contemplation we shall reap in the harvest of action and thus the purpose of contemplation is achieved. There is a transition from one to the other but it is all a single process with one end in view—that God is, after which it returns to what it was before. If I go from one end of this house to the other, it is true, I shall be moving and yet it will be all one motion. In all he does, man has only his one vision of God. One is based on the other and fulfills it. In the unity [one beholds] in contemplation, God foreshadows [variety of] the harvest of action. In contemplation, you serve only yourself. In good works, you serve many people.

The whole life of Christ instructs us in this matter, and the lives of his saints as well, all of whom he sent out into the world to teach the Many the one truth. St. Paul said to Timothy: "Beloved, preach the word!" Did he mean the audible word that beats the air? Certainly not! He referred to the inborn, secret word that lies hidden in the soul. It was this that he preached, so that it might instruct the faculties of people and nourish them, and so that the behavior of men might proclaim it and so that one might be fully prepared to serve the need of his neighbor. It should be in the thoughts, the mind, and the will. It should shine through your deeds. As Christ said: "Let your light so shine before men!" He was thinking of people who care only for the contemplative life and not for the practice of virtue, who say that they have no need for this, for they have got beyond it. Christ did not include such people when he said: "Some seed fell in good ground and brought forth fruit an hundredfold." But he did refer to them when he spoke of "the tree that does not bear fruit and which shall be hewn down."

Now some of you may say: "But, sir, what about the silence of which you have said so much?" Plenty of ideas intrude into that. Each deed follows the pattern of its own idea, whether spiritual or external, whether it be teaching, or giving comfort, or what not. Where, then, is the stillness? If the mind goes on thinking and imagining, and the will keeps on functioning, and the memory: does not this all involve ideation? Let us see.

We have already mentioned the passive and active intellects. The active intellect abstracts ideas from external things and strips them of all that is material or accidental and passes them on to the passive intellect, thus begetting their spiritual counterparts there. So the passive intellect is made pregnant by the active and it knows and cherishes these things. Nevertheless, it cannot continue to know them without the active intellect's continuing, renewing enlightenment. But notice this: all the active intellect does for the natural man, God does and much more too for the solitary person. He removes the active intellect and puts himself in its place and takes over its complete function.

Now, if a person is quite unoccupied, and his mind is stilled, God undertakes its work, and becomes controller of the mind's agents and is himself begotten in the passive intellect. Let us see how this is. The active intellect cannot pass on what it has not received, nor can it entertain two ideas at once. It must take first one and then the other. Even if many forms and colors are shown up by light and air at the same time, you can perceive them only one after the other. It is the same with the active intellect when it acts—but when God acts in lieu of it, he begets many ideas or images at one point. When, therefore, God moves you to a good deed, your [soul's] agents organize at once for good and your heart is set on goodness. All your resources for good take shape and gather at the same instant to the same point. This shows clearly and beyond doubt that it is not your own mind that is working, because it has neither the authority nor the resources required for that. Rather, it is the work which is begotten of him who comprehends all ideas within himself simultaneously. St. Paul says: "I can do all things through him that strengtheneth me and in him; I am not divided." Thus you may know that the ideas back of good deeds are not your own but are from the Superintendent of nature, from whom both the deed and the idea proceed. Do not claim as your own what is his and not yours. It is given you for a little while, but it was born of God, beyond time, in the eternity that is above all ideas or images.

You may, however, ask: "What is to become of my mind, once it has been robbed of its natural function and has neither ideas nor anything else to work on? It must always consist of something and the soul's agents are bound to connect with something on which they will go to work, whether the memory, the reason, or the will."

Here is the answer. The object and existence of the mind are essential and not contingent. The mind has a pure, unadulterated being of its own. When it comes across truth or essence, at once it is attracted and settles down to utter its oracle—for it now has a point of reference. If, however, the intellect does not discover any essential truth or touch some bedrock, so that it can say "this is this and therefore not something else," it has to continue searching and expecting, arrested or attracted by nothing, it can only work on until the end, when it passes out, still searching and still expecting.

Sometimes a year or more is spent in working over a point about nature to discover what it is, and then an equal period has to be spent whittling off what it is not. Having no reference point, the mind can make no statement all this time, for it has no real knowledge of the core of truth. That is why the mind can never rest during this lifetime. For let God reveal himself here ever so much, it is nothing to what he really is. There is Truth at the core of the soul but it is covered up and hidden from the mind, and as long as that is so there is nothing the mind can do to come to rest, as it might if it had an unchanging point of reference.

The mind never rests but must go on expecting and preparing for what is yet to be known and what is still concealed. Meanwhile, man cannot know what God is, even though he be ever so well aware of what God is not; and an intelligent person will reject that. As long as it has no reference point, the mind can only wait as matter waits for form. And matter can never find rest except in form; so, too, the mind can never rest except in the essential truth which is locked up in it—the truth about everything. Essence alone satisfies and God keeps on withdrawing, farther and farther away, to arouse the mind's zeal and lure it on to follow and finally grasp the true good that has no cause. Thus, contented with nothing, the mind clamors for the highest good of all.

Now you may say: "But, sir, you have often told us that the agents should all be still and yet here you have everything setting up a clamor and covetousness in the mind where quiet should be: there is a great hubbub and outcry for what the mind has not. Whether it be desire, or purpose, or praise, or thanks, or whatever is imagined or engendered in the soul, it cannot be the pure peace or complete quiet, of which you have spoken. Rather, the mind is despoiled of its peace."

This requires an answer. When you get rid of selfishness, together with all things and what pertains to them, and have transferred all to God, and united with him, and abandoned all for him in complete trust and love, then whatever your lot, whatever touches you, for better or worse, sour or sweet, none of it is yours but it is all God's to whom you have left it.

Tell me: whose is the Word that is spoken? Is it his who speaks, or his who hears it? Even though it come to him who hears it, it still is his who speaks or conceives it. Take an illustration. The sun radiates its light into the air and the air receives it and transmits it to the earth, and receiving it, we can distinguish one color from another. Now, although light seems to be everywhere in the air, it is really in the sun. The rays are really emitted by the sun and come from it—not from the air. They are only received by the air and passed on to anything that can be lighted up.

It is like this with the soul. God begets his Son or the Word in the soul and, receiving it, the soul passes it on in many forms, through its agents, now as desire, now in good intentions, now in loving deeds, now in gratitude or whatever concerns it. These are all his and not yours at all. Credit God with all he does and take none for yourself, as it is written: "The Holy Spirit maketh intercession for us with groanings which cannot be uttered." It is he that prays in us and not we ourselves. St. Paul says that "no man can say that Jesus is the Lord but by the Holy Ghost."

Above all, claim nothing for yourself. Relax and let God operate you and do what he will with you. The deed is his; the word is his; this birth is his; and all you are is his, for you have surrendered self to him, with all your soul's agents and their functions and even your personal nature. Then at once, God comes into your being and faculties, for you are like a desert, despoiled of all that was peculiarly your own. The Scripture speaks of "the voice of one crying in the wilderness." Let this voice cry in you at will. Be like a desert as far as self and the things of this world are concerned.

Perhaps, however, you object: "What should one do to be as

empty as a desert, as far as self and things go? Should one just wait and do nothing? Or should he sometimes pray, read, or do such virtuous things as listening to a sermon or studying the Bible—of course, not taking these things as if from outside himself, but inwardly, as from God? And if one does not do these things, isn't he missing something?"

This is the answer. External acts of virtue were instituted and ordained so that the outer man might be directed to God and set apart for spiritual life and all good things, and not diverted from them by incompatible pursuits. They were instituted to restrain man from things impertinent to his high calling, so that when God wants to use him, he will be found ready, not needing to be brought back from things coarse and irrelevant. The more pleasure one takes in externalities the harder it is to turn away from them. The stronger the love the greater the pain of parting.

See! Praying, reading, singing, watching, fasting, and doing penance—all these virtuous practices were contrived to catch us and keep us away from strange, ungodly things. Thus, if one feels that the spirit of God is not at work in him, that he has departed inwardly from God, he will all the more feel the need to do virtuous deeds—especially those he finds most pertinent or useful—not for his own personal ends but rather to honor the truth—he will not wish to be drawn or led away by obvious things. Rather, he will want to cleave to God, so that God will find him quickly and not have to look far afield for him when, once more, he wants to act through him.

But when a person has a true spiritual experience, he may boldly drop external disciplines, even those to which he is bound by vows, from which even a bishop may not release him. No man may release another from vows he has made to God—for such vows are contracts between man and God. And also, if a person who has vowed many things such as prayer, fasting, or pilgrimages, should enter an order, he is then free from the vow, for once in the order, his bond is to all virtue and to God himself.

I want to emphasize that. However much a person may have vowed himself to many things, when he enters upon a true spiritual experience he is released from them all. As long as that experience lasts, whether a week, or a month, or a year, none of this time will be lost to the monk or nun, for God, whose prisoners they are, will account for it all. When he returns to his usual nature, however, let him fulfill the vows appropriate to each passing moment as it comes, but let him not think for a moment of making up for the times he seemed to neglect, for God will make up for whatever time he caused you to be idle. Nor should you think it could be made up by any number of creature-deeds, for the least deed of God is more than all human deeds together. This is said for learned and enlightened people who have been illumined by God and the Scriptures.

X THOMAS AQUINAS

Thomas Aquinas is the most outstanding example of medieval scholastic theology. His thought dominates Roman Catholicism to this day. As late as 1879 he was declared by Pope Leo XIII in his encyclical *Aeterni Patris* the standard theologian of that Christian communion. Born in 1225 in the castle of Roccasecca in Italy the son of Count Landolf of Aquino (who had sided with the emperor Frederick II against the Papacy), Thomas spent his life in monasteries and universities studying and teaching. From 1259 to 1268 he was lecturer at the papal curia in Italy. He later taught in Paris and Naples. He died in 1274 on his way to the council of Lyon. Thomas' major contribution is the utilization of the philosophy of Aristotle for a systematic and comprehensive articulation of the Christian faith. In this effort he also dealt creatively with social ethics not only as a theologian but also as a commentator on Aristotle's *Nicomachean Ethics*. Thomas sees the continuity of nature and grace and grace as the transformer of nature and is a most powerful spokesman of those who advocate the Christian transformation of the world.

SELECTION I

Summa Theologica II/1, Question 90, Articles 1 and 2

In the first part of Part II of the *Summa Theologica* Thomas discusses the question of law in great detail. These selections give some impression of his method as well as the content of his argument.

FIRST ARTICLE
WHETHER LAW IS SOMETHING PERTAINING TO REASON?

We proceed thus to the First Article:

Objection 1. It seems that law is not something pertaining to reason. For the Apostle says (Rom. vii. 23): *I see another law in my members,* etc. But nothing pertaining to reason is in the members; since the reason does not make use of a bodily organ. Therefore law is not something pertaining to reason.

Obj. 2. Further, in the reason there is nothing else but power, habit, and act. But law is not the power itself of reason. In like manner, neither is it a habit of reason: because the habits of reason are the intellectual virtues of which we have spoken above (Q. LVII.). Nor again is it an act of reason: because then law would cease, when the act of reason ceases, for instance, while we are asleep. Therefore law is nothing pertaining to reason.

Obj. 3. Further, the law moves those who are subject to it to act aright. But it belongs properly to the will to move to act, as is evident from what has been said above (Q. IX., A. 1). Therefore law pertains, not to the reason, but to the will; according to the words of the Jurist (*Lib.* i. *ff., De Const. Prin.*): *Whatsoever pleaseth the sovereign, has force of law.*

On the contrary, It belongs to the law to command and to forbid. But it belongs to reason to command, as stated above (Q. XVII., A. 1). Therefore law is something pertaining to reason.

I answer that, Law is a rule and measure of acts, whereby man is induced to act or is restrained from acting: for *lex* (law) is derived from *ligare* (to bind), because it binds one to act. Now the rule and measure of human acts is the reason, which is the first principle of human acts, as is evident from what has been stated above (Q. I., A. 1 *ad* 3); since it belongs to the reason to direct to the end, which is the first principle in all matters of action, according to the Philosopher (*Phys.* ii.). Now that which is the principle in any genus, is the rule and measure of that genus: for instance, unity in the genus of numbers, and the first movement in the genus of movements. Consequently it follows that law is something pertaining to reason.

Reply Obj. 1. Since law is a kind of rule and measure, it may be in something in two ways. First, as in that which measures and rules: and since this is proper to reason, it follows that, in this way, law is in the reason alone.—Secondly, as in that which is measured and ruled. In this way, law is in all those things that are inclined to something by reason of some law: so that any inclination arising from a law, may be called a law, not essentially but by participation as it were. And thus the inclination of the members to concupiscence is called *the law of the members.*

Reply Obj. 2. Just as, in external action, we may consider the work and the work done, for instance the work of building and the house built; so in the acts of reason, we may consider the act itself of reason, i.e., to understand and to reason, and something produced by this act. With regard to the speculative reason, this is first of all the definition; secondly, the proposition; thirdly, the syllogism or argument. And since also the practical reason makes use of a syllogism in respect of the work to be done, as stated above (Q. XIII., A. 3; Q. LXXVI., A. 1) and as the Philosopher teaches (*Ethic.* vii.); hence we find in the practical reason something that holds the same position in regard to operations, as, in the speculative intellect, the proposition holds in regard to conclusions. Suchlike universal propositions of the practical intellect that are directed to actions have the nature of law. And these propositions are sometimes under our actual consideration, while sometimes they are retained in the reason by means of a habit.

Reply Obj. 3. Reason has its power of moving from the will, as stated above (Q. XVII., A. 1): for it is due to the fact that one wills the end, that the reason issues its commands as regards things ordained to the end. But in order that the volition of what is commanded may have the nature of law, it needs to be in accord with some rule of reason. And in this sense is to be understood the saying that the will of the sovereign has the force of law; otherwise the sovereign's will would savour of lawlessness rather than of law.

SECOND ARTICLE
WHETHER THE LAW IS ALWAYS DIRECTED TO THE COMMON GOOD?

We proceed thus to the Second Article:

Objection 1. It seems that the law is not always directed to the common good as to its end. For it belongs to law to command and to forbid. But commands are directed to certain individual goods. Therefore the end of the law is not always the common good.

Obj. 2. Further, the law directs man in his actions. But human actions are concerned with particular matters. Therefore the law is directed to some particular good.

Obj. 3. Further, Isidore says (*Etym.* ii.): *If the law is based on reason, whatever is based on reason will be a law*. But reason is the foundation not only of what is ordained to the common good, but also of that which is directed to private good. Therefore the law is not only directed to the good of all, but also to the private good of an individual.

On the contrary, Isidore says (*Etym.* v.) that *laws are enacted for no private profit, but for the common benefit of the citizens.*

I answer that, As stated above (A. 1), the law belongs to that which is a principle of human acts, because it is their rule and measure. Now as reason is a principle of human acts, so in reason itself there is something which is the principle in respect of all the rest: wherefore to this principle chiefly and mainly law must needs be referred.—Now the first principle in practical matters, which are the object of the practical reason, is the last end: and the last end of human life is bliss or happiness, as stated above (Q. II., A. 7; Q. III., A. 1). Consequently the law must needs regard principally the relationship to happiness. Moreover, since every part is ordained to the whole, as imperfect to perfect; and since one man is a part of the perfect community, the law must needs regard properly the relationship to universal happiness. Wherefore the Philosopher, in the above definition of legal matters mentions both happiness and the body politic: for he says (*Ethic.* v.) that we call those legal matters *just, which are adapted to produce and preserve happiness and its parts for the body politic:* since the state is a perfect community, as he says in *Polit.* i.

Now in every genus, that which belongs to it chiefly is the principle of the others, and the others belong to that genus in subordination to that thing: thus fire, which is chief among hot things, is the cause of heat in mixed bodies, and these are said to be hot in so far as they have a share of fire. Consequently, since the law is chiefly ordained to the common good, any other precept in regard to some individual work, must needs be devoid of the nature of a law, save in so far as it regards the common good. Therefore every law is ordained to the common good. . . .

SELECTION 2

Summa Theologica, II/1, Question 91, Articles 1–4

Here Thomas analyzes the various kinds of law.

FIRST ARTICLE
WHETHER THERE IS AN ETERNAL LAW?

We proceed thus to the First Article:

Objection 1. It seems that there is no eternal law. Because every law is imposed on someone. But there was not someone from eternity on whom a law could be imposed: since God alone was from eternity. Therefore no law is eternal.

Obj. 2. Further, promulgation is essential to law. But promulgation could not be from eternity: because there was no one to whom it could be promulgated from eternity. Therefore no law can be eternal.

Obj. 3. Further, a law implies order to an end. But nothing ordained to an end is eternal: for the last end alone is eternal. Therefore no law is eternal.

On the contrary, Augustine says (*De Lib. Arb.* i.): *That Law which is the Supreme Reason cannot be understood to be otherwise than unchangeable and eternal.*

I answer that, As stated above (Q. XC., A. 1 *ad* 2; AA. 3, 4), a law is nothing else but a dictate of practical reason emanating from the ruler who governs a perfect community. Now it is evident, granted that the world is ruled by Divine Providence, as was stated in the First Part (Q. XXII., AA. 1, 2), that the whole community of the universe is governed by Divine Reason. Wherefore the very Idea of the government of things in God the Ruler of the universe, has the nature of a law. And since the Divine Reason's conception of things is not subject to time but is eternal, according to Pro. viii. 23, therefore it is that this kind of law must be called eternal. . . .

SECOND ARTICLE

WHETHER THERE IS IN US A NATURAL LAW?

We proceed thus to the Second Article:

Objection 1. It seems that there is no natural law in us. Because man is governed sufficiently by the eternal law: for Augustine says (*De Lib. Arb.* i.) that *the eternal law is that by which it is right that all things should be most orderly*. But nature does not abound in superfluities as neither does she fail in necessaries. Therefore no law is natural to man.

Obj. 2. Further, by the law man is directed, in his acts, to the end, as stated above (Q. XC., A. 2). But the directing of human acts to their end is not a function of nature, as is the case in irrational creatures, which act for an end solely by their natural appetite; whereas man acts for an end by his reason and will. Therefore no law is natural to man.

Obj. 3. Further, the more a man is free, the less is he under the law. But man is freer than all the animals, on account of his free-will, with which he is endowed above all other animals. Since therefore other animals are not subject to a natural law, neither is man subject to a natural law.

On the contrary, The gloss on Rom. ii. 14: *When the Gentiles, who have not the law, do by nature those things that are of the law,* comments as follows: *Although they have no written law, yet they have the natural law, whereby each one knows, and is conscious of, what is good and what is evil.*

I answer that, As stated above (Q. XC., A. 1 *ad* 1), law, being a rule and measure, can be in a person in two ways: in one way, as in him that rules and measures; in another way, as in that which is ruled and measured, since a thing is ruled and measured, in so far as it partakes of the rule or measure. Wherefore, since all things subject to Divine providence are ruled and measured by the eternal law, as was stated above (A. 1); it is evident that all things partake somewhat of the eternal law, in so far as, namely, from its being imprinted on them, they derive their respective inclinations to their proper acts and ends. Now among all others, the rational creature is subject to Divine providence in the most excellent way, in so far as it partakes of a share of providence, by being provident both for itself and for others. Wherefore it has a share of the Eternal Reason, whereby it has a natural inclination to its proper act and end, and this participation of the eternal law in the rational creature is called the natural law. Hence the Psalmist after saying (Ps. iv. 6): *Offer up the sacrifice of justice,* as though someone asked what the works of justice are, adds: *Many say, Who showeth us good things?* in answer to which question he says: *The light of Thy countenance, O Lord, is signed upon us:* thus implying that the light of natural reason, whereby we discern what is good and what is evil, which is the function of the natural law, is nothing else than an imprint on us of the Divine light. It is therefore evident that the natural law is nothing else than the rational creature's participation of the eternal law. . . .

THIRD ARTICLE
WHETHER THERE IS A HUMAN LAW?

We proceed thus to the Third Article:

Objection 1. It seems that there is not a human law. For the natural law is a participation of the eternal law, as stated above (A. 2). Now through the eternal law *all things are most orderly,* as Augustine states (*De Lib. Arb.* i.). Therefore the natural law suffices for the ordering of all human affairs. Consequently there is no need for a human law.

Obj. 2. Further, a law bears the character of a measure, as stated above (Q. XC., A. 1). But human reason is not a measure of things, but vice versa (*cf. Metaph.* x.). Therefore no law can emanate from human reason.

Obj. 3. Further, a measure should be most certain, as stated in *Metaph.* x. But the dictates of human reason in matters of conduct are uncertain, according to Wis. ix. 14: *The thoughts of mortal men are fearful, and our counsels uncertain.* Therefore no law can emanate from human reason.

On the contrary, Augustine (*De Lib. Arb.* i.) distinguishes two kinds of law, the one eternal, the other temporal, which he calls human.

I answer that, As stated above (Q. XC., A. 1 *ad* 2), a law is a dictate of the practical reason. Now it is to be observed that the same procedure takes place in the practical and in the speculative reason: for each proceeds from principles to conclusions, as stated above (*ibid.*). Accordingly we conclude that just as, in the speculative reason, from naturally known indemonstrable principles, we draw the conclusions of the various sciences, the knowledge of which is not imparted to us by nature, but acquired by the efforts of reason, so too it is from the precepts of the natural law, as from general and indemonstrable principles, that the human reason needs to proceed to the more particular determination of certain matters. These particular determinations, devised by human reason, are called human laws, provided the other essential conditions of law be observed, as stated above (Q. XC., AA. 2, 3, 4). Wherefore Tully says in his *Rhetoric* (*De Invent. Rhet.* ii.) that *justice has its source in nature; thence certain things came into custom by reason of their utility; afterwards these things which emanated from nature and were approved by custom, were sanctioned by fear and reverence for the law. . . .*

FOURTH ARTICLE

WHETHER THERE WAS ANY NEED FOR A DIVINE LAW?

We proceed thus to the Fourth Article:

Objection 1. It seems that there was no need for a Divine law. Because, as stated above (A. 2), the natural law is a participation in us of the eternal law. But the eternal law is a Divine law, as stated above (A. 1). Therefore there is no need for a Divine law in addition to the natural law, and human laws derived therefrom.

Obj. 2. Further, it is written (Ecclus. xv. 14) that *God left man in the hand of his own counsel.* Now counsel is an act of reason, as stated above (Q. XIV., A. 1). Therefore man was left to the direction of his reason. But a dictate of human reason is a human law, as stated above (A. 3). Therefore there is no need for man to be governed also by a Divine law.

Obj. 3. Further, human nature is more self-sufficing than irrational creatures. But irrational creatures have no Divine law besides the natural inclination impressed on them. Much less, therefore, should the rational creature have a Divine law in addition to the natural law.

On the contrary, David prayed God to set His law before him, saying: *Set before me for a law the way of Thy justifications, O Lord.*

I answer that, Besides the natural and the human law it was necessary for the directing of human conduct to have a Divine law. And this for four reasons. First, because it is by law that man is directed how to perform his proper acts in view of his last end. And indeed if man were ordained to no other end than that which is proportionate to his natural faculty, there would be no need for man to have any further direction on the part of his reason, besides the natural law and human law which is derived from it. But since man is ordained to an end of eternal happiness which is inproportionate to man's natural faculty, as stated above (Q. V., A. 5), therefore it was necessary that, besides the natural and the human law, man should be directed to his end by a law given by God.

Secondly, because, on account of the uncertainty of human judgment, especially on contingent and particular matters, different people form different judgments on human acts; whence also different and contrary laws result. In order, therefore, that man may know without any doubt what he ought to do and what he ought to avoid, it was necessary for man to be directed in his proper acts by a law given by God, for it is certain that such a law cannot err.

Thirdly, because man can make laws in those matters of which he is competent to judge. But man is not competent to judge of interior movements, that are hidden, but only of exterior acts which appear: and yet for the perfection of virtue it is necessary for man to conduct himself aright in both kinds of acts. Consequently human law could not sufficiently curb and direct interior acts; and it was necessary for this purpose that a Divine law should supervene.

Fourthly, because, as Augustine says (*De Lib. Arb.* i.), human law cannot punish or forbid all evil deeds: since while aiming at doing away with all evils, it would do away with many good things, and would hinder the advance of the common good, which is necessary for human intercourse. In order, therefore, that no evil might remain unforbidden and unpunished, it was necessary for the Divine law to supervene, whereby all sins are forbidden.

And these four causes are touched upon in Ps. cxviii. 8, where it is said: *The law of the Lord is unspotted,* i.e., allowing no foulness of sin; *converting souls,* because it directs not only exterior, but also interior acts; *the testimony of the Lord is faithful,* because of the certainty of what is true and right; *giving wisdom to little ones,* by directing man to an end supernatural and Divine. . . .

SELECTION 3

Summa Theologica, II/2, Question 58, Articles 1, 11, 12

The typical combination of insights from Greek philosophy and biblical thinking is demonstrated in this discussion of justice.

FIRST ARTICLE
WHETHER JUSTICE IS FITTINGLY DEFINED AS BEING THE PERPETUAL AND CONSTANT WILL TO RENDER TO EACH ONE HIS RIGHT?

We proceed thus to the First Article:

Objection 1. It seems that lawyers have unfittingly defined justice as being *the perpetual and constant will to render to each one his right.* For, according to the Philosopher (*Ethic.* v.), justice is a habit which makes a man *capable of doing what is just, and of being just in action and in intention.* Now will denotes a power, or also an act. Therefore justice is unfittingly defined as being a will.

Obj. 2. Further, Rectitude of the will is not the will; else if the will were its own rectitude, it would follow that no will is unrighteous. Yet, according to Anselm (*De Veritate* xiii.), justice is rectitude. Therefore justice is not the will.

Obj. 3. Further, No will is perpetual save God's. If therefore justice is a perpetual will, in God alone will there be justice.

Obj. 4. Further, Whatever is perpetual is constant, since it is unchangeable. Therefore it is needless in defining justice, to say that it is both *perpetual and constant.*

Obj. 5. Further, It belongs to the sovereign to give each one his right. Therefore, if justice gives each one his right, it follows that it is in none but the sovereign: which is absurd.

Obj. 6. Further, Augustine says (*De Moribus Eccl.* xv.) that *justice is love serving God alone.* Therefore it does not render to each one his right.

I answer that, The aforesaid definition of justice is fitting if understood aright. For since every virtue is a habit that is the principle of a good act, a virtue must needs be defined by means of the good act bearing on the matter proper to that virtue. Now the proper matter of justice consists of those things that belong to our intercourse with other men, as shall be shown further on (A. 2). Hence the act of justice in relation to its proper matter and object is indicated in the words: *Rendering to each one his right,* since, as Isidore says (*Etym.* x.), *a man is said to be just because he respects the rights of others.*

Now in order that an act bearing upon any matter whatever be virtuous, it requires to be voluntary, stable, and firm, because the Philosopher says (*Ethic.* ii.) that in order for an act to be virtuous it needs first of all to be done *knowingly,* secondly to be done *by choice,* and *for a due end,* thirdly to be done *immovably.* Now the first of these is included in the second, since *what is done through ignorance is involuntary* (*Ethic.* iii.). Hence the definition of justice mentions first the *will,* in order to show that the act of justice must be voluntary; and mention is made afterwards of its constancy and perpetuity in order to indicate the firmness of the act.

Accordingly, this is a complete definition of justice; save that the act is mentioned instead of the habit, which takes its species from that act, because habit implies relation to act. And if anyone would reduce it to the proper form of a definition, he might say that *justice is a habit whereby a man renders to each one his due by a constant and perpetual will:* and this is about the same definition as that given by the Philosopher (*Ethic.* v.) who says that *justice is a habit whereby a man is said to be capable of doing just actions in accordance with his choice. . . .*

ELEVENTH ARTICLE
WHETHER THE ACT OF JUSTICE IS TO RENDER TO EACH ONE HIS OWN?

We proceed thus to the Eleventh Article:

Objection 1. It seems that the act of justice is not to render to each one his own. For Augustine (*De Trin.* xiv.) ascribes to justice the act of succouring the needy. Now in succouring the needy we give them what is not theirs but ours. Therefore the act of justice does not consist in rendering to each one his own.

Obj. 2. Further, Tully says (*De Offic.* i.) that *beneficence which we may call kindness or liberality, belongs to justice.* Now it pertains to liberality to give to another of one's own, not of what is his. Therefore the act of justice does not consist in rendering to each one his own.

Obj. 3. Further, It belongs to justice not only to distribute things duly, but also to repress injurious actions, such as murder, adultery and so forth. But the rendering to each one of what is his seems to belong solely to the distribution of things. Therefore the act of justice is not sufficiently described by saying that it consists in rendering to each one his own.

On the contrary, Ambrose says (*De Offic.* i.): *It is justice that renders to each one what is his, and claims not another's property; it disregards its own profit in order to preserve the common equity.*

I answer that, As stated above (AA. 9, 10), the matter of justice is an external operation, in so far as either it or the thing we use by it is made proportionate to some other person to whom we are related by justice. Now each man's own is that which is due to him according to equality of proportion. Therefore the proper act of justice is nothing else than to render to each one his own. . . .

TWELFTH ARTICLE
WHETHER JUSTICE STANDS FOREMOST AMONG ALL MORAL VIRTUES?

We proceed thus to the Twelfth Article:

Objection 1. It seems that justice does not stand foremost among all the moral virtues. Because it belongs to justice to render to each one what is his, whereas it belongs to liberality to give of one's own, and this is more virtuous. Therefore liberality is a greater virtue than justice.

Obj. 3. Further, Virtue is about that which is difficult and good, as stated in *Ethic.* ii. But fortitude is about more difficult things than justice is, since it is about dangers of death, according to *Ethic.* iii. Therefore fortitude is more excellent than justice.

On the contrary, Tully says (*De Offic.* i.): *Justice is the most resplendent of the virtues, and gives its name to a good man.*

I answer that, If we speak of legal justice, it is evident that it stands foremost among all the moral virtues, for as much as the common good transcends the individual good of one person. In this sense the Philosopher declares (*Ethic.* v.) that *the most excellent of the virtues would seem to be justice, and more glorious than the star of eve or dawn.* But, even if we speak of particular justice, it excels the other moral virtues for two reasons. The first reason may be taken from the subject, because justice is in the more excellent part of the soul, viz. the rational appetite or will, whereas the other moral virtues are in the sensitive appetite, whereunto appertain the passions which are the matter of the other moral virtues. The second reason is taken from the object, because the other virtues are commendable in respect of the sole good of the virtuous person, as stated in *Ethic.* v. Hence the Philosopher says (*Rhet.* i.): *The greatest virtues must needs be those which are most profitable to other persons, since virtue is a faculty of doing good to others. For this reason the greatest honours are accorded the brave and the just, since bravery is useful to others in warfare, and justice is useful to others both in warfare and in time of peace. . . .*

SELECTION 4
Summa Theologica, II/2, Question 60, Articles 5–6

Thomas advocates judgment according to written law rather than the fortuitous opinions of men.

FIFTH ARTICLE
WHETHER WE SHOULD ALWAYS JUDGE ACCORDING TO THE WRITTEN LAW?

We proceed thus to the Fifth Article:

Objection 1. It seems that we ought not always to judge according to the written law. For we ought always to avoid judging unjustly. But written laws sometimes contain injustice, according to Isa. x. 1: *Woe to them that make wicked laws, and when they write, write injustice.* Therefore we ought not always to judge according to the written law.

Obj. 2. Further, Judgment has to be formed about individual happenings. But no written law can cover each and every individual happening, as the Philosopher declares (*Ethic.* v.). Therefore it seems that we are not always bound to judge according to the written law.

On the contrary, Augustine says (*De Vera Relig.* xxxi.): *In these earthly laws, though men judge about them when they are making them, when once they are established and passed, the judges may judge no longer of them, but according to them.*

I answer that, As stated above (A. 1), judgment is nothing else but a decision or determination of what is just. Now a thing becomes just in two ways: first by the very nature of the case, and this is called *natural right,* secondly by some agreement between men, and this is called *positive right,* as stated above (Q. LVII., A. 2). Now laws are written for the purpose of manifesting both these rights, but in different ways. For the written law does indeed contain natural right, but it does not establish it, for the latter derives its force, not from the law but from nature: whereas the written law both contains positive right, and establishes it by giving it force of authority.

Hence it is necessary to judge according to the written law, else judgment would fall short either of the natural or of the positive right. . . .

SIXTH ARTICLE

WHETHER JUDGMENT IS RENDERED PERVERSE BY BEING USURPED?

We proceed thus to the Sixth Article:

Objection 1. It seems that judgment is not rendered perverse by being usurped. For justice is rectitude in matters of action. Now truth is not impaired, no matter who tells it, but it may suffer from the person who ought to accept it. Therefore again justice loses nothing, no matter who declares what is just, and this is what is meant by judgment.

Obj. 2. Further, It belongs to judgment to punish sins. Now it is related to the praise of some that they punished sins without having authority over those whom they punished; such as Moses in slaying the Egyptian (Exod. ii. 12), and Phinees the son of Eleazar in slaying Zambri the son of Salu (Num. xxv. 7–14), and *it was reputed to him unto justice* (Ps. cv. 31). Therefore usurpation of judgment pertains not to injustice.

Obj. 3. Further, Spiritual power is distinct from temporal. Now prelates having spiritual power sometimes interfere in matters concerning the secular power. Therefore usurped judgment is not unlawful.

Obj. 4. Further, Even as the judge requires authority in order to judge aright, so also does he need justice and knowledge, as shown above (A. 2). But a judgment is not described as unjust, if he who judges lacks the habit of justice or the knowledge of the law. Neither therefore is it always unjust to judge by usurpation, i.e. without authority.

On the contrary, It is written (Rom. xiv. 4): *Who art thou that judgest another man's servant?*

I answer that, Since judgment should be pronounced according to the written law, as stated above (A. 5), he that pronounces judgment, interprets, in a way, the letter of the law, by applying it to some particular case. Now since it belongs to the same authority to interpret and to make a law, just as a law cannot be made save by public authority, so neither can a judgment be pronounced except by public authority, which extends over those who are subject to the community. Wherefore even as it would be unjust for one man to force another to observe a law that was not approved by public authority, so too it is unjust, if a man compels another to submit to a judgment that is pronounced by other than the public authority. . . .

SELECTION 5
Summa Theologica, II/2, Question 64, Articles 2–3

The notion that killing sinners is lawful is here expressed in a manner which tended to determine all later Christian teaching on this subject.

SECOND ARTICLE
WHETHER IT IS LAWFUL TO KILL SINNERS?

We proceed thus to the Second Article:

Objection 1. It seems that it is not lawful to kill men who have sinned. For Our Lord in the parable (Matth. xiii.) forbade the uprooting of the cockle which denotes wicked men according to a gloss. Now whatever is forbidden by God is a sin. Therefore it is a sin to kill a sinner.

Obj. 2. Further, Human justice is conformed to Divine justice. Now according to Divine justice sinners are kept back for repentance, according to Ezech. xxxiii. 11: *I desire not the death of the wicked, but that the wicked turn from his way and live.* Therefore it seems altogether unjust to kill sinners.

Obj. 3. Further, It is not lawful, for any good end whatever, to do that which is evil in itself, according to Augustine (*Contra Mendac.* vii.) and the Philosopher (*Ethic.* ii.). Now to kill a man is evil in itself, since we are bound to have charity towards all men, and we wish our friends to live and to be, according to *Ethic.* ix. Therefore it is nowise lawful to kill a man who has sinned.

On the contrary, It is written (Exod. xxii. 18): *Wizards thou shalt not suffer to live;* and (Ps. c. 8): *In the morning I put to death all the wicked of the land.*

I answer that, As stated above (A. 1), it is lawful to kill dumb animals, in so far as they are naturally directed to man's use, as the imperfect is directed to the perfect. Now every part is directed to the whole, as imperfect to perfect, wherefore every part is naturally for the sake of the whole. For this reason we observe that if the health of the whole body demands the excision of a member, through its being decayed or infectious to the other members, it will be both praiseworthy and advantageous to have it cut away. Now every individual person is compared to the whole community, as part to whole. Therefore if a man be dangerous and infectious to the community, on account of some sin, it is praiseworthy and advantageous that he be killed in order to safeguard the common good, since *a little leaven corrupteth the whole lump* (I Cor. v. 6). . . .

THIRD ARTICLE
WHETHER IT IS LAWFUL FOR A PRIVATE INDIVIDUAL TO KILL A MAN WHO HAS SINNED?

We proceed thus to the Third Article:

Objection 1. It seems that it is lawful for a private individual to kill a man who has sinned. For nothing unlawful is commanded in the Divine law. Yet, on account of the sin of the molten calf, Moses commanded (Exod. xxxii. 27): *Let every man kill his brother, and friend, and neighbour.* Therefore it is lawful for private individuals to kill a sinner.

Obj. 2. Further, As stated above (A. 2 *ad* 3), man, on account of sin, is compared to the beasts. Now it is lawful for any private individual to kill a wild beast, especially if it be harmful. Therefore for the same reason, it is lawful for any private individual to kill a man who has sinned.

Obj. 3. Further, A man, though a private individual, deserves praise for doing what is useful for the common good. Now the slaying of evildoers is useful for the common good, as stated above (A. 2). Therefore it is deserving of praise if even private individuals kill evildoers.

On the contrary, Augustine says (*De Civ. Dei* i.): *A man who, without exercising public authority, kills an evildoer, shall be judged guilty of murder, and all the more, since he has dared to usurp a power which God has not given him.*

I answer that, As stated above (A. 2), it is lawful to kill an evildoer in so far as it is directed to the welfare of the whole community, so that it belongs to him alone who has charge of the community's welfare. Thus it belongs to a physician to cut off a decayed limb, when he has been entrusted with the care of the health of the whole body. Now the care of the common good is entrusted to persons of rank having public authority: wherefore they alone, and not private individuals, can lawfully put evildoers to death. . . .

SELECTION 6

Summa Theologica, II/2, Question 66, Articles 1–2

Private property has always been problematic for Christians. Thomas' approach became the most widely accepted position.

FIRST ARTICLE

WHETHER IT IS NATURAL FOR MAN TO POSSESS EXTERNAL THINGS?

We proceed thus to the First Article:

Objection 1. It seems that it is not natural for man to possess external things. For no man should ascribe to himself that which is God's. Now the dominion over all creatures is proper to God, according to Ps. xxiii. 1: *The earth is the Lord's,* etc. Therefore it is not natural for man to possess external things.

Obj. 2. Further, Basil in expounding the words of the rich man (Luke xii. 18), *I will gather all things that are grown to me, and my goods,* says: *Tell me: which are thine: where did you take them from and bring them into being?* Now whatever man possesses naturally, he can fittingly call his own. Therefore man does not naturally possess external things.

Obj. 3. Further, According to Ambrose (*De Trin.* i.) *dominion denotes power.* But man has no power over external things, since he can work no change in their nature. Therefore the possession of external things is not natural to man.

On the contrary, It is written (Ps. viii. 8): *Thou hast subjected all things under his feet.*

I answer that, External things can be considered in two ways. First, as regards their nature, and this is not subject to the power of man, but only to the power of God Whose mere will all things obey. Secondly, as regards their use, and in this way, man has a natural dominion over external things, because, by his reason and will, he is able to use them for his own profit, as they were made on his account: for the imperfect is always for the sake of the perfect, as stated above (Q. LXIV., A. 1). It is by this argument that the Philosopher proves (*Polit.* i.) that the possession of external things is natural to man. Moreover, this natural dominion of man over other creatures, which is competent to man in respect of his reason wherein God's image resides, is shown forth in man's creation (Gen. i. 26) by the words: *Let us make man to Our image and likeness: and let him have dominion over the fishes of the sea,* etc.

Reply Obj. 1. God has sovereign dominion over all things: and He, according to His providence, directed certain things to the sustenance of man's body. For this reason man has a natural dominion over things, as regards the power to make use of them.

Reply Obj. 2. The rich man is reproved for deeming external things to belong to him principally, as though he had not received them from another, namely from God.

Reply Obj. 3. This argument considers the dominion over external things as regards their nature. Such a dominion belongs to God alone, as stated above.

SECOND ARTICLE

WHETHER IT IS LAWFUL FOR A MAN TO POSSESS A THING AS HIS OWN?

We proceed thus to the Second Article:

Objection 1. It seems that it is unlawful for a man to possess a thing as his own. For whatever is contrary to the natural law is unlawful. Now according to the natural law all things are common property: and the possession of property is contrary to this community of goods. Therefore it is unlawful for any man to appropriate any external thing to himself.

Obj. 2. Further, Basil in expounding the words of the rich man quoted above (A. 1, Obj. 2), says: *The rich who deem as their own property the common goods they have seized upon, are like to those who by going beforehand to the play prevent others from coming, and appropriate to themselves what is intended for common use.* Now it would be unlawful to prevent others from obtaining possession of common goods. Therefore it is unlawful to appropriate to oneself what belongs to the community.

Obj. 3. Further, Ambrose says (*Serm.* lxiv., *de temp.*): *Let no man call his own that which is common property:* and by *common* he means external things, as is clear from the context. Therefore it seems unlawful for a man to appropriate an external thing to himself.

On the contrary, Augustine says (*De Haeres.* xl.): *The 'Apostolici' are those who with extreme arrogance have given themselves that name, because they do not admit into their communion persons who are married or possess anything of their own, such as both monks and clerics who in considerable number are to be found in the Catholic Church.* Now the reason why these people are heretics is because, severing themselves from the Church, they think that those who enjoy the use of the above things, which they themselves lack, have no hope of salvation. Therefore it is erroneous to maintain that it is unlawful for a man to possess property.

I answer that, Two things are competent to man in respect of exterior things. One is the power to procure and dispense them, and in this regard it is lawful for man to possess property. Moreover this is necessary to human life for three reasons. First because every man is more careful to procure what is for himself alone than that which is common to many or to all: since each one would shirk the labour and leave to another that which concerns the community, as happens where there is a great number of servants. Secondly, because human affairs are conducted in more orderly fashion if each man is charged with taking care of some particular thing himself, whereas there would be confusion if everyone had to look after any one thing indeterminately. Thirdly, because a more peaceful state is ensured to man if each one is contented with his own. Hence it is to be observed that quarrels arise more frequently where there is no division of the things possessed.

The second thing that is competent to man with regard to external things is their use. In this respect man ought to possess external things, not as his own, but as common, so that, to wit, he is ready to communicate them to others in their need. Hence the Apostle says (I Tim. vi. 17, 18): *Charge the rich of this world . . . to give easily, to communicate to others,* etc. . . .

SELECTION 7

Summa Theologica, II/2, Question 78, Article 1

Thomas' attitude towards usury eventually created serious problems in an emerging capitalist society.

FIRST ARTICLE

WHETHER IT IS A SIN TO TAKE USURY FOR MONEY LENT?

We proceed thus to the First Article:

Objection 1. It seems that it is not a sin to take usury for money lent. For no man sins through following the example of Christ. But Our Lord said of Himself (Luke xix. 23): *At My coming I might have exacted it,* i.e. the money lent, *with usury.* Therefore it is not a sin to take usury for lending money.

Obj. 2. Further, According to Ps. xviii. 8, *The law of the Lord is unspotted,* because, to wit, it forbids sin. Now usury of a kind is allowed in the Divine law, according to Deut. xxiii. 19, 20: *Thou shalt not fenerate to thy brother money, nor corn, nor any other thing, but to the stranger:* nay more, it is even promised as a reward for the observance of the Law, according to Deut. xxviii. 12: *Thou shalt fenerate to many nations, and shalt not borrow of any one.* Therefore it is not a sin to take usury.

Obj. 3. Further, In human affairs justice is determined by civil laws. Now civil law allows usury to be taken. Therefore it seems to be lawful.

Obj. 4. Further, The counsels are not binding under sin. But, among other counsels we find (Luke vi. 35): *Lend, hoping for nothing thereby*. Therefore it is not a sin to take usury.

Obj. 5. Further, It does not seem to be in itself sinful to accept a price for doing what one is not bound to do. But one who has money is not bound in every case to lend it to his neighbour. Therefore it is lawful for him sometimes to accept a price for lending it.

Obj. 6. Further, Silver made into coins does not differ specifically from silver made into a vessel. But it is lawful to accept a price for the loan of silver vessel. Therefore it is also lawful to accept a price for the loan of a silver coin. Therefore usury is not in itself a sin.

Obj. 7. Further, Anyone may lawfully accept a thing which its owner freely gives him. Now he who accepts the loan, freely gives the usury. Therefore he who lends may lawfully take the usury.

On the contrary, It is written (Exod. xxii. 25): *If thou lend money to any of thy people that is poor, that dwelleth with thee, thou shalt not be hard upon them as an extortioner, nor oppress them with usuries.*

I answer that, To take usury for money lent is unjust in itself, because this is to sell what does not exist, and this evidently leads to inequality which is contrary to justice.

In order to make this evident, we must observe that there are certain things the use of which consists in their consumption: thus we consume wheat when we use it for food. Wherefore in suchlike things the use of the thing must not be reckoned apart from the thing itself, and whoever is granted the use of the thing, is granted the thing itself; and for this reason, to lend things of this kind is to transfer the ownership. Accordingly if a man wanted to sell wine separately from the use of the wine, he would be selling the same thing twice, or he would be selling what does not exist, wherefore he would evidently commit a sin of injustice. In like manner he commits an injustice who lends wine or wheat, and asks for double payment, viz.

one, the return of the thing in equal measure, the other, the price of the use, which is called usury.

On the other hand there are things the use of which does not consist in their consumption: thus to use a house is to dwell in it, not to destroy it. Wherefore in such things both may be granted: for instance, one man may hand over to another the ownership of his house while reserving to himself the use of it for a time, or vice versa, he may grant the use of the house, while retaining the ownership. For this reason a man may lawfully make a charge for the use of his house, and, besides this, revendicate the house from the person to whom he has granted its use, as happens in renting and letting a house.

Now money, according to the Philosopher (*Ethic.* v.: *Polit.* i.) was invented chiefly for the purpose of exchange: and consequently the proper and principal use of money is its consumption or alienation whereby it is sunk in exchange. Hence it is by its very nature unlawful to take payment for the use of money lent, which payment is known as usury: and just as a man is bound to restore other ill-gotten goods, so is he bound to restore the money which he has taken in usury. . . .

SELECTION 8

Summa Theologica, II/2, Question 40, Article 1

The notion of the just war is here classically defined.

FIRST ARTICLE
WHETHER IT IS ALWAYS SINFUL TO WAGE WAR?

We proceed thus to the First Article:

Objection 1. It seems that it is always sinful to wage war. Because punishment is not inflicted except for sin. Now those who wage war are threatened by Our Lord with punishment, according to Matth. xxvi. 52: *All that take the sword shall perish with the sword.* Therefore all wars are unlawful.

Obj. 2. Further, Whatever is contrary to a Divine precept is a sin. But war is contrary to a Divine precept, for it is written (Matth. v. 39): *But I say to you not to resist evil;* and (Rom.

xii. 19): *Not revenging yourselves, my dearly beloved, but give place unto wrath.* Therefore war is always sinful.

Obj. 3. Further, Nothing, except sin, is contrary to an act of virtue. But war is contrary to peace. Therefore war is always a sin.

Obj. 4. Further, The exercise of a lawful thing is itself lawful, as is evident in scientific exercises. But warlike exercises which take place in tournaments are forbidden by the Church, since those who are slain in these trials are deprived of ecclesiastical burial. Therefore it seems that war is a sin in itself.

On the contrary, Augustine says in a sermon on the son of the centurion (*cf. Ep. ad Marcel.*, cxxxviii.): *If the Christian Religion forbade war altogether, those who sought salutary advice in the Gospel would rather have been counselled to cast aside their arms, and to give up soldiering altogether. On the contrary, they were told: 'Do violence to no man; . . . and be content with your pay.' If he commanded them to be content with their pay, he did not forbid soldiering.*

I answer that, In order for a war to be just, three things are necessary. First, the authority of the sovereign by whose command the war is to be waged. For it is not the business of a private individual to declare war, because he can seek for redress of his rights from the tribunal of his superior. Moreover it is not the business of a private individual to summon together the people, which has to be done in wartime. And as the care of the common weal is committed to those who are in authority, it is their business to watch over the common weal of the city, kingdom or province subject to them. And just as it is lawful for them to have recourse to the sword in defending that common weal against internal disturbances, when they punish evil-doers, according to the words of the Apostle (Rom. xiii. 4): *He beareth not the sword in vain: for he is God's minister, an avenger to execute wrath upon him that doth evil;* so too, it is their business to have recourse to the sword of war in defending the common weal against external enemies. Hence it is said to those who are in authority (Ps. lxxxi. 4): *Rescue the poor: and deliver the needy out of the hand of the sinner;* and for this reason Augustine says (*Contra Faust.* xxii.): *The natural order conducive to peace among mortals demands that the power to declare and counsel war should be in the hands of those who hold the supreme authority.*

Secondly, a just cause is required, namely that those who are attacked, should be attacked because they deserve it on account of some fault. Wherefore Augustine says (Q. X., *super Jos.*): *A just war is wont to be described as one that avenges wrongs, when a nation or state has to be punished, for refusing to make amends for the wrongs inflicted by its subjects, or to restore what it has seized unjustly.*

Thirdly, it is necessary that the belligerents should have a rightful intention, so that they intend the advancement of good, or the avoidance of evil. Hence Augustine says (*De Verb. Dom*): *True religion looks upon as peaceful those wars that are waged not for motives of aggrandisement, or cruelty, but with the object of securing peace, of punishing evil-doers, and of uplifting the good.* For it may happen that the war is declared by the legitimate authority, and for a just cause, and yet be rendered unlawful through a wicked intention. Hence Augustine says (*Contra Faust.* xxii.): *The passion for inflicting harm, the cruel thirst for vengeance, an unpacific and relentless spirit, the fever of revolt, the lust of power, and suchlike things, all these are rightly condemned in war. . . .*

SELECTION 9

Summa Theologica, II/2, Question 182, Articles 1–2

The distinction between the contemplative and the active life and the glorification of the contemplative characterizes medieval ethics.

FIRST ARTICLE

WHETHER THE ACTIVE LIFE IS MORE EXCELLENT THAN THE CONTEMPLATIVE?

We proceed thus to the First Article:

Objection 1. It seems that the active life is more excellent than the contemplative. For *that which belongs to better men would seem to be worthier and better*, as the Philosopher says (*Top.* iii. 1). Now the active life belongs to persons of higher rank, namely prelates, who are placed in a position of honour and power; wherefore Augustine says (*De Civ. Dei,* xix. 19) that *in our actions we must not love honour or power in this life.* Therefore it would seem that the active life is more excellent than the contemplative.

Obj. 2. Further, In all habits and acts, commanding belongs to the more excellent; thus the military art, being the more excellent, commands the art of the bridle-maker. Now it belongs to the active life to direct and command the contemplative, as appears from the words addressed to Moses (Exod. xix. 21), *Go down and charge the people, lest they should have a mind to pass the* fixed *limits to see the Lord.* Therefore the active life is more excellent than the contemplative.

Obj. 3. Further, No man should be taken away from a greater thing in order to be occupied with lesser things: for the Apostle says (I Cor. xii. 31): *Be zealous for the better gifts.* Now some are taken away from the state of the contemplative life to the occupations of the active life, as in the case of those who are transferred to the state of prelacy. Therefore it would seem that the active life is more excellent than the contemplative.

On the contrary, Our Lord said (Luke x. 42): *Mary hath chosen the best part, which shall not be taken away from her.* Now Mary figures the contemplative life. Therefore the contemplative life is more excellent than the active.

I answer that, Nothing prevents certain things being more excellent in themselves, whereas they are surpassed by another in some respect. Accordingly we must reply that the contemplative life is simply more excellent than the active: and the Philosopher proves this by eight reasons (*Ethic.* x. 7, 8). The first is, because the contemplative life becomes man according to that which is best in him, namely the intellect, and according to its proper objects, namely intelligibles; whereas the active life is occupied with externals. Hence Rachel, by whom the contemplative life is signified, is interpreted *the vision of the principle,* whereas as Gregory says (*Moral.* vi. 18) the active life is signified by Lia who was blear-eyed. The second reason is because the contemplative life can be more continuous, although not as regards the highest degree of contemplation, as stated above

(A. CLXXX., A. 8, *ad* 2; Q. CLXXXI., A. 4, *ad* 3), wherefore Mary, by whom the contemplative life is signified, is described as *sitting* all the time *at the Lord's feet*. Thirdly, because the contemplative life is more delightful than the active; wherefore Augustine says (*De Verb. Dom.* xxvi.) that *Martha was troubled, but Mary feasted*. Fourthly, because in the contemplative life man is more self-sufficient, since he needs fewer things for that purpose; wherefore it was said (Luke x. 41): *Martha, Martha, thou art careful and art troubled about many things*. Fifthly, because the contemplative life is loved more for its own sake, while the active life is directed to something else. Hence it is written (Ps. xxvi. 4): *One thing I have asked of the Lord, this will I seek after, that I may dwell in the house of the Lord all the days of my life, that I may see the delight of the Lord*. Sixthly, because the contemplative life consists in leisure and rest, according to Ps. xlv. 11, *Be still and see that I am God*. Seventhly, because the contemplative life is according to Divine things, whereas active life is according to human things; wherefore Augustine says (*De Verb. Dom.* xxvii.): *'In the beginning was the Word:' to Him was Mary hearkening: 'The Word was made flesh:' Him was Martha serving*. Eighthly, because the contemplative life is according to that which is most proper to man, namely his intellect; whereas in the works of the active life the lower powers also, which are common to us and brutes, have their part; wherefore (Ps. xxxv. 8) after the words, *Men and beasts thou wilt preserve, O Lord*, that which is special to man is added (*verse* 10): *In Thy light we shall see light*.

Our Lord adds a ninth reason (Luke x. 42) when He says: *Mary hath chosen the best part, which shall not be taken away from her*, which words Augustine (*De Verb. Dom., loc. cit.*) expounds thus: *Not,—Thou hast chosen badly but,—She has chosen better. Why better? Listen,—Because it shall not be taken away from her. But the burden of necessity shall at length be taken from thee: whereas the sweetness of truth is eternal*.

Yet in a restricted sense and in a particular case one should prefer the active life on account of the needs of the present life. Thus too the Philosopher says (Top. iii. 2): *It is better to be wise than to be rich, yet for one who is in need, it is better to be rich*. . . .

SECOND ARTICLE
WHETHER THE ACTIVE LIFE IS OF GREATER MERIT THAN THE CONTEMPLATIVE?

We proceed thus to the Second Article:

Objection 1. It would seem that the active life is of greater merit than the contemplative. For merit implies relation to meed; and meed is due to labour, according to I Cor. iii. 8, *Every man shall receive his own reward according to his own labour.* Now labour is ascribed to the active life, and rest to the contemplative life; for Gregory says (*Hom.* xiv. *in Ezech.*): *Whosoever is converted to God must first of all sweat from labour, i.e. he must take Lia, that afterwards he may rest in the embraces of Rachel so as to see the principle.* Therefore the active life is of greater merit than the contemplative.

Obj. 2. Further, The contemplative life is a beginning of the happiness to come; wherefore Augustine commenting on Jo. xxi. 22, *So I will have him to remain till I come,* says (*Tract.* cxxiv. *in Joan.*): *This may be expressed more clearly: Let perfect works follow Me conformed to the example of My passion, and let contemplation begun here remain until I come, that it may be perfected when I shall come.* And Gregory says (*loc. cit. in Ezech.*) that *contemplation begins here, so as to be perfected in our heavenly home.* Now the life to come will be a state not of meriting but of receiving the reward of our merits. Therefore the contemplative life would seem to have less of the character of merit than the active, but more of the character of reward.

Obj. 3. Further, Gregory says (*Hom.* xii. *in Ezech.*) that *no sacrifice is more acceptable to God than zeal for souls.* Now by the zeal for souls a man turns to the occupations of the active life. Therefore it would seem that the contemplative life is not of greater merit than the active.

On the contrary, Gregory says (*Moral.* vi.): *Great are the merits of the active life, but greater still those of the contemplative.*

I answer that, As stated above (I.–II., Q. CXIV., A. 4), the root of merit is charity; and, while, as stated above (Q. XXV., A. 1), charity consists in the love of God and our neighbour, the love of God is by itself more meritorious than the love of our neighbour, as stated above (Q. XXVII., A. 8). Wherefore that which pertains more directly to the love of God is generically more meritorious than that which pertains directly to the love of our neighbour for God's sake. Now the contemplative life pertains directly and immediately to the love of God; for Augustine says (*De Civ. Dei,* xix. 19) that *the love of* (the Divine) *truth seeks a holy leisure,* namely of the contemplative life, for it is that truth above all which the contemplative life seeks, as stated above (Q. CLXXXI., A. 4 *ad* 2). On the other hand, the active life is more directly concerned with the love of our neighbour, because it is *busy about much serving* (Luke x. 40). Wherefore the contemplative life is generically of greater merit than the active life. This is moreover asserted by Gregory (*Hom.* iii. *in Ezech.*): *The contemplative life surpasses in merit the active life, because the latter labours under the stress of present work, by reason of the necessity of assisting our neighbour, while the former with heartfelt relish has a foretaste of the coming rest,* i.e. the contemplation of God.

Nevertheless it may happen that one man merits more by the works of the active life than another by the works of the contemplative life. For instance through excess of Divine love a man may now and then suffer separation from the sweetness of Divine contemplation for the time being, that God's will may be done and for His glory's sake. Thus the Apostle said (Rom. ix. 3): *I wished myself to be an anathema from Christ, for my brethren;* which words Chrysostom expounds as follows (*De Compunct.* i. 7): *His mind was so steeped in the love of Christ that, although he desired above all to be with Christ, he despised even this, because thus he pleased Christ. . . .*

XI THE MEDIEVAL PAPACY

In the pagan Roman Empire religion was completely subservient to the state. A person by assuming the office of emperor also acquired divinity. Divinity was, thus, a by-product of absolute political power. It is the almost unbelievable accomplishment of the medieval papacy to have reversed this situation completely. In the view of the medieval papacy absolute political power was a by-product of sitting in Christ's stead on the throne of St. Peter in Rome. Few of the medieval popes were professional theologians. Many were canon lawyers who succeeded because of their administrative skill and personal dynamism; they failed if they were unable to administer the complex machinery of papal government. Their pronouncements profoundly influenced Christian social teaching. In some of them the ambition of the Christian clergy to rule the world finds its most succinct expression.

SELECTION 1

Pope Gregory VII (1073–1085) was involved in a struggle for supremacy over the temporal and the spiritual realms with the Emperor Henry IV (1056–1106). This is the sentence of excommunication hurled against Henry IV on February 22, 1076.

O St. Peter, chief of the Apostles, incline to us, I beg, your holy ear and listen to your servant whom from infancy you have nourished, and whom you have shielded until the present day from the hand of the wicked who have hated me, and who do hate me, for my fidelity to you. Amongst all the saints you and my Lady, the Mother of God, and your brother, St. Paul, are witnesses for me that your Holy Roman Church drew me to its leadership against my will; that I never had any thought of ascending to your chair by violence and I should have preferred to end my life as a pilgrim rather than to have seized your throne by secular means for the sake of worldly glory. And therefore I believe that it is through your grace and not through my own merit that it has pleased and does please you that the Christian people, who have been expressly committed to you, should obey me. And especially to me, as your deputy and through your favour, has God granted the power of binding and loosing in Heaven and earth.

On the basis of this belief, therefore, for the honour and defence of your Church, in the name of Almighty God, Father, Son and Holy Ghost, by your power and authority, I withdraw from Henry the king, son of Henry the Emperor, who has risen against your Church with unheard-of insolence, the rule over the whole kingdom of the Germans and over Italy. And I absolve all Christians from the bonds of the oath which they have taken to him or which they shall in future take; and I forbid any one to serve him as king. For it is fitting that he who strives to lessen the honour of your Church should lose the honour which he possesses. And since he has scorned to obey as a Christian, and has not come back to God whom he has deserted, but has had intercourse with the excommunicated; practised numerous iniquities; spurned my admonitions which I sent to him—as you are witness—for his own salvation; and separated himself from the Church endeavouring to split it. I bind him, in your stead, with the chain of the anathema. And relying upon you, I bind him, so that the people may know that you are Peter, and upon your rock the Son of the living God has built His Church, and the gates of hell shall not prevail against it.

SELECTION 2

As a result of the lengthy conflict between Pope Boniface VIII (1294–1303) and King Philip IV of France (1285–1314) Boniface expressed the legal claims of the papacy in this Bull, *Unam Sanctam* of November 18, 1302.

That there is only one Holy, Catholic and Apostolic Church we are compelled to believe and to hold, our faith urging us and this we do firmly believe and simply confess; and also that there is no salvation or remission of sins outside of her—as the bridegroom proclaims in Canticles: "One is my dove, my perfect one is but one; she is the only one of her mother, the chosen of her that bore her," which represents one mystical body whose head is Christ; and of Christ God is the head. And in it there is "one Lord, one faith, one baptism." At the time of the flood there was, indeed, one ark of Noah, prefiguring one Church; it had been finished in one cubit, had one steersman and commander, namely Noah, and we read that outside of it all things existing on earth were destroyed. This Church we venerate, and this alone, as the Lord says through the prophet: "Deliver, O God, my soul from the sword and my only one from the hand of the dog." He prayed for the soul, that is for Himself—for the head and the body at the same time—which body, namely, He called the one and only Church because of the promised unity of faith, sacraments and charity of the Church. That is the "seamless garment" of the Lord which was not cut but fell by lot. Therefore, in this one and only Church there is one body and one head, not two heads as if it were a monster: namely Christ and Peter, the vicar of Christ, and the successor of Peter; because the Lord said to Peter: "Feed my sheep." "My sheep," He said, speaking generally and not particularly about these or those sheep; so that it must be understood that He committed to him all His sheep. If therefore the Greeks and others say that they were not committed to Peter and his successors, they necessarily confess that they are not of the sheep of Christ, for the Lord says in John: "There shall be one fold and one shepherd."

We are taught by the words of the Gospel that in this Church and in its power there are two swords, a spiritual, to wit, and a temporal. For when the Apostles said, "Behold, here are two swords"—that means in the Church, since the Apostles were speaking—the Lord did not reply that it was too many, but enough. And he who denies that the temporal sword is in the power of Peter, has wrongly understood the word of the Lord when He says: "Put up again thy sword into its place." Wherefore both are in the power of the Church, namely the spiritual and material swords; the one, indeed to be wielded for the Church, the other by the Church; the former by the priest, the latter by the hand of kings and knights, but at the will and sufferance of the priest. For it is necessary that one sword should be under another and that the temporal authority should be subjected to the spiritual. For when the Apostle says, "There is no power but from God and those (powers) that are, are ordained of God," they would not be ordained unless sword were under sword and the inferior, so to speak, were kept back by the other to be led to the most illustrious deeds. Because according to St. Dionysius it is the law of Divinity that the lowest are to be led through the intermediate to the highest. Not therefore, according to the law of the universe, are all things kept in order equally and immediately; but the lowest through the intermediate and the inferior through the superior. But it is necessary that we confess the more clearly that the spiritual power exceeds any earthly power in dignity and nobility, as spiritual things excel temporal ones. This we can, indeed clearly perceive with our eyes from the giving of tithes, from the benediction and sanctification, from the recognition of this power and from the exercise of government over those same things. For, the truth bearing witness, the spiritual power has to establish the earthly power, and to judge it, if it be not good. So is verified the prophecy of the prophet Jeremiah concerning the Church and the power of the Church: "Lo, I have set thee this day over the nations and over kingdoms," etc.

If, therefore, the earthly power err, it shall be judged by the spiritual power; if the lesser spiritual power err, it shall be judged by the higher, competent spiritual power; but if the supreme spiritual power err, it could be judged solely by God, not by man; of which the Apostle is witness: "The spiritual man judgeth all things; and he himself is judged of no man." Because this authority, although given to man and exercised by man, is not human, but rather Divine, being given to Peter at God's mouth and founded for him and his successors on a rock by Him Whom he confessed, when the Lord said to the same Peter: "Whatsoever thou shalt bind," etc. Whoever, therefore, resists this power thus ordained by God, resists the ordination of God, unless he pretends, like the Manicheans, that there are two beginnings; which we judge to be false and heretical, since —as Moses testifies—not in the beginnings, but "in the beginning" God created heaven, and earth. Consequently we declare, state, define and pronounce that it is altogether necessary to salvation for every human creature to be subject to the Roman Pontiff.

Given at the Lateran, in the 8th year of our Pontificate.

XII MARTIN LUTHER

A German Augustinian monk and later university professor at Wittenberg, Luther was the most important of the early leaders of the Protestant Reformation. Born in Eisleben in 1483, he died in 1546 in the very same town while on a journey.

Though he rarely left Saxony and had been outside of Germany only once as a young monk he influenced the entire world with his enormous literary activity. Because of his significance for theology, his importance for Christian social ethics is sometimes overlooked. But from the publication of the *95 Theses* in 1517, designed to stop what he considered the demoralizing effects of the indulgence traffic, to his final journey to Eisleben to settle a conflict between the Counts of Mansfeld concerning some mining property, he was involved in social teaching. The following selections are an attempt to illustrate the character of this teaching from 1517 to the end of his life.

SELECTION 1

In a letter of Luther to Archbishop Albrecht of Mainz which accompanied the *95 Theses* of 1517 Luther expresses his concern for the social consequences of the indulgence traffic. "Works of piety and love are infinitely better than indulgences," he asserts. The *Theses* themselves indicate that Luther considered the sale of indulgences ethically ruinous.

DISPUTATION OF DOCTOR MARTIN LUTHER ON THE POWER AND EFFICACY OF INDULGENCES

OCTOBER 31, 1517

Out of love for the truth and the desire to bring it to light, the following propositions will be discussed at Wittenberg, under the presidency of the Reverend Father Martin Luther, Master of Arts and of Sacred Theology, and Lecturer in Ordinary on the same at that place. Wherefore he requests that those who are unable to be present and debate orally with us, may do so by letter.

In the Name of our Lord Jesus Christ. Amen.

1. Our Lord and Master Jesus Christ, when He said *Poenitentiam agite,* willed that the whole life of believers should be repentance.

2. This word cannot be understood to mean sacramental penance, i.e., confession and satisfaction, which is administered by the priests.

3. Yet it means not inward repentance only; nay, there is no inward repentance which does not outwardly work divers mortifications of the flesh.

4. The penalty [of sin], therefore, continues so long as hatred of self continues; for this is the true inward repentance, and continues until our entrance into the kingdom of heaven.

5. The pope does not intend to remit, and cannot remit any penalties other than those which he has imposed either by his own authority or by that of the canons.

6. The pope cannot remit any guilt, except by declaring that it has been remitted by God and by assenting to God's remission; though, to be sure, he may grant remission in cases reserved to his judgment. If his right to grant remission in such cases were despised, the guilt would remain entirely unforgiven.

7. God remits guilt to no one whom He does not, at the same time, humble in all things and bring into subjection to His vicar, the priest.

8. The penitential canons are imposed only on the living, and, according to them, nothing should be imposed on the dying.

9. Therefore the Holy Spirit in the pope is kind to us, be-

cause in his decrees he always makes exception of the article of death and of necessity.

10. Ignorant and wicked are the doings of those priests who, in the case of the dying, reserve canonical penances for purgatory.

11. This changing of the canonical penalty to the penalty of purgatory is quite evidently one of the tares that were sown while the bishops slept.

12. In former times the canonical penalties were imposed not after, but before absolution, as tests of true contrition.

13. The dying are freed by death from all penalties; they are already dead to canonical rules, and have a right to be released from them.

14. The imperfect health [of soul], that is to say, the imperfect love, of the dying brings with it, of necessity, great fear; and the smaller the love, the greater is the fear.

15. This fear and horror is sufficient of itself alone (to say nothing of other things) to constitute the penalty of purgatory, since it is very near to the horror of despair.

16. Hell, purgatory, and heaven seem to differ as do despair, almost-despair, and the assurance of safety.

17. With souls in purgatory it seems necessary that horror should grow less and love increase.

18. It seems unproved, either by reason or Scripture, that they are outside the state of merit, that is to say, of increasing love.

19. Again, it seems unproved that they, or at least that all of them, are certain or assured of their own blessedness, though we may be quite certain of it.

20. Therefore by "full remission of all penalties" the pope means not actually "of all," but only of those imposed by himself.

21. Therefore those preachers of indulgences are in error, who say that by the pope's indulgences a man is freed from every penalty, and saved;

22. Whereas he remits to souls in purgatory no penalty which, according to the canons, they would have had to pay in this life.

23. If it is at all possible to grant to any one the remission of

all penalties whatsoever, it is certain that this remission can be granted only to the most perfect, that is, to the very fewest.

24. It must needs be, therefore, that the greater part of the people are deceived by that indiscriminate and high-sounding promise of release from penalty.

25. The power which the pope has, in a general way, over purgatory, is just like the power which any bishop or curate has, in a special way, within his own diocese or parish.

26. The pope does well when he grants remission to souls [in purgatory], not by the power of the keys (which he does not possess), but by way of intercession.

27. They preach man who say that so soon as the penny jingles into the money-box, the soul flies out [of purgatory].

28. It is certain that when the penny jingles into the money-box, gain and avarice can be increased, but the result of the intercession of the Church is in the power of God alone.

29. Who knows whether all the souls in purgatory wish to be bought out of it, as in the legend of Sts. Severinus and Paschal.

30. No one is sure that his own contrition is sincere; much less that he has attained full remission.

31. Rare as is the man that is truly penitent, so rare is also the man who truly buys indulgences, i.e., such men are most rare.

32. They will be condemned eternally, together with their teachers, who believe themselves sure of their salvation because they have letters of pardon.

33. Men must be on their guard against those who say that the pope's pardons are that inestimable gift of God by which man is reconciled to Him;

34. For these "graces of pardon" concern only the penalties of sacramental satisfaction, and these are appointed by man.

35. They preach no Christian doctrine who teach that contrition is not necessary in those who intend to buy souls out of purgatory or to buy *confessionalia*.

36. Every truly repentant Christian has a right to full remission of penalty and guilt, even without letters of pardon.

37. Every true Christian, whether living or dead, has part in

all blessings of Christ and the Church; and this is granted him by God, even without letters of pardon.

38. Nevertheless, the remission and participation [in the blessings of the Church] which are granted by the pope are in no way to be despised, for they are, as I have said, the declaration of divine remission.

39. It is most difficult, even for the very keenest theologians, at one and the same time to commend to the people the abundance of pardons and [the need of] true contrition.

40. True contrition seeks and loves penalties, but liberal pardons only relax penalties and cause them to be hated, or at least, furnish an occasion [for hating them].

41. Apostolic pardons are to be preached with caution, lest the people may falsely think them preferable to other good works of love.

42. Christians are to be taught that the pope does not intend the buying of pardons to be compared in any way to works of mercy.

43. Christians are to be taught that he who gives to the poor or lends to the needy does a better work than buying pardons;

44. Because love grows by works of love, and man becomes better; but by pardons man does not grow better, only more free from penalty.

45. Christians are to be taught that he who sees a man in need, and passes him by, and gives [his money] for pardons, purchases not the indulgences of the pope, but the indignation of God.

46. Christians are to be taught that unless they have more than they need, they are bound to keep back what is necessary for their own families, and by no means to squander it on pardons.

47. Christians are to be taught that the buying of pardons is a matter of free will, and not of commandment.

48. Christians are to be taught that the pope, in granting pardons, needs, and therefore desires, their devout prayer for him more than the money they bring.

49. Christians are to be taught that the pope's pardons are

useful, if they do not put their trust in them; but altogether harmful, if through them they lose their fear of God.

50. Christians are to be taught that if the pope knew the exactions of the pardon-preachers, he would rather that St. Peter's church should go to ashes, than that it should be built up with the skin, flesh and bones of his sheep.

51. Christians are to be taught that it would be the pope's wish, as it is his duty, to give of his own money to very many of those from whom certain hawkers of pardons cajole money, even though the church of St. Peter might have to be sold.

52. The assurance of salvation by letters of pardon is vain, even though the commissary, nay, even though the pope himself, were to stake his soul upon it.

53. They are enemies of Christ and of the pope, who bid the Word of God be altogether silent in some Churches, in order that pardons may be preached in others.

54. Injury is done the Word of God when, in the same sermon, an equal or a longer time is spent on pardons than on this Word.

55. It must be the intention of the pope that if pardons, which are a very small thing, are celebrated with one bell, with single processions and ceremonies, then the Gospel, which is the very greatest thing, should be preached with a hundred bells, a hundred processions, a hundred ceremonies.

56. The "treasures of the Church," out of which the pope grants indulgences, are not sufficiently named or known among the people of Christ.

57. That they are not temporal treasures is certainly evident, for many of the vendors do not pour out such treasures so easily, but only gather them.

58. Nor are they the merits of Christ and the Saints, for even without the pope, these always work grace for the inner man, and the cross, death, and hell for the outward man.

59. St. Lawrence said that the treasures of the Church were the Church's poor, but he spoke according to the usage of the word in his own time.

60. Without rashness we say that the keys of the Church, given by Christ's merit, are that treasure;

61. For it is clear that for the remission of penalties and of reserved cases, the power of the pope is of itself sufficient.

62. The true treasure of the Church is the Most Holy Gospel of the glory and the grace of God.

63. But this treasure is naturally most odious, for it makes the first to be last.

64. On the other hand, the treasure of indulgences is naturally most acceptable, for it makes the last to be first.

65. Therefore the treasures of the Gospel are nets with which they formerly were wont to fish for men of riches.

66. The treasures of the indulgences are nets with which they now fish for the riches of men.

67. The indulgences which the preachers cry as the "greatest graces" are known to be truly such, in so far as they promote gain.

68. Yet they are in truth the very smallest graces compared with the grace of God and the piety of the Cross.

69. Bishops and curates are bound to admit the commissaries of apostolic pardons, with all reverence.

70. But still more are they bound to strain all their eyes and attend with all their ears, lest these men preach their own dreams instead of the commission of the pope.

71. He who speaks against the truth of apostolic pardons, let him be anathema and accursed!

72. But he who guards against the lust and license of the pardon-preachers, let him be blessed!

73. The pope justly thunders against those who, by any art, contrive the injury of the traffic in pardons.

74. But much more does he intend to thunder against those who use the pretext of pardons to contrive the injury of holy love and truth.

75 To think the papal pardons so great that they could absolve a man even if he had committed an impossible sin and violated the Mother of God—this is madness.

76. We say, on the contrary, that the papal pardons are not able to remove the very least of venial sins, so far as its guilt is concerned.

77. It is said that even St. Peter, if he were now pope, could

not bestow greater graces; this is blasphemy against St. Peter and against the pope.

78. We say, on the contrary, that even the present pope, and any pope at all, has greater graces at his disposal; to wit, the Gospel, powers, gifts of healing, etc., as it is written in I Corinthians xii.

79. To say that the cross, emblazoned with the papal arms, which is set up [by the preachers of indulgences], is of equal worth with the Cross of Christ, is blasphemy.

80. The bishops, curates and theologians who allow such talk to be spread among the people, will have an account to render.

81. This unbridled preaching of pardons makes it no easy matter, even for learned men, to rescue the reverence due to the pope from slander, or even from the shrewd questionings of the laity.

82. To wit:—"Why does not the pope empty purgatory, for the sake of holy love and of the dire need of the souls that are there, if he redeems an infinite number of souls for the sake of miserable money with which to build a Church? The former reasons would be most just; the latter is most trivial."

83. Again:—"Why are mortuary and anniversary masses for the dead continued, and why does he not return or permit the withdrawal of the endowments founded on their behalf, since it is wrong to pray for the redeemed?"

84. Again:—"What is this new piety of God and the pope, that for money they allow a man who is impious and their enemy to buy out of purgatory the pious soul of a friend of God, and do not rather, because of that pious and beloved soul's own need, free it for pure love's sake?"

85. Again:—"Why are the penitential canons, long since in actual fact and through disuse abrogated and dead, now satisfied by the granting of indulgences, as though they were still alive and in force?"

86. Again:—"Why does not the pope, whose wealth is to-day greater than the riches of the richest, build just this one church of St. Peter with his own money, rather than with the money of poor believers?"

87. Again:—"What is it that the pope remits, and what par-

ticipation does he grant to those who, by perfect contrition, have a right to full remission and participation?"

88. Again:—"What greater blessing could come to the Church than if the pope were to do a hundred times a day what he now does once, and bestow on every believer these remissions and participations?"

89. "Since the pope, by his pardons, seeks the salvation of souls rather than money, why does he suspend the indulgences and pardons granted heretofore, since these have equal efficacy?"

90. To repress these arguments and scruples of the laity by force alone, and not to resolve them by giving reasons, is to expose the Church and the pope to the ridicule of their enemies, and to make Christians unhappy.

91. If, therefore, pardons were preached according to the spirit and mind of the pope, all these doubts would be readily resolved; nay, they would not exist.

92. Away, then, with all those prophets who say to the people of Christ, "Peace, peace," and there is no peace!

93. Blessed be all those prophets who say to the people of Christ, "Cross, cross," and there is no cross!

94. Christians are to be exhorted that they be diligent in following Christ, their Head, through penalties, deaths, and hell;

95. And thus be confident of entering into heaven rather through many tribulations, than through the assurance of peace.

SELECTION 2

In his *Open Letter to the Christian Nobility* of 1520, Luther discussed at great length what he considered the reasons for the sorry state of Christendom. At the end he addressed himself briefly to economic and social reforms.

There is great need of a general law and decree of the German nation against the extravagance and excess in dress, by which so many nobles and rich men are impoverished. God has given to us, as to other lands, enough wool, hair, flax and every thing else which properly serves for the seemly and honorable dress of every rank, so that we do not need to spend and waste such enormous sums for silk and velvet and golden ornaments and other foreign wares. I believe that even if the pope had not robbed us Germans with his intolerable exactions, we should still have our hands more than full with these domestic robbers, the silk and velvet merchants. In the matter of clothes, as we see, everybody wants to be equal to everybody else, and pride and envy are aroused and increased among us, as we deserve. All this and much more misery would be avoided if our curiosity would only let us be thankful, and be satisfied with the goods which God has given us.

In like manner it is also necessary to restrict the spice-traffic which is another of the great ships in which money is carried out of German lands. There grows among us, by God's grace, more to eat and drink than in any other land, and just as choice and good. Perhaps the proposals that I make may seem foolish and impossible and give the impression that I want to suppress the greatest of all trades, that of commerce; but I am doing what I can. If reforms are not generally introduced, then let every one who is willing reform himself. I do not see that many good customs have ever come to a land through commerce, and in ancient times God made His people of Israel dwell away from the sea on this account, and did not let them engage much in commerce.

But the greatest misfortune of the German nation is certainly the traffic in annuities. If that did not exist many a man would have to leave unbought his silks, velvets, golden ornaments, spices and ornaments of every sort. It has not existed much over a hundred years, and has already brought almost all princes, cities, endowed institutions, nobles and their heirs to poverty, misery and ruin; if it shall continue for another hundred years Germany cannot possibly have a *pfennig* left and we shall certainly have to devour one another. The devil invented the practice, and the pope, by confirming it, has injured the whole world.

Therefore I ask and pray that everyone open his eyes to see the ruin of himself, his children and his heirs, which not only stands before the door, but already haunts the house, and that emperor, princes, lords and cities do their part that this trade be condemned as speedily as possible, and henceforth prevented, regardless whether or not the pope, with all his law and unlaw, is opposed to it, and whether or not benefices or church foundations are based upon it. It is better that there should be in a city one living based on an honest freehold or revenue, than a hundred based on an annuity; indeed a living based on an annuity is worse and more grievous than twenty based on freeholds. In truth this traffic in rents must be a sign and symbol that the world, for its grievous sins, has been sold to the devil, so that both temporal and spiritual possessions must fail us, and yet we do not notice it at all.

Here, too, we must put a bit in the mouth of the Fuggers and similar corporations. How is it possible that in the lifetime of a single man such great possessions, worthy of a king, can be piled up, and yet everything be done legally and according to God's will? I am not a mathematician, but I do not understand how a man with a hundred gulden can make a profit of twenty gulden in one year, nay, how with one gulden he can make another; and that, too, by another way than agriculture or cattle-raising, in which increase of wealth depends not on human wits, but on God's blessing. I commend this to the men of affairs. I am a theologian, and find nothing to blame in it except its evil and offending appearance, of which St. Paul says, "Avoid every appearance or show of evil." This I know well, that it would be much more pleasing to God if we increased agriculture and diminished commerce, and that they do much better who, according to the Scriptures, till the soil and seek their living from it, as was said to us and to all men in Adam, "Accursed be the earth when thou laborest therein, it shall bear thee thistles and thorns, and in the sweat of thy face shalt thou eat thy bread." There is still much land lying untilled.

Next comes the abuse of eating and drinking which gives us Germans a bad reputation in foreign lands, as though it were our special vice. Preaching cannot stop it; it has become too common, and has got too firmly the upper hand. The waste of money which it causes would be a small thing, were it not followed by other sins,—murder, adultery, stealing, irreverence and all the vices. The temporal sword can do something to prevent it; or else it will be as Christ says: "The last day shall come like a secret snare, when they shall be eating and drinking, marrying and wooing, building and planting, buying and selling." It is so much like that now that I verily believe the judgment day is at the door, though men are thinking least of all about it.

Finally, is it not a pitiful thing that we Christians should maintain among us open and common houses of prostitution, though all of us are baptised unto chastity? I know very well what some say to this, to wit, that it is not the custom of any one people, that it is hard to break up, that it is better that there should be such houses than that married women, or maidens, or those of more honorable estate should be outraged. But should not the temporal, Christian government consider that in this heathen way the evil is not to be controlled? If the people of Israel could exist without such an abomination, why could not Christian people do as much? Nay, how do many cities, towns and villages exist without such houses? Why should not great cities also exist without them?

In this, and in the other matters above mentioned, I have tried to point out how many good works the temporal government could do, and what should be the duty of every government, to the end that every one may learn what an awful responsibility it is to rule, and to have high station. What good would it do that an overlord were in his own life as holy as St. Peter, if he have not the purpose diligently to help his subjects in these matters? His very authority will condemn him! For it is the duty of the authorities to seek the highest good of their subjects. But if the authorities were to consider how the young people might be brought together in marriage, the hope of entering the married state would greatly help every one to endure and to resist temptation.

But now every man is drawn to the priesthood or the monastic life, and among them, I fear, there is not one in a hundred who has any other reason than that he seeks a living, and doubts that he will ever be able to support himself in the estate of matrimony. Therefore they live wildly enough beforehand, and wish, as they say, to "wear out their lust," but rather wear it in, as experience shows. I find the proverb true, "Despair makes most of the monks and priests"; and so things are as we see them.

My faithful counsel is that, in order to avoid many sins

which have become very common, neither boy nor maid should take the vow of chastity, or of the "spiritual life," before the age of thirty years. It is, as St. Paul says, a peculiar gift. Therefore let him whom God does not constrain, put off becoming a cleric and taking the vows. Nay, I will go farther and say, If you trust God so little that you are not willing to support yourself as a married man, and wish to become a cleric only because of this distrust, then for the sake of your own soul, I beg of you not to become a cleric, but rather a farmer, or whatever else you please. For if to obtain your temporal support you must have one measure of trust in God, you must have ten measures of trust to continue in the life of a cleric. If you do not trust God to support you in the world, how will you trust him to support you in the Church? Alas, unbelief and distrust spoil everything and lead us into all misery, as we see in every estate of life!

Much could be said of this miserable condition. The young people have no one to care for them. They all do as they please, and the government is of as much use to them as if it did not exist; and yet this should be the chief concern of pope, bishops, lords and councils. They wish to rule far and wide, and yet to help no one. O, what a rare bird will a lord and ruler be in heaven just on this account, even though he build a hundred churches for God and raise up all the dead!

SELECTION 3

Luther became deeply involved in the Peasant War of 1525, "the most tragic episode in the history of the Reformation in Germany." First he wrote *An Admonition to Peace* in reply to the *Twelve Articles* of the peasants of Swabia. This was a conciliatory tract. When the peasants threatened to be successful he wrote a violent denunciation *Against the Robbing and Murdering Hordes of Peasants* which alienated even some of his friends. Our selection is taken from a later treatise in which Luther attempts to explain his approach to the rebellion after the peasants had actually been defeated.

An Open Letter Concerning the Hard Book Against the Peasants

Our selection illustrates the distinction between the "two kingdoms," central in Luther's thought, as well as his bitter language against the revolting peasants.

There are two kingdoms, one the kingdom of God, the other the kingdom of the world. I have written this so often that I am surprised that there is anyone who does not know it or note it. One who knows how to distinguish rightly between these two kingdoms will certainly not be offended at my little book, and will also have a right understanding of the sayings about mercy. God's kingdom is a kingdom of grace and mercy, not of wrath and punishment. In it there is only forgiveness, consideration for one another, love, service, the doing of good, peace, joy, etc. But the kingdom of the world is a kingdom of wrath and severity. In it there is only punishment, repression, judgment, and condemnation, for the suppressing of the wicked and the protection of the good. For this reason it has the sword, and a prince or lord is called in Scripture God's wrath, or God's rod (Isaiah xiv).

The words of Scripture that speak of mercy apply to the kingdom of God and to Christians, not to the kingdom of the world, for it is a Christian's duty not only to be merciful, but to endure every kind of suffering—robbery, arson, murder, devil and hell. It goes without saying that he is to smite, slay and recompense no one. But the kingdom of the world is nothing else than the servant of God's wrath upon the wicked, and is a real precursor of hell and everlasting death. It should not be merciful, but strict, severe and wrathful in the fulfilment of its work and duty. Its tool is not a wreath of roses or a flower of love, but a naked sword; and a sword is a symbol of wrath, severity and punishment. It is turned only against the wicked, to hold them in check and keep them at peace, and to protect and save the righteous. Therefore God decrees, in the law of Moses and in Exodus xxii, where He institutes the sword, "Thou shalt take the murderer even from mine altar, and shalt not have mercy on him," and the Epistle to the Hebrews confesses that he who acts against the law shall die without mercy. This shows that in the exercise of their office, worldly rulers cannot and ought not be merciful, though out of grace, they may give their office a holiday.

Now he who would confuse these two kingdoms—as our false fanatics do—would put wrath into God's kingdom and mercy into the world's kingdom; and that is the same as putting the devil in heaven and God in hell. Both of these things these sympathizers with the peasants would like to do. First they wanted to go to work with the sword, fight for the Gospel as "Christian brethren," and kill other people, when it was these others' duty to be merciful and patient. Now that the kingdom of the world has overcome them, they want to have mercy in it; that is to say, they would endure no worldly kingdom, but would not grant God's kingdom to anyone. Can you imagine anything more perverse? Not so, dear friends! If one has deserved wrath in the kingdom of the world, let him submit, and either take his punishment, or humbly sue for pardon; those who are in God's kingdom ought to have mercy on everyone and pray for everyone, and yet not hinder the kingdom of the world in the maintenance of its rights and the performance of its duty, but rather assist it.

Although the severity of the world's kingdom seems unmerciful, nevertheless, when we see it rightly, it is not the smallest of God's mercies. Let everyone think this over and give his own judgment on the following case. Suppose I had a wife and children, a house, servants, and property, and a thief or murderer fell upon me, killed me in my own house, ravished my wife and children, took all that I had, and went unpunished, so that he could do the same thing again, when he wished. Tell me, who would be more in need of mercy in such a case, I or the thief and murderer? Without doubt it would be I who would need most that people should have mercy on me. But how can this mercy be shown to me and my poor, miserable wife and children, except by suppressing such a knave, and protecting me and maintaining my rights, or, if he will not be suppressed and keeps on, by giving him his just dues, and punishing him, so that he must stop it? What fine mercy to me it would be, if we were to have mercy on the thief and murderer, and let him kill, and abuse and rob me!

That kind of mercy which rules and acts through the temporal sword, these peasants' advocates do not consider. They open their eyes and their mouths upon the wrath and the severity only, and say that we are flattering the furious princes and lords, when we teach that they are to punish the wicked. And yet they are themselves ten times worse flatterers of the murderous knaves and wicked peasants; nay, they are bloodthirsty murderers, rebels at heart, for they have no mercy on those whom the peasants overthrew, robbed, dishonored, and subjected to all kinds of injustice. For if the intentions of the peasants had been carried out, no honest man would have been safe from them, but whoever had a *pfennig* more than another would have had to suffer for it. They had already begun that, and it would not have stopped there; women and children would have been put to shame; they would have taken to killing each other, too, and there would have been no peace or safety anywhere. Has anything been heard of that is more unrestrained than a mob of peasants when they are fed full and have got power? As Solomon says, in Proverbs xxx, "Such people the world cannot bear."

On such people are we now to have mercy above others, and let them rage on as they please with everyone's body, life, wife, children, honor and property? Are we to leave them unpunished, and allow the innocent to perish shamefully before our very eyes, without mercy or help or comfort? I hear constant reports that the Bamberg peasants were offered more than they asked, provided only they would keep the peace, and they would not. Margrave Casimir, too, promised his peasants that whatever others won with strife and rebellion, he would give them out of free grace; but that did not help either. It is well known that the Franconian peasants, out of sheer wantonness, planned nothing else than robbing, burning, breaking, and destroying. It is my own experience with the Thuringian peasants that the more they were exhorted and instructed, the more obstinate, the prouder, the madder they became. Their attitude everywhere was so wanton and defiant that it seemed as though they really wanted to be slain without grace or mercy. They scornfully defied God's wrath, and now it is coming upon them, as the cviii Psalm says, "They would not have grace, and now it is far away from them."

The Scriptures, therefore, have fine, clear eyes and see the temporal sword aright. They see that out of great mercy, it must be unmerciful, and from utter kindliness, it must exercise wrath and severity. As Peter and Paul say, it is God's servant for vengeance, wrath, and punishment upon the wicked, but for the protection, praise, and honor of the righteous. It looks upon the righteous and has mercy on them, and in order that they may not suffer, it guards, bites, stabs, cuts, hews, and slays, as has been commanded it by God, whose servant it knows itself to be, even in this. This punishing of the wicked without grace does not occur for its own sake, because the punishment of the wicked is a thing to seek after, not in order that the evil desires that are in their blood may be atoned for, but in order that the righteous may be protected, and peace and safety maintained. And beyond all doubt, these are precious works of mercy, love, and kindness, since there is nothing on earth that is worse than disturbance, insecurity, oppression, violence, and injustice. Who could or would stay alive, if such things were the rule? Therefore the wrath and severity of the sword is just as necessary to a people as eating and drinking, nay, as life itself.

"Nay," say they, "we are not talking about the obdurate peasants who are unwilling to surrender, but of those who have been beaten, or who have given themselves up. To them the princes ought to show mercy, and not treat them so cruelly." I answer; You cannot be a good man if you slander my little book and say that I speak in it of such conquered peasants, or of those who have surrendered, whereas I made it plain that I was speaking of those who were first approached in a friendly way, and would not. All my words were against the obdurate, hardened, blinded peasants, who would neither see nor hear, as anyone may see who reads them; and yet you say that I advocate the slaughter of the poor captured peasants without mercy. If you are going to read books this way and interpret them as you please, what book will have any chance with you? Therefore, as I wrote them so I write now; On the obstinate, hardened, blinded peasants, let no one have mercy, but let everyone, as he is able, hew, stab, slay, lay about him as though among mad dogs, in order that, by so doing, he may show mercy to those who are ruined, driven away, and led astray by these peasants, so that peace and safety may be maintained. It is better to cut off one member without mercy than to have the whole body perish by fire, or by disease. How do you like that? Am I still a preacher of the Gospel who advocates grace and mercy? If you think I am not, it makes little difference, for you are a bloodhound and a rebellious murderer and destroyer of the country, you and your rebellious peasants, whom you are flattering in their rebellion.

SELECTION 4

Luther carried on a voluminous correspondence which he used for ethical teaching. In this selection, a letter of December 28, 1541, he reproves Count Albert of Mansfeld for confiscating property belonging to the miners in his territory.

I desire from the bottom of my heart that you may receive in a Christian and gracious way what I write here. Your Grace knows that I am a native of the territory of Mansfeld. Until now I have naturally loved my native land, for even the books of heathen writers declare that every child has a natural love for his fatherland. Besides, God did many laudable things through Your Grace at the beginning of the gospel: churches, pulpits, and schools were well ordered to the praise and honor of God. And during the peasant uprising God made excellent and glorious use of Your Grace. For these and other reasons I cannot readily forget Your Grace or cease to pray for you and be concerned about you.

But it appears to me, especially from rumors and complaints that have reached me, that Your Grace has fallen away from such good beginnings and has become a very different person. As Your Grace may well believe, this causes me great heartache on your account. Your Grace too must be aware that you have become cold, have given your heart to Mammon, and have the ambition to become rich. According to complaints Your Grace is also sharply and severely oppressive to subjects and proposes to confiscate their forges and goods and to make what amounts to vassals out of them. God will not suffer this. Or if he does, he will allow your land to become impoverished and go to ruin, for he can take away what is his own gift without giving an accounting for it; as Haggai says: "Ye have sown much, and bring in little; and he that earneth wages, earneth wages to put it into a bag with holes."

I have heard some say that it has been proposed to establish in Germany a government like that in France. I should approve of this if it were first determined whether it would be right and agreeable in God's sight. Meanwhile it is well to observe that the kingdom of France, which was once a golden and glorious kingdom, now has nothing to boast of either in people or in goods. In comparison with the former golden kingdom, it has become a leaden and tinnish kingdom. What before was called a Christian kingdom now is friendly with the Turks. This is what happens when God and his Word are despised.

This is, I believe, the last time that I shall be writing to Your Grace, for I am nearer to my grave than may be supposed. I pray again that Your Grace may be more gentle and gracious with your subjects. Let them remain as before. Then Your Grace will also remain, if God wills it, here and hereafter. Otherwise Your Grace will lose both, as the fable of Aesop tells of the man who killed the goose that laid a golden egg every day and so lost both the daily eggs and the goose that was the source of them, or like the dog in Aesop that lost the piece of meat when he snapped at the shadow of the meat in the water. This is certainly true, that he who desires too much will have too little, as Solomon states again and again in the book of Proverbs.

In short, I am concerned about Your Grace's soul. I cannot permit myself to cease praying for you and being concerned about you, for then I am convinced that I would cease being in the Church. Not only the law of Christian love constrains me, but also the dire threat in Ezek., ch. 4, that God will damn us preachers for the sins of others: "If thou givest him not warning, nor speakest to warn the wicked from his wicked way, to save his life; the same wicked man shall die in his iniquity; but his blood will I require at thine hand, for therefore have I made thee a pastor." Your Grace will know how to take this admonition, for I cannot allow myself to be damned for Your

Grace's sin. I desire, rather, that you may be saved together with me, if this be possible. If not, I have at least done my duty and am excused in God's sight.

SELECTION 5

All during his life Luther preached. He used the sermons also for the clarification of Christian ethics. This selection is an example from the year before his death (1545) in which he summarizes his teaching concerning marriage. The language is that of an irascible old man, typical for the style of his old age.

"Let marriage be held in honor among all, and let the marriage bed be undefiled; for God will judge the immoral and adulterous" (Heb. 13:4).

This is a sermon concerning the holy estate of matrimony which is highly necessary, especially among Christians, that all men may know what the holy estate of matrimony really is and where it comes from, so that we shall not go on living so casually from day to day, like the heathen and dumb brutes who neither ask nor think about these things, but simply go on interbreeding and cohabiting promiscuously. No, among Christians, it must not be so; but rather as St. Paul says in I Thess. 4[:3–5], "This is the will of God, your sanctification: that you abstain from immorality; that each one of you know how to take a wife for himself in holiness and honor, not in the passion of lust like heathen who do not know God."

Therefore Christians should live in sanctification, not like swine and animals, nor like the heathen, who neither regard nor honor this estate.

There is much to preach concerning this holy estate and divine ordinance of marriage, for it is the oldest of all estates in the whole world; indeed, all others are derived from that estate in which Adam and Eve, our first parents, were created and ordained and in which they and all their God-fearing children and descendants lived.

For there it is, written in the first book of Moses: "God created man in his own image, in the image of God he created him; male and female he created them. And God blessed them, and God said to them, 'Be fruitful and multiply, and fill the earth and subdue it'" [Gen. 1:27–28].

There it is; these are not my words nor those of any other man, but God's Word. This is the way he created and ordained it, and he who will not believe it, let him leave it. Moreover, the daily birth and arrival of all men proves that God wants his creation and ordinance, the holy estate of matrimony, to be maintained, in that little men and women are born and begin to grow up every day.

So every single one of us must declare and confess that we have not made or created ourselves; nor can we do it, neither could our parents do it. Who, then? The almighty, eternal God, the creator of all things, who first created and ordained little men and women for the marriage estate, he created us too for this estate. For I must freely confess and declare that I was created a male child, another a female child; I must confess that I am not a stone or a stick, but rather born and created a human being, man or woman. . . .

Therefore all men should marry and be married, and since through the fall of our first parents we have been so spoiled that we are not all fit for marriage, yet those who are not fit for the married state should so live that they walk chastely and honorably and give offense to no one, though at the beginning it was not so and all were fit to become married. But now it happens that some do not want to enter the state of matrimony even though they are fit and qualified to marriage. Some, on the other hand, would like to be married and are unable to do so. Neither do I condemn and disapprove of these. The third group, however, who desire and want to be married and are also fit and competent to do so, even though they enter the marriage state contrary to human laws, do what is right, and nobody should be scandalized by what they do. For the married state should not be forbidden to anyone who is competent to be married, but should be free and open to everyone. And this estate should not be condemned and rejected as something foul and unclean, as the pope and his followers do. For to be married is an ordinance and institution of God, since when God created man and woman, he himself placed them in this estate in which they not only could but should live godly, honorable, pure, and chaste lives, bearing children and peopling the world, indeed, the kingdom of God.

Who, then, would be so bold as to tear down the glorious, holy ordinance of God or to say anything against it? Who, then, is so bold as to condemn this ordinance and despise it as useless, unholy, and unnecessary? . . .

The marriage estate is God's ordinance and we shall stick to this no matter whether they hate and persecute us and will neither regard nor listen to us; this bothers us not at all. We have God; he regards us, along with all the angels and heavenly hosts, he also defends us against all the darts of the devil and our adversaries.

Then, if our dear God and Father in heaven grants you children, nurture and care for them, raise them up in the discipline, fear, and admonition of the Lord. Then you will be doing right and performing better and nobler good works than all the monks and nuns; then you will be living in God's vocation and ordinance and they contrary to God's vocation and ordinance. Because I am certain that I have a gracious God, who regards me, nourishes me, and protects me, I do not care that the louse in Rome, the pope, and his lice, the cardinals and bishops, monks and nuns, do not regard or respect me. I pay no attention to it; I am content that God, my dear Father, sees me and has regard for me. . . .

XIII JOHN CALVIN

Calvin was the most important of the second-generation reformers. Born in 1509 at Noyon, France, he first studied law and later came under the influence of humanism and pursued linguistic studies. Soon he joined the cause of the Reformation and became its leader in the French-speaking world by virtue of his authoritative position in Geneva. From here he influenced the Reformation all over the world and made the city the headquarters of Reformed Christendom. He died in 1564.

Calvin's most influential book was his massive *Institutes of the Christian Religion,* the most widely disseminated systematic presentation of classical Protestantism. It went through many editions during his lifetime and contains significant aspects of his social ethics. Calvin has been blamed or praised for his influence on the shape of the modern world, especially the rise of capitalism and popular democracy. In both instances there is no evidence of any direct or conscious influence. The indirect influence of certain Calvinist ideas as modified in the course of time is considerable.

SELECTION I

Institutes, Book II, Chap. II, No. I

Basic for Calvin's ethical teaching is his view of man as totally corrupt. Any ethics which ignores this situation would, according to him, of necessity suggest the wrong remedy.

Having seen that the dominion of sin, ever since the first man was brought under it, not only extends to the whole race, but has complete possession of every soul, it now remains to consider more closely, whether, from the period of being thus enslaved, we have been deprived of all liberty; and if any portion still remains, how far its power extends. In order to facilitate the answer to this question, it may be proper in passing to point out the course which our inquiry ought to take. The best method of avoiding error is to consider the dangers which beset us on either side. Man being devoid of all uprightness, immediately takes occasion from the fact to indulge in sloth, and having no ability in himself for the study of righteousness, treats the whole subject as if he had no concern in it. On the other hand, man cannot arrogate anything, however minute, to himself, without robbing God of his honour, and through rash confidence subjecting himself to a fall. To keep free of both these rocks, our proper course will be, first, to show that man has no remaining good in himself, and is beset on every side by the most miserable destitution; and then teach him to aspire to the goodness of which he is devoid, and the liberty of which he has been deprived: thus giving him a stronger stimulus to exertion than he could have if he imagined himself possessed of the highest virtue. How necessary the latter point is, everybody sees. As to the former, several seem to entertain more doubt than they ought. For it being admitted as incontrovertible that man is not to be denied anything that is truly his own, it ought also to be admitted, that he is to be deprived of everything like false boasting. If man had no title to glory in himself, when, by the kindness of his Maker, he was distinguished by the noblest ornaments, how much ought he to be humbled now, when his ingratitude has thrust him down from the highest glory to extreme ignominy? At the time when he was raised to the highest pinnacle of honour, all which Scripture attributes to him is, that he was created in the image of God, thereby intimating that the blessings in which his happiness consisted were not his own, but derived by divine communication. What remains, therefore, now that man is stript of all his glory, than to acknowledge the God for whose kindness he failed to be grateful, when he was loaded with the riches of his grace? Not having glorified him by the acknowledgment of his blessings, now, at least, he ought to glorify him by the confession of his poverty. In truth, it is no less useful for us to renounce all the praise of wisdom and virtue, than to aim at the glory of God. Those who invest us with more than we possess only add sacrilege to our ruin. For when we are taught to contend in our own strength, what more is done than to lift us up, and then leave us to lean on a reed which immediately gives way? Indeed, our strength is exaggerated when it is compared to a reed. All that foolish men invent and prattle on this subject is mere smoke.

SELECTION 2
Institutes, Book II, Chap. II, No. 13

While man is corrupt, he has not lost the use of his reason for the purposes of this world, where it proves to be a most useful tool.

Still, however, man's efforts are not always so utterly fruitless as not to lead to some result, especially when his attention is directed to inferior objects. Nay, even with regard to superior objects, though he is more careless in investigating them, he makes some little progress. Here, however, his ability is more limited, and he is never made more sensible of his weakness than when he attempts to soar above the sphere of the present life. It may therefore be proper, in order to make it more manifest how far our ability extends in regard to these two classes of objects, to draw a distinction between them. The distinction is, that we have one kind of intelligence of earthly things, and another of heavenly things. By earthly things, I mean those which relate not to God and his kingdom, to true righteousness and future blessedness, but have some connection with the present life, and are in a manner confined within its boundaries. By heavenly things, I mean the pure knowledge of God, the method of true righteousness, and the mysteries of the heavenly kingdom. To the former belong matters of policy and economy, all mechanical arts and liberal studies. To the latter (as to which, see the eighteenth and following sections) belong the knowledge of God and of his will, and the means of framing the life in accordance with them. As to the former, the view to be taken is this: Since man is by nature a social animal, he is disposed, from natural instinct, to cherish and preserve society; and accordingly we see that the minds of all men have impressions of civil order and honesty. Hence it is that every individual understands how human societies must be regulated by laws, and also is able to comprehend the principles of those laws. Hence the universal agreement in regard to such subjects, both among nations and individuals, the seeds of them being implanted in the breasts of all without a teacher or lawgiver. The truth of this fact is not affected by the wars and dissensions which immediately arise, while some, such as thieves and robbers, would invert the rules of justice, loosen the bonds of law, and give free scope to their lust; and while others (a vice of most frequent occurrence) deem that to be unjust which is elsewhere regarded as just, and, on the contrary, hold that to be praiseworthy which is elsewhere forbidden. For such persons do not hate the laws from not knowing that they are good and sacred, but, inflamed with headlong passion, quarrel with what is clearly reasonable, and licentiously hate what their mind and understanding approve. Quarrels of this latter kind do not destroy the primary idea of justice. For while men dispute with each other as to particular enactments, their ideas of equity agree in substance. This, no doubt, proves the weakness of the human mind, which, even when it seems on the right path, halts and hesitates. Still, however, it is true, that some principle of civil order is impressed on all. And this is ample proof that, in regard to the constitution of the present life, no man is devoid of the light of reason.

SELECTION 3

Institutes, Book II, Chap. VIII, No. 39, 41, 45–46

Calvin inserts a detailed discussion of the ten commandments into his *Institutes,* which illustrates his ethical approach. Our selection reproduces part of his commentary on the "second table," the duties to man.

"THOU SHALT NOT KILL."

The purport of this commandment is, that since the Lord has bound the whole human race by a kind of unity, the safety of all ought to be considered as intrusted to each. In general, therefore, all violence and injustice, and every kind of harm from which our neighbour's body suffers, is prohibited. Accordingly, we are required faithfully to do what in us lies to defend the life of our neighbour, to promote whatever tends to his tranquility, to be vigilant in warding off harm, and, when danger comes, to assist in removing it. Remembering that the Divine Lawgiver thus speaks, consider, moreover, that he requires you to apply the same rule in regulating your mind. It were ridiculous, that he, who sees the thoughts of the heart, and has special regard to them, should train the body only to rectitude. This commandment, therefore, prohibits the murder of the heart, and requires a sincere desire to preserve our brother's life. The hand, indeed, commits the murder, but the mind, under the influence of wrath and hatred, conceives it. How can you be angry with your brother, without passionately longing to do him harm? If you must not be angry with him, neither must you hate him, hatred being nothing but inveterate anger. However you may disguise the fact, or endeavour to escape from it by vain pretexts, where either wrath or hatred is, there is an inclination to do mischief. If you still persist in tergiversation, the mouth of the Spirit has declared, that "whosoever hateth his brother is a murderer" (I John iii. 15); and the mouth of our Saviour has declared, that "whosoever is angry with his brother without a cause shall be in danger of the judgment: and whosoever shall say to his brother, Raca, shall be in danger of the council: but whosoever shall say, Thou fool, shall be in danger of hell fire" (Matth. v. 22).

✧ ✧ ✧ ✧

"THOU SHALT NOT COMMIT ADULTERY."

The purport of this commandment is, that as God loves chastity and purity, we ought to guard against all uncleanness. The substance of the commandment therefore, is, that we must not defile ourselves with any impurity or libidinous excess. To this corresponds the affirmative, that we must regulate every part of our conduct chastely and continently. The thing expressly forbidden is adultery, to which lust naturally tends, that its filthiness (being of a grosser and more palpable form, inasmuch as it casts a stain even on the body) may dispose us to abominate every form of lust. As the law under which man was created was not to lead a life of solitude, but enjoy a help-meet for him —and ever since he fell under the curse the necessity for this mode of life is increased—the Lord made the requisite provision for us in this respect by the institution of marriage, which, entered into under his authority, he has also sanctified with his blessing. Hence, it is evident, that any mode of cohabitation different from marriage is cursed in his sight, and that the conjugal relation was ordained as a necessary means of preventing us from giving way to unbridled lust. Let us beware, therefore, of yielding to indulgence, seeing we are assured that the curse of God lies on every man and woman cohabiting without marriage.

✧ ✧ ✧ ✧

"THOU SHALT NOT STEAL."

The purport is, that injustice being an abomination to God, we must render to every man his due. In substance, then, the commandment forbids us to long after other men's goods, and, accordingly, requires every man to exert himself honestly in preserving his own. For we must consider, that what each individual possesses has not fallen to him by chance, but by the distribution of the sovereign Lord of all, that no one can pervert his means to bad purposes without committing a fraud on a divine dispensation. There are very many kinds of theft. One consists in violence, as when a man's goods are forcibly plundered and carried off; another in malicious imposture, as when they are fraudulently intercepted; a third in the more hidden craft which takes possession of them with a semblance of justice; and a fourth in sycophancy, which wiles them away under the pretence of donation. But not to dwell too long in enumerating the different classes, we know that all the arts by which we obtain possession of the goods and money of our neighbours, for sincere affection substituting an eagerness to deceive or injure them in any way, are to be regarded as thefts. Though they may be obtained by an action at law, a different decision is given by God. He sees the long train of deception by which the man of craft begins to lay nets for his more simple neighbour, until he entangles him in its meshes—sees the harsh and cruel laws by which the more powerful oppresses and crushes the feeble—sees the enticements by which the more wily baits the hook for the less wary, though all these escape the judgment of man, and no cognisance is taken of them. Nor is the violation of this commandment confined to money, or merchandise, or lands, but extends to every kind of right; for we defraud our neighbours to their hurt if we decline any of the duties which we are bound to perform towards them. If an agent or an indolent steward wastes the substance of his employer, or does not give due heed to the management of his property; if he unjustly squanders or luxuriously wastes the means intrusted to him; if a servant holds his master in derision, divulges his secrets, or in any way is treacherous to his life or his goods; if, on the other hand, a master cruelly torments his household, he is guilty of theft before God; since every one who, in the exercise of his calling, performs not what he owes to others, keeps back, or makes away with what does not belong to him.

This commandment, therefore, we shall duly obey, if, contented with our own lot, we study to acquire nothing but honest and lawful gain; if we long not to grow rich by injustice, nor to plunder our neighbour of his goods, that our own may thereby be increased; if we hasten not to heap up wealth cruelly wrung from the blood of others; if we do not, by means lawful and unlawful, with excessive eagerness, scrape together whatever may glut our avarice or meet our prodigality. On the other hand, let it be our constant aim faithfully to lend our counsel and aid to all so as to assist them in retaining their property; or if we have to do with the perfidious or crafty, let us rather be prepared to yield somewhat of our right than to contend with them. And not only so, but let us contribute to the relief of those whom we see under the pressure of difficulties, assisting their want out of our abundance. Lastly, let each of us consider how far he is bound in duty to others, and in good faith pay what we owe. In the same way, let the people pay all due honour to their rulers, submit patiently to their authority, obey their laws and orders, and decline nothing which they can bear without sacrificing the favour of God. Let rulers, again, take due charge of their people, preserve the public peace, protect the good, curb the bad, and conduct themselves throughout as those who must render an account of their office to God, the Judge of all. Let the ministers of churches faithfully give heed to the ministry of the words, and not corrupt the doctrine of salvation, but deliver it purely and sincerely to the people of God. Let them teach not merely by doctrine, but by example; in short, let them act the part of good shepherds towards their flocks. Let the people, in their turn, receive them as the messengers and apostles of God, render them the honour which their Supreme Master has bestowed on them, and supply them with such things as are necessary for their livelihood. Let parents be careful to bring up, guide, and teach their children as a trust committed to them by God. Let them not exasperate or alienate them by cruelty, but cherish and embrace them with the lenity and indulgence which becomes their character. The regard due to parents from their children has already been adverted to. Let the young respect those advanced in years, as the Lord has been pleased to make that age honourable. Let the aged also, by their prudence and their experience (in which they are far superior), guide the feebleness of youth, not assailing them with harsh and clamorous invectives, but tempering strictness with ease and affability. Let servants show themselves diligent and respectful in obeying their masters, and this not with eye-service, but from the heart, as the servants of God. Let masters also not be stern and disobliging to their servants, nor harass them with excessive asperity, nor treat them with insult, but rather let them acknowledge them as brethren and fellow-servants of our heavenly Master, whom, therefore, they are bound to treat with mutual love and kindness. Let every one, I say, thus consider what in his own place and order he owes to his neighbours, and pay what he owes. Moreover, we must always have a reference to the Lawgiver, and so remember that the law requiring us to promote and defend the interest and convenience of our fellowmen, applies equally to our minds and our hands.

SELECTION 4
Institutes, Book III, Chap. XXI, No. 7

This is a brief summary of Calvin's most controversial doctrine, "double predestination."

We say, then, that Scripture clearly proves this much, that God by his eternal and immutable counsel determined once for all those whom it was his pleasure one day to admit to salvation, and those whom, on the other hand, it was his pleasure to doom to destruction. We maintain that this counsel, as regards the elect, is founded on his free mercy, without any respect to human worth, while those whom he dooms to destruction are excluded from access to life by a just and blameless, but at the same time incomprehensible judgment. In regard to the elect, we regard calling as the evidence of election, and justification as another symbol of its manifestation, until it is fully accomplished by the attainment of glory. But as the Lord seals his elect by calling and justification, so by excluding the reprobate either from the knowledge of his name or the sanctification of his Spirit, he by these marks in a manner discloses the judgment which awaits them.

SELECTION 5
Institutes, Book IV, Chap. XX, No. 1–3, 8, 24, 31–32

The distinction between spiritual and civil government is central in Calvin's social ethics. He seems to favor a form of government incorporating checks and balances. And, while opposed to any kind of revolution, he seems to advocate the overthrow of tyrants by means of lower magistrates.

. . . Some, on hearing that liberty is promised in the gospel, a liberty which acknowledges no king and no magistrate among men, but looks to Christ alone, think that they can receive no benefit from their liberty so long as they see any power placed over them. Accordingly, they think that nothing will be safe until the whole world is changed into a new form, when there will be neither courts, nor laws, nor magistrates, nor anything of the kind to interfere, as they suppose, with their liberty. But he who knows to distinguish between the body and the soul, between the present fleeting life and that which is future and eternal, will have no difficulty in understanding that the spiritual kingdom of Christ and civil government are things very widely separated. Seeing, therefore, it is a Jewish vanity to seek and include the kingdom of Christ under the elements of this world, let us, considering, as Scripture clearly teaches, that the blessings which we derive from Christ are spiritual, remember to confine the liberty which is promised and offered to us in him within its proper limits. For why is it that the very same apostle who bids us "stand fast in the liberty wherewith Christ hath made us free, and be not again entangled with the yoke of bondage" (Gal. v, 1), in another passage forbids slaves to be solicitous about their state (I Cor. vii, 21), unless it be that spiritual liberty is perfectly compatible with civil servitude? In this sense the following passages are to be understood: "There is neither Jew nor Greek, there is neither bond nor free, there is neither male nor female" (Gal. iii, 28). Again, "there is neither Greek nor Jew, circumcision nor uncircumcision, barbarian, Scythian, bond nor free: but Christ is all and in all" (Col. iii, 11). It is thus intimated, that it matters not what your condition is among men, nor under what laws you live, since in them the kingdom of Christ does not at all consist.

Still the distinction does not go so far as to justify us in supposing that the whole scheme of civil government is matter of pollution, with which Christian men have nothing to do. Fanatics, indeed, delighting in unbridled license, insist and vociferate that, after we are dead by Christ to the elements of this world, and being translated into the kingdom of God sit among the celestials, it is unworthy of us, and far beneath our dignity, to be occupied with those profane and impure cares which relate to matters alien from a Christian man. To what end, they say, are laws without courts and tribunals? But what has a Christian man to do with courts? Nay, if it is unlawful to kill, what have we to do with laws and courts? But as we lately taught that that kind of government is distinct from the spiritual and internal kingdom of Christ, so we ought to know that they are not adverse to each other. The former, in some measure, begins the heavenly kingdom in us, even now upon earth, and in this mortal and evanescent life commences immortal and incorruptible blessedness, while to the latter it is assigned, so long as we live among men, to foster and maintain the external worship of God, to defend sound doctrine and the condition of the Church, to adapt our conduct to human society, to form our manners to civil justice, to conciliate us to each other, to cherish common peace and tranquillity. All these I confess to be superfluous, if the kingdom of God, as it now exists within us, extinguishes the present life. But if it is the will of God that while we aspire to true piety we are pilgrims upon the earth, and if such pilgrimage stands in need of such aids, those who take them away from man rob him of his humanity. As to their allegation that there ought to be such perfection in the Church of God that her guidance should suffice for law, they stupidly imagine her to be such as she never can be found in the community of men. For while the insolence of the wicked is so great, and their iniquity so stubborn, that it can scarcely be curbed by any severity of laws, what do we expect would be done by those whom force can scarcely repress from doing ill, were they to see perfect impunity for their wickedness?

But we shall have a fitter opportunity of speaking of the use of civil government. All we wish to be understood at present is, that it is perfect barbarism to think of exterminating it, its use among men being not less than that of bread and water, light and air, while its dignity is much more excellent. Its object is not merely, like those things, to enable men to breathe, eat, drink, and be warmed (though it certainly includes all these, while it enables them to live together); this, I say, is not its only object, but it is, that no idolatry, no blasphemy against the name of God, no calumnies against his truth, nor other offences to religion, break out and be disseminated among the people; that the public quiet be not disturbed, that every man's property be kept secure, that men may carry on innocent commerce with each other, that honesty and modesty be cultivated; in short, that a public form of religion may exist among Christians, and humanity among men. Let no one be surprised that I now attribute the task of constituting religion aright to human polity, though I seem above to have placed it beyond the will of man, since I no more than formerly allow men at pleasure to enact laws concerning religion and the worship of God, when I approve of civil order which is directed to this end—viz. to prevent the true religion, which is contained in the law of God, from being with impunity openly violated and polluted by public blasphemy.

✧ ✧ ✧ ✧

But as we have hitherto described the magistrate who truly is what he is called—viz. the father of his country, and (as the Poet speaks) the pastor of the people, the guardian of peace, the president of justice, the vindicator of innocence, he is justly to be deemed a madman who disapproves of such authority. And since in almost all ages we see that some princes, careless about all their duties on which they ought to have been intent, live, without solicitude, in luxurious sloth; others, bent on their own interest, venally prostitute all rights, privileges, judgments, and enactments; others pillage poor people of their money, and afterwards squander it in insane largesses; others act as mere robbers, pillaging houses, violating matrons, and slaying the innocent; many cannot be persuaded to recognise such persons for princes, whose command, as far as lawful, they are bound to obey. For while in this unworthy conduct, and among atrocities so alien, not only from the duty of the magistrate, but also of the man, they behold no appearance of the image of God, which ought to be conspicuous in the magistrate, while they see not a vestige of that minister of God, who was appointed to be a praise to the good and a terror to the bad, they cannot recognise the ruler whose dignity and authority Scripture recommends to us. And, undoubtedly, the natural feeling of the human mind has always been not less to assail tyrants with hatred and execration, than to look up to just kings with love and veneration.

✧ ✧ ✧ ✧

Although the Lord takes vengeance on unbridled domination, let us not therefore suppose that that vengeance is committed to us, to whom no command has been given but to obey and suffer. I speak only of private men. For when popular magistrates have been appointed to curb the tyranny of kings (as the Ephori, who were opposed to kings among the Spartans, or Tribunes of the people to consuls among the Romans, or Demarchs to the senate among the Athenians; and perhaps there is something similar to this in the power exercised in each kingdom by the three orders, when they hold their primary diets). So far am I from forbidding these officially to check the undue license of kings, that if they connive at kings when they tyrannise and insult over the humbler of the people, I affirm that their dissimulation is not free from nefarious perfidy, because they fraudulently betray the liberty of the people, while knowing that, by the ordinance of God, they are its appointed guardians.

But in that obedience which we hold to be due to the commands of rulers, we must always make the exception, nay, must be particularly careful that it is not incompatible with obedience to Him to whose will the wishes of all kings should be subject, to whose decrees their commands must yield, to whose majesty their sceptres must bow. And, indeed, how preposterous were it, in pleasing men, to incur the offence of Him for whose sake you obey men! The Lord, therefore, is King of kings. When he opens his sacred mouth, he alone is to be heard, instead of all and above all. We are subject to the men who rule over us, but subject only in the Lord. If they command anything against Him let us not pay the least regard to it, nor be moved by all the dignity which they possess as magistrates—a dignity to which no injury is done when it is subordinated to the special and truly supreme power of God.

XIV THE ANABAPTISTS

In the sixteenth century the name "Anabaptists" was applied to a widely divergent group of reform-minded people who disassociated themselves from Luther and Zwingli and their followers as well as the Roman Catholic Church. While their social teachings varied greatly, from the advocacy of violence and the extermination of the "godless" by Thomas Münzer to the consistent pacifism of the Swiss groups and the followers of Menno Simons, it was the pacifist tradition which survived and whose teachings influenced all of Christendom and the entire development of Western thought. The view of the Church held by most Christians in America owes more to this Anabaptist vision than to the teachings of sixteenth-century Jesuits, Lutherans, or Calvinists.

SELECTION I
The Schleitheim Confession of Faith

The Schleitheim Confession of Faith was prepared at a conference of Swiss Brethren in 1527. The section here reproduced deals with the separation of the true Christians from the wicked and represents the "religion against culture" approach observed also in other periods of Church history.

We are agreed [as follows] on separation: A separation shall be made from the evil and from the wickedness which the devil planted in the world; in this manner, simply that we shall not have fellowship with them [the wicked] and not run with them in the multitude of their abominations. This is the way it is: Since all who do not walk in the obedience of faith, and have not united themselves with God so that they wish to do His will, are a great abomination before God, it is not possible for anything to grow or issue from them except abominable things. For truly all creatures are in but two classes, good and bad, believing and unbelieving, darkness and light, the world and those who [have come] out of the world, God's temple and idols, Christ and Belial; and none can have part with the other.

To us then the command of the Lord is clear when He calls upon us to be separate from the evil and thus He will be our God and we shall be His sons and daughters.

He further admonishes us to withdraw from Babylon and the earthly Egypt that we may not be partakers of the pain and suffering which the Lord will bring upon them.

From all this we should learn that everything which is not united with our God and Christ cannot be other than an abomination which we should shun and flee from. By this is meant all popish and antipopish works and church services, meetings and church attendance, drinking houses, civic affairs, the commitments [made in] unbelief and other things of that kind, which are highly regarded by the world and yet are carried on in flat contradiction to the command of God, in accordance with all the unrighteousness which is in the world. From all these things we shall be separated and have no part with them for they are nothing but an abomination, and they are the cause of our being hated before our Christ Jesus, Who has set us free from the slavery of the flesh and fitted us for the service of God through the Spirit Whom He has given us.

Therefore there will also unquestionably fall from us the unchristian, devilish weapons of force—such as sword, armor and the like, and all their use [either] for friends or against one's enemies—by virtue of the word of Christ, Resist not [him that is] evil.

✧ ✧ ✧ ✧

We are agreed as follows concerning the sword. The sword is ordained of God outside the perfection of Christ. It punishes and puts to death the wicked, and guards and protects the good. In the Law the sword was ordained for the punishment of the wicked and for their death, and the same [sword] is [now] ordained to be used by the worldly magistrates.

In the perfection of Christ, however, only the ban is used for a warning and for the excommunication of the one who has sinned, without putting the flesh to death—simply the warning and the command to sin no more.

Now it will be asked by many who do not recognize [this as] the will of Christ for us, whether a Christian may or should employ the sword against the wicked for the defense and protection of the good, or for the sake of love.

Our reply is unanimously as follows: Christ teaches and commands us to learn of Him, for He is meek and lowly in heart and so shall we find rest to our souls. Also Christ says to the heathenish woman who was taken in adultery, not that one should stone her according to the law of His Father (and yet He says, As the Father has commanded me, thus I do), but in mercy and forgiveness and warning, to sin no more. Such an attitude we also ought to take completely according to the rule of the ban.

Secondly, it will be asked concerning the sword, whether a Christian shall pass sentence in worldly dispute and strife such as unbelievers have with one another. This is our united answer: Christ did not wish to decide or pass judgment between brother and brother in the case of the inheritance, but refused to do so. Therefore we should do likewise.

Thirdly, it will be asked concerning the sword, Shall one be a magistrate if one should be chosen as such? The answer is as follows: They wished to make Christ king, but He fled and did not view it as the arrangement of His Father. Thus shall we do as He did, and follow Him, and so shall we not walk in darkness. For He Himself says, He who wishes to come after me, let him deny himself and take up his cross and follow me. Also, He Himself forbids the [employment of] the force of the sword saying, The worldly princes lord it over them, etc., but not so shall it be with you. Further, Paul says, Whom God did foreknow He also did predestinate to be conformed to the image of His Son, etc. Also Peter says, Christ has suffered (not ruled) and left us an example, that ye should follow His steps.

Finally it will be observed that it is not appropriate for a Christian to serve as a magistrate because of these points: The government magistracy is according to the flesh, but the Christians' is according to the Spirit; their houses and dwelling remain in this world, but the Christians' are in heaven; their citizenship is in this world, but the Christians' citizenship is in heaven; the weapons of their conflict and war are carnal and against the flesh only, but the Christians' weapons are spiritual, against the fortification of the devil. The worldlings are armed with steel and iron, but the Christians are armed with the armor of God, with truth, righteousness, peace, faith, salvation and the Word of God. In brief, as is the mind of Christ toward us, so shall the mind of the members of the body of Christ be through Him in all things, that there may be no schism in the body through which it would be destroyed. For every kingdom divided against itself will be destroyed. Now since Christ is as it is written of Him, His members must also be the same, that His body may remain complete and united to its own advancement and up-building.

We are agreed as follows concerning the oath: The oath is a confirmation among those who are quarreling or making promises. In the Law it is commanded to be performed in God's Name, but only in truth, not falsely. Christ, who teaches the perfection of the Law, prohibits all swearing to His [followers], whether true or false—neither by heaven, nor by the earth, nor by Jerusalem nor by our head,—and that for the reason which He shortly thereafter gives, For you are not able to make one hair white or black. So you see it is for this reason that all swearing is forbidden: we cannot fulfill that which we promise when we swear, for we cannot change [even] the very least thing on us.

Now there are some who do not give credence to the simple command of God, but object with this question: Well now, did not God swear to Abraham by Himself (since He was God) when He promised him that He would be with him and that He would be his God if he would keep His commandments—why then should I not also swear when I promise someone? Answer: Hear what the Scripture says: God, since He wished more abundantly to show unto the heirs the immutability of His counsel, inserted an oath, that by two immutable things (in which it is impossible for God to lie) we might have a strong consolation. Observe the meaning of this Scripture: What

God forbids you to do, He has power to do, for everything is possible for Him. God swore an oath to Abraham, says the Scripture, so that He might show that His counsel is immutable. That is, no one can withstand nor thwart His will; therefore He can keep His oath. But we can do nothing, as is said above by Christ, to keep or perform [our oaths]: therefore we shall not swear at all.

Then others further say as follows: It is not forbidden of God to swear in the New Testament, when it is actually commanded in the Old, but it is forbidden only to swear by heaven, earth, Jerusalem and our head. Answer: Hear the Scripture, He who swears by heaven swears by God's throne and by Him who sitteth thereon. Observe: it is forbidden to swear by heaven, which is only the throne of God: how much more is it forbidden [to swear] by God himself! Ye fools and blind, which is greater, the throne or Him that sitteth thereon?

Further some say, Because evil is now [in the world, and] because man needs God for [the establishment of] the truth, so did the apostles Peter and Paul also swear. Answer: Peter and Paul only testify of that which God promised to Abraham with the oath. They themselves promise nothing, as the example indicates clearly. Testifying and swearing are two different things. For when a person swears he is in the first place promising future things, as Christ was promised to Abraham Whom we a long time afterwards received. But when a person bears testimony he is testifying about the present, whether it is good or evil, as Simeon spoke to Mary about Christ and testified, Behold this (child) is set for the fall and rising of many in Israel, and for a sign which shall be spoken against.

Christ also taught us along the same line when He said, Let your communication be Yea, yea; Nay, nay; for whatsoever is more than these cometh of evil. He says, Your speech or word shall be yea and nay. (However) when one does not wish to understand, he remains closed to the meaning. Christ is simply Yea and Nay, and all those who seek Him simply will understand His Word. Amen.

SELECTION 2

Thomas Münzer: *Sermon Before the Princes*

Thomas Münzer, though not interested in baptism with water, became for many people in the sixteenth century the typical representative of the Anabaptists. In the selections from his sermon of July 13, 1524, here reproduced, he attempted to win the rulers of electoral Saxony for his kind of extremism. It is this kind of preaching which encouraged the Peasant War and produced Luther's reaction. (See above.)

The pitiable corruption of holy Christendom has become so great that at the present time no tongue can tell it all. Therefore a new Daniel must arise and interpret for you your vision and the [prophet], as Moses teaches (Deut. 20:2), must go in front of the army. He must reconcile the anger of the princes and the enraged people. For if you will rightly experience the corruption of Christendom and the deception of the false clerics and the vicious reprobates, you will become so enraged at them that no one can think it through. Without doubt it will vex you and go right to your heart that you have been so kindly after they, with the very sweetest words, misled you into the most shameful conceptions (Prov. 6: 1 ff.) against all established truth. For they have made fools of you so that everyone swears by the saints that the princes are in respect to their office a pagan people. They are said to be able to maintain nothing other than a civil unity. O beloved, yea, the great Stone there is about to fall and strike these schemes of [mere] reason and dash them to the ground, for he says (Matt. 10:34): I am not come to send peace but a sword. What should be done, however, with the same? Nothing different from [what is done with] the wicked who hinder the gospel: Get them out of the way and eliminate them, unless you want to be ministers of the devil rather than of God, as Paul calls you (Rom. 13:4). You need not doubt it. God will strike to pieces all your adversaries who undertake to persecute you, for his hand is by no means shortened, as Isaiah (ch. 59:1) says. Therefore he can still help you and wishes to, as he supported the elect King Josiah and others who defended the name of God. Thus you are angels, when you wish to do justly, as Peter says (II, ch. 1:4). Christ commanded in deep gravity, saying (Luke 19:27): Take mine enemies and strangle them before mine eyes. Why? Ah! because they ruin Christ's government for him and in addition want to defend their rascality under the guise of Christian faith and ruin the whole world with their insidious subterfuge. Therefore Christ our Lord says (Matt. 18:6): Whosoever shall offend one of these little ones, it is better for him that a millstone be hung about his neck and that he be thrown in the depth of the sea. You can gloss over here and there as much as you like—these are the words of Christ. Now if Christ can say, Whosoever offends *one* of the little ones, what should one say then if somebody offends a great multitude in their faith? That is what the archvillains do, who vex the whole world and make it forsake the true Christian faith and say: No one may know the mystery of God. Everyone should behave himself according to their words and not according to their works (cf. Matt. 23:3). They say that it is not necessary for faith to be tried like gold in the fire (I Peter 1:7; Ps. 140:10). But in this way Christian faith would be worse than a dog's faith where he hopes to get a piece of bread because the table is being set. This is the kind of faith the false divines juggle before the blind world. This is not remarkable after all, for they preach only for the stomach's sake (Phil. 3:19). They cannot say anything further from the experiences of their heart (Matt. 12:34). Now if you want to be true governors, you must begin government at the roots, and, as Christ commanded, drive his enemies from the elect. For you are the means to this end. Beloved, don't give us any old jokes about how the power of God should do it without your application of the sword. Otherwise may it rust away for you in its scabbard! May God grant it, whatever any divine may say to you! Christ says it sufficiently (Matt. 7:19; John 15:2, 6): Every tree that bringeth not forth good fruit is rooted out and cast into the fire. If you do away with the mask of the world, you will soon recognize it with a righteous judgment (John 7:24). Perform a righteous judgment at God's command! You have help enough for the purpose (Wisdom of Solomon, ch. 6), for Christ is your Master (Matt. 23:8). Therefore let not the evildoers live longer who make us turn away from God (Deut. 13:5). For the godless person has no right to live when he is in the way of the pious. In Ex. 22:18 God says: Thou shalt not suffer evildoers to live. Saint Paul also means this where he says of the sword of rulers that it is bestowed upon them for the retribution of the wicked as protection for the pious (Rom. 13:4). God is your protection and will teach you to fight against his foes (Ps. 18:34). He will make your hands skilled in fighting and will also sustain you. But you will have to suffer for that reason a great cross and temptation in order that the fear of God may be declared unto you. That cannot happen without suffering, but it costs you no more than the danger of having risked all for God's sake and the useless prattle of your adversaries. For though even pious David was drawn from his castle by Absalom, he finally came again into ascendancy when Absalom got hung up and was stabbed. Therefore, you cherished fathers of Saxony, you must hazard all for the sake of the gospel. But God will chasten you out of love as his most beloved sons (cf. Deut. 1:31) when he in his momentary anger is enraged. Blessed at that time are all who trust in God. Free in the Spirit of Christ, say only (Ps. 3:6): I will not be afraid of a hundred thousand though they have set themselves against me round about. I suppose at this point our learned divines will bring out the goodness of Christ, which they in their hypocrisy apply by force. But over against this [goodness] they ought also to take note of the sternness of Christ (John 2:15–17; Ps. 69:9), when he turned over the roots of idolatry. As Paul says in Col. 3:5–7, because of these the wrath of God cannot be done away with in the congregation. If he, according to our view, tore down the lesser, surely without doubt he would not have spared the idols and images if there had been any. For he himself commanded the same through Moses (Deut. 7:5 f.) where he says: Ye are a holy people. Ye ought not to have pity on account of the superstitious. Break down their altars, smash up their images and burn them up, that I be not angry with you. These words Christ has not abrogated, but rather he wishes to fulfill them for us (Matt. 5:17). There are [of course] all those figures interpreted by the prophets, but these [in Matthew] are bright clear words which must stand forever (Isa. 40:8). God cannot say yes today and tomorrow no, but rather he is unchangeable in his Word (Mal. 3:6; I Sam. 15:10–22; Num., ch. 22). [In reply to the argument] that the apostles of the Gentiles did not disturb the idols, I answer thus. Saint Peter was a timid man (Gal. 2:11–13). If he dissembled with the Gentiles, he was a symbol of all the apostles, so that Christ said of him (John 21:15–19) that he mightily feared death. And, because of this [fear, it] is easy enough to understand that he [gave no occasion] to arouse the pagans by such [action]. But Saint Paul spoke out quite sternly against idolatry. If he had been able to push his teaching to its conclusion among the Athenians (Acts 17:16–31), he would without any doubt have cast it down, as God through Moses has commanded, and as it also happened many times thereafter through [the action of] the martyrs in trustworthy histories. Therefore no justification is given us in the inadequacy and the negligence of the saints to let the godless have their way. Since they with us confess God's name they ought to choose between two alternatives: either to repudiate the Christian faith completely or put idolatry out of the way (Matt. 18:7–9). That our learned divines, however, should come along and, in their godless prevaricating manner, say in reference to Daniel (2:34) that the Antichrist ought to be destroyed without [human] hands is as much as to say he [Antichrist] is already inwardly collapsed, as was the [Canaanite] people when the Chosen were bent on entering the Promised Land, as Joshua (ch. 5:1) writes. He [Joshua] notwithstanding did not spare them [the Canaanites] the sharpness of the sword. Look at Ps. 44:5 and I Chron. 14:11. There you will find the solution in this way. They did not conquer the land by the sword but rather through the power of God. But the sword was the means, as eating and drinking is for us a means of living. In just this way the sword is necessary to wipe out the godless (Rom. 13:4). That this might now take place, however, in an orderly and proper fashion, our cherished fathers, the princes, should do it, who with us confess Christ. If, however, they do not do it, the sword will be taken from them (Dan. 7:26 f.). For they confess him all right with words and deny him with the deed (Titus 1:16). They [the princes], accordingly, should proffer peace to the enemies (Deut. 2:26–30). If the latter wish to be spiritual [in the outmoded sense] and do not give testimony of the knowledge (*kunst*) of God (cf. I Peter 3:9, 12), they should be gotten out of the way (I Cor. 5:13). But I pray for them with the devout David where they are not against God's revelation. Where, however, they pursue the opposition, may they be slain without any mercy as Hezekiah (II Kings 18:22), Josiah (ch. 23:5), Cyrus (cf. II Chron. 36:22 f.), Daniel (ch. 6:27), Elijah (I Kings 18:40) destroyed the priests of Baal, otherwise the Christian church (*kirche*) cannot come back again to its origin. The weeds must be plucked out of the vineyard of God in the time of harvest. Then the beautiful red wheat will acquire substantial rootage and come up properly (Matt. 13:24–30). The angels [v. 39], however, who sharpen their sickles for this purpose are the serious servants of God who execute the wrath of the divine wisdom (Mal. 3:1–6).

Nebuchadnezzar (Dan. 2:46) perceived the divine wisdom in Daniel. He fell down before him after the mighty truth had overcome him. But he was moved like a reed before the wind, as ch. 3 (vs. 5 ff.) proves. Of the same character are many people now, by far the greater number, who accept the gospel with great joy as long as everything is going fine and friendly (Luke 8:13). But when God wishes to put such people to the test or to the trial by fire (I Peter 1:7), oh, how they take offense at the smallest weed, as Christ in Mark (ch. 4:17) prophesied. Without doubt inexperienced people will to such an extent anger themselves over this little book for the reason that I say with Christ (Luke 19:27; Matt. 18:6) and with Paul (I Cor. 5:7, 13) and with the instruction of the whole divine law that the godless rulers should be killed, especially the priests and monks who revile the gospel as heresy for us and wish to be considered at the same time as the best Christians. When hypocritical, spurious (*getichte*) goodness becomes engaged and embittered beyond the average, it then wishes to defend the godless and says Christ killed no one, etc. And since the friends of God thus quite ineffectually command the wind, the prophecy of Paul (II Tim. 3:5) is fulfilled. In the last days the lovers of pleasures will indeed have the form of godliness (*Gütticheit*), but they will denounce its power. Nothing on earth has a better form and mask than spurious goodness. For this reason all corners are full of nothing but hypocrites, among whom not a one is so bold as to be able to say the real truth. Therefore in order that the truth may be rightly brought to the light, you rulers—it makes no difference whether you want to or not—must conduct yourselves according to the conclusion of this chapter (ch. 2:48 f.), namely, that Nebuchadnezzar made the holy Daniel an officer in order that he might execute good, righteous decisions, as the Holy Spirit says (Ps. 58:10 f.). For the godless have no right to live except as the elect wish to grant it to them, as it is written in Ex. 23:29–33. Rejoice, you true friends of God, that for the enemies of the cross their heart has fallen into their breeches. They must do right even though they have never dreamed it. If we now fear God, why do we want to enrage ourselves before slack defenseless people (Num. 14:8 f.; Josh. 11:6)? Be but daring! He who wishes to have rule himself, to him all power on earth and heaven is given (Matt. 28:18). May He preserve you, most beloved, forever. Amen.

SELECTION 3
Menno Simons: *On the Ban: Questions and Answers*

Menno Simons (1496–1561) became the most influential leader of the pacifist Anabaptists. The Ban, here discussed, helped to make the Mennonites a disciplined community.

QUESTION 1. Is separation a command or is it a counsel of God? *Answer.* Let everyone weigh the words of Christ and of Paul [I Cor. 5:11] . . . and he will discover whether it is a divine commandment or whether it is a counsel. Everything which Paul says in regard to separation he generally speaks in the imperative mode, that is, in a commanding manner. *Expurgate,* that is, purge, I Cor. 5:7. *Profligate,* that is, drive out. *Se jungere,* that is, withdraw from, I Tim. 6:5. *Fuge,* that is, flee, Titus 3:9. Again (II Thess. 3:6): We command you, brethren, in the name of our Lord Jesus Christ. I think, brethren, these Scriptures show that it is a command; and even if it were not a command but an advice of God, should we not diligently follow such advice? If my spirit despise the counsel of the Holy Spirit, then I truly acknowledge that my spirit is not of God. And to what end many have come who did not follow God's Spirit, but their own, may be read in many passages of sacred history and may be seen in many instances, at the present time.

QUESTION 2. If any person should not observe this ban and yet be pious otherwise, should such a one be banned on that account? *Answer.* Whoever is pious will show his piety in obedience, and not knowingly or willfully despise and disregard the word, commandment, will, counsel, admonition, and doctrine of God. For if anyone willfully keeps *commercium* with such whose company is forbidden in Scripture, then we must come to the conclusion that he despises the Word of God, yea, is in open rebellion and refractoriness (I speak of those who well know and acknowledge, and yet do not do). For rebellion is as the sin of witchcraft and stubbornness is as iniquity and idolatry (I Sam. 15:23).

Since the Scripture admonishes and commands that we shall not associate with such, nor eat with them, nor greet them, nor receive them into our houses, etc.; and then if somebody should say, I will associate with them, I will eat with them, I will greet them in the Lord, and receive them into my house—he would plainly prove that he did not fear the commandment and admonition of the Lord, but that he despised it, rejected the Holy Spirit, and that he trusted, honored, and followed his own opinion rather than the Word of God. Now judge for yourself what kind of sin it is not to be willing to hear and obey God's Word. Paul says (II Thess. 3:6, 14): Now we command you, brethren, in the name of our Lord Jesus Christ, that ye withdraw yourselves from every brother that walketh disorderly, and not after the tradition which ye received of us; again: And if any man obey not our word by this epistle, note that man, and have no company with him, that he may be ashamed. Inasmuch as the ban was so strictly commanded by the Lord, and practiced by the apostles (Matt. 18:17), therefore we must also use it and obey it, since we are thus taught and enlightened by God, or else we should be shunned and avoided by the congregation of God. This must be acknowledged and confessed.

QUESTION 3. Should husband and wife shun each other on account of the ban—as also parents and children? *Answer.* First, that the rule of the ban is a general rule, and excepts none: neither husband nor wife, neither parent nor child. For God's word judges all flesh with the same judgment and knows no respect of persons. Inasmuch as the rule of the ban is general, excepts none, and is no respecter of persons—therefore it is reasonable and necessary to hear and obey the Word of the Lord in this respect; no matter whether it be husband or wife, parents or children.

Secondly, we say that separation must be made in the congregation; and therefore the husband must consent and vote with the church in the separation of his wife; and the wife in the separation of her husband. If the pious consort must give his consent, then it is also becoming that he also shun her, with the church; for what use is there in the ban when the shunning and avoiding are not connected with it?

Thirdly, we say that the ban was instituted to make ashamed unto reformation. Do not understand this shame as the world is ashamed; but understand as in the conscience, and therefore let it be done with all discretion, reasonableness, and love. If then my husband or wife, parent or child is judged in the church, in the name of and by the power of Christ, to be banned, it becomes us (inasmuch as the evangelical ban is unto reformation), according to the counsel of the Holy Spirit, to seek the reformation of my own body, namely, of my spouse, and also of our nearest kinsfolk as parent or child; for spiritual love must be preferred to anything else. Aside from this I would care for them and provide the temporal necessaries of life, so far as it would be in my power.

Fourthly, we say that the ban was given that we should not be sullied by the leaven of false doctrine or unclean-living flesh, by apostates. And as it is plain that none can corrupt and leaven us more than our own spouses, parents, etc., therefore the Holy Spirit counsels us to shun them, lest they leaven our faith and thus make us ashamed before God. If we love husband or wife, parent or child more than Christ Jesus, we cannot possibly be the disciples of Christ.

Some object to this, saying that there is no divorce but by reason of adultery. This is just what we say; and therefore we do not speak of divorce, but of shunning, and that for the aforementioned reasons. To shunning, Paul (I Cor. 7:10) has decidedly consented, although this is not always coupled with adultery; but not to divorce. For divorce is not allowed by the Scripture except by reason of adultery (Matt. 5:32; Luke 16:18); therefore we shall never consent to it for other reasons.

Therefore we understand it that the husband should shun his wife, the wife her husband, parents their children and the children their parents when they apostatize. For the rule of the ban is general. They [the godly] must consent, with the church, to the sentence; they must aim at Scriptural shame unto reformation and diligently watch, lest they [themselves] be leavened by them, as said above.

My beloved in the Lord, I would here sincerely pray you that you would make a difference between commandment and commandment and not consider all commandments as equally weighty. For adultery, idolatry, shedding blood, and the like shameful and abominable works of the flesh will be punished more severely than a misunderstanding in regard to the ban, and particularly when not committed willfully and perversely. Therefore beware that in this matter of matrimony you press no one farther than he is taught of God in his heart and that he in his conscience can bear, lest you boil the kid while it is still sucking its mother's milk [cf. Deut. 14:21]. On every hand the Scriptures teach that we should bear with the weak. Brethren, it is a delicate matter. I know too well what has been the result of pressing this matter too far by some in my time. Therefore I advise you to point all to the sure and certain ground. And those consciences that are, through the Scripture and the Holy Spirit, free and unencumbered will freely, without the interference of anyone, by the unction of the Holy Spirit and not by human encouragement, do that which he advises, teaches, and commands in the Holy Scripture, if it should be that one's spouse should be banned. For verily I know that whoever obeys the Holy Spirit, with faithful heart will never be made ashamed.

QUESTION 4. Should we greet one that is banned, with the common, everyday greeting, or return our respects at his greeting? For John says (II John 10 f.): If there come any unto you, and bring not this doctrine, receive him not into your house, neither bid him God speed; for he that biddeth him God speed is partaker of his evil deeds. *Answer.* Mildness, politeness, respectfulness and friendliness to all mankind becomes all Christians. If, then, an apostate should greet me with the common greeting of Good Morning or Good Day and I should be silent; if he should be respectful to me and I should turn my face from him, and bear myself austerely and unfriendly toward him, I might well be ashamed of myself, as Sirach says. For how can such a one be convinced, led to repentance, and be moved to do better by such austerity? The ban is not given to destroy but to build up.

If it should be said that John has forbidden such greeting, I for myself would answer that, before my God, I cannot understand that John said this in regard to the everyday greeting, but that he says, if some deceiver should come to us who has left the doctrine of Christ, that we should not receive such a one into our houses, lest he mislead us; and that we should not greet him as a brother lest we have communion with him. But not so with the worldly greeting. For if the worldly greeting have such power in itself that it causes the communion of the vain works of those whom I greet, then it must follow that I would have communion with the fornication, adultery, drunkenness, avarice, idolatry and bloodshed of the world, whenever I should greet a worldly man with the common greeting or return his compliment. Oh no! But the greeting or kiss of peace does signify communion. Yet if one should have conscientious scruples in this matter, with such a one I do not dispute about it. For it is not worth contending about. But I would much rather see all scruples in regard to this matter removed and have Christian discretion, love, politeness, and respectfulness practiced for [our] improvement rather than stubbornness, unfriendliness, malice, and unmercifulness unto disruption. Brethren, beware of discord and controversy. The Lord grant every God-fearing person a wholesome understanding of his holy Word. Amen.

QUESTION 5. Are we allowed to show the banned any charity, love, and mercy? *Answer.* Everyone should consider, (1) the exact meaning of the word *commercium;* (2) for what reason and purpose the ban was ordained by the Holy Spirit in the Scriptures; (3) how a real true Christian is reborn, bred, and endowed; (4) how the merciful Father himself acts with those who are already worthy of his judgment and wrath.

All those who can rightly see into these will doubtlessly not deny necessary services, love, and mercy to the banned. For the word *commercium* does not forbid these, but it forbids daily company, conversation, society and business, as was explained above. The ban is also a work of divine love and not of perverse, unmerciful, heathenish cruelty. A true Christian will serve, aid, and commiserate with everybody; yea, even with his most bitter enemies. Austerity, cruelty, and unmercifulness he hates with all his heart. He has a nature like his Father of whom he is born: for he maketh his sun to rise on the evil and on the good, and sendeth rain on the just and on the unjust. If I, then, be of a different nature than he, I show that I am not his child.

Therefore I say with our faithful brother Dietrich Philips that we should not practice the ban to the destruction of mankind (as the Pharisees did their Sabbath) but to its improvement; and thus we desire to serve the bodies of the fallen, in love, reasonableness, and humility, with our temporal goods when necessary, and their souls with the spiritual goods of the holy Word. And we should rather, with the Samaritan, show mercy to the wounded than to pass by him with the priest and Levite. James says (ch. 2:13): For he shall have judgment without mercy, that hath showed no mercy, and mercy rejoiceth against judgment. Be ye therefore merciful as your Father also is merciful. Blessed are the merciful; for they shall obtain mercy. In short, if we understand the true meaning and nature of the word *commercium*, we understand for what reason and purpose the ban was instituted, how a true Christian is and should be minded; and if we conform ourselves to the example of Christ and of God, then the latter is all helped along. And if we have not this grace, we will shamefully err in this ban and be cruel, unmerciful Christians; from which error and abomination may the gracious Father eternally save all his beloved children.

My brethren, I tell the truth and lie not when I say that I hate with all my heart such unmercifulness and cruel-mindedness. Nor do I wish to be considered a brother of such unmerciful, cruel brethren, if there should be such, unless they desist from such abomination and discreetly follow, in love and mercy, the example of God and Christ. For my heart cannot consent to such unmerciful action which exceeds the cruelty of the heathen and Turks; and by the grace of God I will fight against it with my Lord's sword unto death. For it is against the doctrine of the New Testament, and contrary to the Spirit, mind, and nature of God and Christ, according to which all the Scriptures of the New Testament should be judged and understood. All those who do not understand it thus are already in great error.

But in case my necessary service, charity, love, and mercy should become a *commercium*, or that my soul should thereby be led into corruption, then we confess (the Lord must be praised) that our daily intercourse is forbidden in the Scripture, and that it is better to leave off our charity, love, and mercy than to ensnare our souls thereby and lead them into error. The unction of the Holy Spirit will teach us what we should best do in these matters.

QUESTION 6. Are we allowed to sell to, and buy of, the apostates inasmuch as Paul says (I Cor. 5:11) that we should not have intercourse with them? And yet the disciples bought victuals in Sychar, and the Jews dealt with the Gentiles (John 4:5). *Answer*. That the apostles bought victuals in Sychar proves nothing at all; for many of the Samaritans were a remnant of the ten tribes, as we have sufficiently shown above, from the Holy Scripture. But we do not deny that the Jews dealt with the Gentiles, yet they shunned their *commercium*, that is, their daily association, company, and conversation, and did not eat or drink with them, as the writings of the Evangelist sufficiently and plainly show in many Scriptural passages.

And inasmuch as Christ points us to the Jewish ban or shunning, namely, that as they shunned the Gentiles and sinners, so we should likewise shun an apostate Christian; and as the

Jews had dealings with them, although they shunned their daily intercourse in company, association, and conversation; therefore we say that we cannot maintain, either by the Jewish example to which Christ points or by any explicit Scripture, that we should not in any manner deal with the apostate, if no such daily intercourse arises therefrom. For such intercourse with the apostate is strictly prohibited by Scripture; and since it is prohibited, it is manifest that a pious, God-fearing Christian could have no apostate as a regular buyer or seller. For as I have daily to get my cloth, bread, corn, salt, etc., and exchange for it my grain, butter, etc., it cannot fail but that intercourse will arise therefrom. But with a trading which is conducted without such intercourse this is not the case.

And because such business which is carried on without intercourse cannot be shown to be disallowed by virtue of the Scripture, as was said, therefore we would pray all God-fearing brethren and sisters in the Lord, for the sake of God and of love, to act in this matter, as in all others, as reasonable, good, discreet, wise, and prudent Christians and not as vain, reckless, self-conceited, proud, obdurate, and offensive boasters; for a true Christian should always strive after that which is the best and the surest, and follow the pure, unfeigned love, lest he abuse the freedom which he seems to have, to the injury and hindrance of his own soul, to the affliction and destruction of his beloved brethren, to the scornful boasting of the perverse, and to the shameful defamation of the holy Word and the afflicted church of Christ. Besides, I pray and desire in like manner that none will thus in the least be offended at his brother and mistake and judge him by an unscriptural judgment; as he has in this case no reproving example among the Jews nor forbidding word [in the Scriptures].

O my sincerely beloved brethren, let us sincerely pray for understanding and wisdom that all misunderstanding, error, jealousy, offense, division, and untimely reports may be utterly exterminated, root and branch; that a wholesome understanding, doctrine, friendship, love, edification, and a sound judgment may get under way and prevail. Let everyone look with pure eyes and impartial hearts to the example to which Christ points, and to the wholesome, natural meaning of the holy apostles, and let true, Christian love take precedence; and everyone will know, by the grace of God, how he should act and proceed concerning this matter.

QUESTION 7. Are we allowed to be seated with an apostate in a ship or wagon, or to eat with him at the table of a tavern? *Answer*. The first part of this question . . . we deem childish and useless, since this so often happens without intercourse and must needs happen. As to the second part, namely, [whether] to eat at the table with an apostate, while traveling, we can point the questioner to no surer ground and answer than this, namely, we advise, pray, and admonish every pious Christian, as he loves Christ and his Word, to fear God sincerely, and follow the most certain way, that is, not to eat by or with him; for thereby none can be deceived; and if perchance some God-fearing brother might do so, then let everyone beware, lest he sin against his brother by an unscriptural judgment; for none may judge unless he have the judging word on his side.

Whosoever fears God, whosoever desires to follow after his holy Word, with all his strength loves his brother, seeks to avoid all offense and desires to walk in the house of God in all peace and unity, will act justly in all things and will not offend or afflict his brethren.

QUESTION 8. Who, according to Scripture, should be banned or excommunicated? *Answer*. Christ says (Matt. 18:15–17): If thy brother trespass against thee, etc., and will not hear thee or the witnesses, nor the church, let him be unto thee as a heathen man and a publican. And Paul (I Cor. 5:11): If any man that is called a brother be a fornicator, or covetous, or an idolater, or a railer, or a drunkard, or an extortioner; with such a one do not eat. To this class also belong perjurers, thieves, violent persons, haters, fighters, and all those who walk in open, well-known, damnable works of the flesh, of which Paul enumerates a great many (Rom. 1:29; Gal. 5:19; I Cor. 6:9; Eph. 5:5). Again, disorderly persons, working not at all, but who are busy bodies; such as do not abide in the doctrine of Christ and his apostles and do not walk therein, but are disobedient (II Thess. 3:11, 14). Again, masters of sects. Again, those who give offense, cause dispute and discord concerning the doctrine of Christ and of his apostles. In short, all those who openly lead a shameful, carnal life, and those who are corrupted by a heretical, unclean doctrine (Titus 3:10), and who will not be overcome by the wine and oil of the Holy Spirit, but remain, after they have been admonished and sought to be regained in all love and reasonableness, obdurate in their corrupted walk and opinion. They should, at last, in the name of our Lord Jesus Christ, by the power of the Holy Spirit, that is, by the binding Word of God, be reluctantly but unanimously separated from the church of Christ and thereupon, according to the Scriptures, be shunned in all divine obedience, until they repent.

XV IGNATIUS LOYOLA AND THE JESUITS

The reformation of the Roman Catholic Church by the Council of Trent and the character of post-Tridentine Roman Catholicism were profoundly influenced by the Spanish knight Ignatius of Loyola (1491–1556), the founder of the Jesuit Order (Societas Jesu). After his own conversion in 1521, the care of men's souls and the defense of the papacy became Loyola's main interests. The Order founded by him and approved by Pope Paul III in 1540 was dedicated to absolute obedience to the pope. A mighty educational force in Roman Catholic countries and all over the world, it determined the character of the so-called "Counter Reformation."

The Jesuits were not approved by all Roman Catholics. Especially their ethical teachings and the doctrine of probabilism were bitterly attacked by Blaise Pascal (1623–1662) in his *Provincial Letters*. Nevertheless, the influence of the Jesuits on Christian social teaching has been profound.

SELECTION I

Institutum Societatis Jesu, I, 407 f.

Let us with the utmost pains strain every nerve of our strength to exhibit this virtue of obedience, firstly to the Highest Pontiff, then to the Superiors of the Society; so that in all things, to which obedience can be extended with charity, we may be most ready to obey his voice, just as if it issued from Christ our Lord . . . , leaving any work, even a letter, that we have begun and have not yet finished; by directing to this goal all our strength and intention in the Lord, that holy obedience may be made perfect in us in every respect, in performance, in will, in intellect; by submitting to whatever may be enjoined on us with great readiness, with spiritual joy and perseverance; by persuading ourselves that all things [commanded] are just; by rejecting with a kind of blind obedience all opposing opinion or judgement of our own; and that in all things which are ordained by the Superior where it cannot be clearly held [*definiri*] that any kind of sin intervenes. And let each one persuade himself that they that live under obedience ought to allow themselves to be borne and ruled by divine providence working through their Superiors exactly as if they were a corpse which suffers itself to be borne and handled in any way whatsoever; or just as an old man's stick which serves him who holds it in his hand wherever and for whatever purpose he wish to use it. . . .

SELECTION 2

Francisco de Suárez: *A Treatise on Laws and God the Lawgiver,* Book III, Chap. II

The Jesuits were outstanding moral theologians and produced in Suárez (1548–1619), a leading theologian of Spanish scholasticism, one of the great social philosophers of the Roman Catholic Church. In this selection, Suárez rejects the absolute power of the prince and asserts that since men are born free, the power to make human laws resides in the whole body of mankind.

IN WHAT MEN DOES THIS POWER TO MAKE HUMAN LAWS RESIDE DIRECTLY, BY THE VERY NATURE OF THINGS?

1. The reason for doubt on this point is the fact that the power in question dwells either in individual men; or in all men, that is to say, in the whole body of mankind collectively regarded.

The first alternative cannot be upheld. For it is not true that every individual man is the superior of the rest; nor do certain persons, [simply] by the nature of things, possess the said power in a greater degree than other persons [on some ground apart from general superiority], since there is no reason for thus favouring some persons as compared with others.

The second alternative would also seem to be untenable. For

in the first place, if it were correct, all the laws derived from such power would be common to all men. And secondly, [so the argument runs] no source can be found, from which the whole multitude of mankind could have derived this power; since men themselves cannot be that source—inasmuch as they are unable to give that which they do not possess—and since the power cannot be derived from God, because if it were so derived, it could not change but would necessarily remain in the whole community in a process of perpetual succession, like the spiritual power which God conferred upon Peter and which for that reason necessarily endures in him or in his successors, and cannot be altered by men.

2. It is customary to refer, in connexion with this question, to the opinion of certain canonists who assert that by the very nature of the case this [legislative] power resides in some supreme prince upon whom it has been divinely conferred, and that it must always, through a process of succession, continue to reside in a specific individual. The Gloss (on *Decretum,* Pt. II, causa VII, qu. i, can. ix) is cited [by way of confirmation]; but the passage cited contains simply the statement that the son of a king is lawfully king, which is a very different matter, nor does it assert that this mode of succession was perpetual among men. Another Gloss (on *Decretum,* Pt. I, dist. x, can. viii) is also cited, because it declares that the Emperor receives his power from God alone. But that Gloss, in its use of the exclusive word 'alone,' is intended to indicate simply that the Emperor does not receive his power from the Pope; it is not intended to deny that he receives it from men. For, in this very passage, it is said that the Emperor is set up by the army in accordance with the ancient custom mentioned in the *Decretum* (Pt. I, dist. xciii, can. xxiv). The said opinion, then, is supported neither by authority nor by a rational basis, as will become more evident from what follows.

3. Therefore, we must say that this power, viewed solely according to the nature of things, resides not in any individual man but rather in the whole body of mankind. This conclusion is commonly accepted and certainly true. It is to be deduced from the words of St. Thomas ([I.–II,] qu. 90, art. 3, ad 2 and qu. 97, art. 3, ad 3) in so far as he holds that the prince has the

power to make laws, and that this power was transferred to him by the community. The civil laws (*Digest,* I. iv. 1 and I. ii. 2, § II) set forth and accept the same conclusion. . . .

The basic reason in support of the first part of the conclusion is evident, and was touched upon at the beginning of our discussion, namely, the fact that in the nature of things all men are born free; so that, consequently, no person has political jurisdiction over another person, even as no person has dominion over another; nor is there any reason why such power should, [simply] in the nature of things, be attributed to certain persons over certain other persons, rather than *vice versa.* One might make this assertion only: that at the beginning of creation Adam possessed, in the very nature of things, a primacy and consequently a sovereignty over all men, so that [the power in question] might have been derived from him, whether through the natural origin of primogeniture, or in accordance with the will of Adam himself. For it is so that Chrysostom (on *First Corinthians,* Homily xxxiv [, no. 5]) has declared all men to be formed and pro-created from Adam alone, a subordination to one sole prince being thus indicated. However, by virtue of his creation only and his natural origin, one may infer simply that Adam possessed domestic—not political—power. For he had power over his wife, and later he possessed the *patria potestas* over his children until they were emancipated. In the course of time, he may also have had servants and a complete household with full power over the same, the power called 'domestic.' But after families began to multiply, and the individual heads of individual families began to separate, those heads possessed the same power over their respective households. Political power, however, did not make its appearance until many families began to congregate into one perfect community. Accordingly, since this community had its beginning, not in the creation of Adam nor solely by his will, but rather by the will of all who were assembled therein, we are unable to make any well-founded statement to the effect that Adam, in the [very] nature of things, held a political primacy in the said community. For such an inference cannot be drawn from natural principles, since it is not the progenitor's due, by the sole force of natural law, that he shall also be king over his posterity.

But, granted that this inference does not follow upon natural principles, neither have we sufficient foundation for the assertion that God has bestowed such power upon that [progenitor], through a special donation or act of providence, since we have had no revelation to this effect, nor does Holy Scripture so testify to us. To this argument may be added the point made by Augustine and noted in our preceding Chapter [Chap. i, sect. 1], namely, that God did not say: 'Let us make man that he may have dominion over men,' but rather did He say: [Let us make man that he may have dominion] over other living creatures.

Therefore, the power of political dominion or rule over men has not been granted, directly by God, to any particular human individual.

4. From the foregoing, it is easy to deduce the second part of the assertion [at beginning of Section 3], namely, that the power in question resides, by the sole force of natural law, in the whole body of mankind [collectively regarded].

The proof is as follows: this power does exist in men, and it does not exist in each individual, nor in any specific individual, as has also been shown; therefore, it exists in mankind viewed collectively, for our foregoing division [into the two alternatives] sufficiently covers the case.

SELECTION 3
Suárez: *Disputation XIII: On Charity,* Chap. 1

Suárez's discussion of war illustrates the reasoning which has undergirded non-pacifist Western thought.

ON WAR

An external contest at arms which is incompatible with external peace is properly called war, when carried on between two sovereign princes or between two states. When, however, it is a contest between a prince and his own state, or between citizens and their state, it is termed sedition. When it is between private individuals it is called a quarrel or a duel. The difference between these various kinds of contest appears to be material rather than formal, and we shall discuss them all, as did St. Thomas (II.–II, qq. 40, 41, 42) and others who will be mentioned below.

IS WAR INTRINSICALLY EVIL?

1. The first heresy [in connexion with this subject] consists in the assertion that it is intrinsically evil and contrary to charity to wage war. . . . The second error is the assertion that war is specifically forbidden to Christians, and especially, war against Christians. So Eck maintains (*Enchiridion Locorum Communium*, Chap. xxii); and other persons of our own time, who are heretics, advance the same contention. They distinguish, however, two kinds of war, the defensive and the aggressive, which we shall discuss in Subsection 6 of this Section. The conclusions that follow will elucidate the matter.

2. Our first conclusion is that war, absolutely speaking, is not intrinsically evil, nor is it forbidden to Christians. This conclusion is a matter of faith and is laid down in the Scriptures, for in the Old Testament, wars waged by most holy men are praised (*Genesis,* Chap. xiv [, vv. 19–20]): 'Blessed be Abram [. . . .] And blessed be God by whose protection the enemies are in thy hands.' We find similar passages concerning Moses, Josue, Samson, Gedeon, David, the Machabees, and others, whom God often ordered to wage war upon the enemies of the Hebrews. Moreover, the apostle Paul (*Hebrews,* Chap. xi [, v. 33]) said that by faith the saints conquered kingdoms. The same principle is confirmed by further testimony, that of the Fathers quoted by Gratian (*Decretum,* Pt. II, causa xxiii, qq. 1 and 2), and also that of Ambrose (*On Duties,* various chapters).

However, one may object, in the first place, that the Lord said to David [I *Paralipomenon,* Chap. xxviii, v. 3]: 'Thou shalt not build my temple because thou art a man who has shed blood.'

Secondly, it will be objected that Christ said to Peter (John, Chap. xviii [, v. 11]): 'Put up thy sword into the scabbard,' &c.; and that Isaias also said (*Isaias,* Chap. ii [, v. 4]): 'They shall turn their swords into ploughshares [. . .] neither shall they be exercised any more to war'; and, in another Chapter (Chap. xi [, v. 9]): 'They shall not hurt nor shall they kill in all my holy mountain.' The Prophet is speaking, indeed, of the time of the coming of the Messiah, at which time, especially, it will be made clear, what is permissible and what is not permissible.

Thirdly, at the Council of Nicaea (Chap. xi [, can. xii]), a penalty was imposed upon Christians who, after having received the faith, enrolled themselves for military service. Furthermore, Pope Leo (*Letters,* xcii [Letter clxvii, inquis. xii]) wrote that war was forbidden to Christians, after a solemn penance.

Fourthly, war morally brings with it innumerable sins; and a given course of action is considered in itself evil and forbidden, if it is practically always accompanied by unseemly circumstances and harm to one's neighbours. [Furthermore,] one may add that war is opposed to peace, to the love of one's enemies, and to the forgiveness of injuries.

3. We reply to the first objection that [the Scriptural passage in question] is based upon the unjust slaying of Uriah; and, also, upon the particularly great reverence owed to the Temple.

[As for the second objection, we may answer, first, that] Christ our Lord is speaking of one who on his own initiative wishes to use the sword, and in particular, of one who so desires, against the will of his prince. Moreover, the words of Isaias, especially in Chap. xi, are usually understood as referring to the state of glory. Secondly, it is said that future peace was symbolized in the coming of the Messiah, as is explained by Jerome on this point [on *Isaias,* Chap. xi], Eusebius (*Demonstrations,* Bk. I, Chap. i), and other Fathers [of the Church]; or, at least, that Isaias is referring to the spiritual warfare of the Apostles and of the preachers of the Gospel, who have conquered the world not by a material but by a spiritual sword. This is the interpretation found in Justin Martyr, in his *Second Apology* for the Christians, and in other writers.

The Council of Nicaea, indeed, dealt especially with those Christians who, for a second time, were assuming the uniform of pagan soldiers which they had once cast off. And Pope Leo, as the Gloss (on *Decretum,* Pt. II, causa xxxiii, qu. iii (*De Paenitentia*), dist. v, cans. iv and iii) explains, was speaking of those Christians who, after a public penance had been imposed upon them, were returning to war, before the penance had been completed. Furthermore, it may have been expedient for the early Church to forbid those who had recently been converted to the faith, to engage in military service immediately, in company with unbelievers, and under pagan officers.

To the argument drawn from reason, Augustine replies (*On the City of God*, Bk. XIX, last chapter [Chap. vii]) that he deems it advisable to avoid war in so far as is possible, and to undertake it only in cases of extreme necessity, when no alternative remains; but he also holds that war is not entirely evil, since the fact that evils follow upon war is incidental, and since greater evils would result if war were never allowed.

Wherefore, in reply to the confirmation of the argument in question one may deny that war is opposed to an honourable peace; rather, it is opposed to an unjust peace, for it is more truly a means of attaining peace that is real and secure. Similarly, war is not opposed to the love of one's enemies; for whoever wages war honourably hates, not individuals, but the actions which he justly punishes. And the same reasoning is true of the forgiveness of injuries, especially since this forgiveness is not enjoined under every circumstance, for punishment may sometimes be exacted, by legitimate means, without injustice.

4. Secondly, I hold that defensive war not only is permitted, but sometimes is even commanded. The first part of this proposition follows from the first conclusion, which even the Doctors cited above accept; and it holds true not only for public officials, but also for private individuals, since all laws allow the repelling of force with force (*Decretals*, Bk. V, tit. xxxix, Chap. iii). The reason supporting it is that the right of self-defence is natural and necessary. Whence the second part of our second proposition is easily proved. For self-defence may sometimes be prescribed, at least in accordance with the order of charity; a fact which I have elsewhere pointed out. . . . The same is true of the defence of the state, especially if such defence is an official duty. . . . If any one objects that in the *Epistle to the Romans* (Chap. xii [, v. 19]) these words are found: 'Revenge not yourselves, my dearly beloved', and that this saying is in harmony with the passage (Matthew, Chap. v [, v. 39]): 'If one strike thee on the right cheek, turn to him also the other', we shall reply with respect to the first passage, that the reference is to vengeance. . . .

5. My third conclusion is, that even when war is aggressive,

it is not an evil in itself, but may be right and necessary. This is clear from the passages of Scripture cited above, which make no distinction [between aggressive and defensive wars]. The same fact is evidenced by the custom of the Church, one that has quite frequently been approved by the Fathers and the Popes. . . .

The reason supporting our third conclusion is that such a war is often necessary to a state, in order to ward off acts of injustice and to hold enemies in check. Nor would it be possible, without these wars, for states to be maintained in peace. Hence, this kind of warfare is allowed by natural law; and even by the law of the Gospel, which derogates in no way from natural law, and contains no new divine commands save those regarding faith and the Sacraments. The statement of Luther that it is not lawful to resist the punishment of God is indeed ridiculous; for God does not will the evils [against which war is waged,] but merely permits them; and therefore He does not forbid that they should be justly repelled.

6. It remains for us to explain what constitutes an aggressive war, and what, on the other hand, constitutes a defensive war; for sometimes that which is merely an act of defence may present the appearance of an aggressive act. Thus, for example, if enemies seize the houses or the property of others, but have themselves suffered invasion from the latter, that is no aggression but defence. To this extent, civil laws (*Code*, VIII. iv. 1 and *Digest*, XLIII. xvi. 1 and 3) are justified in conscience also, when they provde that if any one tries to dispossess me of my property, it is lawful for me to repel force with force. For such an act is not aggression, but defence, and may be lawfully undertaken even on one's own authority. The laws in question are extended to apply to him who, while absent, has been ejected from a tenure which they call a natural one, and who, upon his return, is prevented from recovering that tenure. For [the same laws decree] that any one who has been despoiled may, even on his own authority, have recourse to arms, because such an act is not really aggression, but a defence of one's legal possession. This rule is laid down in *Decretals*, Bk. II, tit. xiii, Chap. xii.

Consequently, we have to consider whether the injustice is,

practically speaking, simply about to take place; or whether it has already done so, and redress is sought through war. In this second case, the war is aggressive. In the former case, war has the character of self-defence, provided that it is waged with a moderation of defence which is blameless. Now the injury is considered as beginning, when the unjust act itself, even physically regarded, is beginning; as when a man has not been entirely deprived of his rightful possession; or even when he has been so deprived, but immediately—that is, without noteworthy delay—attempts to defend himself and to reinstate himself in possession. The reason for this is as follows: When any one is, to all intents and purposes, in the very act of resisting, and attempts—in so far as is possible—to protect his right, he is not considered as having, in an absolute sense, suffered wrong, nor as having been deprived of his possession. . . .

7. Our fourth proposition is this: in order that a war may be justly waged, a number of conditions must be observed, which may be grouped under three heads. First, the war must be waged by a legitimate power; secondly, the cause itself and the reason must be just; thirdly, the method of its conduct must be proper, and due proportion must be observed at its beginning, during its prosecution and after victory. All of this will be made clear in the following sections. The underlying principle of this general conclusion, indeed, is that, while a war is not in itself evil, nevertheless, on account of the many misfortunes which it brings in its train, it is one of those undertakings that are often carried on in evil fashion; and that therefore, it requires many justifying circumstances to make it righteous.

XVI PURITANISM

Puritanism is a most complex term which has acquired connotations in modern usage only vaguely related to its original meaning. As the Calvinistically oriented reform-movement in Post-Reformation England and America the social teachings of Puritanism exerted a wide and complex influence on the Anglo-Saxon world. It is not unambiguously a force for freedom and democracy as the writings of John Milton and the Levellers might suggest. Neither is it unambiguously conservative as Richard Baxter's *Holy Commonwealth* would lead us to believe. Typical is the painstaking effort to lead men to a holy and God-pleasing life as illustrated in Cotton Mather's *Essays to Do Good.*

SELECTION I
John Milton: *Areopagitica*

John Milton (1608–1674), the most eloquent spokesman of "Liberal Puritanism," advocated freedom of the press in his *Areopagitica* (1644).

And now the time in speciall is, by priviledge to write and speak what may help to the furder discussing of matters in agitation. The Temple of *Janus* with his two *controversal* faces might now not unsignificantly be set open. And though all the windes of doctrin were let loose to play upon the earth, so Truth be in the field, we do injuriously by licencing and prohibiting to misdoubt her strength. Let her and Falshood grapple; who ever knew Truth put to the wors, in a free and open encounter. Her confuting is the best and surest suppressing. He who hears what praying there is for light and clearer knowledge to be sent down among us, would think of other matters to be constituted beyond the discipline of *Geneva,* fram'd and fabric't already to our hands. Yet when the new light which we beg for shines in upon us, there be who envy, and oppose, if it come not first in at their casements. What a collusion is this, whenas we are exhorted by the wise man to use diligence, *to seek for wisdom as for hidd'n treasures* early and late, that another order shall enjoyn us to know nothing but by statute. When a man hath bin labouring the hardest labour in the deep mines of knowledge, hath furnisht out his findings in all their equipage, drawn forth his reasons as it were a battell raung'd, scatter'd and defeated all objections in his way, calls out his adversary into the plain, offers him the advantage of wind and sun, if he please; only that he may try the matter by dint of argument, for his opponents then to sculk, to lay ambushments, to keep a narrow bridge of licencing where the challenger should passe, though it be valour anough in shouldiership, is but weaknes and cowardise in the wars of Truth. For who knows not the Truth is strong next to the Almighty; she needs no policies, nor stratagems, nor licencings to make her victorious, those are the shifts and the defences that error uses against her power: give her but room, & do not bind her when she sleeps, for then she speaks not true, as the old *Proteus* did, who spake oracles only when he was caught & bound, but then rather she turns herself into all shapes, except her own, and perhaps tunes her voice according to the time, as *Micaiah* did before Ahab, untill she be adjur'd into her own likenes. Yet is it not impossible that she may have more shapes then one. What else is all that rank of things indifferent, wherein Truth may be on this side, or on the other, without being unlike her self. What but a vain shadow else is the abolition of *those ordinances, that hand writing nayl'd to the crosse,* what great purchase is this Christian liberty which *Paul* so often boasts of. His doctrine is, that he who eats or eats not, regards a day, or regards it not, may doe either to the Lord. How many other things might be tolerated in peace, and left to conscience, had we but charity, and were it not the chief strong hold of our hypocrisie to be ever judging one another. I fear yet this iron yoke of outward conformity hath left a slavish print upon our necks; the ghost of a linnen decency yet haunts us. We stumble and are impatient at the least dividing of one visible congregation from another, though it be not in fundamentalls; and through our forwardnes to suppresse, and our backwardnes to recover any enthrall'd peece of truth, which is the fiercest rent and disunion of all. We doe not see that while we still affect by all means a rigid externall formality, we may as soon fall again into a grosse conforming stupidity, a stark and dead congealment of *wood and hay and stubble* forc't and frozen together, which is more to the sudden degenerating of a Church then many *sub-dichotomies* of petty schisms. Not that I can think well of every light separation, or that all in a Church is to be expected *gold and silver and pretious stones:* it is not possible for man to sever the wheat from the tares, the good fish from the other frie; that must be the Angels Ministery at the end of mortall things. Yet if all cannot be of one mind, as who looks they should be? this doubtles is more wholsome, more prudent, and more Christian that many be tolerated, rather then all compell'd. I mean not tolerated Popery, and open superstition, which as it extirpats all religions and civill supremacies, so it self should be extirpat, provided first that all charitable and compassionat means be us'd to win and regain the weak and the misled: that also which is impious or evil absolutely either against faith or maners no law can possibly permit, that intends not to unlaw it self: but those neighboring differences, or rather indifferences, are what I speak of, whether in some point of doctrine or of discipline, which though they may be many, yet need not interrupt *the unity of Spirit,* if we could but find among us *the bond of peace*. In the mean while if any one would write, and bring his helpfull hand to the slow-moving Reformation which we labour under, if Truth have spok'n to him before others, or but seem'd at least to speak, who hath so bejesuited us that we should trouble that man with asking licence to doe so worthy a deed? and not consider this, that if it come to prohibiting, there is not ought more likely to be prohibited then truth it self; whose first appearance to our eyes blear'd and dimm'd with prejudice and custom, is more unsightly and unplausible then many errors, ev'n as the person is of many a great man slight and contemptible to see to. And what doe they tell us vainly of new opinions, when this very opinion of theirs, that none must be heard, but whom they like, is the worst and newest opinion of all others; and is the chief cause why sects and schisms doe so much abound, and true knowledge is kept at distance from us; besides yet a greater danger which is in it. For when God shakes a Kingdome with strong and healthfull commotions to a generall reforming, 'tis not untrue that many sectaries and false teachers are then busiest in seducing; but yet more true it is, that God then raises to his own work men of rare abilities, and more then common industry not only to look back and revise what hath bin taught heretofore, but to gain furder and goe on, some new enlightn'd steps in the discovery of truth. For such is the order of Gods enlightning his Church, to dispense and deal out by degrees his beam, so as our earthly eyes may best sustain it. Neither is God appointed and confin'd, where and out of what place these his chosen shall be first heard to speak; for he sees not as man sees, chooses not as man chooses, lest we should devote our selves again to set places, and assemblies, and outward callings of men; planting our faith one while in the old Convocation house, and another while in the Chappell at Westminster; when all the faith and religion that shall be there canoniz'd, is not sufficient without plain convincement, and the charity of patient instruction to supple the least bruise of conscience, to edifie the meanest Christian, who desires to walk in the Spirit, and not in the letter of human trust, for all the number of voices that can be there made; no though *Harry* the 7. himself there, with all his leige tombs about him, should lend them voices from the dead, to swell their number. And if the men be erroneous who appear to be the leading schismaticks, what withholds us but our sloth, our self-will, and distrust in the right cause, that we doe not give them gentle meetings and gentle dismissions, that we debate not and examin the matter throughly with liberall and frequent audience; if not for their sakes, yet for our own? seeing no man who hath tasted learning, but will confesse the many waies of profiting by those who not contented with stale receits are able to manage, and set forth new positions to the world. And were they but as the dust and cinders of our feet, so long as in that notion they may yet serve to polish and brighten the armoury of Truth, ev'n for that respect they were not utterly to be cast away. But if they be of those whom God hath fitted for the speciall use of these times with eminent and ample gifts, and those perhaps neither among the Priests, nor among the Pharisees, and we in the hast of a precipitant zeal shall make no distinction, but resolve to stop their mouths, because we fear they come with new and dangerous opinions, as we commonly fore-judge them ere we understand them, no lesse then woe to us, while thinking thus to defend the Gospel, we are found the persecutors.

SELECTION 2

An Agreement of the People (Printed Nov. 3, 1647)

The Levellers were theological radicals in the Puritan movement who opposed both the bishops and the state-church ambitions of the Presbyterians. The following selection is from the so-called *First Agreement of the People* (printed Nov. 3, 1647).

In order whereunto we declare:

I. That the people of England, being at this day very unequally distributed by counties, cities, and boroughs, for the election of their deputies in Parliament, ought to be more indifferently proportioned, according to the number of the inhabitants; the circumstances whereof, for number, place, and manner, are to be set down before the end of this present Parliament.

II. That to prevent the many inconveniences apparently arising from the long continuance of the same persons in authority, this present Parliament be dissolved upon the last day of September, which shall be in the year of our Lord 1648.

III. That the people do of course choose themselves a Parliament once in two years, viz., upon the first Thursday in every second March, after the manner as shall be prescribed before the end of this Parliament, to begin to sit upon the first Thursday in April following, at Westminster (or such other place as shall be appointed from time to time by the preceding Representatives), and to continue till the last day of September then next ensuing, and no longer.

IV. That the power of this, and all future Representatives of this nation is inferior only to theirs who choose them, and doth extend, without the consent or concurrence of any other person or persons, to the enacting, altering, and repealing of laws; to the erecting and abolishing of offices and courts; to the appointing, removing, and calling to account magistrates and officers of all degrees; to the making war and peace; to the treating with foreign states; and generally to whatsoever is not expressly or impliedly reserved by the represented to themselves.

Which are as followeth:

1. That matters of religion, and the ways of God's worship, are not at all entrusted by us to any human power, because therein we cannot remit or exceed a tittle of what our consciences dictate to be the mind of God, without wilful sin; nevertheless the public way of instructing the nation (so it be not compulsive) is referred to their discretion.

2. That the matter of impressing and constraining any of us to serve in the wars is against our freedom, and therefore we do not allow it in our representatives; the rather because money (the sinews of war) being always at their disposal, they can never want numbers of men apt enough to engage in any just cause.

3. That after the dissolution of the present Parliament, no person be at any time questioned for anything said or done in reference to the late public differences, otherwise than in execution of the judgments of the present representatives, or House of Commons.

4. That in all laws made, or to be made, every person may be bound alike, and that no tenure, estate, charter, degree, birth, or place, do confer any exemption from the ordinary course of legal preceedings, whereunto others are subjected.

5. That as the laws ought to be equal, so they must be good, and not evidently destructive to the safety and well-being of the people.

These things we declare to be our native rights, and therefore are agreed and resolved to maintain them with our utmost possibilities against all opposition whatsoever, being compelled thereunto not only by the example of our ancestors, whose blood was often spent in vain for the recovery of their freedoms, suffering themselves, through fraudulent accommodations, to be still deluded of the fruit of their victories, but also by our own woeful experience, who, having long expected, and dearly earned, the establishment of these certain rules of government, are yet made to depend for the settlement of our peace and freedom upon him that intended our bondage and brought a cruel war upon us.

SELECTION 3

Gerrard Winstanley: *The Law of Freedom in a Platform* or *True Magistracy Restored*

The most radical movement connected with the revolution in England was that of Gerrard Winstanley (1609–after 1660). An abortive effort, it illustrates nevertheless certain possibilities implicit in the overthrow of the monarchy. Our selection is taken from *The Law of Freedom in a Platform* or *True Magistracy Restored* (1652).

1. The bare letter of the Law established by act of *Parliament* shall be the Rule for *Officer and People,* and the chief Judg of all Actions.

2. He or they who add or diminish from the Law, excepting in the Court of *Parliament,* shall be cashiered his Office, and never bear Office more.

3. No man shall administer the Law for Mony or Reward; he that doth shal dye as a Traytor to *the Commonwealth:* for when Mony must buy and sell Justice, and bear all the sway, there is nothing but *Oppression* to be expected.

4. The Laws shall be read by the Minister to the people four times in the year, *viz.* every *quarter,* that every one may know whereunto they are to yeeld Obedience; then none may dye for want of knowledg.

5. No accusation shall be taken against any man, unless it be proved by two or three witnesses, or his own confession.

6. No man shall suffer any punishment, but for matter of fact, or Reviling words: but no man shall be troubled for his judgment or practise in the things of his God, so he live quiet in the Land.

7. The accuser and accused shall always appear face to face before any Officer, that both sides may be heard, and no wrong to either party.

8. If any Judg of Officer execute his own Will contrary to

the Law, or which there is no Law to warrant him in, he shall be cashiered, and never bear Office more.

9. He who raises an accusation against any man, and cannot prove it, shall suffer the same punishment the other should, if proved. An Accusation is when one man complains of another to an Officer; all other accusations the Law takes no notice of.

10. He who strikes his Neighbor, shall be struck himself by the Executioner blow for blow, and shall lose eye for eye, tooth for tooth, limb for limb, life for life: and the reason is, that men may be tender of one anothers bodies, doing as they would be done by.

11. If any man strike an Officer, he shall be made a servant under the Taskmaster for a whole year.

12. He who endevors to stir up contention among neighbors, by tale-bearing or false reports, shall the first time be reproved openly by the Overseers among all the people: the second time shall be whiped: the third time shall be a servant under the Taskmaster for three Months: and if he continues, he shall be a servant for ever, and lose his Freedom in the Commonwealth.

13. If any give reviling and provoking words, whereby his neighbors spirit is burthened, if complaint be made to the Overseers, they shall admonish the offender privately to forbear: if he continues to offend his neighbor, the next time he shall be openly reproved and admonished before the Congregation, when met together: if he continue, the third time he shall be whipt; the fourth time, if proof be made by witnesses, he shall be a servant under the Taskmaster for twelve Months.

14. He who will rule as a Lord over his brother, unless he be an Officer commanding obedience to the Law, he shall be admonished as aforesaid, and receive like punishment, if he continue.

15. Every household shall keep all Instruments and Tools fit for the tillage of the Earth, either for planting, reaping or threshing. Some households, which have many men in them, shall keep Plows, Carts, Harrows, and such like: other households shall keep Spades, Pick axes, Axes, pruning hooks, and such like, according as every Family is furnished with men to work therewith.

And if any Master or Father of a Family be negligent herein, the Overseer for that Circuit shall admonish him between them two; if he continue negligent, the Overseers shall reprove him before all the people: and if he utterly refuse, then the ordering of that Family shall be given to another, and he shall be a servant under the taskmaster till he conform.

16. Every family shall come into the field, with sufficient assistance, at seed time to plow, dig, and plant, and at harvest time to reap the fruits of the Earth, and carry them into the Storehouses, as the Overseers order the work, and the number of workmen. And if any refuse to assist in this work, The Overseers shall ask the reason, and if it be sickness, or any distemper that hinders them, they are freed from such service; if meer idleness keep them back, they are to suffer punishment, according to the Laws against Idleness.

17. If any refuse to learn a trade, or refuse to work in seedtime, or harvest, or refuse to be a Waiter in Store-houses, and yet will feed and clothe himself with other mens labors; The Overseers shall first admonish him privately; if he continue idle, he shall be reproved openly before all the people by the Overseers; and shall be forbore with a moneth after this reproof: If he still continues idle, he shall then be whipt, and be let go at liberty for a moneth longer; if still he continue idle, he shall be delivered into the taskmasters hand, who shall set him to work for twelve moneths, or till he submit to right Order: And the reason why every young man shall be trained up in some work or other, is to prevent pride and contention; it is for the health of their bodies, it is a pleasure to the minde, to be free in labors one with another; and it provides plenty of food and all necessaries for the Common-wealth.

18. In every Town and City, shall be appointed Store-houses for flax, wool, lether, cloth, and for all such commodities, as come from beyond Seas, and these shall be called general Storehouses, from whence every particular family may fetch such commodities as they want, either for their use in their house, or for to work in their trades; or to carry into the Country Storehouses.

19. Every particular house and shop in a town or city, shall be a particular Store-house or shop, as now they be; and these shops shall either be furnished by the particular labor of that

family according to the trade that family is of, or by the labor of other lesser families of the same trade, as all shops in every town are now furnished.

20. The waiters in Store-houses, shall deliver the goods under their charge, without receiving any money, as they shall receive in their goods without paying any money.

21. If any waiter in a Store-house neglect his office, upon a just complaint the Overseers shall acquaint the Judges Court therewith, and from thence he shall receive his sentence to be discharged that house and office: And to be appointed some other laboring work under the taskmaster; and another shall have his place: For he who may live in freedom and will not, is to taste of servitude.

22. The onely work of every Overseer, is to see the Laws executed; for the Law is the true magistracy of the Land.

23. If any Overseer, favour any in their idleness, and neglect the execution of the Laws, he shall be reproved the first time by the Judges Court; the second time cashiered his Office, and shall never bear office more, but fall back into the rank of young people and servants to be a worker.

24. New Overseers, shall at their first entrance into their office, look back upon the actions of the old Overseers of the last year, to see if they have been faithful in their places, and consented to no breach of Law, whereby Kingly bondage should any ways be brought in.

25. The Overseers for Trades, shall see every family to lend assistance to plant and reap the fruits of the Earth; to work in their Trades, and to furnish the Storehouses; and to see that the Waiters in Storehouses be diligent to receive in, and deliver out any goods, without buying and selling, to any man whatsoever.

26. While any Overseer is in the performance of his place, every one shall assist him, upon pain of open reproof (or cashiered if he be another Officer) or forfeiture of freedom, according to the nature of the business in hand, in which he refused his assistance.

27. If any man entice another to buy and sell, and he who is enticed doth not yield, but makes it known to the Overseer; the enticer shall lose his freedom for twelve moneths, & the Overseer shall give words [of] commendation of him that re-

fused the enticement, before all the Congregation, for his faithfulness to the Commonwealths Peace.

28. If any do buy and sell the Earth or fruits thereof, unless it be to, or with strangers of another nation, according to the Law of Navigation, they shall be both put to death as traytors to the peace of the Commonwealth; because it brings in Kingly bondage again: and is the occasion of all quarrels and oppressions.

29. He or she who calls the Earth his, and not his brothers, shall be set upon a stool, with those words written in his forehead, before all the Congregation; and afterwards be made a servant for twelve moneths under the taskmaster; If he quarrel, or seek by secret perswation, or open rising in arms, to set up such a Kingly propriety, he shall be put to death.

30. The Storehouses shall be every mans substance, and not any ones.

31. No man shall either give hire, or take hire for his work; for this brings in Kingly bondage: If any Freemen want help, there are young people, or such as are common servants, to do it, by the Overseers appointment: He that gives, and he that takes hire for work, shall both lose their Freedom, and become servants, for twelve Months under the Taskmaster.

32. Because other Nations as yet own Monarchy, and will buy and sell; therefore it is convenient, for the peace of our Commonwealth, That our ships do transport our English goods, and exchange for theirs, and conform to the Customs of other Nations in buying and selling: Always provided, That what goods our ships carry out, they shall be the Commonwealths goods; and all their Trading with other Nations shall be upon the common Stock, to enrich the Storehouses.

33. As Silver and Gold is either found out in Mynes in our own Land, or brought by shipping from beyond Sea, it shall not be coyned with a Conquerors stamp upon it, to set up buying and selling under his name, or by his leave; for there shall be no other use of it in the Commonwealth, then to make dishes and other necessaries for the ornament of houses, as now there is use made of Brass, Pewter, and Iron, or any other Metal in their use.

But if in case other Nations, whose commodities we want,

will not exchange with us, unless we give them money, then pieces of Silver and Gold may be stamped with the Commonwealths Arms upon it, for the same use, and no otherwise.

For where money bears all the sway, there is no regard of that golden Rule, *Do as you would be done by:* Justice is bought and sold: nay, Injustice is sometimes bought and sold for money: and it is the cause of all Wars and Oppressions. And certainly the righteous Spirit of the whole Creation did never enact such a Law, That unless his weak and simple men did go from *England* to the *East Indies,* and fetch Silver and Gold to bring in their hands to their Brethren, and give it them for their good-will to let them plant the Earth, and live and enjoy their livelyhood therein, [they should not have the use of the land.]

34. All Overseers and State-Officers shall be chosen new every year, to prevent the rise of Ambition and Covetousness; for the Nations have smarted sufficiently by suffering Officers to continue long in an Office, or to remain in an Office by hereditary succession.

35. A man that is of a turbulent spirit, given to quarreling, and provoking words to his neighbor, shall not be chosen any Officer while he so continues.

36. All men from twenty years of age upwards shall have freedom of voyce to choose Officers, unless they be such as lie under the sentence of the Law.

37. Such shall be chosen Officers, as are rational men of moderate conversation, and who have experience in the Laws of the Commonwealth.

38. All men from forty years of age upwards shall be capable to be chosen State Officers, and none younger, unless any one by his industry and moderate conversation doth move the people to choose him.

39. If any man make suit to move the people to choose him an Officer, that man shall not be chosen at all that time: If another man perswade the people to choose him who makes suit for himself, they shall both lose their freedom at that time, *viz.* they shall neither have a voyce to choose another, nor be chosen themselves.

40. He who professes the service of a righteous God by

preaching and prayer, and makes a Trade to get the possessions of the Earth, shall be put to death for a Witch and a Cheater.

41. He who pretends one thing in words, and his actions declare his intent was another thing, shall never bear Office in the Commonwealth.

Every Freeman shall have a Freedom in the Earth, to plant or build, to fetch from the Storehouses any thing he wants, and shall enjoy the fruits of his labours without restraint from any; he shall not pay Rent to any Landlord, and he shall be capable to be chosen any Officer, so he be above forty years of age, and he shall have a voyce to choose Officers though he be under forty years of age: If he want any young men to be Assistance to him in his Trade or household employment, the Overseers shall appoint him young men or maids to be his servants in his family.

SELECTION 4
Richard Baxter: *A Holy Commonwealth,* Chap. VIII

The conservative side of Puritanism is expressed by Richard Baxter (1615–1691) in his *A Holy Commonwealth* (1659).

At his first creation man was subjected to none but God: though it was provided in Nature, that there should have been government and subjection, though man had continued innocent. But that would have been only a Paternal assisting Government for our good, having nothing in it that is penal, or any way evil. When God immediately ruled, and man obeyed, all went right. Had this continued, the world had not felt those fractures and wounds, nor been troubled with rapines, wars or confusions as it is. God being most perfectly wise and just, could not err in commanding. Man was innocent and able to obey, but free and mutable: and so was tempted from his obedience. Satan, by disobedience having overthrown himself, did know it was the way to overthrow man. God could not be corrupted, nor tempted to unwise or unrighteous government: and if neither King nor subject were corrupted, the Kingdom could not have decayed. But Satan knew which was the weakest link in the chain: Man was frail, though holy; and not confirmed yet, though upright; and therefore defectible. The attempt of breaking his rank, and forsaking his due subjection, was the Devil's fall: and by the same way he assaulted man, incurring in him a desire to be *as God,* and then provoking him to seek it by disobeying God—a foolish means to an impossible or impious end. The breach being thus made between man and his universal King, the joints of holy order were loosed, and a breach was made also between man and himself, and man and the inferior creatures, and enmity and confusion took possession in the world. The creatures rebel against their Master turned rebel; his own passions and appetite rebel against his reason; and the seeds of all the confusions that have followed in the world, were won within us. As the enmity between the woman's and the Serpent's seed, being propagated to posterity, is the great quarrel of the world, so all those vices in which the malignant enmity doth consist, are propagated and by custom receive an increase. The root of them all is *Selfishness,* which much consisteth in pride; still man would be as God. Every man would be highest, and have the eyes of others set upon him, and be the idol of the world. The sin that broke order, is still at work to widen the breach. He that is a subject, would fain be in authority; and he that is of a lower rank, is ambitious to be higher; and he that is in Sovereign Power with just limitations, doth hate restraint, and take it for imprisonment or subjection; and striveth till he hath broke all bonds, and hath no guide but his own understanding, and nothing to moderate his impotent will. So that in all ages and nations, subjects are still disposed to murmurings and rebellions, and Princes to transcend their bounds by tyranny: and all because we are all the aspiring brood of *Adam,* that was made little lower then the Angels, but fell to be too near the Devils, by desiring to become as God. If the advantage of greatness, the gate of temptation, or the warmth of prosperity, do but heighten this ambition, and hatch it to maturity, men will be then the sons of the Coal, and as so many Granadoes thrown by Satan among the people where they live, to enflame and trouble and confound the world. The worm of ambition will restlessly crawl within their stomachs, and make them by a troublous stir to seek for honor as food to quiet it, and keep it from gnawing on their hearts.

But this greedy worm is unsatiable, crying as the horse-leech, *Give, Give*.

The cure of this mischief hath long busied the people and politicians of the world: and yet it is uncured. Princes that have strength, do make some shift with much ado, by severity to restrain the subject from rebellion. But how to restrain the Prince from Tyranny without disabling him from necessary government, is much yet undiscovered, or the discoveries unpracticed. The world hath had more *Dionysiuses* and *Neros* then *Davids, Solomons* or *Constantines*. *Rehoboam* is no warning to them, but hath most imitators, though with bad success. In most of the world, their doleful case doth tell us what their government is; we see among them tyranny is hereditary; and Princes live among their subjects as the pike among the smaller fishes; as if the people were made for them. They divide their interest from their people's; and live as if their people's welfare were not theirs, but rather all that is taken from the subject, is added unto them. The soul and body of most commonwealths fall out, and the head and heart have such diseased obstructions and oppositions, as are their mutual torment, and the prognostic of their hastening dissolution: when the ivy hath killed the tree that bore it, it must perish with it. And if they are first themselves dismounted, they seldom ever get into the saddle, and sit fast after it.

Some nations have thought that the way to prevent this, was to be *free;* that is, to be *Self-governors*. And so when all governed, they found that none governed, but tyranny and all vice did reign in popular confusions; and there was neither peace nor safety to the whole or parts. No waves being greater than the seas, nor any tyrant so cruel as the many-headed tyrant: and it being the surest way to be always miserable, to be governed by them that are always naught—that is, by the multitude, in most parts of the world.

The sense of the mischief of Democracy hath made others think that the best way is to leave Kings to their wills, and let them use their power arbitrarily. They think it costeth the world more to limit Princes then it's worth; and that if they are absolute, their interest will lead them to cherish their people. Or if they should grow cruel, God will protect us, and turn it to the best. A hundred sheep will fly from a little cur, and yet the shepherd takes care that few of them are destroyed. I could the easier digest this Doctrine, were it not for these reasons. 1. The heart of man is deceitful and desperately wicked; and what will it not do, if it may do what it will? 2. When men know that they are liable to no restraint, it will let loose their lusts, and make them worse. 3. We may not tempt them thus into a life of sin, to their own destruction. 4. Nor must we tempt God by pretending to trust him in a neglect of means. 5. It is against the light of Nature that one man's will should ruin a nation. 6. If we may give away our bodily welfare, yet not our soul's. The Prince's interest may lead him to have some regard to the bodily welfare of the people; but he will not regard their souls. Greatness will have great temptations. And when there is no restraint, this will make the greatest to be the worst. And the worst men are inclined to the worst opinions, and to be the greatest enemies to piety and honesty; and so would banish Christianity into corners, or from the earth. 7. If we might give away our own interest, we may not so give away God's nor encourage or suffer every deceived wicked Prince to do as the infidel Princes do, and persecute Christianity out of their dominions. 8. At least we may not be guilty of treason against God, by consenting to an Idol, or usurper that claimeth his prerogative, and pretendeth to an absolute unlimited power, as if he were from under the laws and government of the Almighty: we must know no power but what's from God; and therefore none against his undoubted interest and laws. As it is unlawful to submit to the Pope that thus usurpeth in the Church, so as unlawful to consent to any Anti-Gods' usurpation in the commonwealth. 9. And the experience of the world hath taught them to abhor unlimited government, even as intolerable to the people. For though they should not destroy the *whole people,* yet at their pleasure their *particular Subjects* must be the fuel of their rage and lust. Every man's estate, wife, or daughter that they have a mind to, must be theirs; and their word must command the heads of the best deserving Nobility to the block; and however the distant vulgar speed, those that are nearest them will be as Lambs before the Wolf. 10. And experience hath told the world, that there is many, and very many, bad Kings for one good one throughout the world; and the wicked will do wickedly when they have no restraint; and therefore this were to deliver up the Kingdoms of the earth to Satan, who ruleth by the wicked; when we have a promise that they shall be the *Kingdoms of the Lord and of his Christ,* that *ruleth* especially by the *holy and the just.*

Others have thought it a hopeful way of cure, to have the government elective, and either *quam diu bene se gesserint,* or for a short continuance by rotation. But these have found that the remedy was insufficient. The nations of the earth have but few men that are wise and good: and if those must rule but a little while, the bad will succeed them. And if it must run through many, and so there be many bad Rulers for one good one, the bad ones will do more hurt than the good ones can do good. And it will be next impossible so to temper the government, as that bad rulers may have power to preserve the commonwealth and yet not have power to perpetuate themselves and invade a perpetual Dictatorship with *Caesar.* For armies they must have; and those that can get sufficient interest in them, may use them to their own ends. Some think that the wealthier peoples' bearing arms would prevent all this: for they would never serve a tyrant against their liberties. Much should be done, I confess, more than is, this way, to preserve the people's liberties: but yet the remedy is inconsiderable. For, 1. We must have our Armies abroad, and those will be the poor, and those will be mercenary, and return to serve their Commanders minds. 2. Flattering words will mislead them that are not mercenary. 3. Prosperity and wealth doth effeminate men and make them cowardly. 4. Experience told us in our late Wars, that the Trained Bands were as ready, at least in most places, to follow the stronger side that was in place, as the poorer volunteers were. For they thought they had somewhat more to lose than their younger sons or servants had; and therefore they would not venture to disobey the strongest.

Some think a Lot, being a divine decision, to be the only way to choose the Prince: which hath its place, but solveth not the difficulty without more ado. To use lots among a company of bad or unjust men to find one good one, is a tempting God; and but like the casting a net among frogs to catch fish. The materials must be first prepared, and the main secured.

In a word, many models have been devised, and most of them have their excellencies, and defects. Some of them secure the people's wealth and liberty from a tyrant, and lay them open to an invading enemy. Some of them free the people from oppression by a Prince, and leave them under a multitude of oppressors. Some so secure liberty as to introduce injustice and confusion, and certainly cast away the means of spiritual, everlasting good, in order to preserve their temporal good. And most of them tread under foot the government and interest of the Universal King, and pretend the means against the end. They that can do most to mend the people, and secure us of good rulers, and so to secure us in the main matters of Religion and Peace, are the best politicians, though they leave us many inconveniences. And to that end he that could cull out the best of every mode, and leave the worst, would show his wisdom. Because I pretend not to such skill, nor intend any accurate tract of politic, nor the discovery of an *Utopia,* or *City of the Sun,* nor intend to bestow that time and labor which is necessary to improve that little knowledge that I have, to any such ends, but only to urge upon the world the great divine, neglected principles that we may be secured of the main, I shall readily give place to any of their new devised models that are consistent with these principles, and leave them to beautify the Commonwealth in their own ways, if the life of it may be secured by God's way.

And yet I must say that for ought I see, the government of this Commonwealth is already balanced with as much prudence, caution, and equality (though with less ado) as the curiousest of the models that self-conceited men would obtrude with so much ostentation. Might we but see the *foundation* of Parliaments reformed, by an exclusion of truly *unworthy* persons from the elections (from choosing or being chosen) that so we were out of danger of having impious Parliaments chosen by an impious majority of the people, we should then build all the fabric of our government on a rock, that else will have a foundation of sand. And a multitude of errors would be thus corrected at one, and more done for our happiness than a thousand of the new fanatical devices will accomplish. Of this having spoken before, I shall yet add somewhat more, to show you how the Kingdoms of the world may be made the Kingdoms of the Lord, and of his Christ.

Thes. 190. *The Happiest Commonwealth is that which most attaineth the Ends of Government and Society, which are the public Good, especially in matters of everlasting concernment, and the Pleasing of God the Absolute Lord and King of all.*

SELECTION 5
Cotton Mather: *Essays to Do Good: Miscellaneous Proposals to Gentlemen*

Cotton Mather (1663–1728) represents the development of Puritanism in America. His *Essays to Do Good* were first published in 1710. Our selection is taken from "Miscellaneous Proposals to Gentlemen," and gives some of the flavor of the work.

There is a certain city, in which every house has a box hanging by a chain, on which is written, "remember the poor"; and they seldom conclude a bargain without putting something into the box. The deacons have the key, and once a quarter go round the city, and take out the money. When that city was in imminent danger, a man of moderate character was heard to say, "that he was of opinion, God would preserve that city from being destroyed, if it were only for the great charity which its inhabitants express to the poor." It is the richest city of the richest country, for its size, that ever existed: a city which is thought to spend, annually, in charitable uses, more than all the revenues which the fine country of the grand duke of Tuskany brings into its arbitrary master. "The hands of the poor are the treasury-box of Christ."

When you dispense your alms to the poor, who know what it is to pray, you may oblige them to pray for you by name every day. It is an excellent thing to have the blessing of those who have been ready to perish, thus coming upon you. Observe here a surprising sense, in which you may be "praying always." You are so, even while you are sleeping, if those whom you have thus obliged are praying for you. And now look for the accomplishment of that word: "Blessed is he that considereth the poor: the Lord will preserve him, and keep him alive, and he shall be blessed upon the earth."

Very frequently your alms are dispersed among such persons as very much need admonitions of piety. Cannot you contrive to mingle a spiritual charity with your temporal bounty? Perhaps you may discourse with them about the state of their souls, and may obtain from them, (for which you have now a singular advantage) some declared resolutions to do what they ought to do. Or else you may convey to them little books, or tracts, which they will certainly promise to read, when you thus desire them.

Charity to the *souls* of men is undoubtedly the highest, the noblest, and the most important charity. To furnish the poor with catechisms and Bibles, is to do for them an incalculable service. No one knows how much he may do by dispersing books of piety, and by putting into the hands of mankind such treatises of divinity as may have a tendency to make them wiser or better. It was a noble action of some good men, who, a little while ago, were at the charge of printing thirty thousand of the "Alarm to the Unconverted," written by Joseph Allein, to be given away to such as would promise to read it. A man of no great fortune has been known to give away without much trouble nearly a thousand books of piety, every year for many years together. Who can tell, but that with the expense of less than a shilling, you may "convert a sinner from the error of his ways, and save a soul from death." A worse doom than to be "condemned to the mines" rests upon that soul who had rather hoard up his money than employ it on such a charity.

He who supports the office of the evangelical ministry supports a good work, and performs one; yea, in a secondary way, performs what is done by the skilful, faithful and laborious minister. The servant of the Lord, who is encouraged by you, will do the more good for your assistance: and what you have done for him, and in consideration of the glorious gospel preached by him, you have done for a glorious Christ; and you shall "receive a prophet's reward." Luther said; "what you give to scholars, you give to God himself." This is still more true, when the scholars are become godly and useful preachers.

I have somewhere met with the following passage: "it was for several years the practice of a worthy gentleman, in renewing his leases, instead of making it a condition that his tenants should keep a hawk or a dog for him, to oblige them to keep a Bible in their houses, and to bring up their children to read and to be catechised." *Landlords!* It is worth your consideration whether you may not in your leases insert some clauses that may serve the kingdom of God. You are his tenants in those very freeholds in which you are landlords to other men. Oblige your tenants to worship God in their families.

To take a poor child, especially an orphan, left in poverty, and to bestow a liberal education upon it, is an admirable charity; yea, it may draw after it a long train of good, and may interest you in all the good that shall be done by him whom you have educated.

Hence also, what is done for schools, for colleges, and for hospitals, is done for the general good. The endowment or maintenance of these is at once to do good to many.

But alas! how much of the silver and gold of the world is buried in hands, where it is little better than conveyed back to the mines from whence it came! How much of it is employed to as little purpose as what arrives at Hindoostan, where a great part of it is, after some circulation, carried as to a fatal centre, and by the Moguls lodged in subterraneous caves, never to see the light again! "The Christian, whose faith and hope are genuine, acts not thus."

Sometimes elaborate compositions may be prepared for the press, works of great bulk, and of still greater worth, by which the best interests of knowledge and virtue may be considerably promoted; but they lie, like the impotent man at the pool of Bethseda, in silent neglect; and are likely to continue in that state, till God inspire some wealthy persons nobly to subscribe to their publication, and by this generous application of their property, to bring them abroad. The names of such noble benefactors to mankind ought to live as long as the works themselves: and where the works do any good, what these have done towards the publishing of them, ought to be "told for a memorial" of them.

I will pursue this subject still farther. It has been said the "idle gentlemen, and idle beggars, are the pests of the commonwealth." The saying may seem affronting, but they who are offended at it, must quarrel with the ashes of a bishop, for it was Dr. Sanderson's. Will you then think, sirs, of some honorable and agreeable employments? I will mention one: The Pythagoreans forbade men's "eating their own brains," or "keeping their good thoughts to themselves." The incomparable Boyle observes, that "as to religious books, in general, those which have been written by laymen, and especially by gentlemen, have (*caeteris paribus*) been better received, and more effectual, than those published by clergymen." Mr. Boyle's were certainly so. Men of quality have frequently attained such accomplishments in languages and science, that they have become prodigies of literature. Their libraries also have seen stupendous collections, approaching towards Vatican or Bodleian dimensions. An English gentleman has been sometimes the most "accomplished person in the world." How many of these (besides a Leigh, a Wolsely, or a Polhill) have been benefactors to mankind by their admirable writings! It were much to be wished that persons of wealth and elevation would qualify themselves for the use of the pen as well as of the sword, and deserve this eulogium, "they have written excellent things." An English person of quality, in his treatise, entitled, "A View of the Soul," has the following passage: "It is certainly the highest dignity, if not the greatest happiness, of which human nature is capable in the vale below, to have the soul so far enlightened, as to become the mirror, or conduit, or conveyor of God's truth to others." It is a bad motto for a man of capacity, "my understanding is unfruitful." Gentlemen, consider what subjects may most properly and usefully fall under your cultivation. Your pens will stab atheism and vice more effectually than other men's. If out of your "Tribe" there come forth "those who handle the pen of the writer," they will do uncommon execution. One of them has ingeniously said, "though I know some *functions,* yet I know no *truths* of religion, which, like the shewbread, are only for the priests."

I will present to you but one proposal more, and it is this, that you would wisely choose a friend of good abilities, of warm affections, and of excellent piety, (a minister of such a character if you can) and entreat him, yea, oblige him to study for you and to suggest to you opportunities to do good. Make him, as *Ambrosius* did his *Origen,* your Monitor. Let him advise you from time to time, what good you may do. Let him see that he never gratifies you more than by his advice on this head. If a *David* have a *Seer* to perform such an office for him, one who may search for occasions of doing good, what extensive services may be done for the temple of God in the world!

Let me only add, that when gentlemen occasionally meet together, why should not their conversation correspond with their superior station? They should deem it beneath them to employ the conversation on trifling subjects, or in such a way that, if it were secretly taken in short hand, they would blush to hear it repeated. Sirs, it becomes a gentleman to entertain his company with the finest thoughts on the finest themes; and certainly there cannot be a subject so worthy of a gentleman as this, what good is there to be done in the world? Were this noble subject more frequently started in the conversation of gentlemen, incredible good might be achieved.

I will conclude by saying, you must accept of any public service, of which you are capable, when you are called to it. Honest *Jeans* has this pungent passage: "The world applauds the prudent retirement of those who bury their parts and gifts in an obscure privacy, though they have a fair call, both from God and man, to public engagements: but the terrible censure of these men by Jesus Christ at the last day, will prove them to have been the most arrant fools that ever lived on the face of the earth." The fault of not employing our talent for the public good is justly styled, "a great sacrilege in the temple of the God of Nature." It was a sad age of which Tacitus said, "indolent retirement was wisdom."

XVII THE QUAKERS

The Society of Friends, popularly called Quakers, is a relatively small religious movement which has its roots in the religious excitement of Cromwell's revolution. The original leaders started as Puritans and moved through various transformations (Independents, Baptists) to their final religious vision. The social teachings of the Society of Friends—their pacifism, rejection of slavery and openness to the needs of enemies—have influenced Christendom quite out of proportion to their small numbers.

SELECTION I
Rules of Discipline—Society of Friends

These Advices which were to be read at least once a year in the meetings of the Society give an impression of the spirit of the movement.

Take heed, dear friends, we intreat you, to the convictions of the Holy Spirit, who leads, through unfeigned repentance and living faith in the Son of God, to reconciliation with our Heavenly Father, and to the blessed hope of eternal life, purchased for us by the one offering of our Lord and Saviour Jesus Christ.

Be earnestly concerned in religious meetings reverently to present yourselves before the Lord, and seek, by the help of the Holy Spirit, to worship God through Jesus Christ.

Be in the frequent practice of waiting upon God in private retirement, with prayer and supplication, honestly examining yourselves as to your growth in grace, and your preparation for the life to come.

Be careful to make a profitable and religious use of those portions of time on the first day of the week, which are not occupied by our meetings for worship.

Live in love as Christian brethren, ready to be helpful one to another, and to sympathize with each other in the trials and afflictions of life.

Follow peace with all men, desiring the true happiness of all; and be liberal to the poor, endeavouring to promote their temporal, moral, and religious well-being.

With a tender conscience, and in accordance with the precepts of the Gospel, take heed to the limitations of the Spirit of Truth, in the pursuit of the things of this life.

Maintain strict integrity in all your transactions in trade, and in your other outward concerns, remembering that you will have to account for the mode of acquiring, and the manner of using, your possessions.

Watch, with Christian tenderness, over the opening minds of your offspring; enure them to habits of self-restraint and filial obedience; carefully instruct them in the knowledge of the Holy Scriptures, and seek for ability to imbue their minds with the love of their Heavenly Father, their Redeemer, and their Sanctifier.

Observe simplicity and moderation in the furniture of your houses, and in the supply of your tables, as well as in your personal attire, and that of your families.

Be diligent in the private and daily family reading of the Holy Scriptures; and guard carefully against the introduction of improper books into your families.

Be careful to place out children, of all degrees, with those friends whose care and example will be most likely to conduce to their preservation from evil; prefer such assistants, servants, and apprentices, as are members of our religious society; not demanding exorbitant apprentice fees, lest you frustrate the care of friends in these respects.

Encourage your apprentices and servants of all descriptions to attend public worship, making way for them herein: and exercise a watchful care for their moral and religious improvement.

Be careful to make your wills and settle your outward affairs in time of health; and, when you accept the office of guardian, executor, or trustee, be faithful and diligent in the fulfilment of your trust.

Finally, dear friends, let your conversation be such as becometh the Gospel. Exercise yourselves to have always a conscience void of offence towards God and towards man. Watch over one another for good; and when occasions of uneasiness first appear in any, let them be treated with in privacy and tenderness, before the matter be communicated to another: and friends, every where, are advised to maintain "the unity of the spirit in the bond of peace."

SELECTION 2
Rules of Discipline

The Quaker opposition to war is well known. It was repeatedly expressed in the *Rules of Discipline.*

It has been a weighty concern on this meeting, that our ancient and honourable testimony against being concerned in bearing arms, or fighting, may be maintained; it being a doctrine and testimony agreeable to the nature and design of the Christian religion, and to the universal love and grace of God. This testimony, we desire may be strictly and carefully maintained, by a godly care and concern in all to stand clear therein; so shall we strengthen and comfort one another.

And as it has pleased the Lord, by the breaking forth of the glorious light of his Gospel, and the shedding abroad of his Holy Spirit, to gather us to be a people to his praise, and to unite us in love, not only one unto another, but to the whole creation of God, by subjecting us to the government of his Son our Lord and Saviour Jesus Christ, the Prince of Peace; it behoveth us to hold forth the ensign of the Lamb of God, and by our patience and peaceable behaviour to show, that we walk in obedience to the example and precepts of our Lord and Master, who hath commanded us to love our enemies, and to do good even to them that hate us. Wherefore we intreat all who profess themselves members of our society, to be faithful to that ancient testimony, borne by us ever since we were a people, against bearing arms and fighting; that by a conduct agreeable to our profession, we may demonstrate ourselves to be real followers of the

Messiah, the peaceable Saviour, of the increase of whose government and peace, there shall be no end.

✧ ✧ ✧ ✧

Our general scruple to bear arms is well known; and truly we are satisfied that our testimony in this respect is a testimony for Messiah, of whose reign it is the glory, that "the wolf and the lamb shall feed together." Most, if not all, people admit the transcendent excellency of peace. All who adopt the petition, "Thy kingdom come," pray for its universal establishment. Some people then must begin to fulfil the evangelical promise, and cease to learn war any more. Now, friends, seeing these things cannot be controverted, how do we long that your whole conversation be as becometh the Gospel; and that while any of us are professing to scruple war, they may not in some parts of their conduct be inconsistent with that profession! It is an awful thing to stand forth to the nation as the advocates of inviolable peace; and our testimony loses its efficacy in proportion to the want of consistency in any. And we think we are at this time peculiarly called to let our light shine with clearness, on account of the lenity shown us by government, and the readiness of magistrates to afford us all legal relief under suffering. And we can serve our country in no way more availingly, nor more acceptably to Him who holds its prosperity at his disposal, than by contributing, all that in us lies, to increase the number of meek, humble, and self-denying Christians.

SELECTION 3
Rules of Discipline

Quakers led the way in the abolition of slavery.

It is the sense of this meeting, that the importing of Negroes from their native country and relations by friends, is not a commendable nor allowed practice, and is therefore censured by this meeting.

We fervently warn all in profession with us, that they be careful to avoid being any way concerned in reaping the unrighteous profits arising from the iniquitous practice of dealing in Negroes, and other slaves; whereby, in the original purchase, one man selleth another, as he doth the beast that perisheth, without any better pretension to a property in him, than that of superior force; in direct violation of the Gospel rule, which teacheth all to do as they would be done by, and to do good to all; being the reverse of that covetous disposition, which furnisheth encouragement to those poor ignorant people to perpetuate their savage wars, in order to supply the demands of this most unnatural traffic, whereby great numbers of mankind, free by nature, are subjected to inextricable bondage; and which hath often been observed to fill their possessors with haughtiness, tyranny, luxury, and barbarity, corrupting the minds and debasing the morals of their children, to the unspeakable prejudice of religion and virtue, and the charity, which is the unchangeable nature, and the glory, of true Christianity.

We therefore can do no less, than, with the greatest earnestness, impress it upon friends every where, that they endeavour to keep their hands clear of this unrighteous gain of oppression.

This meeting having reason to apprehend, that divers under our name are concerned in the unchristian traffic in Negroes, doth recommend it earnestly to the care of friends every where, to discourage, as much as in them lies, a practice so repugnant to our Christian profession; and to deal with all such as shall persevere in a conduct so reproachful to Christianity, and to disown them, if they desist not therefrom.

We think it seasonable at this time to renew our exhortation, that friends every where be especially careful to keep their hands clear of giving encouragement in any shape to the slave-trade, it being evidently destructive of the natural rights of mankind; who are all ransomed by one Saviour, and visited by one divine light, in order to salvation; a traffic calculated to enrich and aggrandize some upon the misery of others, in its nature abhorrent to every just and tender sentiment, and contrary to the whole tenour of the Gospel.

It appears that the practice of holding Negroes in oppressive and unnatural bondage, hath been so successfully discouraged by friends in some of the colonies, as to be considerably lessened. We cannot but approve of these salutary endeavours, and earnestly intreat they may be continued, that, through the favour of

Divine Providence, a traffic so unmerciful, and unjust in its nature, to a part of our own species made equally with ourselves for immortality, may come to be considered by all in its proper light, and be utterly abolished, as a reproach to the Christian profession.

Our testimony against the inhuman practice of slave-keeping gains ground amongst our brethren in the American colonies, and hath had some happy influence on the minds of considerate people of other denominations, in opposition to that flagrant injustice to our fellow-creatures; for whom our Saviour shed his precious blood, as well as for others, and to whom he dispenseth a measure of his grace in common with the rest of mankind.

The Christian religion being designed to regulate and refine the natural affections of man, and to exalt benevolence into that charity which promotes peace on earth, and good-will towards all ranks and classes of mankind the world over; under the influence thereof, our minds have been renewedly affected in sympathy with the poor enslaved Africans; whom avarice hath taught some men, laying claim to the character of Christians, to consider as the refuse of the human race, and not entitled to the common privileges of mankind. The contempt in which they are held, and the remoteness of their sufferings from the notice of disinterested observers, have occasioned few advocates to plead their cause. The consideration of their case being brought weightily before the last yearly meeting, friends were engaged to recommend endeavours for putting a stop to a traffic so disgraceful to humanity, and so repugnant to the precepts of the Gospel.

XVIII RATIONALISM

The so-called "Age of Reason" had a profound effect on Christian ethics. In England it found an early and eloquent spokesman sympathetic to the Christian Faith in John Locke (1632–1704). His insistence that one must make the distinction between propositions which are (1) According to reason (2) Above reason and (3) Contrary to reason,[9] and that the teachings of the Christian Faith may be "according to reason" or "above reason" but never "contrary to reason" was the stock in trade of Christian rationalism.

It influenced the social teachings of the Christian Church by insisting that ethics ought to be defended by appeal to reason rather than revelation. While this approach developed first in England and found in the Anglican Bishop Joseph Butler (1692–1752) one of its most eloquent spokesmen, it profoundly influenced both continental Europe and America. It led Thomas Paine (1737–1809) to reject in the name of reason all claims of revelation. That the appeal to the absolute authority of human reason would eventually have this result had always been the opinion of the orthodox whose worst fears were thus confirmed.

SELECTION I

John Locke: *The Reasonableness of Christianity*

Because of the weakness of man, his sin, lust, carelessness and fear, he fails to find God in nature and by reason. Revelation thus provides a surer way to reasonable morality in view of the frailty and weakness of our constitutions.

Next to the knowledge of one God; maker of all things; "a clear knowledge of their duty was wanting "to mankind." This part of knowledge, though cultivated with some care by some of the heathen philosophers, yet got little footing among the people. All men, indeed, under pain of displeasing the gods, were to frequent the temples: every one went to their sacrifices and services: but the priests made it not their business to teach them virtue. If they were diligent in their observations and ceremonies; punctual in their feasts and solemnities, and the tricks of religion; the holy tribe assured them the gods were pleased, and they looked no farther. Few went to the schools of the philosophers to be instructed in their duties, and to know what was good and evil in their actions. The priests sold the better pennyworths, and therefore had all the custom. Lustrations and processions were much easier than a clean conscience, and a steady course of virtue; and an expiatory sacrifice that atoned for the want of it, was much more convenient than a strict and holy life. No wonder then, that religion was everywhere distinguished from, and preferred to virtue; and that it was dangerous heresy and profaneness to think the contrary. So much virtue as was necessary to hold societies together, and to contribute to the quiet of governments, the civil laws of commonwealths taught, and forced upon men that lived under magistrates. But these laws being for the most part made by such, who had no other aims but their own power, reached no farther than those things that would serve to tie men together in subjection; or at most were directly to conduce to the prosperity and temporal happiness of any people. But natural religion, in its full extent, was nowhere, that I know, taken care of, by the force of natural reason. It should seem, by the little that has hitherto been done in it, that it is too hard a task for unassisted reason to establish morality in all its parts, upon its true foundation, with a clear and convincing light. And it is at least a surer and shorter way, to the apprehensions of the vulgar, and mass of mankind, that one manifestly sent from God, and coming with visible authority from him, should, as a king and lawmaker, tell them their duties; and require their obedience; than leave it to the long and sometimes intricate deductions of reason, to be made out to them. Such trains of reasoning the greatest part of mankind have neither leisure to weigh; nor, for want of education and use, skill to judge of. We see how unsuccessful in this the attempts of philosophers were before our Saviour's time. How short their several systems came of the perfection of a true and complete morality, is very visible. And if, since that, the Christian philosophers have much out-done them; yet we may observe, that the first knowledge of the truths they have added, is owing to revelation: though as soon as they are heard and considered, they are found to be agreeable to reason; and such as can by no means be contradicted. Every one may observe a great many truths, which he receives at first from others, and readily assents to, as consonant to reason, which he would have found it hard, and perhaps beyond his strength, to have discovered himself. Native and original truth is not so easily wrought out of the mine, as we, who have it delivered already dug and fashioned into our hands, are apt to imagine. And how often at fifty or threescore years old are thinking men told what they wonder how they could miss thinking of? Which yet their own contemplations did not, and possibly never would have helped them to. Experience shows, that the knowledge of morality, by mere natural light, (how agreeable soever it be to it,) makes but a slow progress, and little advance in the world. And the reason of it is not hard to be found in men's necessities, passions, vices, and mistaken interests; which turn their thoughts another way: and the designing leaders, as well as following herd, find it not to their purpose to employ much of their meditations this way. Or whatever else was the cause, it is plain, in fact, that human reason unassisted failed men in its great and proper business of morality. It never from unquestionable principles, by clear deductions, made out an entire body of the "law of nature." And he that shall collect all the moral rules of the philosophers, and compare them with those contained in the New Testament, will find them to come short of the morality delivered by our Saviour, and taught by his apostles; a college made up, for the most part, of ignorant, but inspired fishermen.

Though yet, if any one should think, that out of the sayings of the wise heathens before our Saviour's time, there might be a collection made of all those rules of morality, which are to be found in the Christian religion; yet this would not at all hinder, but that the world, nevertheless, stood as much in need of our Saviour, and the morality delivered by him. Let it be granted (though not true) that all the moral precepts of the gospel were known by somebody or other, amongst mankind before. But where, of how, or of what use, is not considered. Suppose they may be picked up here and there; some from Solon and Bias in Greece, others from Tully in Italy: and to complete the work, let Confucius, as far as China, be consulted; and Anacharsis, the Scythian, contribute his share. What will all this do, to give the world a complete morality, that may be to mankind the unquestionable rule of life and manners? I will not here urge the impossibility of collecting from men, so far distant from one another, in time and place, and languages. I will suppose there was a Stobeus in those times, who had gathered the moral sayings from all the sages of the world. What would this amount to, towards being a steady rule; a certain transcript of a law that we are under? Did the saying of Aristippus, or Confucius, give it an authority? Was Zeno a law-giver to mankind? If not, what he or any other philosopher delivered, was but a saying of his. Mankind might hearken to it, or reject it, as they pleased; or as it suited their interest, passions, principles or humours. They were under no obligation; the opinion of this or that philosopher was of no authority. And if it were, you must take all he said under the same character. All his dictates must go for law, certain and true; or none of them. And then, if you will take any of the moral sayings of Epicurus (many whereof Seneca quotes with esteem and approbation) for precepts of the law of nature, you must take all the rest of his doctrine for such too; or else his authority ceases: and so no more is to be received from him, or any of the sages of old, for parts of the law of nature, as carrying with it an obligation to be obeyed, but what they prove to be so. But such a body of ethics, proved to be the law of nature, from principles of reason, and teaching all the duties of life; I think nobody will say the world had before our Saviour's time. It is not enough, that there were up and down scattered sayings of wise men, conformable to right reason. The law of nature, is the law of convenience too: and it is no wonder that those men of parts, and studious of virtue, (who had occasion to think on any particular part of it,) should, by meditation, light on the right even from the observable convenience and beauty of it; without making out its obligation from the true principles of the law of nature, and foundations of morality. But these incoherent apophthegms of philosophers, and wise men, however excellent in themselves, and well intended by them; could never make a morality, whereof the world could be convinced; could never rise to the force of a law, that mankind could with certainty depend on. Whatsoever should thus be universally useful, as a standard to which men should conform their manners, must have its authority, either from reason or revelation. It is not every writer of morality, or compiler of it from others, that can thereby be erected into a law-giver to mankind; and a dictator of rules, which are therefore valid, because they are to be found in his books; under the authority of this or that philosopher. He, that any one will pretend to set up in this kind, and have his rules pass for authentic directions, must show, that either he builds his doctrine upon principles of reason, self-evident in themselves; and that he deduces all the parts of it from thence, by clear and evident demonstration: or must show his commission from heaven, that he comes with authority from God, to deliver his will and commands to the world. In the former way, no-body that I know, before our Saviour's time, ever did, or went about to give us a morality. It is true, there is a law of nature: but who is there that ever did, or undertook to give it us all entire, as a law; no more, nor no less, than what was contained in, and had the obligation of that law? Who ever made out all the parts of it, put them together, and showed the world their obligation? Where was there any such code, that mankind might have recourse to, as their unerring rule, before our Saviour's time? If there was not, it is plain there was need of one to give us such a morality; such a law, which might be the sure guide of those who had a desire to go right; and, if they had a mind, need not mistake their duty, but might be certain when they had performed, when failed in it. Such a law of morality Jesus Christ hath given us in the New Testament; but by the latter of these ways, by revelation. We have from him a full and sufficient rule for our direction, and conformable to that of reason. But the truth and obligation of its precepts have their force, and are put past doubt to us, by the evidence of his mission. He was sent by God: his miracles show it; and the authority of God in his precepts cannot be questioned. Here morality has a sure standard, that revelation vouches, and reason cannot gainsay, nor question; but both together witness to come from God the great law-maker. And such an one as this, out of the New Testament, I think the world never had, nor can any one say, is any-where else to be found. Let me ask any one, who is forward to think that the doctrine of morality was full and clear in the world, at our Saviour's birth; whither would he have directed Brutus and Cassius, (both men of parts and virtue, the one whereof believed, and the other disbelieved a future being,) to be satisfied in the rules and obligations of all the parts of their duties; if they should have asked him, Where they might find the law they were to live by, and by which they should be charged, or acquitted, as guilty, or innocent? If to the sayings of the wise, and the declarations of philosophers, he sends them into a wild wood of uncertainty, to an endless maze, from which they should never get out: if to the religions of the world, yet worse: and if to their own reason, he refers them to that which had some light and certainty; but yet had hitherto failed all mankind in a perfect rule; and, we see, resolved not the doubts that had risen amongst the studious and thinking philosophers; nor had yet been able to convince the civilized parts of the world, that they had not given, nor could, without a crime, take away the lives of their children, by exposing them.

✧ ✧ ✧ ✧

A great many things which we have been bred up in the belief of, from our cradles, (and are notions grown familiar, and, as it were, natural to us, under the gospel,) we take for unquestionable obvious truths, and easily demonstrable; without considering how long we might have been in doubt or ignorance of them, had revelations been silent. And many are beholden to revelation, who do not acknowledge it. It is no diminishing to revelation, that reason gives its suffrage too, to the truths revelation has discovered. But it is our mistake to think, that because reason confirms them to us, we had the first certain knowledge of them from thence; and in that clear evidence we now possess them.

SELECTION 2

Joseph Butler: *Upon the Love of Our Neighbors*

Bishop Joseph Butler (1692–1752) developed his social ethics in a series of sermons. A section from his sermon "Upon the Love of Our Neighbors" is here given as an example of his rational approach.

First, It is manifest that nothing can be of consequence to mankind or any creature, but happiness. This then is all which any person can, in strictness of speaking, be said to have a right to. We can therefore *owe no man any thing,* but only to further and promote his happiness, according to our abilities. And therefore a disposition and endeavour to do good to all with whom we have to do, in the degree and manner which the different relations we stand in to them require, is a discharge of all the obligations we are under to them.

As human nature is not one simple uniform thing, but a composition of various parts, body, spirit, appetites, particular passions, and affections; for each of which reasonable self-love would lead men to have due regard, and make suitable provision: so society consists of various parts, to which we stand in different respects and relations; and just benevolence would as surely lead us to have due regard to each of these, and behave as the respective relations require. Reasonable good-will, and right behaviour towards our fellow-creatures, are in a manner the same: only that the former expresseth the principle as it is in the mind; the latter, the principle as it were become external, i.e. exerted in actions.

And so far as temperance, sobriety, and moderation in sensual pleasures, and the contrary vices, have any respect to our fellow-creatures, any influence upon their quiet, welfare, and happiness; as they always have a real, and often a near influence upon it; so far it is manifest those virtues may be produced by the love of our neighbour, and that the contrary vices would be prevented by it. Indeed if men's regard to themselves will not restrain them from excess; it may be thought little probable, that their love to others is not, any more than their regard to themselves, just, and in its due degree. There are however manifest instances of persons kept sober and temperate from regard to their affairs, and the welfare of those who depend upon them. And it is obvious to every one, that habitual excess, a dissolute course of life, implies a general neglect of the duties we owe towards our friends, our families, and our country.

From hence it is manifest that the common virtues, and the common vices of mankind, may be traced up to benevolence, or the want of it. And this entitles the precept, *Thou shalt love thy neighbour as thyself*, to the preeminence given to it; and is a justification of the Apostle's assertion, that all other commandments are comprehended in it; whatever cautions and restrictions there are, which might require to be considered, if we were to state particularly and at length, what is virtue and right behaviour in mankind. But,

Secondly, It might be added, that in a higher and more general way of consideration, leaving out the particular nature of creatures, and the particular circumstances in which they are placed, benevolence seems in the strictest sense to include in it all that is good and worthy; all that is good, which we have any distinct particular notion of. We have no clear conception of any positive moral attribute in the supreme Being, but what may be resolved up into goodness. And, if we consider a reasonable creature or moral agent, without regard to the particular relations and circumstances in which he is placed; we cannot conceive any thing else to come in towards determining whether he is to be ranked in an higher or lower degree in which that principle, and what is manifestly connected with it, prevail in him.

That which we more strictly call piety, or the love of God, and which is an essential part of a right temper, some may perhaps imagine no way connected with benevolence: yet surely they must be connected, if there be indeed in being an object infinitely good. Human nature is so constituted, that every good affection implies the love of itself; i.e. becomes the object of a new affection in the same person. Thus, to be righteous, implies in it the love of righteousness; to be benevolent, the love of benevolence; to be good, the love of goodness; whether this righteousness, benevolence, or goodness, be viewed as in our own mind, or in another's: and the love of God as a being perfectly good, is the love of perfect goodness contemplated in a being or person. Thus morality and religion, virtue and piety, will at last necessarily coincide, run up into one and the same point, and *love* will be in all senses *the end of the commandment.*

SELECTION 3
Gotthold Ephraim Lessing: *The Tale of the Three Rings*

Gotthold Ephraim Lessing (1729–1781) gave the ideas of the Enlightenment their most persuasive popular expression in his play *Nathan the Wise*. In the tale of the three rings, the hero presents Lessing's claim that a rational approach to religious differences is the only truly religious approach.

NATHAN

In days of yore, there dwelt in Eastern lands
A man, who from a valued hand received
A ring of priceless worth. An opal stone
Shot from within an ever-changing hue,
And held its virtue in its form concealed,
To render him of God and man beloved,
Who wore it in this fixed unchanging faith.
No wonder that its Eastern owner ne'er
Withdrew it from his finger, and resolved
That to his house the ring should be secured.
Therefore he thus bequeathed it: first to him
Who was the most beloved of his sons,
Ordaining then that he should leave the ring
To the most dear among his children; then,
That without heeding birth, the fav'rite son,
In virtue of the ring alone, should still
Be lord of all the house. You hear me, Sultan?

SALADIN

I understand. Proceed.

NATHAN

From son to son,
The ring at length descended to a sire
Who had three sons, alike obedient to him,
And whom he loved with just and equal love.
The first, the second, and the third, in turn,
According as they each apart received
The overflowings of his heart, appeared
Most worthy as his heir, to take the ring,
Which, with good-natured weakness, he in turn
Had promised privately to each; and thus
Things lasted for a while. But death approached,
The father now embarrassed, could not bear
To disappoint two sons, who trusted him.
What's to be done? In secret he commands
The jeweller to come, that from the form
Of the true ring, he may bespeak two more.
Nor cost, nor pains are to be spared, to make
The rings alike—quite like the true one. This
The artist managed. When the rings were brought
The father's eye could not distinguish which
Had been the model. Overjoyed, he calls
His sons, takes leave of each apart—bestows
His blessing and his ring on each—and dies.
You hear me?

SALADIN

Ay! I hear. Conclude the tale.

NATHAN

Tis ended, Sultan! All that follows next
May well be guessed. Scarce is the father dead,
When with his ring, each separate son appears,
And claims to be the lord of all the house.
Question arises, tumult and debate—
But all in vain—the true ring could no more
Be then distinguished than—the true faith now.

SALADIN

Is that your answer to my question?

NATHAN

No!
But it may serve as my apology.
I cannot venture to decide between
Rings which the father had expressly made,
To baffle those who would distinguish them.

SALADIN

Rings, Nathan! Come, a truce to this! The creeds
Which I have named have broad, distinctive marks,
Differing in raiment, food, and drink!

NATHAN

'Tis true!
But then they differ not in their foundation.
Are not all built on history alike,
Traditional or written? History
Must be received on trust. Is it not so?
In whom are we most likely to put trust?
In our own people? In those very men
Whose blood we are? who, from our earliest youth
Have proved their love for us, have ne'er deceived,
Except in cases where 'twere better so?
Why should I credit my forefathers less
Than you do yours? or can I ask of you
To charge your ancestors with falsehood, that
The praise of truth may be bestowed on mine?
And so of Christians.

SALADIN

By our Prophet's faith,
The man is right. I have no more to say.

NATHAN

Now let us to our rings once more return.
We said the sons complained; each to the judge
Swore from his father's hand immediately
To have received the ring—as was the case—
In virtue of a promise, that he should
One day enjoy the ring's prerogative.

In this they spoke the truth. Then each maintained
It was not possible that to himself
His father had been false. Each could not think
His father guilty of an act so base.
Rather than that, reluctant as he was
To judge his brethren, he must yet declare
Some treach'rous act of falsehood had been done.

SALADIN

Well! and the judge? I'm curious now to hear
What you will make him say. Go on, go on!

NATHAN

The judge said: If the father is not brought
Before my seat, I cannot judge the case.
Am I to judge enigmas? Do you think
That the true ring will here unseal his lips?
But, hold! You tell me that the real ring
Enjoys the secret power to make the man
Who wears it, both by God and man, beloved.
Let that decide. Who of the three is loved
Best by his brethren? Is there no reply?
What! do these love-exciting rings alone
Act inwardly? Have they no outward charm?
Does each one love himself alone? You're all
Deceived deceivers. All your rings are false.
The real ring, perchance, has disappeared;
And so your father, to supply the loss,
Has caused three rings to fill the place of one.

SALADIN

O, charming, charming!

NATHAN

And,—the judge continued:—
If you insist on judgment, and refuse
My counsel, be it so. I recommend
That you consider how the matter stands.
Each from his father has received a ring:
Let each then think the real ring his own.
Your father, possibly, desired to free

His power from one ring's tyrannous control.
He loved you all with an impartial love,
And equally, and had no inward wish
To prove the measure of his love for one
By pressing heavily upon the rest.
Therefore, let each one imitate this love;
So, free from prejudice, let each one aim
To emulate his brethren in the strife
To prove the virtues of his several ring,
By offices of kindness and of love,
And trust in God. And if, in years to come,
The virtues of the ring shall reappear
Amongst your children's children, then, once more
Come to this judgment-seat. A greater far
Than I shall sit upon it, and decide.
So spake the modest judge.

SALADIN

Oh God, O God!

NATHAN

And if now, Saladin, you think you're he—

SALADIN

This promised judge—I?—Dust! I?—Nought! oh God!

NATHAN

What is the matter, Sultan?

SALADIN

Dearest Nathan!
The judge's thousand years are not yet past;
His judgment-seat is not for me. But go,
And still remain my friend.

SELECTION 4
Thomas Paine: *The Age of Reason*

Thomas Paine's summary of his objections to revealed religion illustrates one direction in which rationalism developed.

First—That the idea or belief of a word of God, existing in print, or in writing, or in speech, is inconsistent in itself for reasons already assigned. These reasons, among many others, are the want of a universal language; the mutability of language; the errors to which translations are subject; the possibility of totally suppressing such a word; the probability of altering it, or of fabricating the whole, and imposing it upon the world.

Secondly—That the Creation we behold is the real and ever existing word of God, in which we cannot be deceived. It proclaims his power, it demonstrates his wisdom, it manifests his goodness and beneficence.

Thirdly—That the moral duty of man consists in imitating the moral goodness and beneficence of God manifested in the Creation towards all his creatures. That seeing as we daily do the goodness of God to all men, it is an example calling upon all men to practise the same towards each other; and, consequently, that every thing of persecution and revenge between man and man, and every thing of cruelty to animals, is a violation of moral duty.

I trouble not myself about the manner of future existence. I content myself with believing, even to positive conviction, that the power that gave me existence is able to continue it, in any form and manner he pleases, either with or without this body; and it appears more probable to me that I shall continue to exist hereafter, than that I should have had existence, as I now have, before that existence began.

It is certain that, in one point, all nations of the earth and all religions agree; all believe in a God; the things in which they disagree, are the redundancies annexed to that belief; and, therefore, if ever a universal religion should prevail, it will not be believing any thing new, but in getting rid of redundancies, and believing as man believed at first. Adam, if ever there was such a man, was created a Deist; but, in the mean time, let every man follow, as he has a right to do, the religion and worship he prefers.

XIX GERMAN PIETISM

The definition of "Pietism" is controversial, but its significance for the development of Christian social thought is massive. Associated with the names of Philip Jacob Spener (1635–1705), August Hermann Francke (1663–1727), and Nicolaus Ludwig Count Zinzendorf (1700–1760), the movement had precursors like Johann Arndt (1555–1621), who, however, considered himself an orthodox Lutheran and was the pastor and teacher of the most impressive dogmatician of Lutheran Orthodoxy, Johann Gerhard (1586–1631). Spener emphasized the importance of the new birth of the Christian, an emphasis which became typical for Pietists who often felt that the date of this new birth should and could be established by the individual believer. It was this individual believer who played an increasingly important part in Pietism and who was gathered in small Bible study groups, the so-called *Collegia Pietatis*.

In its relation to society Pietism was characterized by an apparently contradictory attitude: Pietists rejected the "world" and "worldliness" as a realm of evil. At the same time they made valiant and sometimes effective efforts to change this "evil world." Thus Pietism became the movement which carried Protestantism to the ends of the earth through its missionary efforts and simultaneously tried to change the situation at home through a multitude of schools, hospitals, and other institutions of Christian service. The method was to change the world by changing individuals, especially also those in positions of power. Thus August Hermann Francke established a school specifically designed to educate the sons of the nobility and other leading citizens, and the Moravians became famous for their excellent private schools.

This Pietistic approach of changing the world by changing individuals and especially the leaders of society became widely adopted and quite typical for the Protestant Christian approach to social change. It presents both its greatest strength and weakness and has its roots in the thought of the men here presented.

SELECTION 1
Philip Jacob Spener: *Pia Desideria*

The man who is commonly regarded as the founder of Pietism was born in Alsace and studied at the university of Strasbourg. He read both Johann Arndt's *True Christianity* and many of the Puritan tracts (e.g. Lewis Bayly's *Practice of Piety,* Dyke's *Mystery of Selfedeceit,* Baxter's *Call to the Unconverted*) as well as the writings of Martin Luther. In 1666 he became senior pastor of Frankfurt/Main, where he served for twenty years and attracted a vast number of disciples. Later he served in Dresden and Berlin, where he died in 1705. One of his most influential works is *Pia Desideria,* published during his stay at Frankfurt. Our selection is taken from this booklet and deals with the emphasis upon the spiritual priesthood of all Christians.

PROPOSALS TO CORRECT CONDITIONS IN THE CHURCH

1. Thought should be given to a more extensive use of the Word of God among us. We know that by nature we have no good in us. If there is to be any good in us, it must be brought about by God. To this end the Word of God is the powerful means, since faith must be enkindled through the gospel, and the law provides the rules for good works and many wonderful impulses to attain them. The more at home the Word of God is among us, the more we shall bring about faith and its fruits.

It may appear that the Word of God has sufficiently free course among us inasmuch as at various places (as in this city) there is daily or frequent preaching from the pulpit. When we reflect further on the matter, however, we shall find that with respect to this first proposal, more is needed. I do not at all disapprove of the preaching of sermons in which a Christian congregation is instructed by the reading and exposition of a certain text, for I myself do this. But I find that this is not enough. In the first place, we know that "all scripture is inspired by God and profitable for teaching, for reproof, for correction, and for training in righteousness" (II Tim. 3:16). Accordingly *all* scripture, without exception, should be known by the congregation if we are all to receive the necessary benefit. If we put together all the passages of the Bible which in the course of many years are read to a congregation in one place, they will comprise only a very small part of the Scriptures which have been given to us. The remainder is not heard by the congregation at all, or is heard only insofar as one or another verse is quoted or alluded to in sermons, without, however, offering any understanding of the entire context, which is nevertheless of the greatest importance. In the second place, the people have little opportunity to grasp the meaning of the Scriptures except on the basis of those passages which may have been expounded to them, and even less do they have the opportunity to become as practiced in them as edification requires. Meanwhile, although solitary reading of the Bible at home is in itself a splendid and praiseworthy thing, it does not accomplish enough for most people.

It should therefore be considered whether the church would not be well advised to introduce the people to Scripture in still other ways than through the customary sermons on the appointed lessons.

This might be done, first of all, by diligent reading of the Holy Scriptures, especially of the New Testament. It would not be difficult for every housefather to keep a Bible, or at least a New Testament, handy and read from it every day or, if he cannot read, to have somebody else read. How necessary and beneficial this would be for all Christians in every station of life was splendidly and effectively demonstrated a century ago by Andrew Hyperius, whose two books on this matter were quickly translated into German by George Nigrinus and, after the little work had become quite unknown, were recently brought to the attention of people again in a new edition put out by Dr. Elias

Veyel, my esteemed former fellow student in Strasbourg and my beloved brother in Christ.

Then a second thing would be desirable in order to encourage people to read privately, namely, that where the practice can be introduced the books of the Bible be read one after another, at specified times in the public service, without further comment unless one wished to add brief summaries. This would be intended for the edification of all, but especially of those who cannot read at all, or cannot read easily or well, or of those who do not own a copy of the Bible.

For a third thing it would perhaps not be inexpedient (and I set this down for further and more mature reflection) to reintroduce the ancient and apostolic kind of church meetings. In addition to our customary services with preaching, other assemblies would also be held in the manner in which Paul describes them in I Corinthians 14:26–40. One person would not rise to preach (although this practice would be continued at other times), but others who have been blessed with gifts and knowledge would also speak and present their pious opinions on the proposed subject to the judgment of the rest, doing all this in such a way as to avoid disorder and strife. This might conveniently be done by having several ministers (in places where a number of them live in a town) meet together or by having several members of a congregation who have a fair knowledge of God or desire to increase their knowledge meet under the leadership of a minister, take up the Holy Scriptures, read aloud from them, and fraternally discuss each verse in order to discover its simple meaning and whatever may be useful for the edification of all. Anybody who is not satisfied with his understanding of a matter should be permitted to express his doubts and seek further explanation. On the other hand, those (including the ministers) who have made more progress should be allowed the freedom to state how they understand each passage. Then all that has been contributed, insofar as it accords with the sense of the Holy Spirit in the Scriptures, should be carefully considered by the rest, especially by the ordained ministers, and applied to the edification of the whole meeting. Everything should be arranged with an eye to the glory of God, to the spiritual growth of the participants, and therefore also to their limitations. Any threat of meddlesomeness, quarrelsomeness, self-seeking, or something else of this sort should be guarded against and tactfully cut off especially by the preachers who retain leadership in these meetings.

Not a little benefit is to be hoped for from such an arrangement. Preachers would learn to know the members of their own congregations and their weakness or growth in doctrine and piety, and a bond of confidence would be established between preachers and people which would serve the best interests of both. At the same time the people would have a splendid opportunity to exercise their diligence with respect to the Word of God and modestly to ask their questions (which they do not always have the courage to discuss with their minister in private) and get answers to them. In a short time they would experience personal growth and would also become capable of giving better religious instruction to their children and servants at home. In the absence of such exercises, sermons which are delivered in continually flowing speech are not always fully and adequately comprehended because there is no time for reflection in between or because, when one does stop to reflect, much of what follows is missed (which does not happen in a discussion). On the other hand, private reading of the Bible or reading in the household, where nobody is present who may from time to time help point out the meaning and purpose of each verse, cannot provide the reader with a sufficient explanation of all that he would like to know. What is lacking in both of these instances (in public preaching and private reading) would be supplied by the proposed exercises. It would not be a great burden either to the preachers or to the people, and much would be done to fulfill the admonition of Paul in Colossians 3:16, "Let the word of Christ dwell in you richly, as you teach and admonish one another in all wisdom, and as you sing psalms and hymns and spiritual songs." In fact, such songs may be used in the proposed meetings for the praise of God and the inspiration of the participants.

This much is certain: the diligent use of the Word of God, which consists not only of listening to sermons but also of reading, meditating, and discussing (Ps. 1:2), must be the chief means for reforming something, whether this occurs in the proposed fashion or in some other appropriate way. The Word of God remains the seed from which all that is good in us must grow. If we succeed in getting the people to seek eagerly and diligently in the book of life for their joy, their spiritual life will be wonderfully strengthened and they will become altogether different people.

What did our sainted Luther seek more ardently than to induce the people to a diligent reading of the Scriptures? He even had some misgivings about allowing his books to be published, lest the people be made more slothful thereby in the reading of the Scriptures. His words in Volume I of the Altenburg edition of his works read:

> I should gladly have seen all my books forgotten and destroyed, if only for the reason that I am afraid of the example I may give. For I see what benefit it has brought to the church that men have begun to collect many books and great libraries outside and alongside of the Holy Scriptures, and especially have begun to scramble together, without any distinction, all sorts of "fathers," "councils," and "doctors." Not only has good time been wasted and the study of the Scriptures neglected, but the pure understanding of God's Word is lost. . . . It was our intention and our hope when we began to put the Bible into German that there would be less writing and more studying and reading of the Scriptures. For all other writings should point to the Scriptures. . . . Neither fathers nor councils nor we ourselves will do so well, even when our very best is done, as the Holy Scriptures have done—that is to say, as God himself has done. . . . I only ask in all kindness that the man who at this time wishes to have my books will by no means let them be a hindrance to his own study of the Scriptures, etc.

Luther also wrote similar things elsewhere.

One of the principal wrongs by which papal politics became entrenched, the people were kept in ignorance, and hence complete control of their consciences was maintained was that the papacy prohibited, and insofar as possible continues to prohibit, the reading of the Holy Scriptures. On the other hand, it was one of the major purposes of the Reformation to restore to the people the Word of God which had lain hidden under the bench (and this Word was the most powerful means by which God blessed his work). So this will be the principal means, now that the church must be put in better condition, whereby the aversion to Scripture which many have may be overcome, neglect of its study be counteracted, and ardent zeal for it awakened.

✧ ✧ ✧ ✧

3. Connected with these two proposals is a third: the people must have impressed upon them and must accustom themselves to believing that it is by no means enough to have knowledge of the Christian faith, for Christianity consists rather of practice. Our dear Savior repeatedly enjoined love as the real mark of his disciples (John 13:34–35, 15:12; I John 3:10, 18, 4:7–8, 11–13, 21). In his old age dear John (according to the testimony of Jerome in his letter to the Galatians) was accustomed to say hardly anything more to his disciples than "Children, love one another!" His disciples and auditors finally became so annoyed at this endless repetition that they asked him why he was always saying the same thing to them. He replied, "Because it is the Lord's command, and it suffices if this be done." Indeed, love is the whole life of the man who has faith and who through his faith is saved, and his fulfillment of the laws of God consists of love.

If we can therefore awaken a fervent love among our Christians, first toward one another and then toward all men (for these two, brotherly affection and general love, must supplement each other according to II Peter 1:7), and put this love into practice, practically all that we desire will be accomplished. For all the commandments are summed up in love (Rom. 13:9). Accordingly the people are not only to be told this incessantly, and they are not only to have the excellence of neighborly love and, on the other hand, the great danger and harm in the opposing self-love pictured impressively before their eyes (which is done well in the spiritually minded John Arndt's *True Christianity*, IV, ii, 22 *et seq.*), but they must also practice such love. They must become accustomed not to lose sight of any opportunity in which they can render their neighbor a service of love, and yet while performing it they must diligently search their hearts to discover whether they are acting in true love or out of other motives. If they are offended, they should especially be on their guard, not only that they refrain from all vengefulness but also that they give up some of their rights and insistence on them for fear that their hearts may betray them and feelings of hostility may become involved. In fact, they should diligently seek opportunities to do good to their enemies in order that such self-control may hurt the old Adam, who is otherwise inclined to vengeance, and at the same time in order that love may be more deeply implanted in their hearts.

For this purpose, as well as for the sake of Christian growth in general, it may be useful if those who have earnestly resolved to walk in the way of the Lord would enter into a confidential relationship with their confessor or some other judicious and enlightened Christian and would regularly report to him how they live, what opportunities they have had to practice Christian love, and how they have employed or neglected them. This should be done with the intention of discovering what is amiss and securing such an individual's counsel and instruction as to what ought now to be done. There should be firm resolution to follow such advice at all times unless something is expected that is quite clearly contrary to God's will. If there appears to be doubt whether or not one is obligated to do this or that out of love for one's neighbor, it is always better to incline toward doing it rather than leaving it undone.

SELECTION 2
August Hermann Francke: *Scriptural Rules*

August Hermann Francke (1663–1727) was the organizational genius of German Pietism. In Halle, where he served as professor of theology, he founded a number of institutions (orphanage, school for children of parents unable to pay tuition, Latin school, school for the education of children of the nobility, publishing house, Bible society) which helped him to extend the Pietist influence all over the world. The following selection illustrates one aspect of Pietism, its methodical attempts at self-improvement.

RULES FOR THE PRESERVATION OF CONSCIENCE AND GOOD ORDER IN SOCIAL INTERCOURSE OR SOCIETY (SCRIPTURAL RULES)

(1) Society offers many occasions for sinning. If you want to preserve your conscience, remember always that the great and majestic God by His omnipresence is always the most eminent member of any society. One should show awe in the presence of such a great Lord.

(2) Whatever you do, see to it that nobody (especially not you yourself) disturbs your inner peace and your rest in God.

(3) Never speak of your enemies except in love and to the honor of God and their best interest.

(4) Do not insist on talking much. But if God gives you the opportunity to speak, speak with respect, prudence, gentleness whenever you are certain. Use a loving seriousness and distinct and clear words, in an orderly fashion and without slurring your words, and do not repeat yourself unnecessarily.

(5) Do not presumptuously speak of the things of this world unless God is honored thereby and your neighbor improved and your pressing needs met. It is a word of the Lord: "Whatever you are doing, whether you speak or act, do everything in the name of the Lord Jesus, giving thanks to God the Father through him." (Col. 3:17)

(6) Beware of barbed or sarcastic speech. Avoid all offensive foolish or merely injudicious proverbs and sayings which might give offense. Ask others to tell you whether you tend to use such, for habit results in lack of awareness. Cursing is among the serious sins. He who curses, curses himself and all that is his.

(7) When speaking of God and your Savior speak with deep humility and reverence as if in His very presence. Be ashamed to use the name of Jesus as a mere expression.

(8) When telling stories be very careful, for the spirit of lies rules here. One tends to fill in the details from one's own imagination if memory has not retained everything. One should

examine when telling a story if one does not here and there speak without certainty. Ridiculous and supercilious stories are not appropriate for the Christian. For they are either not true or at least uncertain or they are opposed to love to the neighbor or result in an abuse of spiritual things or cause the suspicion in the other person that he may be meant by the story. They also tend to encourage others to tell similar and even worse stories. Good and true examples of the virtues and those who bear witness to divine Providence, Power, Mercy and Justice one should never forget, for one can edify greatly with such illustrations. But tell them if you are certain of the facts and clearly and in an orderly fashion without adding anything. If you have forgotten some detail do not be ashamed to admit it.

(9) When speaking of yourself watch that you do not speak out of self-love.

(10) Do not change sound subjects incessantly. This is the undoing of most people who cannot talk fully about anything but start talking about one thing and then about another. Stick by your subject as long as it is not burdensome to others and by doing so you will avoid many a misunderstanding. Edify yourself and others and collect a treasure of important subjects and sound arguments which you can discuss in detail when the need arises.

(11) Remember that certain words are of themselves evil, as for example cursing, useless swearing, rude and obscene talk. This is true also of useless words which serve no purpose and have no goal. And even those words are good who are said to honor him who already knows the word that you are about to speak. You should avoid evil and useless words, for you will have to give account of every single one. Good words use eagerly.

(12) Select your company either because there is need or hope for improvement but in any case select them carefully. Some formal contact with godless people cannot be avoided but do not seek their company without compelling reason. It is more likely that they will lead you astray than that you will win them. If you have to have dealings with them be on guard.

(13) Many speeches are sound but not presented in the

right company or place. In church even the best speech may become a stumbling block for the weak.

(14) In the presence of others do not speak secretively or into somebody's ear or in a foreign language. For this causes suspicion and the person excluded assumes that you do not trust him.

(15) When others speak who want to be heard by everybody present do not start an individual conversation with one member of the group, for this causes disorder and annoyance.

(16) If you tell something which you know or have heard through someone else, think first if the source of your remarks would be content to have you repeat it. If you have doubts, be quiet.

(17) If somebody interrupts you be quiet. The other person will be pleased that he is heard also and even if you were to continue he would not really hear you since he is so intent on what he is about to say.

(18) Never interrupt anybody else. For everybody is annoyed if you don't let him finish. Sometimes you may think you have gotten the point and still fail to understand what he wants to say. The other person feels secretly despised if one does not let him finish. You would not interrupt an important man whom you would like to honor. Consider when you interrupt others and you will note that you let your mouth blurt out without real forethought. You will gain the love of everybody much more easily if you listen patiently to everyone.

(19) If someone contradicts you be especially on guard. For this is the occasion for sin in society. If the honor of God and the welfare of your neighbor does not suffer don't argue. There is much argument and when it is finished both sides have less certainty of the matter than they had before. Even if somebody opposes the truth beware of all violent emotion. This is only the eagerness of the flesh. If you have presented the truth clearly and with sound reasons be content. Further quarrelling will gain little. Your opponent will give the matter more thought if he sees that you are sure of your cause and do not want to quarrel. If he learns nothing else from you he learns meekness and modesty from your example.

(20) If games or other entertainment like dancing, etc. be-

gin take thought. You know that much indecent and rough behaviour is connected with such activities and that they are commonly followed by obscene gestures and talk and other even greater sins. It may be more advisable for you to leave quietly rather than remain since the opportunity may lead you astray to give in to such disorderly behaviour or at least make it difficult for you to preserve the peace of God in your soul.

(21) If it is up to you to punish others because of their sins, do not make excuses that the time is inconvenient if it is really fear and timidity that keep you back. Fear and timidity must be overcome like other evil emotions. But always punish yourself first before punishing others so that your punishment will flow from compassion. Punish with love and great care and modesty in order that the other person may somehow be convinced in his conscience that he has done ill. Christ punished with one look when he looked at Peter who had denied him. Yet Peter wept bitterly. Christ would also punish with explicit and plain words. Love must here be your teacher. But do not participate in the sins of others.

(22) When it comes to eating be moderate in the use of food and drink. If you are urged to overindulge remember that these are temptations to sin against your God. Do not let yourself be led to follow the pleasantness of taste and fill your belly to the brim. It would be better for you if you were to eat more frequently but less on each occasion to preserve your soberness of mind and the aptitude to do good rather than stuffing your stomach and lose the lovely and joyful manner of a sober soul. Much eating and drinking overburdens body and soul. Consistent moderation is an important test of your spiritual intelligence. If your mouth waters to select the best food for yourself to fill yourself with dainty morsels because of their taste and to eat and drink inordinately without real hunger or thirst you still are not a moderate person.

(23) Always and in every company beware of indecent facial expressions, movements of the hands and positions of the body. They reveal disorder in the mind and betray your most secret emotions. Your dear Jesus would not have done such, why would you not follow him in outward behaviour which is of all things the least important? Let a good friend

call these things to your attention since you may not be able to recognize them in yourself.

(24) Beware of unnecessary laughter. Not all laughter is forbidden. For it does happen that the most pious person rejoices so deeply because of godly, not worldly, things that his mouth bears witness with a modest laugh of the delight in his mind. But it is easy to sin here and the road is opened for a distraction of the senses (Wisdom 9:15) which soon leads to the awareness that the heart has become too frivolous when it tries to approach in deep humility the omnipresent God. Especially if others laugh at jokes and foolishness beware that you do not laugh with them. It does not please God, why does it please you. If it does not please you, then why are you laughing? If you laugh you share in the sin. If you remain serious you have punished the sin in the conscience of the useless babbler.

(25) If others have gotten off the subject or sidetracked in their discussion, see to it that you correct this with an intelligent remark as soon as possible. Thus you can avoid much diffuseness. Few use this gift yet it is most necessary.

(26) Never place yourself ahead of anyone and do not avoid the place in society which you have to take because of your status in life and to preserve good order. You are dust, the other ashes. Before God you are both equal. Therefore, as far as you are concerned ignore your status. Love is humble and awakens by its humility love in others. A conceited man is a burden to everyone.

(27) Honor all men in society but be afraid of no one. God is greater than you or he. Fear Him!

(28) Do not be sad and irritable when you are with people but rather joyful and delightful for that refreshes everyone.

(29) If you note that a certain social occasion is not necessary for you, or that God's honor could be furthered better some where else, or that love does not constrain you to serve your neighbor by your continued presence do not stay just for the love of company. You must not remain another instant if the only reason for your staying is to waste time. It is unbecoming for a Christian to be bored in the presence of his God. Even

pious people fail here occasionally and spend time in useless words and deeds which later trouble their souls.

(30) Watch whether your heart is the same, be it in solitude or in society. If this is not the case you have much reason to seek solitude rather than society so that you may put your heart first into right order. But if solitude or society are the same to you watch that you who stand do not fall.

SELECTION 3

Nicolaus Ludwig Count Zinzendorf: *Nine Publick Discourses,* and *Maxims, Theological Ideas and Sentences out of the Present Ordinary of the Brethren's Churches Dissertations and Discourses*

Scion of the highest German nobility (*Reichsgraf*), Zinzendorf (1700–1760) developed a Pietism of a somewhat different stamp than that of Spener and Francke. Because of certain personal idiosyncrasies and an unwillingness to take the denominational divisions of Christendom of the eighteenth century as seriously as was the custom, he was bitterly and even viciously attacked by the orthodox and severely criticized by men of similar orientation, like Henry Melchior Muhlenberg in Pennsylvania and John Wesley in England.

Socially significant in Zinzendorf's movement was its great missionary zeal which opened many a foreign country to the Christian message, its excellent private schools, where generations of German leaders received their secondary education (e.g. Schleiermacher) and its success in permeating some of the established churches of Europe with the spirit of the "Community of Brethren" (*Brüdergemeinde*).

In those countries where Zinzendorf's followers became a separate denomination (e.g. Moravians in U.S.A.) their influence on the total religious scene has been much less impressive.

Our selection, taken from sermons which Zinzendorf preached during an extended stay in London in the 1740s, illustrates the ecumenical inclusiveness of the count which makes him a pioneer of the ecumenical movement that has come to flourish in the twentieth century.

The genuine Character of a Christian consists absolutely herein, that, when he speaks with our Saviour, when he speaks with his Brethren, when he has any thing to transact with God the Father, when he stands in need of the Ministry of the Angels, when he shall at the Day of the Lord present himself to hold the Judgment jointly with him, over Quick and Dead; that he absolutely does not appeal to his Religion, but to his Nature, to his Descent; for the most difficult Objection on this Day is, I know you not, whence you are.

This is that *Crinomenon,* which on that Day, and in all its Circumstances, will be decisive, whereupon all depends, that one is received, and the other cast away; our Saviour does, or does not call a Person to Mind. I will confess him, I will say, I know thee.

Therefore it is a Rule absolutely belonging to the Character of a true Christian, that properly he is neither Lutheran nor Calvinian, neither of this nor of the other Persuasion, nor even Christian itself. What can be said more plain and positive? What Reformer, be it Huss or Luther, or Wicklef, or whatever his Name may be, will be so presumptuous as to maintain, that Men are saved for this Reason, because they are his Followers, when Paul excludes Christ himself, when he says, "Not of Paul, not of Apollos, not of Caphas, not of Christ."

✧ ✧ ✧ ✧

There is no surer Way to divert Men from proceeding to find out in Him their Creator, than to describe our Saviour's Manhood as a superior Essence having some sort of Divine Qualities. No, the Man must remain Man: but then this ordinary Personage is (as you are obliged to look and ask farther) the God over all, who thus truly assumed our Nature. Hereat the Mind of Man starts; but when it approves itself to the Heart, Faith has taken Root for a whole Eternity.

The whole Doctrine of the New Testament is a Mystery, and to our short Reason, Foolishness: But yet there is one Method more suitable than another, to lead the Mind Step by Step into it. I am of Opinion, that in speaking to Heathens, one should at first not even mention any thing Divine, when one mentions the Saviour; but purely raise in them such a Kind of Tenderness towards him, as the Disciples had at the Beginning, when their Thoughts of Him were perhaps pretty much Socinian as yet. Were we to tell them directly, that God himself redeemed them with his Blood, (they have a Notion of God, without our demonstrating his Existence to them) it would not be the Way that would work best on Minds in their situation: But we must tell them, "You are bought with the Saviour's Blood," (as simply, as if they knew already the Necessity of a Redemption) and for some time hold Him and his Sufferings before them, till their Heart is drawn forth in Love and Gratitude to this Benefactor. Then, as People are apt to enquire, after falling in Love with a Person, (to use such a Comparison) what Family and Birth she is of? and are glad, if it proves to be noble: So, when they already are tenderly affected towards Him, who sacrificed his Life for the human Race, to recover them from their Misery and Condemnation, and make them happy Creatures; it will at last be quite seasonable, to give them the full Light of the first Chapter of St. John's Gospel. Accordingly we ask them, "Do you know, who that was and is?" Or perhaps rather, they will have asked of their own accord, How a mere Man could be able to effect such great Things, and redeem the whole World? Thereupon we tell them, "My dear Child! this is even such a Man who made all Mankind at the first, and built the Universe: It is that same Great Being or God, of whom thou hast often had some Perception." Then such a one rejoices indeed!

And thus indeed all Men who have grown up in Ignorance of his Greatness, are sure to become Worshippers of Christ as their God and Maker, the Moment they experience the Benefit of his Wounds. This has been verified in not a few Socinians, who were such by mere Education, and had not been Men of Study; nor indeed can these always be concluded Enemies to him, since they are often conscientious Observers of his Sayings. But Arianism in general (and learned Socinianism does not differ much) proves, that the Person has made Enquiry, found himself compelled by the Scripture to consider our Saviour as

God, but, by starting some Medium or other, will diminish as much as possible the Reality and Propriety of the Name.

As for us, our affectionate Attachment to Jesus must needs become known in the World: If He is not a true Saviour and God, in whom our All is wrapped up, we are of all Men the widest mistaken! this every one will think at the very Threshold, whether he enters into the Merits of the Cause or no. And then he must also think, "They are happy People however! For what is the Pleasure of gilded Palaces and all earthly State, to that of a Man, who can believe that his Maker is his Husband, and that He himself will wipe away all his Tears, anoint him with Oil of Gladness, vindicate his human Frame to Honour, and unite it in some near Manner with his own Divinity, as He once united himself to our Humanity!

XX JOHN WESLEY

The founder of the Methodist movement was born in Epworth, England, on June 17, 1703, and died in London on March 2, 1791. After studies at Oxford he was ordained in 1728 as a priest in the Church of England. Even at Oxford he had participated in study groups concerned not only with personal piety but social improvement which they expressed by visiting jails, caring for the poor and instructing underprivileged children. Contact with German Pietists (Salzburger Lutherans and Moravians) modified his theological heritage and influenced him in the development of his own theological position after his conversion experience at Aldersgate (May 24, 1738).

Wesley's ethics is characterized by an activistic emphasis on sanctification and Christian perfection. This impressed itself upon the Methodist movement and to some extent all Anglo-Saxon Christianity. Wesley's social teachings are a peculiar combination of political conservatism and social activism. He shares with other Pietists a tendency to seek individualistic solutions to social evils and to deal with the symptoms of prevailing evils rather than their causes. Nevertheless, his influence for change was great. Though Wesley was conservative to the core, his humanitarian interests made Methodism a far more radical force for social change than its founder had anticipated.

SELECTION I
The Use of Money

Wesley's life spanned the eighteenth century. It was an age of the industrial revolution and of great social dislocation. Some of the results of these changes are depicted by the artist William Hogarth, a contemporary of Wesley. Wesley's call to personal responsibility is expressed in his sermon on "The Use of Money."

"I say unto you, Make yourselves friends of the mammon of unrighteousness; that when ye fail, they may receive you into everlasting habitations." (Luke XVI, 9).

✧ ✧ ✧ ✧

An excellent branch of Christian wisdom is here inculcated by our Lord on all his followers, namely, The right use of money;—a subject largely spoken of, after their manner, by men of the world; but not sufficiently considered by those whom God hath chosen out of the world. These, generally, do not consider, as the importance of the subject requires, the use of this excellent talent. Neither do they understand how to employ it to the greatest advantage; the introduction of which into the world, is one admirable instance of the wise and gracious providence of God. It has, indeed, been the manner of poets, orators, and philosophers, in almost all ages and nations, to rail at this, as the grand corrupter of the world, the bane of virtue, the pest of human society. But is not all this mere empty rant? Is there any solid reason therein? By no means. For, let the world be as corrupt as it will, is gold or silver to blame? "The love of money," we know, "is the root of all evil;" but not the thing itself. The fault does not lie in the money, but in them that use it. It may be used ill: and what may not? But it may likewise be used well: it is full as applicable to the best, as to the worst uses. It is of unspeakable service to all civilized nations, in all the common affairs of life: it is a most compendious instrument of transacting all manner of business, and (if we use it according to Christian wisdom) of doing all manner of Good. It is true, were man in a state of innocence, or were all men "filled with the Holy Ghost," so that, like the infant church at Jerusalem, "no man counted any thing he had his own," but "distribution was made to every one as he had need," the use of it would be superseded; as we cannot conceive there is any thing of the kind among the inhabitants of heaven. But, in the present state of mankind, it is an excellent gift of God, answering the noblest ends. In the hands of his children, it is food for the hungry, drink for the thirsty, raiment for the naked: it gives to the traveller and the stranger where to lay his head. By it we may supply the place of a husband to the widow, and of a father to the fatherless. We may be a defence for the oppressed, a means of health to the sick, of ease to them that are in pain; it may be as eyes to the blind, as feet to the lame; yea, a lifter up from the gates of death!

It is, therefore, of the highest concern, that all who fear God, know how to employ this valuable talent; that they be instructed how it may answer these glorious ends, and in the highest degree. And, perhaps, all the instructions which are necessary for this, may be reduced to three plain rules, by the exact observance whereof we may approve ourselves faithful stewards of "the mammon of unrighteousness."

The first of these is, (he that heareth, let him understand!) "Gain all you can." Here we may speak like the children of the world: we meet them on their own ground. And it is our bounden duty to do this: we ought to gain all we can gain, without buying gold too dear, without paying more for it than it is worth. But this it is certain we ought not to do; we ought not to gain money at the expense of life, nor (which is in effect the same thing) at the expense of our health. Therefore, no gain whatsoever should induce us to enter into, or to continue in, any employ, which is of such a kind, or is attended with so hard or so long labour as to impair our constitution. Neither should we begin or continue in any business, which necessarily deprives us of proper seasons for food and sleep, in such a proportion as our nature requires. Indeed there is a great difference here. Some employments are absolutely and totally unhealthy; as those which imply the dealing much with arsenic, or other equally hurtful minerals, or the breathing an air tainted with steams of melting lead, which must at length destroy the firmest constitution. Others may not be absolutely unhealthy, but only to persons of a weak constitution. Such are those which require many hours spent in writing; especially if a person write sitting, and lean upon his stomach, or remain long in an uneasy posture. But whatever it is which reason or experience shows to be destructive of health or strength, that we may not submit to;

seeing "the life is more [valuable] than meat, and the body than raiment:" and, if we are already engaged in such an employ, we should exchange it, as soon as possible for some, which, if it lessen our gain, will, however, not lessen our health.

We are, secondly, to gain all we can without hurting our mind, any more than our body. For neither may we hurt this: we must preserve, at all events, the spirit of a healthful mind. Therefore, we may not engage or continue in any sinful trade; any that is contrary to the law of God, or of our country. Such are all that necessarily imply our robbing or defrauding the king of his lawful customs. For it is, at least, as sinful to defraud the king of his right, as to rob our fellow subjects: and the king has full as much right to his customs, as we have to our houses and apparel. Other businesses there are, which, however innocent in themselves, cannot be followed with innocence now; at least, not in England; such, for instance, as will not afford a competent maintenance, without cheating or lying, or conformity to some custom which is not consistent with a good conscience: these, likewise, are sacredly to be avoided, whatever gain they may be attended with provided we follow the custom of the trade; for, to gain money, we must not lose our souls. There are yet others which many pursue with perfect innocence, without hurting either their body or mind; and yet, perhaps, you cannot: either they may entangle you in that company which would destroy your soul; and by repeated experiments it may appear, that you cannot separate the one from the other; or there may be an idiosyncrasy,—a peculiarity in your constitution of soul, (as there is in the bodily constitution of many,) by reason whereof that employment is deadly to you, which another may sagely follow. So I am convinced, from many experiments, I could not study, to any degree of perfection, either mathematics, arithmetic, or algebra, without being a deist, if not an atheist: and yet others may study them all their lives, without sustaining any inconvenience. None, therefore, can here determine for another; but every man must judge for himself, and abstain from whatever he, in particular, finds to be hurtful to his soul.

We are, thirdly, to gain all we can, without hurting our neighbour. But this we cannot do, if we love our neighbour as ourselves. We cannot, if we love every one as ourselves, hurt any one *in his substance*. We cannot devour the increase of his lands, and perhaps the lands and houses themselves, by gaming, by over grown bills, (whether on account of physic, of law, or any thing else,) or by requiring or taking such interest, as even the laws of our country forbid. Hereby all pawnbroking is excluded: seeing whatever good we might do thereby, all unprejudiced men see with grief to be abundantly overbalanced by the evil. And if it were otherwise, yet we are not allowed to "do evil that good may come." We cannot, consistent with brotherly love, sell our goods below the market price; we cannot study to ruin our neighbour's trade, in order to advance our own; much less can we entice away, or receive, any of his servants or workmen whom he has need of. None can gain by swallowing up his neighbour's substance, without gaining the damnation of hell!

Neither may we gain by hurting our neighbour *in his body*. Therefore we may not sell any thing which tends to impair health. Such is, eminently, all that liquid fire, commonly called drams, or spirituous liquors. It is true, these may have a place in medicine; they may be of use in some bodily disorders; although there would rarely be occasion for them, were it not for the unskilfulness of the practitioner. Therefore such as prepare and sell them only for this end, may keep their conscience clear. But who are they? Who prepare them only for this end? Do you know ten such distillers in England? Then excuse these. But all who sell them in the common way, to any that will buy, are poisoners general. They murder his Majesty's subjects by wholesale, neither does their eye pity or spare. They drive them to hell like sheep: and what is their gain? Is it not the blood of these men?

✧ ✧ ✧ ✧

And are not they partakers of the same guilt, though in a lower degree, whether surgeons, apothecaries, or physicians, who play with the lives or health of men, to enlarge their own gain? Who purposely lengthen the pain or disease, which they are able to remove speedily? Who protract the cure of their patient's body, in order to plunder his substance? Can any man be clear before God, who does not shorten every disorder, "as much as he can," and remove all sickness and pain, "as soon as he can?" He cannot: for nothing can be more clear, than that he does not "do unto others, as he would they should do unto himself."

This is dear bought gain. And so is whatever is procured by hurting our neighbour *in his soul;* by ministering, suppose, either directly or indirectly, to his unchastity or intemperance; which certainly none can do, who has any fear of God, or any real desire of pleasing him. It nearly concerns all those to consider this, who have any thing to do with taverns, victualling houses, opera houses, play houses, or any other places of public, fashionable diversion. If these profit the souls of men, you are clear; your employment is good, and your gain innocent: but if they are either sinful in themselves, or natural inlets to sin of various kinds, then, it is to be feared, you have a sad account to make. Oh beware, lest God say in that day, "These have perished in their iniquity, but their blood do I require at thy hands!"

These cautions and restrictions being observed, it is the bounden duty of all, who are engaged in worldly business, to observe that first and great rule of Christian wisdom, with respect to money, "Gain all you can." Gain all you can by honest industry. Use all possible diligence in your calling. Lose no time. If you understand yourself, and your relation to God and man, you know you have none to spare. If you understand your particular calling, as you ought, you will have no time that hangs upon your hands. Every business will afford some employment sufficient for every day and every hour. That wherein you are placed, if you follow it in earnest, will leave you no leisure for silly, unprofitable diversions. You have always something better to do, something that will profit you, more or less. And "whatsoever thy hand findeth to do, do it with thy might."

✧ ✧ ✧ ✧

Gain all you can, by common sense, by using in your business all the understanding which God has given you. It is amazing to observe, how few do this; how men run on in the same dull track with their forefathers.

✧ ✧ ✧ ✧

Having gained all you can, by honest wisdom, and unwearied diligence, the second rule of Christian prudence is, "save all you can." Do not throw the precious talent into the sea: leave that folly to heathen philosophers. Do not throw it away in idle expenses, which is just the same as throwing it into the sea. Expend no part of it merely to gratify the desire of the flesh, the desire of the eye, or the pride of life.

Do not waste any part of so precious a talent, merely in gratifying the desires of the flesh; in procuring the pleasures of sense of whatever kind; particularly, in enlarging the pleasure of tasting. I do not mean, avoid gluttony and drunkenness only: an honest heathen would condemn these. But there is a regular, reputable kind of sensuality, an elegant epicurism, which does not immediately disorder the stomach, nor (sensibly at least) impair the understanding; and yet (to mention no other effects of it now) it cannot be maintained without considerable expense. Cut off all this expense! Despise delicacy and variety, and be content with what plain nature requires.

Do not waste any part of so precious a talent, merely in gratifying the desire of the eye, by superfluous or expensive apparel, or by needless ornaments. Waste no part of it in curiously adorning your houses; in superfluous or expensive furniture; in costly pictures, painting, gilding, books; in elegant rather than useful gardens. Let your neighbours, who know nothing better, do this: "Let the dead bury their dead." But "what is that to thee?" says our Lord: "Follow thou me." Are you willing? Then you are able so to do!

Lay out nothing to gratify the pride of life, to gain the admiration or praise of men. This motive of expense is frequently interwoven with one or both of the former. Men are expensive in diet, or apparel, or furniture, not barely to please their appetite, or to gratify their eye, or their imagination, but their vanity too. . . .

Who would expend any thing in gratifying these desires, if he considered, that to gratify them is to increase them. Nothing can be more certain than this: daily experience shows, the more they are indulged, they increase the more. Whenever, therefore, you expend any thing to please your taste or other senses, you pay so much for sensuality. When you lay out money to please your eye, you give so much for an increase of curiosity,—for a stronger attachment to these pleasures which perish in the using. While you are purchasing any thing which men use to applaud, you are purchasing more vanity. Had you not then enough of vanity, sensuality, curiosity, before? Was there need of any addition? And would you pay for it too? What manner of wisdom is this? Would not the literally throwing your money into the sea be a less mischievous folly?

And why should you throw away money upon your children, any more than upon yourself, in delicate food, in gay or costly apparel, in superfluities of any kind? Why should you purchase for them more pride or lust, more vanity, or foolish and hurtful desires? They do not want any more; they have enough already; nature has made ample provision for them; why should you be at farther expense to increase their temptations and snares, and to pierce them through with many sorrows?

Do not leave it to them to throw away. If you have good reason to believe they would waste what is now in your possession, in gratifying, and thereby increasing, the desire of the flesh, the desire of the eye, or the pride of life; at the peril of theirs and your own soul, do not set these traps in their way. Do not offer your sons or your daughters unto Belial, any more than unto Moloch.

"What then would you do if you were in my case? If you had a considerable fortune to leave?" Whether I *would* do it or no, I know what I *ought* to do: this will admit of no reasonable question. If I had one child, elder or younger, who knew the value of money, one who, I believed, would put it to the true use, I should think it my absolute indispensable duty, to leave that child the bulk of my fortune, and to the rest just so much as would enable them to live in the manner they had been accustomed to do. "But what if all your children were equally ignorant of the true use of money?" I ought then, (hard saying! who can hear it?) to give each what would keep him above want; and to bestow all the rest in such a manner as I judged would be most for the glory of God.

But let not any man imagine that he has done any thing, barely by going thus far, by "gaining and saving all he can," if he were to stop here. All this is nothing, if a man go not forward, if he does not point all this at a farther end. Nor, indeed, can a man properly be said to save any thing, if he only lays it up. You may as well throw your money into the sea, as bury it in the earth. And you may as well bury it in the earth, as in your chest, or in the bank of England. Not to use, is effectually to throw it away. If, therefore, you would indeed "make yourselves friends of the mammon of unrighteousness," add the third rule to the two preceding. Having first gained all you can, and secondly saved all you can, then "give all you can."

In order to see the ground and reason of this, consider, when the Possessor of heaven and earth brought you into being, and placed you in this world, he placed you here not as a proprietor, but a steward: as such he entrusted you for a season with goods of various kinds: but the sole property of these still rests in him, nor can ever be alienated from him. As you yourself are not your own, but his, such is, likewise, all that you enjoy. Such is your soul and your body, not your own, but God's. And so is your substance in particular. And he has told you in the most clear and express terms, how you are to employ it for him, in such a manner, that it may be all a holy sacrifice, acceptable through Christ Jesus. And this light, easy service, he hath promised to reward with an eternal weight of glory.

The directions which God has given us, touching the use of our worldly substance, may be comprised in the following particulars. If you desire to be a faithful and a wise steward, out of that portion of your Lord's goods, which he has for the present lodged in your hands, but with the right of resuming whenever it pleases him, first, provide things needful for yourself; food to eat, raiment to put on, whatever nature moderately requires for preserving the body in health and strength. Secondly, provide these for your wife, your children, your servants, or any others who pertain to your household. If, when this is done, there be an overplus left, then "do good to them that are of the household of faith." If there be an overplus still, "as you have opportunity, do good unto all men." In so doing, you give all you can; nay, in a sound sense, all you have: for all that is laid out in this manner, is really given to God. You "render unto God the things that are God's," not only by what you give to the poor, but also by that which you expend in providing things needful for yourself and your household.

If then a doubt should at any time arise in your mind concerning what you are going to expend, either on yourself or any part of your family, you have an easy way to remove it. Calmly and seriously inquire, 1. In expending this, am I acting according to my character? Am I acting herein, not as a proprietor, but as a steward of my Lord's goods? 2. Am I doing this in obedience to his word? In what scripture does he require me so to do? 3. Can I offer up this action, this expense, as a sacrifice to God through Jesus Christ? 4. Have I reason to believe, that for this very work I shall have a reward at the resurrection of the just? You will seldom need any thing more to remove any doubt which arises on this head; but, by this four fold consideration, you will receive clear light as to the way wherein you should go.

If any doubt still remain, you may farther examine yourself by prayer, according to those heads of inquiry. Try whether you can say to the Searcher of hearts, your conscience not condemning you, "Lord, thou seest I am going to expend this sum, on that food, apparel, furniture. And thou knowest, I act therein with a single eye, as a steward of thy goods, expending this portion of them thus, in pursuance of the design thou hadst in entrusting me with them. Thou knowest I do this in obedience to thy word, as thou commandest, and because thou commandest it. Let this, I beseech thee, be a holy sacrifice, acceptable through Jesus Christ! And give me a witness in myself, that for this labour of love, I shall have a recompense, when thou rewardest every man according to his works." Now if your conscience bear you witness in the Holy Ghost, that this prayer is well pleasing to God, then have you no reason to doubt, but that expense is right and good, and such as will never make you ashamed.

SELECTION 2
Thoughts on Slavery

In this eloquent pamphlet against slavery, Wesley first describes the conditions and life of the Africans, denying the claim that they are better off as slaves. They come from fertile lands which they administer justly. He then discusses the brutal manner of their capture and the demoralizing effect of the slave-trade on Africans and Europeans alike. Against the claim that all this is done "legally" he says:

The grand plea is, "They are authorized by law." But can law, human law, change the nature of things? Can it turn darkness into light, or evil into good? By no means. Notwithstanding ten thousand laws, right is right, and wrong is wrong still. There must still remain an essential difference between justice and injustice, cruelty and mercy. So that I still ask, Who can reconcile this treatment of the Negroes, first and last, with either mercy or justice?

Where is the justice of inflicting the severest evils on those that have done us no wrong? of depriving those that never injured us in word or deed, of every comfort of life? of tearing them from their native country, and depriving them of liberty itself, to which an Angolan has the same natural right as an Englishman, and on which he sets as high a value? Yea, where is the justice of taking away the lives of innocent, inoffensive men; murdering thousands of them in their own land, by the hands of their own countrymen; many thousands, year after year, on shipboard, and then casting them like dung into the sea; and tens of thousands in that cruel slavery to which they are so unjustly reduced?

But waiving, for the present, all other considerations, I strike at the root of this complicated villany, I absolutely deny all slave holding to be consistent with any degree of natural justice.

I cannot place this in a clearer light than that great ornament of his profession, Judge Blackstone, has already done.

That slave holding is utterly inconsistent with mercy, is almost too plain to need a proof. Indeed, it is said, "that these Negroes being prisoners of war, our captains and factors buy them, merely to save them from being put to death. And is not this mercy?" I answer, (1.) Did Sir John Hawkins, and many others, seize upon men, women, and children, who were at peace in their own fields or houses, merely to save them from death? (2.) Was it to save them from death, that they knocked out the brains of those they could not bring away? (3.) Who occasioned and fomented those wars, wherein those poor creatures were taken prisoners? Who excited them by money, by drink, by every possible means, to fall upon one another? Was it not themselves? They know in their own conscience it was, if they have any conscience left. But, (4.) To bring the matter to a short issue, can they say before God, that they ever took a single voyage, or bought a single Negro, from this motive? They cannot; they well know, to get money, not to save lives, was the whole and sole spring of their motions.

But if this manner of procuring and treating Negroes is not consistent either with mercy or justice, yet there is a plea for it which every man of business will acknowledge to be quite sufficient. Fifty years ago, one meeting an eminent statesman in the lobby of the house of commons, said, "You have been long talking about justice and equity. Pray which is this bill; equity or justice?" He answered very short and plain, "D—n justice; it is necessity." Here also the slave holder fixes his foot; here he rests the strength of his cause. "If it is not quite right, yet it must be so; there is an absolute necessity for it. It is necessary we should procure slaves; and when we have procured them, it is necessary to use them with severity, considering their stupidity, stubbornness, and wickedness."

I answer, you stumble at the threshold; I deny that villany is ever necessary. It is impossible that it should ever be necessary for any reasonable creature to violate all the laws of justice, mercy, and truth. No circumstances can make it necessary for a man to burst in sunder all the ties of humanity. It can never be necessary for a rational being to sink himself below a brute. A man can be under no necessity of degrading himself into a wolf. The absurdity of the supposition is so glaring, that one would wonder any one can help seeing it.

SELECTION 3

Thoughts on the Present Scarcity of Provision

Wesley's essay is an excellent example of his very deep social concern as well as his somewhat superficial analysis of economic conditions.

Many excellent things have been lately published concerning the present scarcity of provisions; and many causes have been assigned for it, by men of experience and reflection. But may it not be observed, there is something wanting still, in most of those publications? One writer assigns and insists on one cause, another on one or two more. But who assigns all the causes that manifestly concur to produce this melancholy effect? at the same time pointing out, how each particular cause affects the price of each particular sort of provision?

I would willingly offer to candid and benevolent men a few hints on this important subject; proposing a few questions, and subjoining to each what seems to be the plain and direct answer.

I ask, First, Why are thousands of people starving, perishing for want, in every part of the nation? The fact I know; I have seen it with my eyes, in every corner of the land. I have known those who could only afford to eat a little coarse food once every other day. I have known one in London (and one that a few years before had all the conveniences of life) picking up from a dunghill stinking sprats, and carrying them home for herself and her children. I have known another gathering the bones which the dogs had left in the streets, and making broth of them, to prolong a wretched life! I have heard a third artlessly declare, "Indeed I was very faint, and so weak I could hardly walk, until my dog, finding nothing at home, went out, and brought in a good sort of bone, which I took out of his mouth, and made a pure dinner!" Such is the case at this day of multitudes of people, in a land flowing as it were, with milk and honey! abounding with all the necessaries, the conveniences, the superfluities of life!

Now, why is this? Why have all these nothing to eat? Because they have nothing to do. The plain reason why they have no meat is because they have no work.

But why have they no work? Why are so many thousand people, in London, in Bristol, in Norwich, in every county, from one end of England to the other, utterly destitute of employment?

Because the persons that used to employ them cannot afford to do it any longer. Many that employed fifty men, now scarce employ ten; those that employed twenty now employ one, or none at all. They cannot, as they have no vent for their goods; food being so dear, that the generality of people are hardly able to buy any thing else.

But why is food so dear? To come to particulars: Why does bread corn bear so high a price? To set aside partial causes, (which indeed, all put together, are little more than the fly upon the chariot wheel,) the grand cause is, because such immense quantities of corn are continually consumed by distilling. Indeed, an eminent distiller near London, hearing this, warmly replied, "Nay, my partner and I generally distil but a thousand quarters a week." Perhaps so. And suppose five-and-twenty distillers, in and near the town, consume each only the same quantity: here are five-and-twenty thousand quarters a week, that is, above twelve hundred and fifty thousand a year, consumed in and about London! Add the distillers throughout England, and have we not reason to believe, that (not a thirtieth or a twentieth part only, but) little less than half the wheat produced in the kingdom is every year consumed, not by so harmless a way as throwing it into the sea, but by converting it into deadly poison; poison that naturally destroys not only the strength and life, but also the morals, of our countrymen?

It may be objected, "This cannot be. We know how much corn is distilled by the duty that is paid. And hereby it appears, that scarce three hundred thousand quarters a year are distilled throughout the kingdom." Do we know certainly, how much corn is distilled by the duty that is paid? Is it indisputable, that the full duty is paid for all the corn that is distilled? not to insist upon the multitude of private stills, which pay no duty at all. I have myself heard the servant of an eminent distiller occasionally aver, that for every gallon he distilled which paid duty, he distilled six which paid none. Yea, I have heard distillers themselves affirm, "We must do this, or we cannot live." It plainly follows, we cannot judge, from the duty that is paid, of the quantity of corn that is distilled.

"However, what is paid brings in a large revenue to the king." Is this an equivalent for the lives of his subjects? Would his majesty sell a hundred thousand of his subjects yearly to Algiers for four hundred thousand pounds? Surely no. Will he then sell them for that sum, to be butchered by their own countrymen? "But otherwise the swine for the navy cannot be fed." Not unless they are fed with human flesh! Not unless they are fatted with human blood! O, tell it not in Constantinople, that the English raise the royal revenue by selling the flesh and blood of their countrymen!

But why are oats so dear? Because there are four times as many horses kept (to speak within compass) for coaches and chaises in particular, as were a few years ago. Unless, therefore, four times the oats grew now that grew then, they cannot be at the same price. If only twice as much is produced, (which, perhaps, is near the truth,) the price will naturally be double to what it was.

And as the dearness of grain of one kind will always raise the price of another, so whatever causes the dearness of wheat and oats must raise the price of barley too. To account, therefore, for the dearness of this, we need only remember what has been observed above; although some particular causes may concur in producing the same effect.

Why are beef and mutton so dear? Because many considerable farmers, particularly in the northern counties, who used to breed large numbers of sheep, or horned cattle, and very frequently both, now breed none at all: they no longer trouble themselves with either sheep, or cows, or oxen; as they can turn their land to far better account by breeding horses alone. Such is the demand, not only for coach and chaise horses, which are bought and destroyed in incredible numbers, but much more for bred horses, which are yearly exported by hundreds, yea, thousands, to France.

But why are pork, poultry, and eggs so dear? Because of the monopolizing of farms; perhaps as mischievous a monopoly as was ever introduced into these kingdoms. The land which was some years ago divided between ten or twenty little farmers, and enabled them comfortably to provide for their families, is now generally engrossed by one great farmer. One farms an estate of a thousand a year, which formerly maintained ten or twenty. Every one of these little farmers kept a few swine, with some quantity of poultry; and, having little money, was glad to send his bacon, or pork, or fowls and eggs to market continually. Hence the markets were plentifully served; and plenty created cheapness. But at present, the great, the gentlemen farmers are above attending to these little things. They breed no poultry or swine, unless for their own use; consequently they send none to market. Hence it is not strange if two or three of these, living near a market town, occasion such a scarcity of these things, by preventing the former supply, that the price of them is double or treble to what it was before. Hence, (to instance in a small article,) in the same town wherein, within my memory, eggs were sold six or eight a penny, they are now sold six or eight a groat.

Another cause (the most terrible one of all, and the most destructive both of personal and social happiness) why not only beef, mutton, and pork, but all kinds of victuals, are so dear, is luxury. What can stand against this? Will it not waste and destroy all that nature and art can produce? If a person of quality will boil down three dozen of neats' tongues, to make two or three quarts of soup, (and so proportionably in other things,) what wonder that provisions fail? Only look into the kitchens of the great, the nobility and gentry, almost without exception; (considering withal, that "the toe of the peasant treads upon the heel of the courtier;") and when you have observed the amazing waste which is made there, you will no longer wonder at the scarcity, and consequently dearness, of the things which they use so much art to destroy.

But why is land so dear? Because on all these accounts, gentlemen cannot live as they have been accustomed to do without increasing their income; which most of them cannot do, but by raising their rents. And then the farmer, paying a higher rent for the land, must have a higher price for the produce of it. This again tends to raise the price of land; and so the wheel runs round.

But why is it, that not only provisions and land, but well nigh every thing else, is so dear? Because of the enormous taxes, which are laid on almost every thing that can be named. Not only abundant taxes are raised from earth, and fire, and water; but in England, the ingenious statesmen have found a way to lay a tax upon the very light! Yet one element remains: And surely some man of honour will find a way to tax this also. For how long shall the saucy air strike a gentleman on the face, nay, a lord, without paying for it?

But why are the taxes so high? Because of the national debt. They must be so while this continues. I have heard that the national expense, seventy years ago, was, in time of peace, three millions a year. And now the bare interest of the public debt amounts yearly to above four millions! to raise which, with the other stated expenses of government, those taxes are absolutely necessary.

To sum up the whole: Thousands of people throughout the land are perishing for want of food. This is owing to various causes; but above all, to distilling, taxes, and luxury.

Here is the evil, and the undeniable causes of it. But where is the remedy?

Perhaps it exceeds all the wisdom of man to tell: But it may not be amiss to offer a few hints on the subject.

What remedy is there for this sore evil,—many thousand poor people are starving? Find them work, and you will find them meat. They will then earn and eat their own bread.

But how can the masters give them work without ruining themselves? Procure vent for what is wrought, and the masters will give them as much work as they can do. And this would be done by sinking the price of provisions; for then people would have money to buy other things too.

But how can the price of wheat and barley be reduced? By prohibiting for ever, by making a full end of that bane of health, that destroyer of strength, of life, and of virtue,—distilling. Perhaps this alone might go a great way toward answering the whole design. It is not improbable, it would speedily sink the price of corn, at least one part in three. If any thing more were required, might not all starch be made of rice, and the importation of this, as well as of corn, be encouraged?

How can the price of oats be reduced? By reducing the number of horses. And may not this be effectually done, (without affecting the ploughman, the waggoner, or any of those who keep horses for common work,) (1.) By laying a tax of ten pounds on every horse exported to France, for which (notwithstanding an artful paragraph in a late public paper) there is as great a demand as ever? (2.) By laying an additional tax on gentlemen's carriages? Not so much on every wheel, (barefaced, shameless partiality!) but five pounds yearly upon every horse. And would not these two taxes alone supply near as much as is now paid for leave to poison his majesty's liege subjects?

How can the price of beef and mutton be reduced? By increasing the breed of sheep and horned cattle. And this would soon be increased seven-fold, if the price of horses was reduced; which it surely would be, half in half, by the method above mentioned.

How can the price of pork and poultry be reduced? Whether it ever will, is another question. But it can be done, (1.) By letting no farms of above a hundred pounds a year: (2.) By repressing luxury; whether by laws, by example, or by both. I had almost said by the grace of God; but to mention this has been long out of fashion.

How may the price of land be reduced? By all the methods above named, as each tends to lessen the expense of housekeeping: But especially the last; by restraining luxury, which is the grand and general source of want.

How may the taxes be reduced? (1.) By discharging half the national debt, and so saving, by this single means, above two millions a year. (2.) By abolishing all useless pensions, as fast as those who now enjoy them die: Especially those ridiculous ones given to some hundreds of idle men, as governors of forts or castles; which forts have answered no end for above these hundred years, unless to shelter jackdaws and crows. Might not good part of a million more be saved in this very article?

But will this ever be done? I fear not: At least, we have no reason to hope for it shortly; for what good can we expect (suppose the Scriptures are true) for such a nation as this, where there is no fear of God, where there is such a deep, avowed, thorough contempt of all religion, as I never saw, never heard or read of, in any other nation, whether Christian, Mohammedan, or Pagan? It seems as if God must shortly arise and maintain his own cause. But, if so, let us fall into the hands of God, and not into the hands of men.

XXI JONATHAN EDWARDS

Born at East-Windsor, Connecticut, in 1703, Jonathan Edwards became the most important American theologian and philosopher of the eighteenth century. He represents an orthodox Calvinism willing to use idealistic philosophy in its articulation of the faith. The intellectual power of his presentation helped to give him a dominant influence in the shaping of the American mind. As Professor Frankena has stated: "For over a hundred years the Edwardian ethics was stated and restated by such men as Samuel Hopkins, Joseph Bellamy, Timothy Dwight, N. W. Taylor, C. G. Finney, Mark Hopkins and J. H. Fairchild."[10]

For the social teachings of the Christian Church, Edwards' concern with the establishment of the Kingdom of God and his interest in Christian charity are of particular importance since they centrally affected the character of American Christianity. Edwards died in Princeton, New Jersey, on March 22, 1758, as a result of smallpox vaccination.

SELECTION I
Pressing into the Kingdom of God

No ethical concern has been more typically American than the establishment of the Kingdom of God. Edwards' contribution to this development is illustrated in this selection.

"The law and the prophets were until John: since that time the kingdom of God is preached, and every man presseth into it." (Luke 16, 16).

✧ ✧ ✧ ✧

The use I would make of this doctrine, is of *exhortation* to all Christless persons to press into the kingdom of God. Some of you are inquiring what you shall do? You seem to desire to know what is the way wherein salvation is to be sought, and how you may be likely to obtain it. You have now heard the way that the holy word of God directs to. Some are seeking, but it cannot be said of them that they are *pressing* into the kingdom of heaven. There are many that in time past have sought salvation, but not in this manner, and so they never obtained, but are now gone to hell. Some of them sought it year after year, but failed of it, and perished at last. They were overtaken with divine wrath, and are now suffering the fearful misery of damnation, and have no rest day nor night, having no more opportunity to seek, but must suffer and be miserable throughout the never-ending ages of eternity. Be exhorted, therefore, not to seek salvation as they did, but let the kingdom of heaven suffer violence from you.

Here I would first answer an *objection* or two, and then proceed to give some *directions* how to press into the kingdom of God.

Object. 1. Some may be ready to say, we cannot do this of ourselves; that strength of desire, and firmness of resolution, that have been spoken of, are out of our reach. If I endeavour to resolve and to seek with engagedness of spirit, I find I fail: my thoughts are presently off from the business, and I feel myself dull, and my engagedness relaxed in spite of all I can do.

Ans. 1. Though earnestness of mind be not immediately in your power, yet the consideration of what has been now said of the *need* of it, may be a means of stirring you up to it. It is true, persons never will be thoroughly engaged in this business, unless it be by God's influence; but God influences persons by means. Persons are not stirred up to a thorough earnestness without some considerations that move them to it. And if persons can but be made sensible of the necessity of salvation, and also duly consider the exceeding difficulty of it, and the greatness of the opposition, and how short and uncertain the time is, but yet are sensible that they have an opportunity, and that there is a possibility of their obtaining, they will need no more in order to their being thoroughly engaged and resolved in this matter. If we see persons slack and unresolved, and unsteady, it is because they do not enough consider these things.

2. Though strong desires and resolutions of mind be not in your power, yet painfulness of endeavours is in your power. It is in your power to take pains in the use of means, yea very great pains. You can be very painful and diligent in watching your own heart, and striving against sin. Though there is all manner of corruption in the heart continually ready to work, yet you can very laboriously watch and strive against these corruptions; and it is in your power with great diligence, to attend the matter of your duty towards God and towards your neighbour. It is in your power to attend all ordinances, and all public and private duties of religion, and to do it with your might. It would be a contradiction to suppose that a man cannot do these things with all the might he has, though he cannot do them with more might than he has. The dulness and deadness of the heart, and slothfulness of disposition, do not hinder men being able to take pains though it hinders their being willing. That is one thing wherein your laboriousness may appear, even striving against your own dulness. That men have a dead and sluggish heart, does not argue that they be not able to take pains; it is so far from that, that it gives occasion for pains. It is one of the difficulties in the way of duty, that persons have to strive with, and that gives occasion for struggling and labour. If there were no difficulties attending seeking salvation, there would be no occasion for striving; a man would have nothing to strive about. There is indeed a great deal of difficulty attending all duties required of those that would obtain heaven. It is an exceeding difficult thing for them to keep their thoughts; it is a difficult thing seriously, or to any good purpose, to consider matters of the greatest importance; it is a difficult thing to hear, or read, or pray attentively. But it does not argue that a man cannot strive in these things because they are difficult; nay, he could not strive therein if there were not difficulty in them. For what is there excepting difficulties that any can have to strive or struggle with in any affair or business? Earnestness of mind, and diligence of endeavour, tend to promote each other. He that has a heart earnestly engaged, will take pains; and he that is diligent and painful in all duty, probably will not be so

long before he finds the sensibleness of his heart and earnestness of his spirit greatly increased.

Object. 2. Some may object, that if they are earnest, and take a great deal of pains, they shall be in danger of trusting to what they do; they are afraid of doing their duty for fear of making a righteousness of it.

Ans. There is ordinarily no kind of seekers that trust so much to what they do, as slack and dull seekers. Though all seeking salvation, that have never been the subjects of a thorough humiliation, do trust in their own righteousness; yet some do it much more fully than others. Some, though they *trust* in their own righteousness, yet are not *quiet* in it. And those who are most disturbed in their self-confidence, (and therefore in the likeliest way to be wholly brought off from it,) are not such as go on in a remiss way of seeking, but such as are most earnest and thoroughly engaged; partly because in such a way conscience is kept more sensible. A more awakened conscience will not rest so quietly in moral and religious duties, as one that is less awakened. A dull seeker's conscience will be in a great measure satisfied and quieted with his own works and performances; but one that is thoroughly awakened cannot be stilled or pacified with such things as these. In this way persons gain much more knowledge of themselves, and acquaintance with their own hearts, than in a negligent slight way of seeking; for they have a great deal more experience of themselves. It is experience of ourselves, and finding what we are, that God commonly makes use of as the means of bringing us off from all dependence on ourselves. But men never get acquaintance with themselves so fast, as in the most earnest way of seeking. They that are in this way have more to engage them to think of their sins, and strictly to observe themselves, and have much more to do with their own hearts, than others. Such a one has much more experience of his own weakness, than another that does not put forth and try his strength; and will therefore sooner see himself dead in sin. Such a one, though he hath a disposition continually to be flying to his own righteousness, yet finds rest in nothing; he wanders about from one thing to another, seeking something to ease his disquieted conscience; he is driven from one refuge to another, goes from mountain to hill, seeking rest and finding none; and therefore will the sooner prove that there is no rest to be found, nor trust to be put in any creature whatsoever.

It is therefore quite a wrong notion that some entertain, that the more they do, the more they shall depend on it. Whereas the reverse is true; the more they do, or the more thorough they are in seeking, the less will they be likely to rest in their doings, and the sooner will they see the vanity of all that they do. So that persons will exceedingly miss it, if ever they neglect to do any duty either to God or man, whether it be any duty of religion, justice, or charity, under a notion of its exposing them to trust in their own righteousness. It is very true, that it is a common thing for persons, when they earnestly seek salvation, to trust in the pains that they take: but yet commonly those that go on in a more slight way, trust a great deal more securely to their dull services, than he that is pressing into the kingdom of God does to his earnestness. Men's slackness in religion, and their trust in their own righteousness, strengthen and establish one another.—Their trust in what they have done, and what they now do, settles them in a slothful rest and ease, and hinders their being sensible of their need of rousing up themselves and pressing forward. And on the other hand, their negligence tends so to benumb them, and keep them in such ignorance of themselves, that the most miserable refuges are stupidly rested in as sufficient. Therefore we see, that when persons have been going on for a long time in such a way, and God afterwards comes more thoroughly to awaken them, and to stir them up to be in good earnest, he shakes all their old foundations, and rouses them out of their old resting-places; so that they cannot quiet themselves with those things that formerly kept them secure.

I would now proceed to give some *directions* how you should press into the kingdom of God.

1. Be directed to sacrifice *every thing* to your soul's eternal interest. Let seeking this be so much your bent, and what you are so resolved in, that you will make every thing give place to it. Let nothing stand before your resolution of seeking the kingdom of God. Whatever it be that you used to look upon as a convenience, or comfort, or ease, or thing desirable on any account, if it stands in the way of this great concern, let it be

dismissed without hesitation; and if it be of that nature that it is likely always to be an hinderance, then wholly have done with it, and never entertain any expectation from it more. If in time past you have, for the sake of worldly gain, involved yourself in more care and business than you find to be consistent with your being so thorough in the business of religion as you ought to be, then get into some other way, though you suffer in your worldly interest by it. Or if you have heretofore been conversant with company that you have reason to think have been, and will be a snare to you, and an hinderance to this great design in any wise, break off from their society, however it may expose you to reproach from your old companions, or let what will be the effect of it. Whatever it be that stands in the way of your most advantageously seeking salvation—whether it be some dear sinful pleasure, or strong carnal appetite, or credit and honour, or the good-will of some persons whose friendship you desire, and whose esteem and liking you have highly valued—and though there be danger, if you do as you ought, that you shall be looked upon by them as odd and ridiculous, and become contemptible in their eyes—or if it be your ease and indolence, and aversion to continual labour, or your outward convenience in any respect, whereby you might avoid difficulties of one kind or other—*let all go;* offer up all such things together, as it were, in one sacrifice, to the interest of your soul. Let nothing stand in competition with this, but make every thing to fall before it. If the flesh must be crossed, then cross it, spare it not, crucify it, and do not be afraid of being too cruel to it. Gal. v. 24. "They that are Christ's have crucified the flesh, with the affections and lusts." Have no dependence on any worldly enjoyment whatsoever. Let salvation be the one thing with you.

2. Be directed to *forget the things that are behind;* that is, not to keep thinking and making much of what you have done, but let your mind be wholly intent on what you have to do. In some sense you ought to look back on your sins. Jer. ii. 23. "See thy way in the valley, know what thou hast done." You should look back on the wretchedness of your religious performances, and consider how you have fallen short of them; how exceedingly polluted all your duties have been, and how

justly God might reject and loathe them, and you for them. But you ought not to spend your time in looking back, as many persons do, thinking how much they have done for their salvation; what great pains they have taken, how that they have done what they can, and do not see how they can do more; how long a time they have been seeking, and how much more they have done than others, and even than such and such who have obtained mercy.

✧ ✧ ✧ ✧

Do not thus spend your time in looking on what is past, but look forward, and consider what is before you; consider what it is that you can do, and what it is necessary that you should do, and what God calls you still to do, in order to order your own salvation.

✧ ✧ ✧ ✧

3. Labour to get your *heart thoroughly disposed* to go on and hold out to the end. Many that seem to be earnest have not a heart thus disposed. It is a common thing for persons to appear greatly affected for a little while; but all is soon past away, and there is no more to be seen of it. Labour therefore to obtain a thorough willingness and preparation of spirit, to continue seeking, in the use of your utmost endeavours, without limitation; and do not think your whole life too long. And in order to this, be advised to two things.

1. Remember that if ever God bestows mercy upon you, he will use his sovereign pleasure about the *time when*. He will bestow it on some in a little time, and on others not till they have sought it long. If other persons are soon enlightened and comforted, while you remain long in darkness, there is no other way but for you to wait. God will act arbitrarily in this manner, and you cannot help it. You must even be content to wait, in a way of laborious and earnest striving, till his time comes. If you refuse, you will but undo yourself; and when you shall hereafter find yourself undone, and see that your case is past remedy, how will you condemn yourself for foregoing a great probability of salvation, only because you had not patience to

hold out, and was not willing to be at the trouble of a persevering labour? And what will it avail before God or your own conscience to say, that you could not bear to be obliged to seek salvation so long, when God bestowed it on others that sought it but for a very short time? Though God may have bestowed the testimonies of his favour on others in a few days or hours after they have begun earnestly to seek it, how does that alter the case as to you, if there proves to be a necessity of your laboriously seeking many years before you obtain them? Is salvation less worth taking a great deal of pains for, because, through the sovereign pleasure of God, others have obtained it with comparatively little pains?

✧ ✧ ✧ ✧

2. Endeavour now thoroughly to weigh in your mind the difficulty, and to *count the cost* of perseverance in seeking salvation. You that are now setting out in this business, (as there are many here who have very lately set about it—Praised be the name of God that he has stirred you up to it!) be exhorted to attend this direction. Do not undertake in this affair with any other thought, but of giving yourself wholly to it for the remaining part of your life, and going through many and great difficulties in it. Take heed that you do not engage secretly upon this condition, that you shall obtain in a little time, promising yourself that it shall be within this present season of the pouring out of God's Spirit, or with any other limitation of time whatsoever. Many, when they begin (seeming to set out very earnestly) do not expect that they shall need to seek very long, and so do not prepare themselves for it. And therefore, when they come to find it otherwise, and meet with unexpected difficulty, they are found unguarded, and easily overthrown. But let me advise you all who are now seeking salvation, not to entertain any self-flattering thoughts; but weigh the utmost difficulties of perseverance, and be provided for them, having your mind fixed in it to go through them, let them be what they will. Consider now beforehand, how tedious it would be, with utmost earnestness and labour, to strive after salvation for many years, in the meantime receiving no joyful or comfortable evidence of your having obtained. Consider what a great temp-

tation to discouragement there probably would be in it; how apt you would be to yield the case; how ready to think that it is vain for you to seek any longer, and that God never intends to shew you mercy, in that he has not yet done it; how apt you would be to think with yourself, "What an uncomfortable life do I live! how much more unpleasantly do I spend my time than others that do not perplex their minds about the things of another world, but are at ease, and take the comfort of their worldly enjoyments!" Consider what a temptation there would probably be in it, if you saw others brought in that began to seek the kingdom of heaven long after you, rejoicing in a hope and sense of God's favour, after but little pains and a short time of awakening; while you, from day to day, and from year to year, seemed to labour in vain. Prepare for such temptations now. Lay in beforehand for such trials and difficulties, that you may not think any strange thing has happened when they come.

I hope that those who have given attention to what has been said, have by this time conceived, in some measure, what is signified by the expression in the text, and after what manner they ought to press into the kingdom of God. Here is this to induce you to a compliance with what you have been directed to; if you sit still, you die; if you go backward, behold you shall surely die; if you go forward, you may live. And though God has not bound himself to any thing that a person does while destitute of faith, and out of Christ, yet there is great probability, that in a way of hearkening to this counsel you will live; and that by pressing onward, and persevering, you will at last, as it were by violence, take the kingdom of heaven. Those of you who have not only heard the directions given, but shall, through God's merciful assistance, practise according to them, are those that probably will overcome. These we may well hope at last to see standing with the Lamb on Mount Sion, clothed in white robes, with palms in their hands; when all your labour and toil will be abundantly compensated, and you will not repent that you have taken so much pains, and denied yourself so much, and waited so long. This self-denial, this waiting, will then look little, and vanish into nothing in your eyes, being all swallowed up in the first minute's enjoyment of that glory that you will then possess, and will uninterruptedly possess and enjoy to all eternity.

SELECTION 2
Obligations to Charity

Edwards claimed "that it is the absolute and indispensable duty of the people of God to give bountifully and willingly for supplying the wants of the needy." This aspect of the Christian life which undergirds concern with "good works" so prevalent in America is eloquently described in the following selection:

Of the Obligation of Christians to perform the duty of Charity to the poor.

This duty is absolutely commanded, and much insisted on in the word of God. Where have we any command in the Bible laid down in stronger terms, and in a more peremptory urgent manner, than the command of giving to the poor? We have the same law in a positive manner laid down in Levit. xxv. 35 &c. "And if thy brother be waxen poor, and fallen in decay with thee, then thou shalt relieve him; yea, though he be a stranger or a sojourner, that he may live with thee." And at the conclusion of ver. 38, God enforces it with saying, *I am the Lord thy God.*

It is mentioned in scripture, not only as a duty, but a great duty. Indeed it is generally acknowledged to be a duty, to be kind to the needy; but by many it seems not to be looked upon as a duty of great importance. However it is mentioned in scripture as one of the greater and more essential duties of religion: Micah vi. 8. "He hath showed thee, O man, what is good; and what doth the Lord thy God require of thee, but to do justly, *to love mercy*, and to walk humbly with thy God?" Here *to love mercy* is mentioned as one of the three great things that are the sum of all religion. So it is mentioned by the Apostle James, as one of the two things wherein pure and undefiled religion consists: James i. 27. "Pure religion, and undefiled, before God and the Father, is this, To visit the fatherless and widows in their affliction, and to keep himself unspotted from the world."

So Christ tells us, it is one of the weightier matters of the law: Matth. xxii. 23. "Ye have omitted the weightier matters of the law, judgment, mercy, and faith." The scriptures again and again teach us, that it is a more weighty and essential thing than the attendance on the outward ordinances of worship: Hos. vi. 6. "I desired mercy, and not sacrifice;" Matth. ix. 13 and xii. 7. I know of scarce any duty which is so much insisted on, so pressed and urged upon us, both in the Old Testament and New, as this duty of charity to the poor.

The reason of the thing strongly obliges to it. It is not only very positively and frequently insisted on by God, but it is most reasonable in itself; and so, on this account, there is reason why God should much insist upon it.

1. It is most reasonable, considering the general state and nature of mankind. This is such as renders it most reasonable that we should love our neighbour as ourselves; for men are made in the image of our God, and on this account are worthy of our love. Besides, we are all nearly allied one to another by nature. We have all the same nature, like faculties, like dispositions, like desires of good, like needs, like aversion to misery, and are made of one blood; and we are made to subsist by society and union one with another. God hath made us with such a nature, that we cannot subsist without the help of one another. Mankind in this respect are as the members of the natural body, one cannot subsist alone, without an union with, and the help of the rest.

Now, this state of mankind shows how reasonable and suitable it is, that men should love their neighbours; and that we should not look every one at his own things, but every man also at the things of others, Phil. ii. 4. A selfish spirit is very unsuitable to the nature and state of mankind. He who is all for himself, and none for his neighbours, deserves to be cut off from the benefit of human society, and to be turned out among wild beasts, to subsist by himself as well as he can. A private niggardly spirit is more suitable for wolves, and other beasts of prey, than for human beings.

To love our neighbour as ourselves, is the sum of the moral

law respecting our fellow-creatures; and to help them, and to contribute to their relief, is the most natural expression of this love. It is vain to pretend to a spirit of love to our neighbours, when it is grievous to us to part with any thing for their help, when under calamity. They who love only in word, and in tongue, and not in deed, have no love in truth. Any profession without it is a vain pretence. To refuse to give to the needy, is unreasonable, because we therein do to others contrary to what we would have others to do to us in like circumstances. We are very sensible of our own calamities; and when we suffer, are ready enough to think, that our state requires the compassion and help of others; and are ready enough to think it hard, if others will not deny themselves in order to help us when in straits.

2. It is especially reasonable, considering our circumstances, under such a dispensation of grace as that of the gospel. Consider how much God hath done for us, how greatly he hath loved us, what he hath given us, when we were so unworthy, and when he could have no addition to his happiness by us. Consider that silver, and gold, and earthly crowns, were in his esteem but mean things to give us, and he hath therefore given us his own Son. Christ loved and pitied us, when we were poor, and he laid out himself to help, and even did shed his own blood for us without grudging. He did not think much to deny himself, and to be at great cost for us vile wretches, in order to make us rich, and to clothe us with kingly robes, when we were naked; to feast us at his own table with dainties infinitely costly, when we were starving; to advance us from the dunghill, and set us among princes, and make us to inherit the throne of his glory, and so to give us the enjoyment of the greatest wealth and plenty to all eternity; agreeably to 2 Cor. viii. 9. "For ye know the grace of our Lord Jesus Christ, that though he was rich, yet for your sakes he became poor, that ye through his poverty might be rich." Considering all those things, what a poor business will it be, that those who hope to share these benefits, yet cannot give something for the relief of a poor neighbour without grudging! that it should grieve them to part with a small matter, to help a fellow-servant in calamity, when Christ did not grudge to shed his holy blood for them!

How unsuitable is it for us, who live only by kindness, to be unkind! What would have become of us, if Christ had been so saving of his blood, and loth to bestow it, as many men are of their money or goods? or if he had been as ready to excuse himself from dying for us, as men commonly object to performing deeds of charity to their neighbour, he would have found enough of them.

Besides, Christ, by his redemption, has brought us into a more near relation one to another, hath made us children of God, children in the same family. We are all brethren, having God for our common Father; which is much more than to be brethren in any other family. He hath made us all one body; therefore we ought to be united, and subserve one another's good, and bear one another's burdens, as is the case with the members of the same natural body. If one of the members suffer, all the other members bear the burden with it, 1 Cor. xii. 26. If one member be diseased or wounded, the other members of the body will minister to it, and help it. So surely it should be in the body of Christ: Gal. vi. 2. "Bear ye one another's burdens, and so fulfil the law of Christ."

Apply these things to yourselves; and inquire, whether you do not lie under guilt on account of the neglect of this duty, in withholding that charity which God requires of you towards the needy? You have often been put upon examining yourselves, whether you do not live in some way displeasing to God. Perhaps at such times it never came into your minds, whether you did not lie under guilt on this account.—But this neglect certainly brings guilt upon the soul in the sight of God, as is evident by the text: "Beware that thine eye be not evil against thy poor brother, and thou givest him nought, and he cry unto the Lord against thee, and it be sin unto thee," ver. 9. This is often mentioned as one of the sins of Judah and Jerusalem, for which God was about to bring such terrible judgments upon them; and it was one of the sins of Sodom, for which that city was destroyed, that she did not give to supply the poor and needy, Ezek. xvi. 49. "This was the iniquity of thy sister Sodom, pride, fulness of bread, and abundance of idleness in her, and in her daughters; neither did she strengthen the hand of the poor and needy."

And have we not reason to fear, that much guilt lies upon this land on this very account? We have a high conceit of ourselves for religion: but do not many other countries shame us? Do not the Papists shame us in this respect? So far as I can understand the tenor of the Christian religion, and the rules of the word of God, the same are in no measure in this respect answered by the general practice of most people in this land. There are many who make a high profession of religion; but do not many of them need to be informed by the Apostle James, what true religion is?

Let every one examine himself, whether he do not lie under guilt in this matter. Have you not forborn to give, when you have seen your brother in want? Have you not shut up the bowels of your compassion towards him, and forborn to deny yourselves a little for his relief? Or when you have given, have you not done it grudgingly? And has it not inwardly hurt and grieved you? You have looked upon what you have given, as lost: So that what you have given, has been, as the apostle expresses it, a matter of covetousness, rather than of bounty. Have not occasions of giving been unwelcome to you? Have you not been uneasy under them? Have you not felt a considerable backwardness to give? Have you not, from a grudging, backward spirit, been apt to raise objections against giving, and to excuse yourselves? Such things as these bring guilt upon the soul, and often bring down the curse of God upon the persons in whom these things are found, as we may show more fully hereafter.

XXII ROMANTICISM

The theology of the nineteenth century is deeply influenced by the spirit of Romanticism, a revolt against the rationalism of the Enlightenment. When reason proved a feeble tool in man's effort to reach beyond himself, when Kant had demonstrated the human imprisonment in the world of phenomena, Romanticism enabled man again to make contact with the ultimate by looking into the depth of his being. In its understanding of Christianity, romanticism emphasizes the mystery of faith, the "feeling of absolute dependence" (Schleiermacher).

Belief in divine immanence and the dynamism of nature made the Romantics conservative in their respect for the laws of nature and critical of an industrial modernity that seemed insensitive to the mysterious character of life. In social ethics they demanded a recovery of the values of the past as well as the realization of the organic character of life and God's support for existence in all its manifold forms. Their influence on Schleiermacher, who was by all odds the most important theologian of the nineteenth century, resulted in a romantic element in the character of later Protestant theology.

SELECTION I
Herder: *God, Some Conversations*

Johann Gottfried Herder (1744–1803), student of Kant and Hamann, studied theology and philosophy and made the insights of the previous philosophical generation fruitful for later theology. In the following selection, the influence of Spinoza is pronounced:

I. The highest Existence knew of nothing higher than existence to give His creatures.

II. The Deity in whom there is but one essential force which we call power, wisdom and goodness could produce nothing else than a living impression of the same, which is itself therefore, power, wisdom and goodness, and which must inseparably form the essence of every existence appearing in the world.

III. All the forces of nature function organically. Every organization is nothing else than a system of living forces, which serve a principal force in accordance with eternal laws of wisdom, goodness and beauty.

IV. The laws according to which the one rules and the others serve, are: Inherent persistence of every being; union of likes and separation of opposites; finally, assimilation to self and reproduction of one's nature in another. They are activities through which the Deity has revealed Himself, and no other, nor higher ones are conceivable.

V. There is no death in creation, but metamorphosis. Metamorphosis in accordance with the wisest, best law of necessity by which every force in the realm of change seeks to maintain itself ever-new and ever-active, and thus through attraction and repulsion, through friendship and enmity, incessantly changes its organic garb.

VI. There is no rest in creation, for an inactive rest would be death. Every living force is active and continues active. Thus, with every continuation of activity, it progresses and perfects itself according to inner eternal laws of wisdom and goodness, which are urged upon it and inherent in it.

VII. The more it augments itself, the more it works upon others, enlarges its limits, organizes and impresses them with the image of the goodness and beauty that dwells in it. Thus in the whole of nature one necessary law rules, to the effect that order emerges from chaos, that active forces emerge from dormant capacities. The activity of this law is not to be restrained.

VIII. Thus nothing evil which could have reality exists in the realm of God. All that is evil is a nonentity. But we call evil that which is limitation, or opposition, or transition, and none of the three deserves this name. Theophron, I thirst to discuss this point with you. I have in mind a Theodicy of wise necessity.

IX. But, as limits appertain to the measure of every existence in space and time, and, as in the realm of God where everything exists, opposites must also exist, so it appertains to the highest goodness of this realm that opposites themselves help and need each other; because only through the union of the two does a world come into being in every substance, that is to say, an existing, whole being, complete in goodness as well as in beauty.

X. The errors of men also are good to an intelligent mind, for they must soon show themselves as errors to him, and thus help him, by way of contrast, to more light, to purer goodness and truth. Nor is this all arbitrary, but according to eternal laws of reason, order and goodness.

SELECTION 2
Schleiermacher: *On Religion*

Friedrich Schleiermacher (1768–1834) was deeply touched by Romanticism in his early years. This influence is still very strong in his sermons, *On Religion, Speeches to Its Cultured Despisers*. It is somewhat ironic that Schleiermacher, who contributed so much to the "Prussian Union," the combination of Lutherans and Reformed into one ecclesiastical organization under the dominion of the Prussian state, expressed deep misgivings about any state-church in this early work. Addressing the "cultured despisers" he wrote:

Listen to what may possibly seem an unholy wish that I can hardly suppress. Would that the most distant presentiment of religion had forever remained unknown to all heads of states, to all successful and skilful politicians! Would that not one of them had ever been seized by the power of that infectious enthusiasm! The source of all corruption has been, that they did not know how to separate their deepest, most personal life from their office and public character. Why must they bring their petty vanity and marvellous presumption into the assembly of the saints, as if the advantages they have to give were valid everywhere without exception? Why must they take back with them into their palaces and judgment-halls the reverence due to the servants of the sanctuary? Probably you are right in wishing that the hem of a priestly garment had never touched the floor of a royal chamber: but let us wish that the purple had never kissed the dust on the altar, for had this not happened the other would not have followed. Had but no prince ever been allowed to enter the temple, till he had put off at the gate the most beautiful of his royal ornaments, the rich cornucopia of all his favours and tokens of honour! But they have employed it here as elsewhere. They have presumed to decorate the simple grandeur of the heavenly structure with rags from their earthly splendour, and instead of fulfilling holy vows, they have left worldly gifts as offerings to the Highest.

As soon as a prince declared a church to be a community with special privileges, a distinguished member of the civil world, the corruption of that church was begun and almost irrevocably decided. And if the society of believing persons, and of persons desiring belief, had not been mixed after a wrong manner, that is always to the detriment of the former, this could not have happened, for otherwise no religious society could ever be large enough to draw the attention of the governor.

Such a constitutional act of political preponderance works on the religious society like the terrible head of Medusa. As soon as it appears everything turns to stone—though without connection, everything that is for a moment combined, is now inseparably welded together; accidental elements that might easily have been ejected are now established for ever; drapery and body are made from one block and every unseemly fold is eternal. The greater and spurious society can no more be separated from the higher and smaller. It can neither be divided nor dissolved. It can neither alter its form nor its articles of faith. Its views and usages are all condemned to abide in their existing state.

But that is not all. The members of the true church the visible church may contain, are forcibly excluded from all share in its government, and are not in a position to do for it even the little that might still be done. There is more to govern than they either could or would do. There are worldly things now to order and manage, and privileges to maintain and make good. And even though in their domestic and civil affairs, they did know how to deal with such things, yet they cannot treat matters of this sort as a concern of their priestly office. That is an incongruity that their sense will not see into and to which they cannot reconcile themselves. It does not accord with their high and pure idea of religion and religious fellowship. They cannot understand what they are to make out of houses and lands and riches, either for the true church to which they belong, or for the larger society which they should conduct. By this unnatural state of affairs the members of the true church are distracted and perplexed.

But besides all this, persons are attracted who otherwise would for ever have remained without. If it is the interest of the proud, the ambitious, the covetous, the intriguing to press into the church, where otherwise they would have felt only the bitterest ennui, and if they begin to pretend interest and intelligence in holy things to gain the earthly reward, how can the truly religious escape subjection? And who bears the blame if unworthy men replace ripe saints, and if, under their supervision, everything creeps in and establishes itself that is most contrary to the spirit of religion? Who but the state with its ill-considered magnanimity?

But in a still more direct way, the state is the cause why the bond between the true church and the visible religious society has been loosened. After showing to the church this fatal kindness, it believed it had a right to its active gratitude, and transferred to it three of its weightiest commissions. More or less it has committed to the church the care and oversight of education. Under the auspices of religion and in the form of a congregation, it demands that the people be instructed in those duties that cannot be set forth in the form of law, that they be stirred up to a truly citizenlike way of thinking, and that, by the power of religion, they be made truthful in their utterances. As a recompense for those services, it robs it of its freedom, as is now to be seen in all parts of the civilized world where there is a state and a church. It treats the church as an institution of its own appointment and invention—and indeed its faults and abuses are almost all its own inventing; and it alone presumes to decide who is fit to come forward in this society as exemplar and as priest. And do you still charge it to religion that the visible church does not consist entirely of pious souls?

SELECTION 3
Chateaubriand: *The Genius of Christianity*

Francois August René de Chateaubriand (1768–1848) produced in his *The Genius of Christianity* a grandly conceived and comprehensive apology for the Christian religion in its Roman Catholic form. Appealing to the imagination in true romantic fashion, he attributed to Christianity all the advances of mankind. The following selection is from the summary chapter of the work.

GENERAL RECAPITULATION

It is not without a certain degree of fear that we approach the conclusion of our work. The serious reflections which induced us to undertake it, the hazardous ambition which has led us to decide, as far as lay in our power, the question respecting Christianity,—all these considerations alarm us. It is difficult to discover how far it is pleasing to the Almighty that men should presume to take into their feeble hands the vindication of his eternity, should make themselves advocates of the Creator at the tribunal of the creature, and attempt to defend by human arguments those counsels which gave birth to the universe. Not without extreme diffidence, therefore, convinced as we are of the incompetency of our talents, do we here present the general recapitulation of this work.

Every religion has its mysteries. All nature is a secret.

The Christian mysteries are the most sublime that can be; they are the archetypes of the system of man and of the world.

The sacraments are moral laws, and present pictures of a highly poetical character.

Faith is a force, charity a love, hope complete happiness, or, as religion expresses it, a complete virtue.

The laws of God constitute the most perfect code of natural justice.

The fall of our first parents is a universal tradition.

A new proof of it may be found in the constitution of the moral man, which is contrary to the general constitution of beings.

The prohibition to touch the fruit of knowledge was a sublime command, and the only one worthy of the Almighty.

All the arguments which pretend to demonstrate the antiquity of the earth may be contested.

The doctrine of the existence of a God is demonstrated by the wonder of the universe. A design of Providence is evident in the instincts of animals and in the beauty of nature.

Morality of itself proves the immortality of the soul. Man feels a desire of happiness, and is the only creature who cannot attain it; there is consequently a felicity beyond the present life; for we cannot wish for what does not exist.

The system of atheism is founded solely on exceptions. It is not the body that acts upon the soul, but the soul that acts upon the body. Man is not subject to the general laws of matter; he diminishes where the animal increases.

Atheism can benefit no class of people:—neither the unfortunate, whom it bereaves of hope, nor the prosperous, whose joys it renders insipid, nor the soldier, of whom it makes a coward, nor the woman, whose beauty and sensibility it mars, nor the mother who has a son to lose, nor the rulers of men, who have no surer pledge of the fidelity of their subjects than religion.

The punishments and rewards which Christianity holds out in another life are consistent with reason and the nature of the soul.

In literature, characters appear more interesting and the passions more energetic under the Christian dispensation than they were under polytheism. The latter exhibited no dramatic feature, no struggles between natural desire and virtue.

Mythology contracted nature, and for this reason the ancients had no descriptive poetry. Christianity restores to the wilderness both its pictures and its solitudes.

The Christian marvellous may sustain a comparison with the marvellous of fable. Then ancients founded their poetry on

Homer, while the Christians found theirs on the Bible: and the beauties of the Bible surpass the beauties of Homer.

To Christianity the fine arts owe their revival and their perfection.

In philosophy it is not hostile to any natural truth. If it has sometimes opposed the sciences, it followed the spirit of the age and the opinions of the greatest legislators of antiquity.

In history we should have been inferior to the ancients but for the new character of images, reflections, and thoughts, to which Christianity has given birth. Modern eloquence furnishes the same observation.

The relics of the fine arts, the solitude of monasteries, the charms of ruins, the pleasing superstitions of the common people, the harmonies of the heart, religion, and the desert, lead to the examination of the Christian worship.

This worship everywhere exhibits a union of pomp and majesty with a moral design and with a prayer either affecting or sublime. Religion gives life and animation to the sepulchre. From the laborer who reposes in a rural cemetery to the king who is interred at St. Dennis, the grave of the Christian is full of poetry. Job and David, reclining upon the Christian tomb, sing in their turn the sleep of death by which man awakes to eternity.

We have seen how much the world is indebted to the clergy and to the institutions and spirit of Christianity. If Schoonbeck, Bonnani, Giustiniani, and Helyot, had followed a better order in their laborious researches, we might have presented here a complete catalogue of the services rendered by religion to humanity. We would have commenced with a list of all the calamities incident to the soul or the body of man, and mentioned under each affliction the Christian order devoted to its relief. It is no exaggeration to assert that, whatever distress or suffering we may think of, religion has, in all probability, anticipated us and provided a remedy for it. From as accurate a calculation as we were able to make, we have obtained the following results:—

There are computed to be on the surface of Christian Europe about four thousand three hundred towns and villages. Of these four thousand three hundred towns and villages, three thousand two hundred and ninety-four are of the first, second, third, and fourth rank. Allowing one hospital to each of these three thousand two hundred and ninety-four places, (which is far below the truth,) you will have three thousand two hundred and ninety-four hospitals, almost all founded by the spirit of Christianity, endowed by the Church, and attended by religious orders. Supposing that, upon an average, each of these hospitals contains one hundred beds, or, if you please, fifty beds for two patients each, you will find that religion, exclusively of the immense number of poor which she supports, has afforded daily relief and subsistence for more than a thousand years to about three hundred and twenty-nine thousand four hundred persons.

On summing up the colleges and universities, we find nearly the same results; and we may safely assert that they afford instruction to at least three hundred thousand youths in the different states of Europe.

In this statement we have not included either the Christian hospitals and colleges in the other three quarters of the globe, or the female youth educated by nuns.

To these results must be added the catalogue of the celebrated men produced by the Church, who form nearly two-thirds of the distinguished characters of modern times. We must repeat, as we have shown, that to the Church we owe the revival of the arts and sciences and of letters; that to her are due most of the great modern discoveries, as gunpowder, clocks, the mariner's compass, and, in government, the representative system; that agriculture and commerce, the laws and political science, are under innumerable obligations to her; that her missions introduced the arts and sciences among civilized nations and laws among savage tribes; that her institution of chivalry powerfully contributed to save Europe from an invasion of new barbarians; that to her mankind is indebted for

The worship of one only God;

The more firm establishment of the belief in the existence of that Supreme Being;

A clearer idea of the immortality of the soul, and also of a future state of rewards and punishments;

A more enlarged and active humanity;

A perfect virtue, which alone is equivalent to all the others—Charity.

A political law and the law of nations, unknown to the ancients, and, above all, the abolition of slavery.

Who is there but must be convinced of the beauty and the grandeur of Christianity? Who but must be overwhelmed with this stupendous mass of benefits?

XXIII THE AMERICAN DEVELOPMENT IN THE NINETEENTH CENTURY

The nineteenth century saw America begin to take its place among the major nations of the world. After abandoning the theocracy of the Puritan establishment even in New England, the place of Christian social teaching became problematical. The fears of religious leaders were expressed by men like Horace Bushnell. A more unbiased and detached opinion came from Alexis de Tocqueville. A most subtle expression of the nonclerical yet profoundly Christian character of American social teaching was submitted by Abraham Lincoln. An entirely different, yet no less influential, aspect of the American development is the proclamation of the Gospel of Wealth by the churches as illustrated by the writings of Bishop Lawrence, who claimed that "godliness is in league with riches."

SELECTION I
Horace Bushnell: *Politics Under the Law of God*

Horace Bushnell, 1802–1876, pastor in Hartford, Connecticut, was an influential American theologian (for example, his book *Christian Nurture*) who emphasized the importance of religious experience for theology. Our selection is from his *Politics Under the Law of God.*

We have taken up, in this country, almost universally, theories of government which totally forbid the entrance of moral considerations. Government, we think, is a social compact or agreement—a mere human creation, having as little connection with God, as little of a moral quality, as a ship of war or a public road. We do not say that government, when exerted and fashioned by man, in whatever manner, is forthwith taken by God to be his instrument and ordinance—that it is molded below and authorized or clothed with authority from above—giving thus to law a moral force, and to the civil constitution the prerogatives of a settled or established order. Rejecting such views of government, or never learning to conceive them, it results that law expresses nothing but human will, and that no one is *morally* bound by it. If he chooses to break it and take the penalty, or if he can shun the penalty by concealment, he is guilty of no moral wrong. It also results that a majority may at any time, and in any way, rise up to change the fundamental compact; for there is no such thing as an established order of the past, endued with a moral authority to bind their actions and determine their legitimate functions. The nefarious doctrine advanced to justify the Rhode Island rebellion, is, I grieve to say, nothing but the shallow theory of government generally prevalent in this country, *carried out* to its legitimate conclusions.[11] Holding such views of government, it would be wonderful if we did not separate its functions practically from God, as far as we separate them in theory. If our nature were not wiser than our philosophy, we could never feel one sentiment of moral obligation in regard to our duties as citizens. There would be no crevice left through which a sense of public virtue could leak into our minds. That the views of which I complain are atheistical in their origin, is a well known fact of history, and they show the fact in their face. That they have operated powerfully to effect the disastrous separation of politics from the constraints of duty and responsibility to God, is too evident.

The neglect of the pulpit to assert the dominion of moral principles over what we do as citizens, has hastened and aggravated the evil I complain of. The false notion has taken possession extensively of the public mind, and received the practical assent, too generally, of the ministers of religion themselves, that they must not meddle with politics. Nothing is made of the obvious distinction between the *moral principles* of politics and those questions of election and of State policy which are to be decided by no moral tests. It is the solemn duty of the ministers of religion to make their people feel the presence of God's law every where—and especially here, where so many of the dearest interests of life—nay, the interests of virtue and religion are themselves at stake. This is the manner of the Bible. There is no one subject on which it is more full and abundant than it is in reference to the moral duty of rulers and citizens. Command, reproof, warning, denunciation—every instrument is applied to keep them under a sense of obligation to God. Some of the ministers of religion, I am afraid, want the courage to discharge their whole duty in this matter. Their position between two fiery and impetuous torrents of party feeling, is often one, I know, of great weakness, and they need to consider, when they put on their armor, whether they can meet one that cometh against them with twenty thousand. But it cannot be necessary that the duties of the ministry in this field, should be totally neglected, as they have been in many places hitherto, or if it be, we may well despair of our country!

✧ ✧ ✧ ✧

What then shall be done?—this is the great practical question to which we are brought—a question which every good citizen, every lover of his country, every Christian, should ponder with earnestness and trembling of spirit—What shall be done?

Three things, I answer, must be done, and we cannot begin too soon. First of all, we must open our eyes to what we *have* done. We must see our sin, as a people, and repent of it with shame and fasting. As citizens and Christians, we must be willing to go before God, confess that we as a people have done wickedly, and ask Him to deliver us from the mischiefs we have already worked by casting off His law, and desecrating the principles of His throne. Gather the people, sanctify the congregation, assemble the elders—let the ministers of the Lord weep between the porch and the altar, and let them say, as the common prayer of all—Spare thy people, O Lord, and give not their heritage to reproach! Then—

Let every man take back his personality and set up his conscience, to do in all public matters what is right and well-pleasing to God. Require it of your rulers to cease from the prostitution of their office to effect the reign of their party. Require them to say what is true and do what is right, and the moment they falter, forsake them. At the same time, in the choice of your rulers, be determined to choose no man who is without character and virtue. If you have an eye that will look on a partizan, without principle, pluck it out and cast it from you. If you have a hand that will vote for wickedness, cut it off. Hear the law of God, and swear that it shall be faithfully observed and kept. *Thou shalt provide out of all the people able men, such as fear God, men of truth, hating covetousness, and place such to be rulers.*

First, let them be able men—men equal to the cares of government and policy. Think it not enough, with some who demand your vote, that a man, a man of principle, is offered to your choice—there are many such whom God never made to rule the nation. Wicked rulers are not the only curse. Woe unto thee, O land! when the king is a child; and God himself threatens it as one of his severest judgments against his people, that children shall rule over them. Besides it is nothing but an insult to principle to set it up beggared of all capacity, in the candidate, and ask your vote because it is principle. There is no readier way to make principle itself contemptible. Choose able men.

When you come to the question of moral character, the answer is more difficult, or it has, at least, become so. I do not say with some, that we are to vote for none but Christians. There are many who do not pass by that name, who are governed by the fear of God, as truly as many who do. If we proceeded by this rule, we should make religion itself a partizan, setting it in public array as a wrangler for office and power, and thus make it odious to all who are not its disciples. The fundamental law which ought to govern us, I consider to be this: That we have no right to set up, in the government below, a man who is against the government above. If we do, we put our trust in wickedness, look to wickedness to defend our rights and constitutions, and expect that wickedness will do as well for us below, as God above—all which is a moral offence to God. We need not go into the heart—we cannot. But we must look for an outwardly right man, one who, in his manners and conduct, acknowledges what is right and good—a man of truth, integrity, principle; who fears God in his walk, who is just, pure, humane—in one word, *righteous*. We have no right in any case whatever to vote for another. Principle forbids it, and principle can bend to nothing.

We have a way of saying—I begin to hear it on all sides, and it seems to be taking the force of a moral maxim—that we must not require the men for whom we vote to conform to any moral standard—we must choose between evils, and take the least of the two. Whether this maxim is propounded in reference to an existing case or alternative, it is not for me to say. I leave you to judge. If it be, I will only say that I most deeply pity such an alternative. Merciful God! has it come to this, that in choosing rulers, we are simply to choose whether the nation shall be governed by seven devils or ten! Is this the alternative offered to our consciences and our liberties! Have we simply to choose between Sodom and Gomorrah? Hear the word of the Lord, ye rulers of Sodom, give ear unto the law of our God, ye people of Gomorrah. There is your standard—the *word* of the Lord, the *law* of your God. And whether we be of Sodom or of Gomorrah, let us go forth and hear and obey this law.

But you will say, if we do not choose the least evil, we endanger the success of the greatest—we do, in effect, vote for the greatest. That is not your fault, but the fault of those who offer you the alternative. You may choose between physical evils, and take the least. Half the wisdom of life consists in doing it. But in the case of moral evils, as between adultery and incest, blasphemy and perjury, murder and treason, you have no right to choose either, or the person guilty of either; and if you do, you are implicated, before God, in the choice you make. There was never a maxim more corrupt, more totally bereft of principle, than this—that, between bad men, you are to choose the least wicked of the two. The word of God in the rule just cited, expressly excludes it. It does not say that we are to choose for rulers the least impious and wicked of two—but such as fear God—men of truth, hating covetousness. And who is it that fears God? the man who is second in wickedness to the most wicked? Who is a man of truth? one who only is not as notoriously false as another? Who is clear of covetousness? the man who is only not as greedy of the spoils as another? Besides, if you wish to have this choice of evils offered you at every election, as long as the nation exists, you have only to bow your soul to it and do what is bid you. Grant that by withholding your vote in the case supposed, you allow the worse to triumph.

You have not of course done evil to your country. Look to the remoter consequences and future effects. A vote is by no means thrown away because it does not go into the balance of the main question. Give it in as a visible token of innocence and incorruptible principle—*a piece of clean white paper*. Let it be known that bad candidates must lose so many votes—that they are not available—that there are so many righteous men who fear God and will not, therefore, support them. It is too much to ask that the good citizens only shall comply, and take the lead of the wicked. If a candidate is unavailable because he is a righteous man, let it be seen that he may also be unavailable because he is a wicked and ungodly man. This is wisdom—this is the true part of dignity—this is due to principle itself—this only will ever suffice to save our nation from the abyss of moral anarchy and the curse of God's judgments.

Once more, you have a duty as citizens in respect to that dismal institution which is corrupting and blighting all that is fair and sound in the public virtue. Slavery is the curse of this nation—I blush to think how tamely we have suffered its encroachments. The time has come to renounce our pusillanimity, and take counsel of God and our own dignity. We have made a farce of American liberty long enough. God's frown is upon us, and the scorn of the world is settling on our name in the earth. No politician, no citizen who loves his country, can be blind to our shame and dishonor longer. We have let that thing, which our fathers would not name in their constitution, rule and overrule us, and be the characteristic of our country. It is poisoning all the elements of law, and dissolving the constraints of public virtue. And the question is now coming upon us, whether we shall not, by one more act of submission, ordain the perpetuity of this hideous power in our country, and give it a final and fixed predominance! I will not trust myself to speak on this subject. I have no words to speak what I feel. I will only say that if, by this treaty with Egypt, a new territory large enough for an empire is to be added to the domain of slavery, without some qualifications or restrictions that will neutralize the evil, our doom as a nation is, to human appearance, sealed. God, I know, is gracious, and how much he will bear I cannot tell. He is also just, and how long his justice can suffer, is past human foresight. We may never absolutely despair of the nation, till we see its pillars prostrate. But if we will obstinately hope, we must not be obstinately blind. And if we dare to look on the moral debauchery of this institution as an element of the political fabric, we cannot think it possible to make our country safe and happy in its liberties as a perpetual slavedom. I intended to speak, in closing, of the disastrous effects of our party politics, in their divorce from moral law and principle, on the general interests of religion and the church. This you will see at a glance. Our politics are now our greatest immorality, and, what is most of all fearful, the immorality sweeps through the church of God, and taints the very disciples of the Redeemer. Let us go to God this day, and ask him with our earnest tears and supplications, in public and in private, to save our beloved country from its perils and avert the doom its sins provoke!

SELECTION 2
Alexis de Tocqueville: *American Institutions*

Alexis de Tocqueville, 1805–1859, came to the United States in 1831 to study the penal system, which enabled him to write eventually, 1835–1840, *Democracy in America*, a brilliant analysis of the influence of popular government on an entire society. The following selection is from his *American Institutions*.

The philosophers of the eighteenth century explained the gradual decay of religious faith in a very simple manner. Religious zeal, said they, must necessarily fail, the more generally liberty is established and knowledge diffused. Unfortunately, facts are by no means in accordance with their theory. There are certain populations in Europe whose unbelief is only equalled by their ignorance and their debasement, while in America one of the freest and most enlightened nations in the world fulfils all the outward duties of religion with fervor.

Upon my arrival in the United States, the religious aspect of the country was the first thing that struck my attention; and the longer I stayed there, the more did I perceive the great political consequences resulting from this state of things, to which I was unaccustomed. In France I had almost always seen the spirit of religion and the spirit of freedom pursuing courses diametrically opposed to each other; but in America I found that they were intimately united, and that they reigned in common over the same country. My desire to discover the causes of this phenomenon increased from day to day. In order to satisfy it, I questioned the members of all the different sects; and I more especially sought the society of the clergy, who are the depositaries of the different persuasions, and who are more especially interested in their duration. As a member of the Roman catholic church I was more particularly brought into contact with several of its priests, with whom I became intimately acquainted. To each of these men I expressed my astonishment and I explained my doubts: I found that they differed upon matters of detail alone; and that they mainly attributed the peaceable dominion of religion in their country, to the separation of church and state. I do not hesitate to affirm that during my stay in America, I did not meet with a single individual, of the clergy or of the laity, who was not of the same opinion upon this point.

This led me to examine more attentively than I had hitherto done, the station which the American clergy occupy in political society. I learned with surprise that they fill no public appointments; not one of them is to be met with in the administration, and they are not even represented in the legislative assemblies. In several states the law excludes them from political life; public opinion in all. And when I came to inquire into the prevailing spirit of the clergy, I found that most of its members seemed to retire of their own accord from the exercise of power, and that they made it the pride of their profession to abstain from politics.

I heard them inveigh against ambition and deceit, under whatever political opinions these vices might chance to lurk; but I learned from their discourses that men are not guilty in the eye of God for any opinions concerning political government, which they may profess with sincerity, any more than they are for their mistakes in building a house or in driving a furrow. I perceived that these ministers of the gospel eschewed all parties, with the anxiety attendant upon personal interest. These facts convinced me that what I had been told was true; and it then became my object to investigate their causes, and to inquire how it happened that the real authority of religion was increased by a state of things which diminished its apparent force: these causes did not long escape my researches.

The short space of threescore years can never content the imagination of man; nor can the imperfect joys of this world satisfy his heart. Man alone, of all created beings, displays a natural contempt of existence, and yet a boundless desire to exist; he scorns life, but he dreads annihilation. These different feelings incessantly urge his soul to the contemplation of a future state, and religion directs his musings thither. Religion, then, is simply another form of hope; and it is no less natural to the human heart than hope itself. Men cannot abandon their religious faith without a kind of aberration of intellect, and a sort of violent distortion of their true natures; but they are invincibly brought back to more pious sentiments; for unbelief is an accident, and faith is the only permanent state of mankind. If we only consider religious institutions in a purely human point of view, they may be said to derive an inexhaustible element of strength from man himself, since they belong to one of the constituent principles of human nature.

I am aware that at certain times religion may strengthen this influence, which originates in itself, by the artificial power of the laws, and by the support of those temporal institutions which direct society. Religions, intimately united to the governments of the earth, have been known to exercise a sovereign authority derived from the twofold source of terror and of faith; but when a religion contracts an alliance of this nature, I do not hesitate to affirm that it commits the same error, as a man who should sacrifice his future to his present welfare; and in obtaining a power to which it has no claim, it risks that authority which is rightfully its own. When a religion founds its empire upon the desire of immortality which lives in every human heart, it may aspire to universal dominion: but when it connects itself with a government, it must necessarily adopt maxims which are only applicable to certain nations. Thus, in forming an alliance with a political power, religion augments its authority over a few, and forfeits the hope of reigning over all.

As long as a religion rests upon those sentiments which are the consolation of all affliction, it may attract the affections of mankind. But if it be mixed up with the bitter passions of the world, it may be constrained to defend allies whom its interests, and not the principle of love, have given to it; or to repel as antagonists men who are still attached to its own spirit, however opposed they may be to the powers to which it is allied. The church cannot share the temporal power of the state, without being the object of a portion of that animosity which the latter excites.

The political powers which seem to be most firmly established have frequently no better guarantee for their duration, than the opinions of a generation, the interests of the time, or the life of an individual. A law may modify the social condition which seems to be most fixed and determinate; and with the social condition everything else must change. The powers of society are more or less fugitive, like the years which we spend upon the earth; they succeed each other with rapidity like the fleeting cares of life; and no government has ever yet been founded upon an invariable disposition of the human heart, or upon an imperishable interest.

As long as religion is sustained by those feelings, propensities, and passions, which are found to occur under the same forms at all the different periods of history, it may defy the efforts of time; or at least it can only be destroyed by another religion. But when religion clings to the interests of the world, it becomes almost as fragile a thing as the powers of the earth. It is the only one of them all which can hope for immortality; but if it be connected with their ephemeral authority, it shares their fortunes, and may fall with those transient passions which supported them for a day. The alliance which religion contracts with political powers must needs be onerous to itself; since it does not require their assistance to live, and by giving them its assistance it may be exposed to decay.

The danger which I have just pointed out always exists, but it is not always equally visible. In some ages governments seem to be imperishable, in others the existence of society appears to be more precarious than the life of man. Some constitutions plunge the citizens into a lethargic somnolence, and others rouse them to feverish excitement. When government appears to be so strong, and laws so stable, men do not perceive the dangers which may accrue from a union of church and state. When governments display so much inconstancy, the danger is self-evident, but it is no longer possible to avoid it; to be effectual, measures must be taken to discover its approach.

In proportion as a nation assumes a democratic condition of society, and as communities display democratic propensities, it becomes more and more dangerous to connect religion with political institutions; for the time is coming when authority will be bandied from hand to hand, when political theories will succeed each other, and when men, laws and constitutions, will disappear or be modified from day to day, and this not for a season only, but unceasingly. Agitation and mutability are inherent in the nature of democratic republics, just as stagnation and inertness are the law of absolute monarchies.

If the Americans, who change the head of the government once in four years, who elect new legislators every two years, and renew the provincial officers every twelvemonth; if the Americans, who have abandoned the political world to the attempts of innovators, had not placed religion beyond their reach, where could it abide in the ebb and flow of human opinions? where would that respect which belongs to it be paid, amid the struggles of faction? and what would become of its immortality in the midst of perpetual decay? The American clergy were the first to perceive this truth, and to act in conformity with it. They saw that they must renounce their religious influence, if they were to strive for political power; and they chose to give up the support of the state, rather than to share in its vicissitudes.

In America, religion is perhaps less powerful than it has been at certain periods in the history of certain peoples; but its influence is more lasting. It restricts itself to its own resources, but of those none can deprive it: its circle is limited to certain principles, but those principles are entirely its own, and under its undisputed control.

SELECTION 3

Abraham Lincoln: *Second Inaugural Address*—March 4, 1865

Fellow-countrymen: At this second appearing to take the oath of the presidential office, there is less occasion for an extended address than there was at the first. Then a statement, somewhat in detail, of a course to be pursued, seemed fitting and proper. Now, at the expiration of four years, during which public declarations have been constantly called forth on every point and phase of the great contest which still absorbs the attention and engrosses the energies of the nation, little that is new could be presented. The progress of our arms, upon which all else chiefly depends, is as well known to the public as to myself; and it is, I trust, reasonably satisfactory and encouraging to all. With high hope for the future, no prediction in regard to it is ventured.

On the occasion corresponding to this four years ago, all thoughts were anxiously directed to an impending civil war. All dreaded it—all sought to avert it. While the inaugural address was being delivered from this place, devoted altogether to saving the Union without war, insurgent agents were in the city seeking to destroy it without war—seeking to dissolve the Union, and divide effects, by negotiation. Both parties deprecated war; but one of them would make war rather than let the nation survive; and the other would accept war rather than let it perish. And the war came.

One-eighth of the whole population were colored slaves, not distributed generally over the Union, but localized in the Southern part of it. These slaves constituted a peculiar and powerful interest. All knew that this interest was, somehow, the cause of the war. To strengthen, perpetuate, and extend this interest was the object for which the insurgents would rend the Union, even by war; while the government claimed no right to do more than to restrict the territorial enlargement of it.

Neither party expected for the war the magnitude or the duration which it has already attained. Neither anticipated that the cause of the conflict might cease with, or even before, the conflict itself should cease. Each looked for an easier triumph, and a result less fundamental and astounding. Both read the same

Bible, and pray to the same God; and each invokes his aid against the other. It may seem strange that any men should dare to ask a just God's assistance in wringing their bread from the sweat of other men's faces; but let us judge not, that we be not judged. The prayers of both could not be answered—that of neither has been answered fully.

The Almighty has his own purposes. "Woe unto the world because of offenses! for it must needs be that offenses come; but woe to that man by whom the offense cometh." If we shall suppose that American slavery is one of those offenses which, in the providence of God, must needs come, but which, having continued through his appointed time, he now wills to remove, and that he gives to both North and South this terrible war, as the woe due to those by whom the offense came, shall we discern therein any departure from those divine attributes which the believers in a living God always ascribe to him? Fondly do we hope—fervently do we pray—that this mighty scourge of war may speedily pass away. Yet, if God wills that it continue until all the wealth piled by the bondsman's two hundred and fifty years of unrequited toil shall be sunk, and until every drop of blood drawn with the lash shall be paid by another drawn with the sword, as was said three thousand years ago, so still it must be said, "The judgments of the Lord are true and righteous altogether."

With malice toward none; with charity for all; with firmness in the right, as God gives us to see the right, let us strive on to finish the work we are in; to bind up the nation's wounds; to care for him who shall have borne the battle, and for his widow, and his orphan—to do all which may achieve and cherish a just and lasting peace among ourselves, and with all nations.

SELECTION 4
William Lawrence: *The Relation of Wealth to Morals*

William Lawrence, 1850–1941, an Episcopalian Bishop of Massachusetts (1893–1926), became one of the most eloquent spokesmen of the benefits of capitalism for human society and its compatibility with Christianity.

There is a certain distrust on the part of our people as to the effect of material prosperity on their morality. We shrink with some foreboding at the great increase of riches, and question whether in the long run material prosperity does not tend toward the disintegration of character.

History seems to support us in our distrust. Visions arise of their fall from splendor of Tyre and Sidon, Babylon, Rome, and Venice, and of great nations too. The question is stated whether England is not to-day, in the pride of her wealth and power, sowing the wind from which in time she will reap the whirlwind.

Experience seems to add its support. Is it not from the ranks of the poor that the leaders of the people have always risen? Recall Abraham Lincoln and patriots of every generation.

The Bible has sustained the same note. Were ever stronger words of warning uttered against the deceitfulness of riches than those spoken by the peasant Jesus, who Himself had no place to lay His head? And the Church has through the centuries upheld poverty as one of the surest paths to Heaven: it has been a mark of the saint.

To be sure, in spite of history, experience, and the Bible, men have gone on their way making money and hailing with joy each age of material prosperity. The answer is: "This only proves the case; men are of the world, riches are deceitful, and the Bible is true; the world is given over to Mammon. In the increase of material wealth and the accumulation of riches the man who seeks the higher life has no part."

In the face of this comes the statement of the chief statistician of our census—from one, therefore, who speaks with authority: "The present census, when completed, will unquestionably show that the visible material wealth in this country now has a value of ninety billion dollars. This is a saving greater than all the people of the Western Continent had been able to make from the discovery of Columbus to the breaking out of the Civil War."

If our reasoning from history, experience, and the Bible is correct, we, a Christian people, have rubbed a sponge over the pages of the Bible and are in for orgies and a downfall to which the fall of Rome is a very tame incident.

May it not be well, however, to revise our inferences from history, experience, and the Bible? History tells us that, while riches have been an item and an indirect cause of national decay, innumerable other conditions entered in. Therefore, while wealth has been a source of danger, it has not necessarily led to demoralization.

That leaders have sprung from the ranks of the poor is true and always will be true, so long as force of character exists in every class. But there are other conditions than a lack of wealth at the source of their uprising.

And as to the Bible:—while every word that can be quoted against the rich is as true as any other word, other words and deeds are as true; and the parables of our Lord on the stewardship of wealth, His association with the wealthy, strike another and complementary note. Both notes are essential to the harmony of His life and teachings. His thought was not of the conditions, rich or poor, but of a higher life, the character rising out of the conditions—fortunately, for we are released from that subtle hypocrisy which has beset the Christian through the ages, bemoaning the deceitfulness of riches and, at the same time, working with all his might to earn a competence, and a fortune if he can.

Now we are in a position to affirm that neither history, experience, nor the Bible necessarily sustains the common distrust of the effect of material wealth on morality. Our path of study is made more clear. Two positive principles lead us out on our path.

The first is that man, when he is strong, will conquer Nature, open up her resources, and harness them to his service. This is his play, his exercise, his divine mission.

"Man," says Emerson, "is born to be rich. He is thoroughly related, and is tempted out by his appetites and fancies to the conquest of this and that piece of Nature, until he finds his well-being in the use of the planet, and of more planets than his own. Wealth requires, besides the crust of bread and the roof, the freedom of the city, the freedom of the earth." "The strong race is strong on these terms."

Man draws to himself material wealth as surely, as naturally, and as necessarily as the oak draws the elements into itself from the earth.

The other principle is that, in the long run, it is only to the man of morality that wealth comes. We believe in the harmony of God's Universe. We know that it is only by working along His laws natural and spiritual that we can work with efficiency. Only by working along the lines of right thinking and right living can the secrets and wealth of Nature be revealed. We, like the Psalmist, occasionally see the wicked prosper, but only occasionally.

Put two men in adjoining fields, one man strong and normal, the other weak and listless. One picks up his spade, turns over the earth, and works till sunset. The other turns over a few clods, gets a drink from the spring, takes a nap, and loafs back to his work. In a few years one will be rich for his needs, and the other a pauper dependent on the first, and growling at his prosperity.

Put ten thousand immoral men to live and work in one fertile valley and ten thousand moral men to live and work in the next valley, and the question is soon answered as to who wins the material wealth. Godliness is in league with riches.

Now we return with an easier mind and clearer conscience to the problem of our twenty-five billion dollars in a decade.

My question is: Is the material prosperity of this Nation favorable or unfavorable to the morality of the people?

The first thought is, Who has prospered? Who has got the money?

I take it that the loudest answer would be, "The millionaires, the capitalists, and the incompetent but luxurious rich;" and, as we think of that twenty-five billion, our thoughts run over the yachts, the palaces, and the luxuries that flaunt themselves before the public.

As I was beginning to write this paper an Irishman with his horse and wagon drew up at my back door. Note that I say *his* horse and wagon. Twenty years ago that Irishman, then hardly twenty years old, landed in Boston, illiterate, uncouth, scarcely able to make himself understood in English. There was no symptom of brains, alertness, or ambition. He got a job to tend a few cows. Soon the American atmosphere began to take hold. He discovered that here every man has his chance. With his first earnings he bought a suit of clothes; he gained self-respect. Then he sent money home; then he got a job to drive a horse; he opened an account at the savings bank; then evening school; more money in the bank. He changed to a better job, married a thrifty wife, and to-day he owns his house, stable, horse, wagon, and bicycle; has a good sum at the bank, supports five children, and has half a dozen men working under him. He is a capitalist, and his yearly earnings represent the income of $30,000. He had no "pull"; he has made his own way by grit, physical strength, and increasing intelligence. He has had material prosperity. His older brother, who paid his passage over, has had material prosperity, and his younger brother, whose passage my friend paid, has had material prosperity.

Now we are beginning to get an idea as to where the savings are. They are in the hands of hundreds of thousands of just such men, and of scores of thousands of men whose incomes ten years ago were two and five thousand, and are now five and ten thousand; and of thousands of others whose incomes have risen from ten to thirty thousand. So that, when you get to the multi-millionaires, you have only a fraction to distribute among them. And of them the fact is that only a small fraction of their income can be spent upon their own pleasure and luxury; the bulk of what they get has to be reinvested, and becomes the means whereby thousands earn their wages. They are simply trustees of a fraction of the national property.

When, then, the question is asked, "Is the material prosperity of this nation favorable or unfavorable to the morality of the people?" I say with all emphasis, "In the long run, and by all means, favorable!"

In other words, to seek for and earn wealth is a sign of a natural, vigorous, and strong character. Wherever strong men are, there they will turn into the activities of life. In the ages of chivalry you will find them on the crusades or seeking the Golden Fleece; in college life you will find them high in rank, in the boat, or on the athletic field; in an industrial age you will find them eager, straining every nerve in the development of the great industries. The race is to the strong. The search for material wealth is therefore as natural and necessary to the man as is the pushing out of its roots for more moisture and food to the oak. This is man's play, his exercise, the expression of his powers, his personality. You can no more suppress it than you can suppress the tide of the ocean. For one man who seeks money for its own sake there are ten who seek it for the satisfaction of the seeking, the power there is in it, and the use they can make of it. There is the exhilaration of feeling one's self grow in one's surroundings; the man reaches out, lays hold of this, that, and the other interest, scheme, and problem. He is building up a fortune? Yes, but his joy is also that he is building up a stronger, abler, and more powerful man. There are two men that have none of this ambition: the gilded, listless youth and the ragged, listless pauper to whom he tosses a dime; they are in the same class.

XXIV THE SOCIAL ENCYCLICALS

To a world being rapidly changed by the industrial and scientific revolution of the nineteenth century the Roman Catholic Church addressed itself through the encyclicals of the popes. Men like Pope Leo XIII (1810–1903) spoke to most of the political and social problems of his time, expressing a critical and prophetic point of view. Some of the ideas which he developed in *Rerum Novarum* were taken up again forty years later by Pius XI (1879–1939) in his *Quadragesimo Anno*. He also spoke out against Nazism (*Mit brennender Sorge*) and Communism (*Divini Redemptoris*).

His successor, Pius XII (1876–1958), also addressed the problem of the modern state (*Summi Pontificatus*). In all these pronouncements a basic conservatism and a deep concern for the welfare of all people are combined. In none of these statements is there as passive an acceptance of the new economic order as shown for example by Bishop Lawrence (see above, Chapter XXIII) or as radical a critique of the new social order as expressed by the spokesmen of the Social Gospel (see below, Chapter XXV).

SELECTION I

Leo XIII: From *Diuturnum,* June 29, 1881

In 1881 the Russian Tsar Alexander II was murdered in St. Petersburg. This papal letter, influenced by this event, shows the dependence of political power upon God.

The long-continued and most bitter war waged against the divine authority of the Church has reached the culmination to which it was tending, the common danger, namely, of human society, and especially of the civil power on which the public safety chiefly reposes. In our own times most particularly this result is apparent. For popular passions now reject, with more boldness than formerly, every restraint of authority. So great is the license on all sides, so frequent are seditions and tumults, that not only is obedience often refused to those who rule states, but a sufficiently safe guarantee of security does not seem to have been left to them.

✧ ✧ ✧ ✧

These perils to commonwealths, which are before Our eyes, fill Us with grave anxiety, when We behold the security of rulers and the tranquillity of empires, together with the safety of nations, put in peril almost from hour to hour. Nevertheless, the divine power of the Christian religion has given birth to excellent principles of stability and order for the State, while at the same time it has penetrated into the customs and institutions of States. And of this power not the least nor last fruit is a just and wise proportion of mutual rights and duties in both princes and peoples. For in the precepts and examples of Christ our Lord there is a wonderful force for restraining in their duty as much those who obey as those who rule; and for keeping between them that agreement which is most according to nature, and that concord of wills, so to speak, from which arises a course of administration tranquil and free from all disturbance. Wherefore, being, by the favor of God, entrusted with the government of the Catholic Church, and made guardian and interpreter of the doctrines of Christ, We judge that it belongs to Our jurisdiction, venerable brethren, publicly to set forth what Catholic truth demands of every one in this sphere of duty; thus making clear also by what way and by what means measures may be taken for the public safety in so critical a state of affairs.

✧ ✧ ✧ ✧

And, indeed, nature, or rather God who is the Author of nature, wills that man should live in a civil society; and this is clearly shown both by the faculty of language, the greatest medium of intercourse, and by numerous innate desires of the mind, and the many necessary things, and things of great importance, which men isolated cannot procure, but which they can procure when joined and associated with others. But now, a society can neither exist nor be conceived in which there is no one to govern the wills of individuals, in such a way as to make, as it were, one will out of many, and to impel them rightly and orderly to the common good; therefore, God has willed that in a civil society there should be some to rule the multitude. And this also is a powerful argument, that those by whose authority the State is administered must be able so to compel the citizens to obedience that it is clearly a sin in the latter not to obey. But no man has in himself or of himself the power of constraining the free will of others by fetters of authority of this kind. This power resides solely in God, the Creator and Legislator of all things; and it is necessary that those who exercise it should do it as having received it from God. "There is one lawgiver and judge, who is able to destroy and deliver." And this is clearly seen in every kind of power. That that which resides in priests comes from God is so acknowledged that among all nations they are recognized as, and called, the ministers of God. In like manner, the authority of fathers of families preserves a certain impressed image and form of authority which is in God, "of whom all paternity in heaven and earth is named." But in this way different kinds of authority have between them wonderful resemblances, since, whatever there is of government and authority, its origin is derived from one and the same Creator and Lord of the world, who is God.

SELECTION 2

Leo XIII: From *Immortale Dei,* November 1, 1885

The Roman Catholic doctrine of the distinction of church and state is here definitively stated and the political responsibility of the Catholic citizen is outlined.

The Almighty, therefore, has given the charge of the human race to two powers, the ecclesiastical and the civil, the one being set over divine, and the other over human, things. Each in its kind is supreme, each has fixed limits within which it is contained, limits which are defined by the nature and special object of the province of each, so that there is, we may say, an orbit traced out within which the action of each is brought into play by its own native right. But, inasmuch as each of these two powers has authority over the same subjects, and as it might come to pass that one and the same thing—related differently, but still remaining one and the same thing—might belong to the jurisdiction and determination of both, therefore God, who foresees all things, and who is the author of these two powers, has marked out the course of each in right correlation to the other. "For the powers that are, are ordained of God." Were this not so, deplorable contentions and conflicts would often arise, and, not infrequently, men, like travelers at the meeting of two roads, would hesitate in anxiety and doubt, not knowing what course to follow. Two powers would be commanding contrary things, and it would be a dereliction of duty to disobey either of the two.

✧ ✧ ✧ ✧

Secondly, action may relate to private and domestic matters, or to matters public. As to private affairs, the first duty is to conform life and conduct to the gospel precepts, and to refuse to shrink from this duty when Christian virtue demands some sacrifice slightly more difficult to make. All, moreover, are bound to love the Church as their common mother, to obey her laws, promote her honor, defend her rights, and to endeavor to make her respected and loved by those over whom they have authority. It is also of great moment to the public welfare to take a prudent part in the business of municipal administration, and to endeavor above all to introduce effectual measures, so that, as becomes a Christian people, public provision may be made for the instruction of youth in religion and true morality. Upon these things the well-being of every State greatly depends.

Furthermore, it is in general fitting and salutary that Catholics should extend their efforts beyond this restricted sphere, and give their attention to national politics. We say "in general" because these Our precepts are addressed to all nations. However, it may in some places be true that, for most urgent and just reasons, it is by no means expedient for Catholics to engage in affairs or to take an active part in politics. Nevertheless, as

We have laid down, to take no share in public matters would be as wrong as to have no concern for, or to bestow no labor upon, the common good, and the more so because Catholics are admonished, by the very doctrines which they profess, to be upright and faithful in the discharge of duty, while, if they hold aloof, men whose principles offer but small guarantee for the welfare of the State will the more readily seize the reins of government. This would tend also to the injury of the Christian religion, forasmuch as those would come into power who are badly disposed toward the Church, and those who are willing to befriend her would be deprived of all influence.

It follows clearly, therefore, that Catholics have just reasons for taking part in the conduct of public affairs. For in so doing they assume not nor should they assume the responsibility of approving what is blameworthy in the actual methods of government, but seek to turn these very methods, so far as is possible, to the genuine and true public good, and to use their best endeavors at the same time to infuse, as it were, into all the veins of the State the healthy sap and blood of Christian wisdom and virtue. The morals and ambitions of the heathens differed widely from those of the Gospel, yet Christians were to be seen living undefiled everywhere in the midst of pagan superstition, and, while always true to themselves, coming to the front boldly wherever an opening was presented. Models of loyalty to their rulers, submissive, so far as was permitted, to the sovereign power, they shed around them on every side a halo of sanctity; they strove to be helpful to their brethren, and to attract others to the wisdom of Jesus Christ, yet were bravely ready to withdraw from public life, nay, even to lay down their life, if they could not without loss of virtue retain honors, dignities, and offices. For this reason, Christian ways and manners speedily found their way not only into private houses but into the camp, the senate, and even into the imperial palaces. "We are but of yesterday," wrote Tertullian, "yet we swarm in all your institutions, we crowd your cities, islands, villages, towns, assemblies, the army itself, your wards and corporations, the palace, the senate, and the law courts." So that the Christian faith, when once it became lawful to make public profession of the Gospel, appeared in most of the cities of Europe, not like an infant crying in its cradle, but already grown up and full of vigor.

SELECTION 3

Leo XIII: From *Rerum Novarum*, May 15, 1891

The encyclical *Rerum Novarum* of May 15, 1891 is an appeal to the solidarity of all classes against the doctrine of class-war. "Nothing," he states, "is more useful than to look at the world as it really is, and at the same time to seek elsewhere, as we have said, for the solace to its troubles."

That the spirit of revolutionary change, which has long been disturbing the nations of the world, should have passed beyond the sphere of politics and made its influence felt in the cognate sphere of practical economics is not surprising. The elements of the conflict now raging are unmistakable, in the vast expansion of industrial pursuits and the marvelous discoveries of science; in the changed relations between masters and workmen; in the enormous fortunes of some few individuals, and the utter poverty of the masses; in the increased self-reliance and closer mutual combination of the working classes; and also, finally, in the prevailing moral degeneracy. The momentous gravity of the state of things now obtaining fills every mind with painful apprehension; wise men are discussing it; practical men are proposing schemes; popular meetings, legislatures, and rulers of nations are all busied with it—actually there is no question which has taken a deeper hold on the public mind.

✧ ✧ ✧ ✧

Therefore, those whom fortune favors are warned that riches do not bring freedom from sorrow and are of no avail for eternal happiness, but rather are obstacles; that the rich should tremble at the threatenings of Jesus Christ—threatenings so unwonted in the mouth of our Lord—and that a most strict account must be given to the Supreme Judge for all we possess. The chief and most excellent rule for the right use of money is one which the heathen philosophers hinted at, but which the Church has traced out clearly, and has not only made known to men's minds, but has impressed upon their lives. It rests on the principle that it is one thing to have a right to use money as one wills. Private ownership, as we have seen, is the natural right of man, and to exercise that right, especially as members of society, is not only lawful, but absolutely necessary. "It is lawful," says St. Thomas Aquinas, "for a man to hold private property; and it is also necessary for the carrying on of human existence." But if the question be asked: How must one's possessions be used?—the Church replies without hesitation in the words of the same holy Doctor: "Man should not consider his material possessions as his own, but as common to all, so as to share them without hesitation when others are in need. Whence the Apostle saith, 'Command the rich of this world . . . to offer with no stint, to apportion largely.'" True, no one is commanded to distribute to others that which is required for his own needs and those of his household; nor even to give away what is reasonably required to keep up becomingly his condition in life, "for no one ought to live other than becomingly." But, when what necessity demands has been supplied, and one's standing fairly taken thought for, it becomes a duty to give to the indigent out of what remains over. "Of that which remaineth, give alms." It is a duty, not of justice (save in extreme cases), but of Christian charity—a duty not enforced by human law. But the laws and judgments of men must yield place to the laws and judgments of Christ the true God, who in many ways urges on His followers the practice of almsgiving—"It is more blessed to give than to receive"; and who will count a kindness done or refused to the poor as done or refused to Himself—"As long as you did it to one of My least brethren you did it to Me." To sum up, then, what has been said: Whoever has received from the divine bounty a large share of temporal blessings, whether they be external and material, or gifts of the mind, has received them for the purpose of using them for the perfecting of his own nature, and, at the same time, that he may employ them, as the steward of God's providence, for the benefit of others. "He that hath a talent," said St. Gregory the Great, "let him see that he hide it not; he that hath abundance, let him quicken himself to mercy and generosity; he that hath art and skill, let him do his best to share the use and the utility hereof with his neighbor."

As for those who possess not the gifts of fortune, they are taught by the Church that in God's sight poverty is no disgrace, and that there is nothing to be ashamed of in earning their bread by labor. This is enforced by what we see in Christ Himself, who, "whereas He was rich, for our sakes became poor"; and who, being the Son of God, and God Himself, chose to seem and to be considered the son of a carpenter—nay, did not disdain to spend a great part of His life as a carpenter Himself. "Is not this the carpenter, the son of Mary?"

From contemplation of this divine Model, it is more easy to understand that the true worth and nobility of man lie in his moral qualities, that is, in virtue; that virtue is, moreover, the common inheritance of men, equally within the reach of high and low, rich and poor; and that virtue, and virtue alone, wherever found, will be followed by the rewards of everlasting happiness. Nay, God Himself seems to incline rather to those who suffer misfortune; for Jesus Christ calls the poor "blessed"; He lovingly invites those in labor and grief to come to Him for solace; and He displays the tenderest charity toward the lowly and the oppressed. These reflections cannot fail to keep down the pride of the well-to-do, and to give heart to the unfortunate; to move the former to be generous and the latter to be moderate in their desires. Thus, the separation which pride would set up tends to disappear, nor will it be difficult to make rich and poor join hands in friendly concord.

✧ ✧ ✧ ✧

Whenever the general interest or any particular class suffers, or is threatened with harm, which can in no other way be met or prevented, the public authority must step in to deal with it. Now, it is to the interest of the community, as well as of the individual, that peace and good order should be maintained; that all things should be carried on in accordance with God's laws and those of nature; that the discipline of family life should be observed and that religion should be obeyed; that a high standard of morality should prevail, both in public and private life; that justice should be held sacred and that no one should injure another with impunity; that the members of the commonwealth should grow up to man's estate strong and robust, and capable, if need be, of guarding and defending their country. If by a strike of workers or concerted interruption of work there should be imminent danger of disturbance to the public peace; or if circumstances were such as that among the working class the ties of family life were relaxed; if religion were found to suffer through the workers not having time and opportunity afforded them to practice its duties; if in workshops and factories there were danger to morals through the mixing of the sexes or from other harmful occasions of evil; or if employers laid burdens upon their workmen which were unjust, or degraded them with conditions repugnant to their dignity as human beings; finally, if health were endangered by excessive labor, or by work unsuited to sex or age—in such cases, there can be no question but that, within certain limits, it would be right to invoke the aid and authority of the law. The limits must be determined by the nature of the occasion which calls for the law's interference—the principle being that the law must not undertake more, nor proceed further, than is required for the remedy of the evil or the removal of the mischief.

Rights must be religiously respected wherever they exist, and it is the duty of the public authority to prevent and to punish injury, and to protect every one in the possession of his own. Still, when there is question of defending the rights of individuals, the poor and badly off have a claim to especial consideration. The richer class have many ways of shielding themselves, and stand less in need of help from the State; whereas the mass of the poor have no resources of their own to fall back upon, and must chiefly depend upon the assistance of the State. And it is for this reason that wage-earners, since they mostly belong in the mass of the needy, should be specially cared for and protected by the government.

✧ ✧ ✧ ✧

We now approach a subject of great importance, and one in respect of which, if extremes are to be avoided, right notions are absolutely necessary. Wages, as we are told, are regulated by free consent, and therefore the employer, when he pays what was agreed upon, has done his part and seemingly is not called upon to do anything beyond. The only way, it is said, in which injustice might occur would be if the master refused to pay the whole of the wages, or if the workman should not complete the work undertaken; in such cases the public authority should intervene, to see that each obtains his due, but not under any other circumstances.

To this kind of argument a fair-minded man will not easily or entirely assent; it is not complete, for there are important considerations which it leaves out of account altogether. To labor is to exert oneself for the sake of procuring what is necessary for the various purposes of life, and chief of all for self-preservation. "In the sweat of thy face thou shalt eat bread." Hence, a man's labor necessarily bears two notes or characters. First of all, it is *personal,* inasmuch as the force which acts is bound up with the personality and is the exclusive property of him who acts, and, further, was given to him for his advantage. Secondly, man's labor is *necessary;* for without the result of labor a man cannot live, and self-preservation is a law of nature, which it is wrong to disobey. Now, were we to consider labor merely in so far as it is personal, doubtless it would be within the workman's right to accept any rate of wages whatsoever; for in the same way as he is free to work or not, so is he free to accept a small wage or even none at all. But our conclusion must be very different if, together with the personal element in a man's work, we consider the fact that work is also necessary for him to live: these two aspects of his work are separable in thought, but not in reality. The preservation of life is the bounden duty of one and all, and to be wanting therein is a crime. It necessarily follows that each one has a natural right to procure what is required in order to live, and the poor can procure that in no other way than by what they can earn through their work.

Let the working man and the employer make free agreements, and in particular let them agree freely as to the wages; nevertheless, there underlies a dictate of natural justice more imperious and ancient than any bargain between man and man, namely that wages ought not to be insufficient to support a frugal and well-behaved wage-earner. If through necessity or fear of a worse evil the workman accept harder conditions because an employer or contractor will afford him no better, he is made the victim of force and injustice. In these and similar questions, however—such as, for example, the hours of labor in different trades, the sanitary precautions to be observed in factories and workshops, etc.—in order to supersede undue interference on the part of the State, especially as circumstances, times, and localities differ so widely, it is advisable that recourse be had to societies or boards such as We shall mention presently, or to some other mode of safe-guarding the interests of the wage-earners; the State being appealed to, should circumstances require, for its sanction and protection.

If a workman's wages be sufficient to enable him comfortably to support himself, his wife, and his children, he will find it easy, if he be a sensible man, to practice thrift, and he will not fail, by cutting down expenses, to put by some little savings and thus secure a modest source of income. Nature itself would urge him to this. We have seen that this great labor question cannot be solved save by assuming as a principle that private ownership must be held sacred and inviolable. The law, therefore, should favor ownership, and its policy should be to induce as many as possible of the people to become owners.

SELECTION 4
Pius XI: From *Mit brennender Sorge,* March 14, 1937

The Vatican had negotiated a concordat with Hitler in 1933, the first foreign power to do so. In fact, the Nazi government ignored the concordat.

It is with deep anxiety and growing surprise that We have long been following the painful trials of the Church and the increasing vexations which afflict those who have remained loyal in heart and action in the midst of a people that once received from St. Boniface the bright message and the Gospel of Christ and God's Kingdom. . . .

When, in 1933, We consented, Venerable Brethren, to open negotiations for a concordat, which the Reich Government proposed on the basis of a scheme of several years' standing; and when, to your unanimous satisfaction, We concluded the negotiations by a solemn treaty, We were prompted by the desire, as it behooved Us, to secure for Germany the freedom of the Church's beneficent mission and the salvation of the souls in her care, as well as by the sincere wish to render the German people a service essential for its peaceful development and prosperity. Hence, despite many and grave misgivings, We then decided not to withhold Our consent, for We wished to spare the Faithful of Germany, as far as it was humanly possible, the trials and difficulties they would have had to face, given the circumstances, had the negotiations fallen through. . . .

. . . Whoever has left in his soul an atom of love for truth, and in his heart a shadow of a sense of justice, must admit that, in the course of these anxious and trying years following upon the conclusion of the concordat, every one of Our words, every one of Our acts, has been inspired by the binding law of treaties. At the same time, anyone must acknowledge, not without surprise and reprobation, how the other contracting party emasculated the terms of the treaty, distorted their meaning, and eventually considered its more or less official violation as a normal policy. The moderation We showed in spite of all this was not inspired by motives of worldly interest, still less by unwarranted weakness, but merely by Our anxiety not to draw out the wheat with the cockle; not to pronounce open judgement, before the public was ready to see its force; not to impeach other people's honesty, before the evidence of events should have torn the mask off the systematic hostility leveled at the Church. Even now that a campaign against the confessional schools, which are guaranteed by the concordat, and the destruction of free election, where Catholics have a right to their children's Catholic education, afford evidence, in a matter so essential to the life of the Church, of the extreme gravity of the situation and the anxiety of every Christian conscience; even now Our responsibility for Christian souls induces Us not to overlook the last possibilities, however slight, of a return to fidelity to treaties, and to any arrangement that may be acceptable to the episcopate. We shall continue without failing, to stand before the rulers of your people as the defender of violated rights, and in obedience to Our Conscience and Our pastoral mission, whether We be successful or not, to oppose the policy which seeks, by open or secret means, to strangle rights guaranteed by a treaty. . . .

Take care, Venerable Brethren, that above all, faith in God, the first and irreplaceable foundation of all religion, be preserved in Germany pure and unstained. The believer in God is not he who utters the name in his speech, but he for whom this sacred word stands for a true and worthy concept of the Divinity. Whoever identifies, by pantheistic confusion, God and the universe, by either lowering God to the dimensions of the world, or raising the world to the dimensions of God, is not a believer in God. Whoever follows that so-called pre-Christian Germanic conception of substituting a dark and impersonal destiny for the personal God, denies thereby the Wisdom and Providence of God. . . .

Whoever exalts race, or the people, or the State, or a particular form of State, or the depositories of power, or any other fundamental value of the human community—however necessary and honorable be their function in worldly things—whoever raises these nations above their standard value and divinizes them to an idolatrous level, distorts and perverts an order of the world planned and created by God: he is far from the true faith in God and from the concept of life which that faith upholds.

Beware, Venerable Brethren, of that growing abuse, in speech as in writing, of the name of God as though it were a meaningless label, to be affixed to any creation, more or less arbitrary, of human speculation. Use your influence on the Faithful, that they refuse to yield to this aberration. Our God is the Personal God, supernatural, omnipotent, infinitely perfect, one in the Trinity of Persons, tri-personal in the unity of divine essence, the Creator of all existence, Lord, King and ultimate Consummator of the history of the world, who will not, and cannot, tolerate a rival god by His side.

This God, this Sovereign Master, has issued commandments whose value is independent of time and space, of country and race. As God's sun shines on every human face, so His law knows neither privilege nor exception. Rulers and subjects, crowned and uncrowned, rich and poor, are equally subject to His word. From the fulness of the Creator's right there naturally arises the fulness of His right to be obeyed by individuals and communities, whoever they are. This obedience permeates all branches of activity in which moral values claim harmony with the law of God, and pervades all integration of the ever-changing laws of man into the immutable laws of God.

None but superficial minds could stumble into concepts of a national God, of a national religion; or attempt to lock within the frontiers of a single people, within the narrow limits of a single race, God, the Creator of the universe, King and Legislator of all nations, before whose immensity they are "as a drop of a bucket" (Isaiah xl, 15). . . .

SELECTION 5

Pius XI: From *Divini Redemptoris*, March 28, 1937

In his attack against Communism, Pope Pius XI observes its "false messianic idea" and its aggressive atheism.

The promise of a Redeemer brightens the first page of the history of mankind, and the confident hope aroused by this promise softened the keen regret for a paradise which had been lost. It was this hope that accompanied the human race on its weary journey, until in the fullness of time the expected Saviour came to begin a new universal civilization, the Christian civilization, far superior even to that which up to this time had been laboriously achieved by certain more privileged nations.

Nevertheless, the struggle between good and evil remained in the world as a sad legacy of the original fall. Nor has the ancient tempter ever ceased to deceive mankind with false promises. It is on this account that one convulsion following upon another has marked the passage of the centuries, down to the revolution of our own days. This modern revolution, it may be said, has actually broken out or threatens everywhere, and it exceeds in amplitude and violence anything yet experienced in the preceding persecutions launched against the Church. Entire peoples find themselves in danger of falling back into a barbarism worse than that which oppressed the greater part of the world at the coming of the Redeemer.

This all too imminent danger, Venerable Brethren, as you have already surmised, is bolshevistic and atheistic communism, which aims at upsetting the social order and at undermining the very foundations of Christian civilization.

✧ ✧ ✧ ✧

The communism of today, more emphatically than similar movements in the past, conceals in itself a false messianic idea. A pseudo-ideal of justice, of equality and fraternity in labor impregnates all its doctrine and activity with a deceptive mysticism, which communicates a zealous and contagious enthusiasm to the multitudes entrapped by delusive promises. This is especially true in an age like ours, when unusual misery has resulted from the unequal distribution of the goods of this world. This pseudo-ideal is even boastfully advanced as if it were responsible for a certain economic progress. As a matter of fact, when such progress is at all real, its true causes are quite different, as for instance the intensification of industrialism in countries which were formerly almost without it, the exploitation of immense natural resources, and the use of the most brutal methods to insure the achievement of gigantic projects with a minimum of expense.

The doctrine of modern communism, which is often concealed under the most seductive trappings, is in substance based on the principles of dialectical and historical materialism previously advocated by Marx, of which the theoreticians of bolshevism claim to possess the only genuine interpretation. According to this doctrine there is in the world only one reality, matter, the blind forces of which evolve into plant, animal and man. Even human society is nothing but a phenomenon and form of matter, evolving in the same way. By a law of inexorable necessity and through a perpetual conflict of forces, matter moves towards the final synthesis of a classless society. In such a doctrine, as is evident, there is no room for the idea of God; there is no difference between matter and spirit, between soul and body; there is neither survival of the soul after death nor any hope in a future life. Insisting on the dialectical aspect of their materialism, the communists claim that the conflict which carries the world towards its final synthesis can be accelerated by man. Hence they endeavor to sharpen the antagonisms which arise between the various classes of society. Thus the class struggle with its consequent violent hate and destruction takes on the aspect of a crusade for the progress of humanity. On the other hand, all other forces whatever, as long as they resist such systematic violence, must be annihilated as hostile to the human race.

Communism, moreover, strips man of his liberty, robs human personality of all its dignity, and removes all the moral restraints that check the eruptions of blind impulse. There is no recognition of any right of the individual in his relations to the collectivity; no natural right is accorded to human personality, which is a mere cog-wheel in the communist system. In man's relations with other individuals, besides, communists hold the principle of absolute equality, rejecting all hierarchy and divinely constituted authority, including the authority of parents. What men call authority and subordination is derived from the community as its first and only font. Nor is the individual granted any property rights over material goods or the means of production, for inasmuch as these are the source of further wealth, their possession would give one man power over another. Precisely on this score, all forms of private property must be eradicated, for they are at the origin of all economic enslavement.

Refusing to human life any sacred or spiritual character, such a doctrine logically makes of marriage and the family a purely artificial and civil institution, the outcome of a specific economic system. There exists no matrimonial bond of a juridico moral nature that is not subject to the whim of the individual or of the collectivity. Naturally, therefore, the notion of an indissoluble marriage tie is scouted. Communism is particularly characterized by the rejection of any link that binds woman to the family and the home, and her emancipation is proclaimed as a basic principle. She is withdrawn from the family and the care of her children, to be thrust instead into public life and collective production under the same conditions as man. The care of home and children then devolves upon the collectivity.

Finally, the right of education is denied to parents, for it is conceived as the exclusive prerogative of the community, in whose name and by whose mandate alone parents may exercise this right.

What would be the condition of a human society based on such materialistic tenets? It would be a collectivity with no other hierarchy than that of the economic system. It would have only one mission: the production of material things by means of collective labor, so that the goods of this world might be enjoyed in a paradise where each would "give according to his powers" and would "receive according to his needs." Communism recognizes in the collectivity the right, or rather, unlimited discretion, to draft individuals for the labor of the collectivity with no regard for their personal welfare; so that even violence could be legitimately exercised to dragoon the recalcitrant against their wills. In the communistic commonwealth morality and law would be nothing but a derivation of the existing economic order, purely earthly in origin and unstable in character. In a word, the communists claim to inaugurate a new era and a new civilization which is the result of blind evolutionary forces culminating in a "humanity without God."

When all men have finally acquired the collectivist mentality in this Utopia of a really classless society, the political State, which is now conceived by communists merely as the instrument by which the proletariat is oppressed by the capitalists, will have lost all reason for its existence and will "wither away." However, until that happy consummation is realized, the State and the powers of the State furnish communism with the most efficacious and most extensive means for the achievement of its goal.

Such, Venerable Brethren, is the new gospel which bolshevistic and atheistic communism offers the world as the glad tidings of deliverance and salvation! It is a system full of errors and sophisms. It is in opposition both to reason and to divine Revelation. It subverts the social order, because it means the destruction of its foundations; because it ignores the true origin and purpose of the State; because it denies the rights, dignity and liberty of human personality.

✧ ✧ ✧ ✧

. . . Where communism has been able to assert its power—and here We are thinking with special affection of the people of Russia and Mexico—it has striven by every possible means, as its champions openly boast, to destroy Christian civilization and the Christian religion by banishing every remembrance of them from the hearts of men, especially of the young. Bishops and priests were exiled, condemned to forced labor, shot and done to death in inhuman fashion: laymen suspected of defending their religion were vexed, persecuted, dragged off to trial and thrown into prison. . . .

✧ ✧ ✧ ✧

. . . For the first time in history we are witnessing a struggle, cold-blooded in purpose and mapped out to the least detail, between man and "all that is called God." Communism is by its nature antireligious. It considers religion as "the opiate of the people" because the principles of religion which speak of a life beyond the grave dissuade the proletariat from the dream of a soviet paradise which is of this world.

But the law of nature and its Author cannot be flouted with impunity. Communism has not been able, and will not be able, to achieve its objectives even in the merely economic sphere. It is true that in Russia it has been a contributing factor in rousing men and materials from the inertia of centuries, and in obtaining by all manner of means, often without scruple, some measure of material success. Nevertheless We know from reliable and even very recent testimony that not even there, in spite of slavery imposed on millions of men, has communism reached its promised goal. After all, even the sphere of economics needs some morality, some moral sense of responsibility, which can find no place in a system so thoroughly materialistic as communism. Terrorism is the only possible substitute, and it is terrorism that reigns today in Russia, where former comrades in revolution are exterminating each other. Terrorism, having failed despite all to stem the tide of moral corruption, cannot even prevent the dissolution of society itself.

In making these observations it is no part of Our intention to condemn *en masse* the peoples of the Soviet Union. For them We cherish the warmest paternal affection. We are well aware that not a few of them groan beneath the yoke imposed on them by men who in very large part are strangers to the real interests of the country. We recognize that many others were deceived by fallacious hopes. We blame only the system, with its authors and abettors who considered Russia the best-prepared field for experimenting with a plan elaborated decades ago, and who from there continue to spread it from one end of the world to the other.

✧ ✧ ✧ ✧

. . . In the plan of the Creator, society is a natural means which man can and must use to reach his destined end. Society is for man and not vice versa. This must not be understood in the sense of liberalistic individualism, which subordinates society to the selfish use of the individual; but only in the sense that by means of an organic union with society and by mutual collaboration the attainment of earthly happiness is placed within the reach of all. In a further sense, it is society which affords the opportunities for the development of all the individual and social gifts bestowed on human nature. These natural gifts have a value surpassing the immediate interests of the moment, for in society they reflect the divine perfection, which would not be true were man to live alone. But on final analysis, even in this latter function society is made for man, that he may recognize the reflection of God's perfection, and refer it in praise and adoration to the Creator. Only man, the human person, and not society in any form is endowed with reason and a morally free will.

Man cannot be exempted from his divinely imposed obligations toward civil society, and the representatives of authority have the right to coerce him when he refuses without reason to do his duty. Society, on the other hand, cannot defraud man of his God-granted rights, the most important of which We have indicated above. Nor can society systematically void these rights by making their use impossible. It is therefore according to the dictates of reason that ultimately all material things should be ordained to man as a person, that through his mediation they may find their way to the Creator. . . .

✧ ✧ ✧ ✧

In view of this organized common effort towards peaceful living, Catholic doctrine vindicates to the State the dignity and authority of a vigilant and provident defender of those divine and human rights on which the Sacred Scriptures and the Fathers of the Church insist so often. It is not true that all have equal rights in civil society. It is not true that there exists no lawful social hierarchy. . . . The enslavement of man despoiled of his rights, the denial of the transcendental origin of the State and its authority, the horrible abuse of public power in the service of a collectivistic terrorism, are the very contrary of all that corresponds with natural ethics and the will of the Creator. Both man and civil society derive their origin from the Creator, Who has mutually ordained them one to the other. Hence neither can be exempted from their correlative obligations, nor deny or diminish each other's rights. The Creator Himself has regulated this mutual relationship in its fundamental lines, and it is by an unjust usurpation that communism arrogates to itself the right to enforce, in place of the divine law based on the immutable principles of truth and charity, a partisan political program which derives from the arbitrary human will and is replete with hate. . . .

✧ ✧ ✧ ✧

It was Christianity that first affirmed the real and universal brotherhood of all men of whatever race and condition. This doctrine she proclaimed by a method, and with an amplitude and conviction, unknown to preceding centuries; and with it she potently contributed to the abolition of slavery. Not bloody revolution, but the inner force of her teaching made the proud Roman matron see in her slave a sister in Christ. It is Christianity that adores the son of God, made Man for love of man, and become not only the "Son of a Carpenter" but Himself a "Carpenter." It was Christianity that raised manual labor to its true dignity. . . .

✧ ✧ ✧ ✧

It may be said in all truth that the Church, like Christ, goes through the centuries doing good to all. There would be today neither socialism nor communism if the rulers of the nations had not scorned the teachings and maternal warnings of the Church. On the bases of liberalism and laicism they wished to build other social edifices which, powerful and imposing as they seemed at first, all too soon revealed the weakness of their foundations, and today are crumbling one after another before our eyes, as everything must crumble that is not grounded on the one corner stone which is Christ Jesus. . . .

SELECTION 6

Pius XII: From *Summi Pontificatus*, October 20, 1939

Pope Pius XII, who as Vatican Secretary of State negotiated the concordat with Hitler, knew the centrality of the church-state problem and addressed himself to it in his first encyclical. A former professor of law, he appeals to what he calls "principles of international natural law."

. . . What age has been, for all its technical and purely civic progress, more tormented than ours by spiritual emptiness and deep-felt interior poverty?

✧ ✧ ✧ ✧

As Vicar of Him Who in a decisive hour pronounced before the highest earthly authority of that day, the great words: "For this was I born, and for this came I into the world; that I should give testimony to the truth. Every one that is of the truth, heareth my voice." (*St. John xviii:*37), We feel We owe no greater debt to Our office and to Our time than to testify to the truth with Apostolic firmness: "to give testimony to the truth." This duty necessarily entails the exposition and confutation of errors and human faults; for these must be made known before it is possible to tend and to heal them, "you shall know the truth, and the truth shall make you free" (*St. John viii:*32). . . .

✧ ✧ ✧ ✧

. . . Before all else, it is certain that the radical and ultimate cause of the evils which We deplore in modern society is the denial and rejection of a universal norm of morality as well for individual and social life as for international relations; We mean the disregard, so common nowadays, and the forgetfulness of the natural law itself, which has its foundation in God, Almighty Creator and Father of all, supreme and absolute Lawgiver, all-wise and just Judge of human actions. When God is hated, every basis of morality is undermined; the voice of conscience is stilled or at any rate grows very faint, that voice which teaches even to the illiterate and to uncivilized tribes what is good and what is bad, what lawful, what forbidden, and makes men feel themselves responsible for their actions to a Supreme Judge.

The denial of the fundamentals of morality had its origin, in Europe, in the abandonment of that Christian teaching of which the Chair of Peter is the depository and exponent. That teaching had once given spiritual cohesion to a Europe which, educated, ennobled and civilized by the Cross, had reached such a degree of civil progress as to become the teacher of other peoples, of other continents. But, cut off from the infallible teaching authority of the Church, not a few separated brethren have gone so far as to overthrow the central dogma of Christianity, the Divinity of the Saviour, and have hastened thereby the progress of spiritual decay. . . .

✧ ✧ ✧ ✧

Among the many errors which derive from the poisoned source of religious and moral agnosticism, We would draw your attention, Venerable Brethren, to two in particular, as being those which more than others render almost impossible or at least precarious and uncertain, the peaceful intercourse of peoples.

The first of these pernicious errors, widespread today, is the forgetfulness of that law of human solidarity and charity which is dictated and imposed by our common origin and by the equality of rational nature in all men, to whatever people they belong, and by the redeeming Sacrifice offered by Jesus Christ on the Altar of the Cross to His Heavenly Father on behalf of sinful mankind. . . .

✧ ✧ ✧ ✧

In the light of this unity of all mankind, which exists in law and in fact, individuals do not feel themselves isolated units, like grains of sand, but united by the very force of their nature and by their internal destiny, into an organic, harmonious mutual relationship which varies with the changing of times.

And the nations, despite a difference of development due to diverse conditions of life and of culture, are not destined to break the unity of the human race, but rather to enrich and embellish it by the sharing of their own peculiar gifts and by that reciprocal interchange of goods which can be possible and efficacious only when a mutual love and a lively sense of charity unite all the sons of the same Father and all those redeemed by the same Divine Blood.

The Church of Christ, the faithful depository of the teaching of Divine Wisdom, cannot and does not think of deprecating or disdaining the particular characteristics which each people, with jealous and intelligible pride, cherishes and retains as a precious heritage. Her aim is a supernatural union in all-embracing love, deeply felt and practiced, and not the unity which is exclusively external and superficial and by that very fact weak. . . .

✧ ✧ ✧ ✧

In accordance with these principles of equality, the Church devotes her care to forming cultured native clergy and gradually increasing the number of native Bishops. And in order to give external expression of these, Our intentions, We have chosen the forthcoming Feast of Christ the King to raise to the Episcopal dignity at the Tomb of the Apostles twelve representatives of widely different peoples and races. In the midst of the disruptive contrasts which divide the human family, may this solemn act proclaim to all Our sons, scattered over the world, that the spirit, the teaching and the word of the Church can never be other than that which the Apostle of the Gentiles preached: "putting on the new [man], him who is renewed unto knowledge, according to the image of him that created him. Where there is neither Gentile nor Jew, circumcision nor uncircumcision, Barbarian nor Scythian, bond nor free. But Christ is all, and in all" (*Colossians iii:10, 11*).

Nor is there any fear lest the consciousness of universal brotherhood aroused by the teaching of Christianity, and the spirit which it inspires, be in contrast with love of traditions or the glories of one's fatherland, or impede the progress of prosperity or legitimate interests. For that same Christianity teaches that in the exercise of charity we must follow a God-given order, yielding the place of honor in our affections and good works to those who are bound to us by special ties. Nay, the Divine Master Himself gave an example of this preference for His Own country and fatherland, as He wept over the coming destruction of the Holy City. But legitimate and well-ordered love of our native country should not make us close our eyes to the all-embracing nature of Christian charity, which calls for consideration of others and of their interests in the pacifying light of love. . . .

✧ ✧ ✧ ✧

But there is yet another error no less pernicious to the well-being of the nations and to the prosperity of that great human society which gathers together and embraces within its confines all races. It is the error contained in those ideas which do not hesitate to divorce civil authority from every kind of dependence upon the Supreme Being—First Source and absolute Master of man and of society—and from every restraint of a Higher Law derived from God as from its First Source. Thus they accord the civil authority an unrestricted field of action that is at the mercy of the changeful tide of human will, or of the dictates of casual historical claims, and of the interests of a few.

Once the authority of God and the sway of His law are denied in this way, the civil authority as an inevitable result tends to attribute to itself that absolute autonomy which belongs exclusively to the Supreme Maker. It puts itself in the place of the Almighty and elevates the State or group into the last end of life, the supreme criterion of the moral and juridical order, and therefore forbids every appeal to the principles of natural reason and of the Christian conscience. . . .

✧ ✧ ✧ ✧

. . . It is the noble prerogative and function of the State to control, aid and direct the private and individual activities of national life that they converge harmoniously towards the common good. That good can neither be defined according to arbitrary ideas nor can it accept for its standard primarily the material prosperity of society, but rather it should be defined according to the harmonious development and the natural perfection of man. It is for this perfection that society is designed by the Creator as a means.

To consider the State as something ultimate to which everything else should be subordinated and directed, cannot fail to harm the true and lasting prosperity of nations. This can happen either when unrestricted dominion comes to be conferred on the State as having a mandate from the nation, people, or even a social order, or when the State arrogates such dominion to itself as absolute master, despotically, without any mandate whatsoever. If, in fact, the State lays claim to and directs private enterprises, these, ruled as they are by delicate and complicated internal principles which guarantee and assure the realization of their special aims, may be damaged to the detriment of the public good, by being wrenched from their natural surroundings, that is, from responsible private action. . . .

✧ ✧ ✧ ✧

True courage and a heroism worthy in its degree of admiration and respect, are often necessary to support the hardships of life, the daily weight of misery, growing want and restrictions on a scale never before experienced, whose reason and necessity are not always apparent. Whoever has the care of souls and can search hearts knows the hidden tears of mothers, the resigned sorrow of so many fathers, the countless bitternesses of which no statistics tell or can tell. He sees with sad eyes the mass of sufferings ever on the increase; he knows how the powers of disorder and destruction stand on the alert ready to make use of all these things for their dark designs. No one of good-will and vision will think of refusing the State, in the exceptional conditions of the world today, correspondingly wider and exceptional rights to meet the popular needs. But even in such emergencies, the moral law, established by God, demands that the lawfulness of each such measure and its real necessity be scrutinized with the greatest rigor according to the standards of the common good.

In any case, the more burdensome the material sacrifices demanded of the individual and the family by the State, the more must the rights of conscience be to it sacred and inviolable. Goods, blood it can demand; but the soul redeemed by God, never. The charge laid by God on parents to provide for the material and spiritual good of their offspring and to procure for them a suitable training saturated with the true spirit of religion, cannot be wrested from them without grave violations of their rights. . . .

✧ ✧ ✧ ✧

The idea which credits the State with unlimited authority is not simply an error harmful to the internal life of nations, to their prosperity, and to the larger and well-ordered increase in their well-being, but likewise it injures the relations between peoples, for it breaks the unity of supranational society, robs the law of nations of its foundation and vigor, leads to violation of others' rights and impedes agreement and peaceful intercourse.

A disposition, in fact, of the divinely sanctioned natural order divides the human race into social groups, nations or States, which are mutually independent in organization and in the direction of their internal life. But for all that, the human race is bound together by reciprocal ties, moral and juridical, into a great commonwealth directed to the good of all nations and ruled by special laws which protect its unity and promote its prosperity.

Now no one can fail to see how the claim to absolute autonomy for the State stands in open opposition to this natural way that is inherent in man—nay, denies it utterly—and therefore leaves the stability of international relations at the mercy of the will of rulers, while it destroys the possibility of true union and fruitful collaboration directed to the general good.

So, Venerable Brethren, it is indispensable for the existence of harmonious and lasting contacts and of fruitful relations, that the peoples recognize and observe these principles of international natural law which regulate their normal development and activity. Such principles demand respect for corresponding rights to independence, to life and to the possibility of continuous development in the paths of civilization; they demand, further, fidelity to compacts agreed upon and sanctioned in conformity with the principles of the law of nations.

The indispensable presupposition, without doubt, of all peaceful intercourse between nations, and the very soul of the juridical relations in force among them, is mutual trust: the expectation and conviction that each party will respect its plighted word; the certainty that both sides are convinced that "Better is wisdom, than weapons of war" (*Ecclesiastes ix: 18*), and are ready to enter into discussion and to avoid recourse to force or to threats of force in case of delays, hindrances, changes or disputes, because all these things can be the result not of bad-will, but of changed circumstances and of genuine interests in conflict.

But on the other hand, to tear the law of nations from its anchor in Divine law, to base it on the autonomous will of States, is to dethrone that very law and deprive it of its noblest and strongest qualities. Thus it would stand abandoned to the fatal drive of private interest and collective selfishness exclusively intent on the assertion of its own rights and ignoring those of others.

Now, it is true that with the passage of time and the substantial change of circumstances, which were not and perhaps could not have been foreseen in the making of a treaty, such a treaty or some of its clauses can in fact become, or at least seem to become, unjust, impracticable or too burdensome for one of the parties. It is obvious that should such be the case, recourse should be had in good time to a frank discussion with a view to modifying the treaty or making another in its stead. But to consider treaties on principle as ephemeral and tacitly to assume the authority of rescinding them unilaterally when they are no longer to one's advantage, would be to abolish all mutual trust among States. In this way, natural order would be destroyed and there would be seen dug between different peoples and nations trenches of division impossible to refill.

Today, Venerable Brethren, all men are looking with terror into the abyss to which they have been brought by the errors and principles which We have mentioned, and by their practical consequences. Gone are the proud illusions of limitless progress. . . .

XXV THE SOCIAL GOSPEL

Recurrent depressions, social conflict and the problems of urbanization made many Protestants towards the end of the nineteenth century doubt Bishop Lawrence's assertion that "godliness is in league with riches." (See above.) To find an answer to the new problems resulting from the industrial and social revolution surrounding it, American Protestantism produced a movement commonly called the Social Gospel. A fairly complex reaction to the new situation, it had its conservative and radical wings. It opposed the naive glorification of the profit motive and advocated justice for the industrial worker and all kinds of political reforms. There was also a strong undercurrent of moralism and a concern with symptomatic relief as expressed in the vastly popular novel *In His Steps* by Charles M. Sheldon which popularized the movement.

Washington Gladden (1836–1918) is often considered the first major voice of this tradition. Walter Rauschenbusch (1861–1918) was probably its most eloquent and prominent exponent. The Social Gospel dominated American Protestantism until the Great Depression and World War II undermined some of its more utopian hopes. Nevertheless, even its most perceptive critics were deeply affected by it (cf. Reinhold Niebuhr, below) and in a slightly transformed version the Social Gospel has experienced a renaissance in the second half of the twentieth century among the advocates of "Secular Christianity."

SELECTION 1

Washington Gladden: *Social Salvation*

Washington Gladden, 1836–1918, a Congregational minister and prolific author (forty books), was one of the earlier spokesmen of the so-called "Social Gospel," which attempted to "realize the Kingdom of God in this world." In his Lyman Beecher lectures, Washington Gladden summarized some of his ideas under the heading *Social Salvation*. The following selection is taken from these lectures.

The first thing for us to understand is that God is in his world, and that we are workers together with him. In all this industrial struggle he is present in every part of it, working according to the counsel of his perfect will. In the gleams of light which sometimes break forth from the darkness of the conflict we discern his inspiration; in the stirrings of good-will which temper the wasting strife we behold the evidence of his presence; in the sufferings and losses and degradations which wait upon every violation of his law of love we witness the retributions with which that law goes armed. In the weltering masses of poverty; in the giddy throngs that tread the paths of vice; in the multitudes distressed and scattered as sheep having no shepherd; in the brutalized ranks marching in lock-step through the prison yard; in the groups of politicians scheming for place and plunder,—in all the most forlorn and untoward and degrading human associations, the One who is never absent is that divine Spirit which brooded over the chaos at the beginning, nursing it to life and beauty, and which is

> "nearer to every creature he hath made,
> Than anything unto itself can be."

Nay, there is not one of these hapless, sinning multitudes in whose spirit he is not present to will and to work according to his good pleasure; never overpowering the will, but gently pressing in, by every avenue open to him, his gifts of love and truth. As he has for every man's life a plan, so has he for the common life a perfect social order into which he seeks to lead his children, that he may give them plenty and blessedness and abundance of peace as long as the moon endureth. Surely he has a way for men to live in society; he has a way of organizing industry; he has a way of life for the family, and for the school, and for the shop, and for the city, and for the state; he has a way for preventing poverty, and a way for helping and saving the poor and the sick and the sinful; and it is his way that we are to seek and point out and follow. We cannot know it perfectly, but if we are humble and faithful and obedient, we shall come to understand it better and better as the years go by. The one thing for us to be sure of is that God has a way for human beings to live and work together, just as truly as he has a way for the stars over our heads and the crystals under our feet; and that it is man's chief end to find this way and follow it. "What the world really wants," says the teacher I have quoted, "is men who have news from the land of the ideal, who have God's life within them, who open afresh the springs of living water that quench the thirst of the soul." Nothing can be truer. But for what kind of news from the land of the ideal are men hungering and thirsting? For the news that brings the ideal down to earth; that makes it no mere dreamy possibility of far-off good, but the lamp of our feet and the light of our path now and here. For all this common life of ours there are ideals that uplift and transfigure and ennoble it. There is an ideal for the home and for the church, for the school and for the shop, for the factory and for the city; and the one refreshing and inspiring experience of life is to get sight of it, and believe in it. The ideal in all these social organizations is nothing else but God's way,—the way that he has ordained for human beings to live and work together. The thing for us to do is first to discern it ourselves, and then to get men to see it, and believe in it, and work for it with heart and soul and mind and strength. It will not be realized all at once; it will take long years of labor and patience; but it is the

> "far-off divine event
> To which the whole creation moves,"

and we know that there can be no permanent peace or welfare but that to which it beckons us.

I trust, my brethren, that I have made plain to you my own deep conviction that the work of the ministry in these days must be deeply concerned with social questions. I trust that you will all find in your own hearts a growing interest in these questions, and that you will be able to communicate that interest to the people to whom you are sent; to kindle in their hearts the enthusiasm of humanity, and to guide them in their thoughts and labors for their fellow men. And I trust that you can also see that this social teaching and social service is not something outside of religion; that religion is and must be the heart and soul of it all; that it means nothing but religion coming to reality in everyday life; the divine ideal descending upon human society and transforming it from glory to glory, even as by the spirit of the Lord. If there is any treatment of social questions in the pulpit which has any other aim or inspiration than this, I have no faith in it. If any minister thinks that he can wisely separate these questions from religion and treat them upon the basis of economic theory or political expediency, I do not agree with him. I do not, for my own part, expect to see any radical or permanent cure discovered for poverty or pauperism, for grinding monopoly or municipal corruption, for bribery or debauchery or crime, except as men's minds and hearts are opened to receive the truths of the spiritual world; except as they are brought into conscious and vital relations with things unseen and eternal. There can be no adequate social reform save that which springs from a genuine revival of religion; only it must be a religion which is less concerned about getting men to heaven than about fitting them for their proper work on the earth; which does not set itself over against the secular life and subdues it by its power and rules it by its law, and transfigures it by its light. For any other kind of religion than this I do not think that the world has any longer very much use.

May God fill your lives with it, and teach you how to bring home its truth and reality to the hearts of men.

SELECTION 2

Francis Peabody: *The Approach to the Social Question*

Francis Greenwood Peabody, Professor of Christian Morals at Harvard University, expressed the hope of the Social Gospel in this work of 1909.

What a strange scene the modern world thus presents, of theoretical indifference and of practical loyalty; of people who think themselves without religion and yet daily testify to the motives of religion! Never were so many minds repelled by the technicalities of religion; yet never were there so many people of whom the great words could be spoken: "Not every one that saith unto me, Lord, Lord, . . . but he that doeth the will of my Father"; never so many who might ask in surprise: "When saw we thee an hungred, and fed thee, or . . . a stranger, and took thee in?" and are fit to receive the answer: "Inasmuch as ye have done it unto these, . . . ye have done it unto me"; never so many unconscious Christians, willing to do the will, but neither knowing nor caring to know the doctrine:—

"Sweet souls, without reproach or blot,
Who do Thy work and know it not."

At such a time, what is the task of teachers of religion but to clarify and interpret these impulses of service, to indicate their religious life, not as an alternative to social duty, but as its natural and logical fulfilment. What, in a word, is this worldwide and compelling summons to the creation of a better world but the premonition of a revival of faith in man as the instrument, and faith in the world as the object, of redemption? Here is no abandonment of religion, or substitute for religion, but a way—not yet wholly clear, but not impassable—along which the life of the present age may reach a religion appropriate to its own needs. It is perhaps not the most direct way, but it is at least not without the approval of modern philosophy, or without the commendation of Jesus Christ, and for many persons under the conditions of the present age the way most immediately open; and it is not so important in the ascent of faith what way one should take, as it is to start from the point where one finds himself, and not stop till the summit is won.

Such seems to be the relation of the Social Question to the religious life. The two are not competitors or alternatives, but the successive experiences, logical steps in the education of the human race. And if this conclusion is legitimate, there follow from it two practical consequences which are of the utmost significance, alike to social service and to religious faith. The first may be described as the spiritualization of the Social Question, and the second may be described as the socialization of the religious life.

What, on the one hand, is the most immediate peril which threatens the Social Question? It is, as has been more than once observed, the peril of a practical materialism; the interpretation of a great human movement in terms of machinery; the expectation that a change in economic methods will of itself produce a change of the human heart. And what, to state the case from the other side, is the chief source of hope and courage in the movement of social service? It is the discovery, which many minds at many points of this great adventure are now making, that beneath the forms of economic change there is proceeding a spiritual enterprise which the present age is called to undertake.

A charity-visitor, for example, enlists in the service of relief, and the problems which confront her—of wages, housing, idleness, food, and drink—seem wholly concerned with economic conditions and material wants. The squalid facts of her task may almost extinguish its spiritual significance, as a flame flickers and dies where the atmosphere is foul. "What room is there," she may ask, "for ethical idealism among these sordid and commercial needs?" "Give me the luxuries of life," the historian, Motley, humorously said, "and I can dispense with its necessities"; and it may well seem to this servant of the poor that philosophy and religion are offering her the luxuries of life, while the necessities of existence are still unsupplied. Must she not abandon her idealism and apply herself to the terribly concrete conditions of her immediate work? On the contrary, her philosophy of charity is essential to her efficiency and courage in the practice of relief. Nothing can redeem the work of charity from dulness and despondency except the capacity for spiritual vision. Let the agent of relief forget her idealism, and she becomes a social mechanic, an official, a statistician, and is on the highroad to discouragement, perfunctoriness, and despair. The mechanism of her task can be endured only as she discerns the meaning of her task. Her philosophy is not a luxury, but a necessity. She is patient with the real because she beholds the ideal. The dull and unresponsive life before her becomes a symbol of her faith, and is transfigured by her idealism into interest, picturesqueness, and sanctity. Her social service has passed the limits of duty and entered the region of privilege. She walks by faith, not by sight; and her faith saves both her and her work from condescension, impatience, and hopelessness. Sir Launfal, seeking the Holy Grail, passed the leper at his own door; but, returning from the distant quest, found the ideal he had sought revealed to him in the duty he had ignored:—

> "And the leper no longer crouched at his side,
> But stood before him glorified,
> Shining and tall and fair and straight
> As the pillar that stood by the Beautiful Gate."

The same story may be told in the language of the industrial world; of many an employer, whose way of business promotes justice, fraternalism, and peace; and of many an employed, whose fidelity and efficiency are such as no wage-system can buy. These men may fancy themselves far from any contact with the religious life; they may listen but languidly to the preachers of other worldliness; they may even conceive of the Christian ministry as a useless caste, and of the Christian Church as a capitalist-club. They are too busy to be pious and too worldly to be saints. And yet, if the Christian character is to have any place in modern life, it must be precisely where these men are set, in the heat of the world's work and under the load of the world's care; and the worst of disasters, alike for religion and for business, is to separate the one from the other. When Jesus looked about him for the habit of life which he desired to commend, he found it most conspicuously in those people who were doing, as it should be done, the common work of the business world. The investor with his talents, the porter at the gate, the farmer in the field, the merchant with his pearls, the woman at her house-work,—how common and worldly, how far from the religion of the Scribes and Pharisees were these types of holiness! Yet of these commonplace people, who had thus spiritualized their Social Question, so that their daily business could meet the test of Christ, he said: The kingdom of heaven is like these. It is the same to-day. Each invention or enterprise which lifts the industrial burden or promotes industrial efficiency; each character forged in the fire of business temptation; each movement of industrial justice, brotherhood, partnership, or peace, is nothing less than the new language in which the men of the present age are uttering their great confession, "We are laborers together with God."

Laurence Oliphant once said that the greatest need of modern England was a spiritually-minded man of the world,—a man, that is to say, who could be in the world, yet not subdued to that he worked in, and who found it not impossible to do the world's work with a spiritual mind. He is like a potter, sitting before the clay which it is his task to mould. He does not wash his hands of it because it soils him, or dabble in it like a little boy for the sake of getting dirty; but he takes it, just as it is, and shapes it into the forms of use or beauty which are possible under the limits of the clay. Precisely such material is the modern business world, and the spiritually-minded man of the world does not dabble in it, or run away from it, but moulds it to the use and beauty to which, just as it is, it may be applied. No harder test was ever offered to the religious life than this demand that it shall adapt itself to the material conditions of an industrial democracy. It must be shaped out of the common clay of commercial conditions and hardened in the fire of industrial temptation. It is called to spiritualize the Social Question, and to make it an instrument of rational and consistent faith. It uses the coarse material of modern life to teach, as Dante said, "How man eternalizes himself."

And if it is the part of religion to spiritualize the Social Question, so, on the other hand, the Social Question is called to socialize the religious life. The religion of the individual, it is true, remains the permanent centre of spiritual experience. No organization or authority can supplant the right to immediate communion of the individual soul with the living God. The religious life is most directly transmitted by the contagion of the spirit, the communicative power of consecrated souls. Nothing that may happen to religion can convert it into a sociological or economic scheme, which substitutes a change in social conditions for a change in human hearts. Socialism may be religious, but religion is not socialism. "The kingdom of God is within you."

To hold fast to this central thought of personal religion is not, however, to desocialize religion. The religion of the individual is not the religion of individualism. The one makes the person the beginning of the religious process; the other makes him the end of it. Individual religion is the most powerful of social dynamics; individualistic religion, on the other hand, is unapplied power, like an engine which has its proper fuel, but is unattached to moving wheels. The difference is not one of origin or power, but of the transmission of energy. No age can safely subordinate the religion of the individual; yet nothing is more obvious than the fact that the present age has completely outgrown the religion of individualism. The age of the Social Question involves the socialization of the religious life. It is no longer possible to think of religion as a personal possession, or security, or joy; for the mind of the time turns inevitably to the further question of utilization, applicability, and service. Thus the centre of religious experience remains where it always has been, but the radius of religious experience is enormously expanded, toward the ever widening circle of social obligations, hopes, and dreams.

This extension of the sphere of religion is, in fact, occurring in every human interest and aim. The religion of individualism is but sharing the fate of the economics and the politics of individualism. Precisely as the modern miracles of intercommunication have transformed the world into an organism where the progress or decadence of one nation is felt, like pain at the extremities of a body, at the remotest parts; precisely as a new economics and a new politics have issued from this new thought of the unity of the world,—so the circle of religious experience has widened from the problem of personal redemption to the problem of a world to be redeemed; and the individual, instead of being called to save his soul from a lost world, is called to set his soul to save the world. The religion of the twentieth century must contemplate the world, not as a chaos of competing atoms, but as an organic and indivisible whole. It must socialize its hopes, and save people, not singly but together, the poor with the prosperous, the employed with the employer, the Oriental with the Occidental, the Black with the White.

SELECTION 3
Walter Rauschenbusch: *A Theology for the Social Gospel*

Walter Rauschenbusch, 1861–1918, was a Baptist clergyman and professor of theology who became the major spokesman of the "Social Gospel" (*Christianity and the Social Crisis,* 1907; and *A Theology for the Social Gospel,* 1917; etc.). For him the "Kingdom of God" and its establishment were central. What this meant to him is set forth clearly in this selection.

If theology is to offer an adequate doctrinal basis for the social gospel, it must not only make room for the doctrine of the Kingdom of God, but give it a central place and revise all other doctrines so that they will articulate organically with it.

This doctrine is itself the social gospel. Without it, the idea of redeeming the social order will be but an annex to the orthodox conception of the scheme of salvation. It will love like a Negro servant family in a detached cabin back of the white man's house in the South. If this doctrine gets the place which has always been its legitimate right, the practical proclamation and application of social morality will have a firm footing.

To those whose minds live in the social gospel, the Kingdom of God is a dear truth, the marrow of the gospel, just as the incarnation was to Athanasius, justification by faith alone to Luther, and the sovereignty of God to Jonathan Edwards. It was just as dear to Jesus. He too lived in it, and from it looked out on the world and the work he had to do.

Jesus always spoke of the Kingdom of God. Only two of his reported sayings contain the word "Church," and both passages are of questionable authenticity. It is safe to say that he never thought of founding the kind of institution which afterward claimed to be acting for him.

Yet immediately after his death, groups of disciples joined and consolidated by inward necessity. Each local group knew that it was part of a divinely founded fellowship mysteriously spreading through humanity, and awaiting the return of the Lord and the establishing of his Kingdom. This universal

Church was loved with the same religious faith and reverence with which Jesus had loved the Kingdom of God. It was the partial and earthly realization of the divine Society, and at the Parousia the Church and the Kingdom would merge.

But the Kingdom was merely a hope, the Church a present reality. The chief interest and affection flowed toward the Church. Soon, through a combination of causes, the name and idea of "the Kingdom" began to be displaced by the name and idea of "the Church" in the preaching, literature, and theological thought of the Church. Augustine completed this process in his *De Civitate Dei*. The Kingdom of God which has, throughout human history, opposed the Kingdom of Sin, is today embodied in the Church. The millennium began when the Church was founded. This practically substituted the actual, not the ideal Church for the Kingdom of God. The beloved ideal of Jesus became a vague phrase which kept intruding from the New Testament. Like Cinderella in the kitchen, it saw the other great dogmas furbished up for the ball, but no prince of theology restored it to its rightful place. The Reformation, too, brought no renascence of the doctrine of the Kingdom; it had only eschatological value, or was defined in blurred phrases borrowed from the Church. The present revival of the Kingdom idea is due to the combined influence of the historical study of the Bible and of the social gospel.

When the doctrine of the Kingdom of God shriveled to an undeveloped and pathetic remnant in Christian thought, this loss was bound to have far-reaching consequences. We are told that the loss of a single tooth from the arch of the mouth in childhood may spoil the symmetrical development of the skull and produce malformations affecting the mind and character. The atrophy of that idea which had occupied the chief place in the mind of Jesus, necessarily affected the conception of Christianity, the life of the Church, the progress of humanity, and the structure of theology. I shall briefly enumerate some of the consequences affecting theology. This list, however, is by no means complete.

1. Theology lost its contact with the synoptic thought of Jesus. Its problems were not at all the same which had occupied his mind. It lost his point of view and became to some extent

incapable of understanding him. His ideas had to be rediscovered in our time. Traditional theology and the mind of Jesus Christ became incommensurable quantities. It claimed to regard his revelation and the substance of his thought as divine, and yet did not learn to think like him. The loss of the Kingdom idea is one key to this situation.

2. The distinctive ethical principles of Jesus were the direct outgrowth of his conception of the Kingdom of God. When the latter disappeared from theology, the former disappeared from ethics. Only persons having the substance of the Kingdom ideal in their minds, seem to be able to get relish out of the ethics of Jesus. Only those church bodies which have been in opposition to organized society and have looked for a better city with its foundations in heaven, have taken the Sermon on the Mount seriously.

3. The Church is primarily a fellowship for worship; the Kingdom is a fellowship of righteousness. When the latter was neglected in theology, the ethical force of Christianity was weakened; when the former was emphasized in theology, the importance of worship was exaggerated. The prophets and Jesus had cried down sacrifices and ceremonial performances, and cried up righteousness, mercy, solidarity. Theology now reversed this, and by its theoretical discussions did its best to stimulate sacramental actions and priestly importance. Thus the religious energy and enthusiasm which might have saved mankind from its great sins, were used up in hearing and endowing masses, or in maintaining competitive church organizations, while mankind is still stuck in the mud. There are nations in which the ethical condition of the masses is the reverse of the frequency of the masses in the churches.

4. When the Kingdom ceased to be the dominating religious reality, the Church moved up into the position of the supreme good. To promote the power of the Church and its control over all rival political forces was equivalent to promoting the supreme ends of Christianity. This increased the arrogance of churchmen and took the moral check off their policies. For the Kingdom of God can never be promoted by lies, craft, crime or war, but the wealth and power of the Church have often been promoted by these means. The medieval ideal of the supremacy of the

Church over the State was the logical consequence of making the Church the highest good with no superior ethical standard by which to test it. The medieval doctrines concerning the Church and the Papacy were the direct theological outcome of the struggles for Church supremacy, and were meant to be weapons in that struggle.

5. The Kingdom ideal is the test and corrective of the influence of the Church. When the Kingdom ideal disappeared, the conscience of the Church was muffled. It became possible for the missionary expansion of Christianity to halt for centuries without creating any sense of shortcoming. It became possible for the most unjust social conditions to fasten themselves on Christian nations without awakening any consciousness that the purpose of Christ was being defied and beaten back. The practical undertakings of the Church remained within narrow lines, and the theological thought of the Church was necessarily confined in a similar way. The claims of the Church were allowed to stand in theology with no conditions and obligations to test and balance them. If the Kingdom had stood as the purpose for which the Church exists, the Church could not have fallen into such corruption and sloth. Theology bears part of the guilt for the pride, the greed, and the ambition of the Church.

6. The Kingdom ideal contains the revolutionary force of Christianity. When this ideal faded out of the systematic thought of the Church, it became a conservative social influence and increased the weight of the other stationary forces in society. If the Kingdom of God had remained part of the theological and Christian consciousness, the Church could not, down to our times, have been salaried by autocratic class governments to keep the democratic and economic impulses of the people under check.

7. Reversely, the movements for democracy and social justice were left without a religious backing for lack of the Kingdom idea. The Kingdom of God as the fellowship of righteousness, would be advanced by the abolition of industrial slavery and the disappearance of the slums of civilization; the Church would only indirectly gain through such social changes. Even today many Christians can not see any religious importance in social

justice and fraternity because it does not increase the number of conversions nor fill the churches. Thus the practical conception of salvation, which is the effective theology of the common man and minister, has been cut back and crippled for lack of the Kingdom ideal.

8. Secular life is belittled as compared with church life. Services rendered to the Church get a higher religious rating than services rendered to the community. Thus the religious value is taken out of the activities of the common man and the prophetic services to society. Wherever the Kingdom of God is a living reality in Christian thought, any advance of social righteousness is seen as a part of redemption and arouses inward joy and the triumphant sense of salvation. When the Church absorbs interest, a subtle asceticism creeps back into our theology and the world looks different.

9. When the doctrine of the Kingdom of God is lacking in theology, the salvation of the individual is seen in its relation to the Church and to the future life, but not in its relation to the task of saving the social order. Theology has left this important point in a condition so hazy and muddled that it has taken us almost a generation to see that the salvation of the individual and the redemption of the social order are closely related, and how.

10. Finally, theology has been deprived of the inspiration of great ideas contained in the idea of the Kingdom and in labor for it. The Kingdom of God breeds prophets; the Church breeds priests and theologians. The Church runs to tradition and dogma; the Kingdom of God rejoices in forecasts and boundless horizons. The men who have contributed the most fruitful impulses to Christian thought have been men of prophetic vision, and their theology has proved most effective for future times where it has been most concerned with past history, with present social problems, and with the future of human society. The Kingdom of God is to theology what outdoor color and light are to art. It is impossible to estimate what inspirational impulses have been lost to theology and to the Church, because it did not develop the doctrine of the Kingdom of God and see the world and its redemption from that point of view.

These are some of the historical effects which the loss of the doctrine of the Kingdom of God has inflicted on systematic theology. The chief contribution which the social gospel has made and will make to theology is to give new vitality and importance to that doctrine. In doing so it will be a reformatory force of the highest importance in the field of doctrinal theology, for any systematic conception of Christianity must be not only defective but incorrect if the idea of the Kingdom of God does not govern it.

The restoration of the doctrine of the Kingdom has already made progress. Some of the ablest and most voluminous works of the old theology in their thousands of pages gave the Kingdom of God but a scanty mention, usually in connection with eschatology, and saw no connection between it and the Calvinistic doctrines of personal redemption. The newer manuals not only make constant reference to it in connection with various doctrines, but they arrange their entire subject matter so that the Kingdom of God becomes the governing idea.

In the following brief propositions I should like to offer a few suggestions, on behalf of the social gospel, for the theological formulation of the doctrine of the Kingdom. Something like this is needed to give us "a theology for the social gospel."

1. The Kingdom of God is divine in its origin, progress, and consummation. It was initiated by Jesus Christ, in whom the prophetic spirit came to its consummation, it is sustained by the Holy Spirit, and it will be brought to its fulfillment by the power of God in his own time. The passive and active resistance of the Kingdom of Evil at every stage of its advance is so great, and the human resources of the Kingdom of God so slender, that no explanation can satisfy a religious mind which does not see the power of God in its movements. The Kingdom of God, therefore, is miraculous all the way, and is the continuous revelation of the power, the righteousness, and the love of God. The establishment of a community of righteousness in mankind is just as much a saving act of God as the salvation of an individual from his natural selfishness and moral inability. The Kingdom of God, therefore, is not merely ethical, but has a rightful place in theology. This doctrine is absolutely necessary to establish that organic union between religion and morality, between theology and ethics, which is one of the char-

acteristics of the Christian religion. When our moral actions are consciously related to the Kingdom of God they gain religious quality. Without this doctrine we shall have expositions of schemes of redemption and we shall have systems of ethics, but we shall not have a true exposition of Christianity. The first step to the reform of the Churches is the restoration of the doctrine of the Kingdom of God.

2. The Kingdom of God contains the teleology of the Christian religion. It translates theology from the static to the dynamic. It sees, not doctrines or rites to be conserved and perpetuated, but resistance to be overcome and great ends to be achieved. Since the Kingdom of God is the supreme purpose of God, we shall understand the Kingdom so far as we understand God, and we shall understand God so far as we understand his Kingdom. As long as organized sin is in the world, the Kingdom of God is characterized by conflict with evil. But if there were no evil, or after evil has been overcome, the Kingdom of God will still be the end to which God is lifting the race. It is realized not only by redemption, but also by the education of mankind and the revelation of his life within it.

3. Since God is in it, the Kingdom of God is always both present and future. Like God it is in all tenses, eternal in the midst of time. It is the energy of God realizing itself in human life. Its future lies among the mysteries of God. It invites and justifies prophecy, but all prophecy is fallible; it is valuable in so far as it grows out of action for the Kingdom and impels action. No theories about the future of the Kingdom of God are likely to be valuable or true which paralyze or postpone redemptive action on our part. To those who postpone, it is a theory and not a reality. It is for us to see the Kingdom of God as always coming, always pressing in on the present, always big with possibility, and always inviting immediate action. We walk by faith. Every human life is so placed that it can share with God in the creation of the Kingdom, or can resist and retard its progress. The Kingdom is for each of us the supreme task and the supreme gift of God. By accepting it as a task, we experience it as a gift. By laboring for it we enter into the joy and peace of the Kingdom as our divine fatherland and habitation.

4. Even before Christ, men of God saw the Kingdom of God as the great end to which all divine leadings were pointing. Every idealistic interpretation of the world, religious or philosophical, needs some such conception. Within the Christian religion the idea of the Kingdom gets its distinctive interpretation from Christ. (a) Jesus emancipated the idea of the Kingdom from previous nationalistic limitations and from the debasement of lower religious tendencies, and made it world-wide and spiritual. (b) He made the purpose of salvation essential in it. (c) He imposed his own mind, his personality, his love and holy will on the idea of the Kingdom. (d) He not only foretold it but initiated it by his life and work. As humanity more and more develops a racial consciousness in modern life, idealistic interpretations of the destiny of humanity will become more influential and important. Unless theology has a solidaristic vision higher and fuller than any other, it cannot maintain the spiritual leadership of mankind, but will be outdistanced. Its business is to infuse the distinctive qualities of Jesus Christ into its teachings about the Kingdom, and this will be a fresh competitive test of his continued headship of humanity.

5. The Kingdom of God is humanity organized according to the will of God. Interpreting it through the consciousness of Jesus we may affirm these convictions about the ethical relations within the Kingdom: (a) Since Christ revealed the divine worth of life and personality, and since his salvation seeks the restoration and fulfillment of even the least, it follows that the Kingdom of God, at every stage of human development, tends toward a social order which will best guarantee to all personalities their freest and highest development. This involves the redemption of social life from the cramping influence of religious bigotry, from the repression of self-assertion in the relation of upper and lower classes, and from all forms of slavery in which human beings are treated as mere means to serve the ends of others. (b) Since love is the supreme law of Christ, the Kingdom of God implies a progressive reign of love in human affairs. We can see its advance wherever the free will of love supersedes the use of force and legal coercion as a regulative of the social order. This involves the redemption of society

from political autocracies and economic oligarchies; the substitution of redemptive for vindictive penology; the abolition of constraint through hunger as part of the industrial system; and the abolition of war as the supreme expression of hate and the completest cessation of freedom. (c) The highest expression of love is the free surrender of what is truly our own, life, property, and rights. A much lower but perhaps more decisive expression of love is the surrender of any opportunity to exploit men. No social group or organization can claim to be clearly within the Kingdom of God which drains others for its own ease, and resists the effort to abate this fundamental evil. This involves the redemption of society from private property in the natural resources of the earth, and from any condition in industry which makes monopoly profits possible. (d) The reign of love tends toward the progressive unity of mankind, but with the maintenance of individual liberty and the opportunity of nations to work out their own national peculiarities and ideals.

6. Since the Kingdom is the supreme end of God, it must be the purpose for which the Church exists. The measure in which it fulfills this purpose is also the measure of its spiritual authority and honor. The institutions of the Church, its activities, its worship, and its theology must in the long run be tested by its effectiveness in creating the Kingdom of God. For the Church to see itself apart from the Kingdom, and to find its aims in itself, is the same sin of selfish detachment as when an individual selfishly separates himself from the common good. The Church has the power to save in so far as the Kingdom of God is present in it. If the Church is not living for the Kingdom, its institutions are part of the "world." In that case it is not the power of redemption but its object. It may even become an anti-Christian power. If any form of church organization which formerly aided the Kingdom now impedes it, the reason for its existence is gone.

7. Since the Kingdom is the supreme end, all problems of personal salvation must be reconsidered from the point of view of the Kingdom. It is not sufficient to set the two aims of Christianity side by side. There must be a synthesis, and theology must explain how the two react on each other. (Noted in an earlier chapter.) The entire redemptive work of Christ must

also be reconsidered under this orientation. Early Greek theology saw salvation chiefly as the redemption from ignorance by the revelation of God and from earthliness by the impartation of immortality. It interpreted the work of Christ accordingly, and laid stress on his incarnation and resurrection. Western theology saw salvation mainly as forgiveness of guilt and freedom from punishment. It interpreted the work of Christ accordingly, and laid stress on the death and atonement. If the Kingdom of God was the guiding idea and chief end of Jesus —as we now know it was—we may be sure that every step in His life, including His death, was related to that aim and its realization, and when the idea of the Kingdom of God takes its due place in theology, the work of Christ will have to be interpreted afresh.

8. The Kingdom of God is not confined within the limits of the Church and its activities. It embraces the whole of human life. It is the Christian transfiguration of the social order. The Church is one social institution alongside of the family, the industrial organization of society, and the state. The Kingdom of God is in all these, and realizes itself through them all. During the Middle Ages all society was ruled and guided by the Church. Few of us would want modern life to return to such a condition. Functions which the Church used to perform, have now far outgrown its capacities. The Church is indispensable to the religious education of humanity and to the conservation of religion, but the greatest future awaits religion in the public life of humanity.

XXVI REINHOLD NIEBUHR

The most widely influential native American theologian in the twentieth century is Reinhold Niebuhr, who was born in 1892. His unsentimental social analysis, which uses the insights of his Christian heritage in a critical and original manner, influenced a generation of Americans outside as well as inside the churches. He felt that the illusions of liberalism in regard to man destroy any possibility of an effective social ethics. If the reality of sin is ignored all social teachings are reduced to pious and irrelevant incantations.

Expressing these views over many years in a multitude of ways, he changed positions frequently, always holding on to his basic insights. While selections from his most important work, *The Nature and Destiny of Man,* might reveal his social ethics clearly, it is easiest to approach a writer like Niebuhr by using his many shorter works where he was forced to articulate his position in a compressed form.

SELECTION I
An Interpretation of Christian Ethics

The relevance of an impossible ethical ideal shows Niebuhr's basic approach. He stresses the importance of "the law of love as a basis of even the most minimal social standards," yet calls it "an impossible possibility."

Prophetic Christianity faces the difficulty that its penetration into the total and ultimate human situation complicates the problem of dealing with the immediate moral and social situations which all men must face. The common currency of the moral life is constituted of the "nicely calculated less and more" of the relatively good and the relatively evil. Human happiness in ordinary intercourse is determined by the difference between a little more and a little less justice, a little more and a little less freedom, between varying degrees of imaginative insight with which the self enters the life and understands the interests of the neighbor. Prophetic Christianity, on the other hand, demands the impossible; and by that very demand emphasizes the impotence and corruption of human nature, wresting from man the cry of distress and contrition, "The good that I would, I do not: but the evil that I would not, that I do. . . . Woe is me . . . who will deliver me from the body of this death." Measuring the distance between mountain peaks and valleys and arriving at the conclusion that every high mountain has a "timber line" above which life cannot maintain itself, it is always tempted to indifference toward the task of building roads up the mountain-side, and of coercing its wilderness into a sufficient order to sustain human life. The latter task must consequently be assumed by those who are partly blind to the total dimension of life and, being untouched by its majesties and tragedies, can give themselves to the immediate tasks before them.

Thus prophetic religion tends to disintegrate into two contrasting types of religion. The one inclines to deny the relevance of the ideal of love to the ordinary problems of existence, certain that the tragedy of human life must be resolved by something more than moral achievement. The other tries to prove the relevance of the religious ideal to the problems of everyday existence by reducing it to conformity with the prudential rules of conduct which the common sense of many generations and the experience of the ages have elaborated. Broadly speaking, the conflict between these two world views is the conflict between orthodox Christianity and modern secularism. In so far as liberal Christianity is a compound of prophetic religion and secularism it is drawn into the debate in a somewhat equivocal position but, on the whole, on the side of the secularists and naturalists.

Against orthodox Christianity, the prophetic tradition in Christianity must insist on the relevance of the ideal of love to the moral experience of mankind on every conceivable level.

It is not an ideal magically superimposed upon life by a revelation which has no relation to total human experience. The whole conception of life revealed in the Cross of Christian faith is not a pure negation of, or irrelevance toward, the moral ideals of "natural man." While the final heights of the love ideal condemn as well as fulfill the moral canons of common sense, the ideal is involved in every moral aspiration and achievement. It is the genius and the task of prophetic religion to insist on the organic relation between historic human existence and that which is both the ground and the fulfillment of this existence, the transcendent.

Moral life is possible at all only in a meaningful existence. Obligation can be felt only to some system of coherence and some ordering will. Thus moral obligation is always an obligation to promote harmony and to overcome chaos. But every conceivable order in the historical world contains an element of anarchy. Its world rests upon contingency and caprice. The obligation to support and enhance it can therefore only arise and maintain itself upon the basis of a faith that it is the partial fruit of a deeper unity and the promise of a more perfect harmony than is revealed in any immediate situation. If a lesser faith than this prompts moral action, it results in precisely those types of moral fanaticism which impart unqualified worth to qualified values and thereby destroy even their qualified worth. The prophetic faith in a God who is both the ground and the ultimate fulfillment of existence, who is both the creator and the judge of the world, is thus involved in every moral situation. Without it the world is seen either as being meaningless or as revealing unqualifiedly good and simple meanings. In either case the nerve of moral action is ultimately destroyed. The dominant attitudes of prophetic faith are gratitude and contrition; gratitude for Creation and contrition before Judgment; or, in other words, confidence that life is good in spite of its evil and that it is evil in spite of its good. In such a faith both sentimentality and despair are avoided. The meaningfulness of life does not tempt to premature complacency, and the chaos which always threatens the world of meaning does not destroy the tension of faith and hope in which all moral action is grounded.

The prophetic faith, that the meaningfulness of life and existence implies a source and end beyond itself, produces a morality which implies that every moral value and standard is grounded in and points toward an ultimate perfection of unity and harmony, not realizable in any historic situation. An analysis of the social history of mankind validates this interpretation.

In spite of the relativity of morals every conceivable moral code and every philosophy of morals enjoins concern for the life and welfare of the other and seeks to restrain the unqualified assertion of the interests of the self against the other. There is thus a fairly universal agreement in all moral systems that it is wrong to take the life or the property of the neighbor, though it must be admitted that the specific applications of these general principles vary greatly according to time and place. This minimal standard of moral conduct is grounded in the law of love and points toward it as ultimate fulfillment. The obligation to affirm and protect the life of others can arise at all only if it is assumed that life is related to life in some unity and harmony of existence. In any given instance motives of the most calculating prudence rather than a high sense of obligation may enforce the standard. Men may defend the life of the neighbor merely to preserve those processes of mutuality by which their own life is protected. But that only means that they have discovered the inter-relatedness of life through concern for themselves rather than by an analysis of the total situation. This purely prudential approach will not prompt the most consistent social conduct, but it will nevertheless implicitly affirm what it ostensibly denies—that the law of life is love.

Perhaps the clearest proof, that the law of love is involved as a basis of even the most minimal social standards, is found in the fact that every elaboration of minimal standards into higher standards makes the implicit relation more explicit. Prohibitions of murder and theft are negative. They seek to prevent one life from destroying or taking advantage of another. No society is content with these merely negative prohibitions. Its legal codes do not go much beyond negatives because only minimal standards can be legally enforced. But the moral codes and ideals of every advanced society demand more than mere prohibition of theft and murder. Higher conceptions of justice are developed. It is recognized that the right to live implies the right to secure the goods which sustain life. This right immediately involves more than mere prohibition of theft. Some obligation is felt, however dimly, to organize the common life so that the neighbor will have fair opportunities to maintain his life. The various schemes of justice and equity which grow out of this obligation, consciously or unconsciously imply an ideal of equality beyond themselves. Equality is always the regulative principle of justice; and in the ideal of equality there is an echo of the law of love, "Thou shalt love thy neighbor AS THYSELF." If the question is raised to what degree the neighbor has a right to support his life through the privileges and opportunities of the common life, no satisfactory, rational answer can be given to it, short of one implying equalitarian principles: He has just as much right as you yourself.

This does not mean that any society will ever achieve perfect equality. Equality, being a rational, political version of the law of love, shares with it the quality of transcendence. It ought to be, but it never will be fully realized. Social prudence will qualify it. The most equalitarian society will probably not be able to dispense with special rewards as inducements to diligence. Some differentials in privilege will be necessary to make the performance of certain social functions possible. While a rigorous equalitarian society can prevent such privileges from being perpetuated from one generation to another without regard to social function, it cannot eliminate privileges completely. Nor is there any political technique which would be a perfect guarantee against abuses of socially sanctioned privileges. Significant social functions are endowed by their very nature with a certain degree of social power. Those who possess power, however socially restrained, always have the opportunity of deciding that the function which they perform is entitled to more privilege than any ideal scheme of justice would allow. The ideal of equality is thus qualified in any possible society by the necessities of social cohesion and corrupted by the sinfulness of men. It remains, nevertheless, a principle of criticism under which every scheme of justice stands and a symbol of the principle of love involved in all moral judgments.

But the principle of equality does not exhaust the possibilities of the moral ideal involved in even the most minimal standards of justice. Imaginative justice leads beyond equality to a consideration of the special needs of the life of the other. A sensitive parent will not make capricious distinctions in the care given to different children. But the kind of imagination which governs the most ideal family relationships soon transcends this principle of equality and justifies special care for a handicapped child and, possibly, special advantages for a particularly gifted one. The "right" to have others consider one's unique needs and potentialities is recognized legally only in the most minimal terms and is morally recognized only in very highly developed communities. Yet the modern public school, which began with the purpose of providing equal educational opportunities for all children, has extended its services so that both handicapped and highly gifted children receive special privileges from it. Every one of these achievements in the realm of justice is logically related, on the one hand, to the most minimal standards of justice, and on the other to the ideal of perfect love—*i.e.*, to the obligation of affirming the life and interests of the neighbor as much as those of the self. The basic rights to life and property in the early community, the legal minima of rights and obligations of more advanced communities, the moral rights and obligations recognized in these communities beyond those which are legally enforced, the further refinement of standards in the family beyond those recognized in the general community—all these stand in an ascending scale of moral possibilities in which each succeeding step is a closer approximation of the law of love.

The history of corrective justice reveals the same ascending scale of possibilities as that of distributive justice. Society begins by regulating vengeance and soon advances to the stage of substituting public justice for private vengeance. Public justice recognizes the right of an accused person to a more disinterested judgment than that of the injured accuser. Thus the element of vengeance is reduced, but not eliminated, in modern standards of punitive justice. The same logic which forced its reduction presses on toward its elimination. The criminal is recognized to have rights as a human being, even when he has violated his obligations to society. Therefore modern criminology, using psychiatric techniques, seeks to discover the cause of anti-social conduct in order that it may be corrected. The reformatory purpose attempts to displace the purely punitive intent. This development follows a logic which must culminate in the command, "Love your enemies." The more imaginative ideals of the best criminologists are, of course, in the realm of unrealized hopes. They will never be fully realized. An element of vindictive passion will probably corrupt the corrective justice of even the best society. The collective behavior of mankind is not imaginative enough to assure more than minimal approximations of the ideal. Genuine forgiveness of the enemy requires a contrite recognition of the sinfulness of the self and of the mutual responsibility for the sin of the accused. Such spiritual penetration is beyond the capacities of collective man. It is the achievement of only rare individuals. Yet the right to such understanding is involved in the most basic of human rights and follows logically if the basic right to life is rationally elaborated. Thus all standards of corrective justice are organically related to primitive vengeance on the one hand, and the ideal of forgiving love on the other. No absolute limit can be placed upon the degree to which human society may yet approximate the ideal. But it is certain that every achievement will remain in the realm of approximation. The ideal in its perfect form lies beyond the capacities of human nature.

Moral and social ideals are always a part of a series of infinite possibilities not only in terms of their purity, but in terms of their breadth of application. The most tender and imaginative human attitudes are achieved only where consanguinity and contiguity support the unity of life with life, and nature aids spirit in creating harmony. Both law and morality recognize rights and obligations within the family which are not recognized in the community, and within the community which are not accepted beyond the community. Parents are held legally responsible for the neglect of their children but not for the neglect of other people's children. Modern nations assume qualified responsibilities for the support of their unemployed, but not for the unemployed of other nations. Such a sense of responsibility may be too weak to function adequately without the support of political motives, as, for instance, the fear that hungry men may disturb the social peace. But weak as it is, it is yet strong enough to suggest responsibilities beyond itself. No modern people is completely indifferent toward the responsibility for all human life. In terms of such breadth the obligation is too weak to become the basis for action, except on rare occasions. The need of men in other nations must be vividly portrayed and dramatized by some great catastrophe before generosity across national boundaries expresses itself. But it can express itself, even in those rare moments, only because all human life is informed with an inchoate sense of responsibility toward the ultimate law of life—the law of love. The community of mankind has no organs of social cohesion and no instruments for enforcing social standards (and it may never have more than embryonic ones); yet that community exists in a vague sense of responsibility toward all men which underlies all moral responsibilities in limited communities.

As has been observed in analyzing the ethic of Jesus, the universalism of prophetic ethics goes beyond the demands of rational universalism. In rational universalism obligation is felt to all life because human life is conceived as the basic value of ethics. Since so much of human life represents only potential value, rational universalism tends to qualify its position. Thus in Aristotelian ethics the slave does not have the same rights as the freeman because his life is regarded as of potentially less value. Even in Stoicism, which begins by asserting the common divinity of all men by reason of their common rationality, the obvious differences in the intelligence of men prompts Stoic doctrine to a certain aristocratic condescension toward the "fools." In prophetic religion the obligation is toward the loving will of God; in other words, toward a more transcendent source of unity than any discoverable in the natural world, where men are always divided by various forces of nature and history. Christian universalism, therefore, represents a more impossible possibility than the universalism of Stoicism. Yet it is able to prompt higher actualities of love, being less dependent upon obvious symbols of human unity and brotherhood. In prophetic ethics the transcendent unity of life is an article of faith. Moral obligation is to this divine unity; and therefore it is more able to defy the anarchies of the world. But this difference between prophetic and rational universalism must not obscure a genuine affinity. In both cases the moral experience on any level of life points toward an unrealizable breadth of obligation of life to life.

If further proof were needed of the relevance of the love commandment to the problems of ordinary morality it could be found by a negative argument: Natural human egoism, which is sin only from the perspective of the law of love, actually results in social consequences which prove this religious perspective to be right. This point must be raised not against Christian orthodoxy, which has never denied this negative relevance of the law of love to all human situations, but against a naturalism which regards the law of love as an expression of a morbid perfectionism, and declares "we will not aim so high or fall so low." According to the thesis of modern naturalism, only excessive egoism can be called wrong. The natural self-regarding impulses of human nature are accepted as the data of ethics; and the effort is made to construct them into forces of social harmony and cohesion. Prophetic Christianity, unlike modern liberalism, knows that the force of egoism cannot be broken by moral persuasion and that on certain levels qualified harmonies must be achieved by building conflicting egoisms into a balance of power. But, unlike modern naturalism, it is unable to adopt a complacent attitude toward the force of egoism. It knows that it is sin, however natural and inevitable it may be, and its sinfulness is proved by the social consequences. It is natural enough to love one's family more than other families and no amount of education will ever eliminate the inverse ratio between the potency of love and the breadth and extension in which it is applied. But the inevitability of narrow loyalties and circumscribed sympathy does not destroy the moral and social peril which they create. A narrow family loyalty is a more potent source of injustice than pure individual egoism, which, incidentally, probably never exists. The special loyalty which men give their limited community is natural enough; but it is also the root of international anarchy. Moral idealism in terms of the presuppositions of a particular class is also natural and inevitable; but it is the basis of tyranny and hypocrisy. Nothing is more natural and, in a sense, virtuous, than the desire of parents to protect the future of their children by bequeathing the fruits of their own toil and fortune to them. Yet this desire results in laws of testation by which social privilege is divorced from social function. The social injustice and conflicts of human history spring neither from a pure egoism nor from the type of egoism which could be neatly measured as excessive or extravagant by some rule of reason. They spring from those virtuous attitudes of natural man in which natural sympathy is inevitably compounded with natural egoism. Not only excessive jealousy, but the ordinary jealousy, from which no soul is free, destroys the harmony of life with life. Not only excessive vengeance, but the subtle vindictiveness which insinuates itself into the life of even the most imaginative souls, destroys justice. Wars are the consequence of the moral attitudes not only of unrighteous but of righteous nations (righteous in the sense that they defend their interests no more than is permitted by all the moral codes of history). The judgment that "whosoever seeketh to gain his life will lose it" remains true and relevant to every moral situation even if it is apparent that no human being exists who does not in some sense lose his life by seeking to gain it.

A naturalistic ethics, incapable of comprehending the true dialectic of the spiritual life, either regards the love commandment as possible of fulfillment and thus slips into utopianism, or it is forced to relegate it to the category of an either harmless or harmful irrelevance. A certain type of Christian liberalism interprets the absolutism of the ethics of the sermon of the mount as Oriental hyperbole, as a harmless extravagance. Thus Sigmund Freud writes: "The cultural super-ego . . . does not trouble enough about the mental constitution of human beings; it enjoins a command and never asks whether it is possible for them to obey it. It presumes, on the contrary, that a man's ego is psychologically capable of anything that is required of it, that it has unlimited power over the id. This is an error; even in normal people the power of controlling the id cannot be increased beyond certain limits. If one asks more of them one produces revolt or neurosis in individuals and makes them unhappy. The command to love the neighbor as ourselves is the strongest defense there is against human aggressiveness and it is a superlative example of the unpsychological attitude of the cultural super-ego. The command is impossible to fulfill; such an enormous inflation of the ego can only lower its value and not remedy its evil. This is a perfectly valid protest against a too moralistic and optimistic love perfectionism. But it fails to meet the insights of a religion which knows that the law of love is an impossible possibility and knows how to confess, "There is a law in my members which wars against the law that is in my mind." Freud's admission that the love commandment is "the strongest defense against human aggressiveness" is, incidentally, the revelation of a certain equivocation in his thought. The impossible command is admitted to be a necessity, even though a dangerous one. It would be regarded as less dangerous by Freud if he knew enough about the true genius of prophetic religion to realize that it has resources for relaxing moral tension as well as for creating it.

If the relevance of the love commandment must be asserted against both Christian orthodoxy and against certain types of naturalism, the impossibility of the ideal must be insisted upon against all those forms of naturalism, liberalism, and radicalism which generate utopian illusions and regard the love commandment as ultimately realizable because history knows no limits of its progressive approximations.

SELECTION 2
Justice and Love

This is an essay dealing with one of Niebuhr's central concerns and indicating the gulf that separates him from an earlier Social Gospel.

"A Christian," declared an eager young participant in a symposium on Christianity and politics, "always considers the common welfare before his own interest." This simple statement reveals a few of the weaknesses of moralistic Christianity in dealing with problems of justice. The statement contains at least two errors, or perhaps one error and one omission.

The first error consists in defining a Christian in terms which assume that consistent selflessness is possible. No Christian, even the most perfect, is able "always" to consider the common interest before his own. At least he is not able to do it without looking at the common interest with eyes colored by his own ambitions. If complete selflessness were a simple possibility, political justice could be quickly transmuted into perfect love; and all the frictions, tensions, partial co-operations, and overt and covert conflicts could be eliminated. If complete selflessness without an admixture of egoism were possible, many now irrelevant sermons and church resolutions would become relevant. Unfortunately there is no such possibility for individual men; and perfect disinterestedness for groups and nations is even more impossible.

The other error is one of omission. To set self-interest and the general welfare in simple opposition is to ignore nine tenths of the ethical issues that confront the consciences of men. For these are concerned not so much with the problem of the self against the whole as with problems of the self in its relation to various types of "general welfare." "What do you mean by common interest?" retorted a shrewd businessman in the symposium referred to. Does it mean the family or the nation? If I have to choose between "my family" and "my nation," is the Christian choice inevitably weighted in favor of the nation since it is the larger community? And if the choice is between "my" nation and another nation, must the preference always be for the other nation on the ground that concern for my own nation represents collective self-interest? Was the young pacifist idealist right who insisted that if we had less "selfish concern for our own civilization" we could resolve the tension between ourselves and Russia, presumably by giving moral preference to a communist civilization over our own?

Such questions as these reveal why Christian moralism has made such meager contributions to the issues of justice in modern society. Justice requires discriminate judgments between conflicting claims. A Christian justice will be particularly critical of the claims of the self as against the claims of the other, but it will not dismiss them out of hand. Without this criticism all justice becomes corrupted into a refined form of self-seeking. But if the claims of the self (whether individual or collective) are not entertained, there is no justice at all. There is an ecstatic form of agape which defines the ultimate heroic possibilities of human existence (involving, of course, martyrdom) but not the common possibilities of tolerable harmony of life with life.

In so far as justice admits the claims of the self, it is something less than love. Yet it cannot exist without love and remain justice. For without the "grace" of love, justice always degenerates into something less than justice.

But if justice requires that the interests of the self be entertained, it also requires that they be resisted. Every realistic system of justice must assume the continued power of self-interest, particularly of collective self-interest. It must furthermore assume that this power will express itself illegitimately as well as legitimately. It must therefore be prepared to resist illegitimate self-interest, even among the best men and the most just nations. A simple Christian moralism counsels men to be unselfish. A profounder Christian faith must encourage men to create systems of justice which will save society and themselves from their own selfishness.

But justice arbitrates not merely between the self and the other, but between the competing claims upon the self by various "others." Justice seeks to determine what I owe this segment as against that segment of a community. One of the strange moral anomalies of our times is that there are businessmen and men of affairs who have a more precise sense of justice in feeling their way through the endless relativities of human relations than professional teachers of morals. Practical experience has made them sensitive to the complex web of values and interests in which human decisions are reached, while the professional teachers of religion and morals deal with simple counters of black and white. This certainly is one of the reasons why the pulpit frequently seems so boring and irrelevant to the pew. At his worst the practical man of affairs is morally heedless and considers only his own interest, mistaking collective self-interest for selfless virtue. At his best he has been schooled in justice, while his teacher confuses the issue by moral distinctions which do not fit the complexities of life.

The realm of justice is also a realm of tragic choices, which are seldom envisaged in a type of idealism in which all choices are regarded as simple. Sometimes we must prefer a larger good to a smaller one, without the hope that the smaller one will be preserved in a larger one. Sometimes we must risk a terrible evil (such as an atomic war) in the hope of avoiding an imminent peril (such as subjugation to tyranny). Subsequent events may prove the risk to have been futile and the choice to have been wrong. If there is enough of a world left after such a wrong choice we will be taxed by the idealists for having made the wrong choice; and they will not know that they escaped an intolerable evil by our choice. Even now we are taxed with the decision to resist nazism, on the ground that the war against nazism has left us in a sad plight. The present peril of communism seems to justify an earlier capitulation to nazism. But since we are men and not God, we could neither anticipate all the evils that would flow from our decision to resist nazism, nor yet could we have capitulated to the immediate evil because another evil was foreshadowed.

The tragic character of our moral choices, the contradiction between various equal values of our devotion, and the incompleteness in all our moral striving, prove that "if in this life only we had hoped in Christ, we are of all men most miserable." No possible historic justice is sufferable without the Christian hope. But any illusion of a world of perfect love without these imperfect harmonies of justice must ultimately turn the dream of love into a nightmare of tyranny and injustice.

SELECTION 3
Christian Faith and Natural Law

Natural Law has been a stand-by for Christian social teaching. Here Niebuhr gives his version of this concept as over against classical Roman Catholic and Protestant views.

In his challenging article entitled "Theology Today," the Archbishop of York presents several questions which in his opinion require a fresh answer in the light of contemporary history. One of these questions is: "Is there a natural order which is from God, as Catholic tradition holds, or is there only natural disorder, the fruit of sin, from which Christ delivers us, as Continental Protestantism has held?" I should like to address myself to this question and suggest that the facts of human history are more complex than either the traditional Catholic or Protestant doctrines of natural order and natural law suggest.

According to Thomistic doctrine, the Fall robbed man of a *donum superadditum* but left him with a *pura naturalia,* which includes a capacity for natural justice. What is lost is a capacity for faith, hope, and love—that is, the ability to rise above the natural order and have communion with divine and supernatural order, to know God and, in fellowship with him, to be delivered of the fears, anxieties, and sins which result from this separation from God. The fallen man is thus essentially an incomplete man, who is completed by the infusion of sacramental grace, which restores practically, though not quite, all of the supernatural virtues which were lost in the Fall. The Fall does not seriously impair man's capacity for natural justice. Only this is an incomplete perfection, incapable of itself to rise to the heights of love.

According to Protestant theology, the Fall had much more serious consequences. It left man "totally corrupt" and "utterly leprous and unclean." The very reason which in Catholic thought is regarded as the instrument and basis of natural justice is believed in Protestant thought to be infected by the Fall and incapable of arriving at any true definition of justice. Calvin is slightly more equivocal about the effects of sin upon reason than Luther, and as a consequence Calvinism does not relegate the natural law and the whole problem of justice so completely to the background as does Lutheranism. Nevertheless, the theory of total depravity is only slightly qualified in Calvinism.

I should like to maintain that the real crux of the human situation is missed in both the Catholic and the Protestant version of the effect of sin upon man's capacity for justice. Something more than a brief paper would be required to prove such a thesis; I must content myself therefore with suggesting the argument in general outline.

The Biblical conception of man includes three primary terms: (a) he is made in the image of God, (b) he is a creature, and (c) he is a sinner. His basic sin is pride. If this pride is closely analyzed, it is discovered to be man's unwillingness to acknowledge his creatureliness. He is betrayed by his greatness to hide his weakness. He is tempted by his ability to gain his own security to deny his insecurity, and refuses to admit that he has no final security except in God. He is tempted by his knowledge to deny his ignorance. (This is the source of all "ideological taint" in human knowledge.) It is not that man in his weakness has finite perspectives that makes conflicts between varying perspectives so filled with fanatic fury in all human history; it is that man denies the finiteness of his perspectives that tempts him to such fanatic cruelty against those who hold convictions other than his own. The quintessence of sin is, in short, that man "changes the glory of the incorruptible God into the image of corruptible man." He always usurps God's place and claims to be the final judge of human actions.

The loss of man's original perfection therefore never leaves him with an untarnished though incomplete natural justice. All statements and definitions of justice are corrupted by even the most rational men through the fact that the definition is colored by interest. This is the truth in the Marxist theory of rationalization and in its assertion that all culture is corrupted by an ideological taint. The unfortunate fact about the Marxist theory is that it is used primarily as a weapon in social conflict. The enemy is charged with this dishonesty, but the Marxist himself claims to be free of it. This is, of course, merely to commit the final sin of self-righteousness and to imagine ourselves free of the sin which we discern in the enemy. The fact that we do not discern it in ourselves is a proof of our sin and not of our freedom from sin. Christ's parable of the mote and the beam is a perfect refutation of this illusion.

The fact remains, nevertheless, that reason is not capable of defining any standard of justice that is universally valid or acceptable. Thus Thomistic definitions of justice are filled with specific details which are drawn from the given realities of a feudal social order and may be regarded as "rationalizations" of a feudal aristocracy's dominant position in society. (The much-praised Catholic prohibition of usury could be maintained only as long as the dominant aristocratic class were borrowers rather than lenders of money. When the static wealth of the landowners yielded to the more dynamic wealth of the financiers and industrialists, the prohibition of usury vanished. Catholics hold Protestantism responsible for this development, but it is significant that the Catholic Church makes no effort to impose the prohibition of usury upon its own bourgeois members.)

Bourgeois idealists of the eighteenth century invented new natural law theories and invested them with bourgeois rather than feudal-aristocratic content. The natural law of the eighteenth century was supposed to be descriptive rather than prescriptive. It was, more exactly, a "law of nature" rather than a "law of reason." But its real significance lay in its specific content. The content of this law justified the bourgeois classes in their ideals, just as the older law justified the feudal aristocrats. In short, it is not possible to state a universally valid concept of justice from any particular sociological locus in history. Nor is it possible to avoid either making the effort or making pretenses of universality which human finiteness does not justify. This inevitable pretense is the revelation of "original sin" in history. Human history is consequently more tragic than Catholic theology assumes. It is not an incomplete world yearning for completion, and finding it in the incarnation. It is a tragic world, troubled not by finiteness so much as by "false eternals" and false absolutes, and expressing the pride of these false absolutes even in the highest reaches of its spirituality. It is not the incarnation as such that is the good news of the gospel, but rather the revelation of a just God who is also merciful; this is the true content of the incarnation. That is, it is the atonement that fills the incarnation with meaning.

But Catholic thought not only fails to do justice to the positive character of the sinful element in all human definitions and realizations of natural justice. It also fails to do justice to the relation of love to justice. In its conception, natural justice is good as far as it goes, but it must be completed by the supernatural virtue of love. The true situation is that anything short of love cannot be perfect justice. In fact, every definition of justice actually presupposes sin as a given reality. It is only because life is in conflict with life, because of sinful self-interest, that we are required carefully to define schemes of justice which prevent one life from taking advantage of another. Yet no scheme of justice can do full justice to all the variable factors which the freedom of man introduces into human history. Significantly, both eighteenth century and medieval conceptions of natural law are ultimately derived from Stoic conceptions. And it is the very nature of Stoic philosophy that it is confused about the relation of nature to reason. This confusion is due to the fact that it does not fully understand the freedom of man. In all Greco-Roman rationalism, whether Platonic, Aristotelian, or Stoic, it is assumed that man's freedom is secured by his rational transcendence over nature. Since reason and freedom are identified, it is assumed that the freedom that man has over nature is held in check and disciplined by his reason. The real situation is that man transcends his own reason, which is to say that he is not bound in his actions by reason's coherences and systems. His freedom consists in a capacity for self-transcendence in infinite regression. There is therefore no limit in reason for either his creativity or his sin. There is no possibility of giving a rational definition of a just relation between man and man or nation and nation short of a complete love in which each life affirms the interests of the other. Every effort to give a definition of justice short of this perfect love invariably introduces contingent factors, conditions of time and place, into the definition.

Love is the only final structure of freedom. Human personality as a system of infinite potentialities makes it impossible to define absolutely what I owe to my fellow man, since nothing that he now is exhausts what he might be. Human personality as capacity for infinite self-transcendence makes it impossible from my own standpoint to rest content in any ordered relation with my fellow men. There is no such relation that I cannot transcend to imagine a better one in terms of the ideal of love. Provisional definitions of justice short of this perfect love, are, of course, necessary. But they are much more provisional than any natural law theory, whether medieval or modern, realizes. The freedom of man is too great to make it possible to define any scheme of justice absolutely in terms of "necessary" standards.

According to Catholic theology, it is this structure of ultimate freedom that is lost in the Fall just as the accompanying virtue of love is lost. The real situation is that "original justice" in the sense of a mythical "perfection before the Fall" is never completely lost. It is not a reality in man but always a potentiality.

It is always what he ought to be. It is the only goodness completely compatible with his own and his fellow man's freedom—that is, with their ultimate transcendence over all circumstances of nature. Man is neither as completely bereft of "original justice" nor as completely in possession of "natural justice" as the Catholic theory assumes.

Protestant theory, on the other hand, partly because of Luther's nominalistic errors, has no sense of an abiding structure at all. Luther's theory of total depravity is, in fact, more intimately related to his nominalism than is generally realized. Only in nominalistic terms, in which love is regarded as good by the fiat of God and not because it is actually the structure of freedom, can it be supposed that life could be completely at variance with itself. "Sin," said Saint Augustine quite truly, "cannot tear up nature by the roots." Injustice has meaning only against a background of a sense of justice. What is more, it cannot maintain itself without at least a minimal content of justice. The "ideological taint" in all human truth could have no meaning except against the background of a truth that is not so tainted. Men always jump to the erroneous conclusion that because they can conceive of a truth and a justice that completely transcend their interests, they are therefore also able to realize such truth and such justice. Against this error of the optimists, Protestant pessimism affirms the equally absurd proposition that sin has completely destroyed all truth and justice.

Protestantism has been betrayed into this error partly by its literalism, by which it defines the Fall as a historic event and "perfection before the Fall" as a perfection existing in a historical epoch before the Fall. When Luther essays to define this perfection he indulges in all kinds of fantastic nonsense. The perfection before the Fall is always an ideal possibility before the act. It describes a dimension of human existence rather than a period of history. It is the vision of health which even a sick man has. It is the structure of the good without which there would be no evil. The anarchy of Europe is evil only because it operates against an ideal possibility and necessity of order in Europe. The blindness of the eye is evil only because the ideal possibility is sight.

Protestant pessimism has been rightfully accused by Catholic thinkers of leading to obscurantism in culture and to antinomianism in morals; and it would be difficult to estimate to what degree our present anarchy is due to Protestant errors. But Catholics forget that Protestant pessimism is but a corrupted form of a prophetic criticism which Christianity must make even against its own culture, and that the medieval culture was subject to such a criticism by reason of its inability to recognize to what degree Christianity as a culture and as an institution is involved not only in the finiteness of history but in the sin of history—that is, precisely in the effort to hide finiteness and to pretend a transcendent perfection which cannot be achieved in history.

It may be useful to apply to contemporary history the theory that all human life stands under an ideal possibility purer than the natural law, and that at the same time it is involved in sinful reality much more dubious than the natural justice that Catholic thought declares to be possible. I will choose one specific example, prompted by the Archbishop of York's splendid wireless address in October last in favor of a "negotiated" rather than an "imposed" peace. The Peace of Versailles was an imposed peace. Its territorial provisions were really more just than is sometimes supposed at the present moment. But among its provisions it contained the forced admission of guilt by the vanquished, a piece of psychological cruelty which reveals self-righteousness at its worst. (It is interesting how our worst sins are always derived from self-righteousness, which is what gives Christ's contest with the Pharisees such relevance.) Against such a peace his Grace, and with him many others, are now pleading for a negotiated peace. They rightly believe that only in such a peace can Europe find security.

Yet it must be recognized that there is no definition of natural justice that can give us a really adequate outline of a just peace. Justice cannot be established in the world by pure moral suasion. It is achieved only as some kind of decent equilibrium of power is established. And such an equilibrium is subject to a thousand contingencies of geography and history. We cannot make peace with Hitler now because his power dominates the Continent, and his idea of a just peace is one that leaves him in the security of that dominance. We believe, I think rightly, that a more just peace can be established if that dominance is broken.

But in so far as the Hitlerian imperial will must be broken first, the new peace will be an imposed peace. We may hope that a chastened Germany will accept it and make it its own. But even if vindictive passions are checked, as they were not in 1918, the fact that Germany will be defeated will rob her of some ideal possibilities in Europe, which she might have had but for her defeat in the war.

Nor is it possible for us to be sure that our conception of peace in Europe, in even our most impartial moments, could do full justice to certain aspects of the European situation that might be seen from the German but not from our perspective. On the other hand, we must assume that even the most chastened Germany would not be willing, except as she is forced, to accept certain provisions for the freedom of Poland and Czechoslovakia and the freedom of small nations generally. The inclination of the strong to make themselves the sponsors of the weak, and to claim that they are doing this not for their own but for the general good, is not a German vice. The Germans have merely accentuated a common vice of history and one that influences every concrete realization of justice. The concretion of justice in specific historic instances always depends upon a certain equilibrium of forces, which prevents the organizing will of the strong from degenerating into tyranny. Without resistance even the best ruler, oligarchy, or hegemonous nation would be tempted to allow its creative function of organization to degenerate into tyranny. Furthermore, even the most resolute moral resistance against vindictive passion cannot prevent retributive justice from degenerating into vindictiveness, if the foe is so thoroughly defeated as to invite the type of egotism which expresses itself in vindictiveness. It is significant, moreover, that no "rational" standard of retributive justice can be defined. What is worked out in each particular instance is always some *ad hoc* compromise between vindictiveness on the one hand and forgiveness on the other. This is particularly true of international disputes in which there are no genuinely impartial courts of adjudication. (Neutral nations are interested in the particular balance of power that emerges out of each conflict.) The structure of justice that emerges from each overt conflict must therefore be established to a very considerable degree by the disputants in the conflict, more particularly by the victors.

Yet men are not completely blinded by self-interest or lost in this maze of historical relativity. What always remains with them is not some uncorrupted bit of reason, which gives them universally valid standards of justice. What remains with them is something higher—namely, the law of love, which they dimly recognize as the law of their being, as the structure of human freedom, and which, in Christian faith, Christ clarifies and redefines, which is why he is called the "second Adam." It is the weakness of Protestant pessimism that it denies the reality of this potential perfection and its relevance in the affairs of politics.

The effort of the Christian church in Britain at the present moment to stem the tide of vindictiveness, which it rightly anticipates as an inevitable danger after the war, is a truer expression of the Christian spirit than pacifist disavowals of the war as such. It is not possible to disavow war absolutely without disavowing the task of establishing justice. For justice rests upon a decent equilibrium of power; and all balances of power involve tension; and tension involves covert conflict; and there will be moments in history when covert conflict becomes overt. But it is possible to transcend a conflict while standing in it. Forgiveness is such a possibility. But forgiveness to the foe is possible only if I know myself to be a sinner—that is, if I do not have some cheap or easy sense of moral transcendence over the sinful reality of claims and counterclaims which is the very stuff of history.

This does not mean that it would ever be possible to establish a justice based upon perfect forgiveness after a war. The sinfulness of human nature will relativize every ideal possibility. Vindictiveness (which is an egoistic corruption of justice) cannot be completely eliminated. But the quality of justice that can be achieved in a war will depend upon the degree to which a "Kingdom of God" perspective can be brought upon the situation. It is this higher imagination rather than some unspoiled rational definition of retributive justice that pulls justice out of the realm of vindictiveness.

Human nature is, in short, a realm of infinite possibilities of good and evil because of the character of human freedom.

The love that is the law of its nature is a boundless self-giving. The sin that corrupts its life is a boundless assertion of the self. Between these two forces all kinds of *ad hoc* restraints may be elaborated and defined. We may call this natural law. But we had better realize how very tentative it is. Otherwise we shall merely sanction some traditional relation between myself and my fellow man as a "just" relation, and quiet the voice of conscience which speaks to me of higher possibilities. What is more, we may stabilize sin and make it institutional; for it will be discovered invariably that my definition of justice guarantees certain advantages to myself to which I have no absolute right, but with which I have been invested by the accidents of history and the contingencies of nature and which the "old Adam" in me is only too happy to transmute into absolute rights.

SELECTION 4
The Hydrogen Bomb

The courageous way in which Niebuhr is willing to address specific and highly complex issues is illustrated in this comment on the hydrogen bomb.

Each age of mankind brings forth new perils and new possibilities. Yet they are always related to what we have known before. The age of atomic bombs, suddenly developing into a thousand times more lethal hydrogen bombs, is very different from the age of scythe and plowshare. It confronts us with the possibility of mutual mass annihilation. Yet we are no different from our fathers. Our present situation is a heightened and more vivid explication of the human situation.

One basic similarity between ourselves and our fathers is that our power over the course of human history is limited. We had imagined that the very technics that finally produced atomic destruction would make us the masters of history. But they merely produce an increased amount of power over nature that has a dubious role in the affairs of men. When we confront the problem of bringing the destructive possibilities of this power under moral control, the whole ambiguity of the human situation is more fully revealed.

Consider the facts. We had the knowledge to produce the

more lethal bomb four years ago, but wisely did not exploit it. Then, when the news came that the Russians had the A-bomb, we were certain that they would be, as we were, on the way to achieving the more deadly H-bomb. There seemed, therefore, nothing to do but give orders to develop it. The fact that this was done without public debate represents a real threat to the democratic substance of our life. This merely accentuates the danger in which we have been ever since secret weapons have been developed. It is, at any rate, fairly certain that, had the President submitted the matter to Congress, the decision would have been identical with the one he made. Thus we have come into the tragic position of developing a form of destruction which, if used by our enemies against us, would mean our physical annihilation; and if used by us against our enemies, would mean our moral annihilation. What shall we do?

The pacifists have a simple answer. Let us simply renounce the use of such a weapon, together with our enemies if possible, alone if necessary. This answer assumes that it is possible to summon the human will to defy historical development with a resounding no. But where is this "human will" which could rise to such omnipotence? Unfortunately we do not have moral access to the Russian will. We have to limit ourselves to the will of America and of the Western world. Could we possibly, as a nation, risk annihilation or subjugation for the sake of saying no to this new development of destruction? Could we risk letting the Russians have the bomb while we are without it? The answer is that no responsible statesman will risk putting his nation in that position of defenselessness. Individuals may, but nations do not, thus risk their very existence. Would a gesture of defenselessness possibly soften the Russian heart? That is the other possibility implied in the pacifist solution. The answer is that we have no such assurance. Granted the Russian hope and belief that it has the possibility of bringing its peculiar redemption to the whole world, it is not likely to be impressed by any "moral" gesture from what it believes to be a decadent world. In other words, our will is neither powerful enough nor good enough to accomplish the miracle expected of us in the pacifist solution.

Yet we are never the prisoners of historical destiny, even

though all pretensions of being its master have crumbled. What shall we do within the limits of our power? Perhaps, since the so-called Baruch plan has become obsolete through the loss of our monopoly in atomic destruction, the thing to do is to revise our proposals and make another effort to secure agreement with the Russians. This course of action is widely approved; and it probably ought to be tried. But it has little prospect of success. The Russians are almost certain to demand general disarmament as the price for any agreement in the field of atomic energy. That means that they believe it possible to dominate Europe politically if the military defenses against its encroachments are removed. We cannot pay that price because we cannot afford to deliver Europe over to communism.

Perhaps the most feasible possibility is that proposed by a group of eleven scientists who have suggested that we produce the H-bomb but make a solemn covenant never to use it first. This proposal has several merits. It would serve to allay some of the apprehensions that the world feels about our possible use of the bomb. It would also restrain those elements in our defense department who are placing undue reliance on the bomb and who may, if we are not careful, so develop our defenses that we could not win a war without using the bomb. It would also tend to counteract all those tendencies in our national life which make for the subordination of moral and political strategy to military strategy. We must not forget that, though we must be prepared to defend ourselves in case of war, it is more important to overcome communism by moral, economic, and political measures. In that case we would not have to fight the war for which the strategists are preparing our defenses. For this reason the proposals of Senator McMahon, looking toward a tremendous expansion of our aid to the Western world, are of great significance.

The refusal to use the bomb first is not of itself a sufficient strategy. But such a refusal would tend to encourage all the more positive strategies for preserving both peace and civilization. Yet the refusal to use the bomb first does have a further significance. We would be saying by such a policy that even a nation can reach the point where it can purchase its life too dearly. If we had to use this kind of destruction in order to save our lives, would we find life worth living? Even nations can reach a point where the words of our Lord, "Fear not them which are able to kill the body but rather fear them that are able to destroy both soul and body in hell," become relevant.

The point of moral transcendence over historical destiny is not as high as moral perfectionists imagine. But there is such a point, though cynics and realists do not recognize it. We must discern that point clearly. A nation does not have the power to say that it would rather be annihilated than to produce a certain weapon. For, as the scientists have asserted, the production of that weapon may serve to guarantee that it will never be used. But to use such a weapon first represents a quite different moral hazard. It ought not to be impossible to nations to meet that hazard successfully.

XXVII PAUL TILLICH

Born in Germany in 1886, Paul Tillich had made a name for himself as a leading philosopher and theologian in that country before he came to the United States and Union Theological Seminary in 1933 as a result of the Nazi take-over of Germany.

A citizen of the United States since 1940, where he died in 1965, Tillich has been the most influencial philosophical theologian on the American scene. He considered himself a man "at the frontier" relating Christian theology to many different areas of human life. Our selection is taken from his book *Love, Power and Justice,* published in 1954, and the chapter where he addresses himself to the unity of power, justice, and love in social relations. It illustrates his method and the seminal character of his thought.

SELECTION I
Love, Power and Justice

Structures of power are always centred in inorganic beings like crystals, molecules, atoms, as well as in organic beings. In the latter ones the centredness increases and reaches in man the state of self-consciousness. Then a new centred structure appears; the social group, or, as it is called if it has a manifest centre, a social organism. An organism is the more developed and has a greater power of being, the more different elements are united around an acting centre. Therefore, man produces the richest, most universal and most powerful social organisms. But the individuals who constitute this organism are each independent centres for themselves, and so they can resist the unity of the social organism to which they belong. And here the limits of the analogy between biological and social organisms become visible. In a biological organism the parts are nothing without the whole to which they belong. This is not the case in social organisms. The destiny of an individual who is separated from the group to which he belongs may be miserable but the separation is not necessarily fatal. The fate of a limb which is cut off from the living organism to which it belongs is decay. In this sense no human group is an organism in the biological sense. Neither is the family the cell of a quasi-biological organism, nor is the nation something like a biological organism.

This statement is politically significant. Those who like to speak of social organisms do it usually with a reactionary tendency. They want to keep dissenting groups in conformity and they use for this purpose biological metaphors in a literal sense. Prussian conservatism and Roman Catholic family glorification agree at this point. But the individual person is not a limb of a body; he is an ultimate, independent reality, with both personal and social functions. The individual man is a social being, but the society does not create the individual. They are interdependent.

This decides also against the widespread method of personifying a group. A State has often been described as a person who has emotions, thoughts, intentions, decisions like an individual person. But there is a difference which makes all this impossible: the social organism does not have an organic centre, in which the whole being is united so that central deliberations and decisions are possible. The centre of a social group is those who represent it, the rulers or the parliaments, or those who have the real power behind the scene without being official representatives. The analogy has been driven to the point where the representative centres of social power are equated with the deliberating and deciding centre of a personality. But this is what one could call 'a deception of the metaphor.' The analogy can be carried through metaphorically but not properly. For the deciding centre of a group is always a part of the group. It is not the group which decides, but those who have the power to speak for the group and force their decisions upon all the members of the group. And they may do this without the (at least) silent consent of the group. The importance of this analysis is visible whenever one makes a group responsible for what the deciding centre has forced upon the group. This gives a solution to the painful question of the moral guilt of a nation (e.g. Nazi Germany). It is never the nation which is directly guilty for what is done by the nation. It is always the ruling group. But all individuals in a nation are responsible for the existence of the ruling group. Not many individuals in Germany are directly guilty of Nazi atrocities. But all of them are responsible for the acceptance of a government which was willing and able to do such things. Those who represent the power of a social group are a representative but not an actual centre. A group is not a person.

Nevertheless it has a structure of power. It is centred. Therefore social power is hierarchical power, power in degrees. Social power, centred and therefore hierarchical, has many forms in which it can appear. It can appear in the control of a society by a feudal group, a military caste, a high bureaucracy, an economic upper class, a priestly hierarchy, an individual ruler with or without constitutional restrictions, the ruling committees of a parliament, a revolutionary vanguard.

The ruling group shares the tensions of power, especially the tension between power by acknowledgement and power by enforcement. Both are always present, and no power structure can stand if one of them is lacking. The silent acknowledgement of the people appears when they reflect: 'those who represent us represent us by divine order or by historical destiny. No question can be raised about it. No criticism is allowed.' Or: 'Those who represent us are chosen by us: now we must accept them as long as they are in legal power, even if they misuse it, otherwise the system as such with the chances it gives to us also would fall down.' The ruling group is safe as long as this kind of acknowledgement is subconscious or half-conscious—metaphorically speaking, silent. Danger for the system appears if the acknowledgement becomes conscious and doubt must be suppressed. Then the moment may come when the suppression no longer works and a revolutionary situation develops. It is noticeable that even in such a situation the law is valid that power has centred or hierarchical character: the bearers of the revolutionary situation are a small group of people who have decided to withdraw acknowledgement. Marx has called them, with a militaristic image, the vanguard. They are the centre of power in a revolutionary situation, the objects of severest suppression in the pre-revolutionary stage, the ruling group in the post-revolutionary stage.

For enforcement is the other side of the hierarchical power structure. It also works well as long as it works silently in the overwhelming majority of the group. This is done by internalized law, a smooth administration and a conformistic attitude. But this is an ideal case and depends on many favourable factors (e.g. in England). Usually the compulsory element is much stronger. There is an easy deception in the mind of idealists about the situation. They experience the small number of enforcing officials in a big city, and that even this small number has to do actual enforcement only occasionally. So they feel the absence of enforcement more than its presence. But most enforcement is done by the threat of enforcement, if it is a real threat. Examples for this can be increased indefinitely even with respect to the best educated citizen (taxes). You cannot remove silent acknowledgement and you cannot remove manifest enforcement from any structure of power.

The ruling minority in a social group are both objects of the silent acknowledgement by the majority and the agents of the enforcement of the law against the wilfulness of any member of the group. This latter position produces all the problems which disturb and possibly ruin a social organism. The situation would be simple, if the law the ruling group is supposed to represent and to enforce were unambiguous. But actually it is burdened with all the ambiguities of justice. An archaic acknowledgement of this fact is the idea that the ruler is above the law, because it is his function to make decisions where the law necessarily remains indefinite. Although modern constitutions avoid an open expression of such a translegal position, they cannot exclude actions of the ruling group which follow the same principle. And this position 'above the law' is neither in ancient nor in modern times a denial of the law. On the contrary, it is meant as a way of making the application of the law possible. The law must be given in a creative act, and it is given by members of the ruling group. It must be applied to the concrete situation in a daring decision, and the decision is made by members of the ruling group. It must be changed in a foreseeing risk; and the risk is taken by members of the ruling group. This analysis shows that those who are in power always do two things: they express the power and justice of being of the whole group; and, at the same time, they express the power and the claim for justice of themselves as the ruling group. This situation has induced Christian as well as Marxist anarchists to accept the ideal of a society without a power structure. But being without a power structure means being without a centre of action. It means an agglomeration of individuals without a united power of being and without a uniting form of justice. A State-like organization cannot be avoided, and if it is given, no checks and balances, not even those of the American Constitution, can prevent the ruling groups from expressing their own power and justice of being in the justice and power of the whole group. Those who belong to the ruling group pay a price for it and have a justification for it. They pay the price of identifying their own destiny with the destiny of the whole group. The power of being of the group constitutes their own power of being. They stand and fall with it. And they have the justification that they are acknowledged by the whole group in whatever constitutional terms this may be expressed. They cannot exist if the whole group definitely withdraws its acknowledgement. They can prolong their power by physical and psychological compulsion, but not for ever.

The silent acknowledgement received by a ruling group from the whole group cannot be understood without an element which is derived neither from justice nor from power but from love, namely from love under guidance of its *erōs* and *philia* qualities. It is the experience of community within the group. Every social group is a community, potentially and actually; and the ruling minority not only expresses the power and justice of being of the group, it also expresses the communal spirit of the group, its ideals and valuations. Every organism, natural as well as social, is a power of being and a bearer of an intrinsic claim for justice because it is based on some form of reuniting love. It removes as organism the separatedness of some parts of the world. The cell of a living body, the members of a family, the citizens of a nation, are examples. This communal self-affirmation, on the human level, is called the spirit of the group. The spirit of the group is expressed in all its utterances, in its laws and institutions, in its symbols and myths, in its ethical and cultural forms. It is normally represented by the ruling classes. And this very fact is perhaps the most solid foundation of their power. Every member of the group sees in the members of the ruling minority the incarnation of those ideals which he affirms when he affirms the group to which he belongs. This incarnation may be a king or a bishop, a big landowner or a big business man, a union leader or a revolutionary hero. Therefore every ruling minority preserves and presents and propagates those symbols in which the spirit of the group is expressed. They guarantee the permanence of a power structure more than the strictest methods of enforcement. They guarantee what I have called the silent acknowledgement of the ruling group by the whole group. In this way, the power and justice of being in a social group is dependent on the spirit of the community, and this means on the uniting love which creates and sustains the community.

In our description of the encounter of power of being with power of being we have limited our task to the encounter of individuals with individuals. We must now extend our description to the encounter of social groups with social groups. If we do so we find the same marks of power encounters, the pushing ahead and withdrawing, the absorbing and throwing out, the amalgamation and separation. This is unavoidable. For every power group experiences growth and disintegration. It tries to transcend itself and to preserve itself at the same time. Nothing is determined *a priori*. It is a matter of trial, risk, and decision. And this trial has elements of intrinsic power united with compulsion whether the group or their representatives want it or not. These encounters are the basic material of history. In them man's political destiny is decided. What is their character? The basis of all power of a social group is the space it must provide for itself. Being means having space or, more exactly, providing space for oneself. This is the reason for the tremendous importance of geographical space and the fight for its possession by all power groups. Our time gives a striking example for this fact. In the necessity of having space the Zionist fight is rooted. Israel lost its independent power of being and often its power of being altogether, when it lost its space. Now it has its space and has shown a rather strong power of being. But perhaps something is lost: the intimate relation to time which made Israel the elected nation and which belongs to the problem of the resignation of power.

The struggle about space is not simply the attempt to remove another group from a given space. The real purpose is to draw this space into a larger power field, to deprive it of a centre of its own. If this happens, it is not the individual power of being which has changed, but the way in which the individual participates in the centre, in which way he influences the law and the spiritual substance of the new, larger power organization.

It is, however, not only geographical space which gives power and being to a social organism. It is also the radiation of power into the larger space of mankind. One of these radiations which enlarge one's own space without reducing that of others is economic expansion. Another is technical expansion or the spread of science and civilization. In none of these cases is a preceding calculation possible. Every factor is changing, the number of the population, the productive power, new discoveries, movements, emigration, competition, the rise of new countries, the disintegration of old ones. History, so to speak, tries what will be its next constellation. And in these trials nations and empires are sacrificed, and others are called into existence. The power of being of each political power group is measured by its encounter with the power of being of other power groups.

But now we must remember that power is never only physical force, but it is also the power of symbols and ideas in which the life of a social group expresses itself. The consciousness of such a spiritual substance *can* become, and in the most important cases of history *does* become, the feeling of a special vocation. If we look at European history we find a series of expressions of such a vocational consciousness, and we find tremendous historical consequences following from it. In an indistinguishable unity of power drive and vocational consciousness the

Romans subjected the Mediterranean world to the Roman law and the order of the Roman empire, based on this law. In the same way Alexander brought Greek culture to nations which were subjected in terms of both arms and language. Considering the fact that these two imperial drives in their amalgamation created the *oikoumenē,* the condition and frame of the spread of Christianity, we cannot say that their vocational consciousness was wrong. The same must be said about the medieval German empire, which, on the basis of the power drives of the Germanic tribes and the vocational consciousness of the Germanic kings, created the structure for the united Christian body with all the glory of medieval religion and culture. After the end of the Middle Ages the European nations combined power drives with vocational consciousness of different character. Spain's world-conquering imperialism was united with the fanatical belief in being the divine tool of the Counter-Reformation. England's vocational consciousness was rooted partly in the Calvinistic idea of world politics for the preservation of pure Christianity, partly in a Christian-humanistic feeling of responsibility for the colonial countries and for a solid balance of power between the civilized nations. This was inseparably united with an economic and political power drive and produced the largest Empire of all times and almost eighty years of European peace. The vocational consciousness of France was based on its cultural superiority in the seventeenth and eighteenth centuries. Modern Germany was under the impact of the so-called *Real-Politik,* without a vocational consciousness. Her ideology was the struggle for *Lebensraum,* partly in competition with the colonial nations and therefore in conflict with them. Hitler's use of an obviously absurd vocational idea, that of Nordic blood, was artificially imposed and only reluctantly accepted, because there was no genuine vocational symbol. To-day two great imperialistic systems fight with each other in terms of both force and vocational consciousness: Russia and America. The Russian vocational consciousness was based on its religious feeling that it had a mission towards the West, namely, to save the disintegrating Western civilization through Eastern mystical Christianity. This was the claim of the Slavophile movement in the nineteenth century.

Present-day Russia has a similar missionary consciousness towards the West and at the same time towards the Far East. Her power drive, which in the official counter-propaganda appears as the desire for world domination, is not understandable without her fanatical vocational consciousness, which must be compared with that of all other imperialistic movements. America's vocational consciousness has been called 'the American dream,' namely to establish the earthly form of the kingdom of God by a new beginning. The old forms of oppressive power were left behind and a new start was made. In the Constitution and the living democracy (both are quasi-religious concepts in the United States) the will is embodied to actualize what is felt as the American vocation. This was originally meant for America alone. Now it is meant explicitly for one-half of the world and implicitly for the whole world. The actual power drive working together with this vocational feeling is still rather limited. But the historical situation increases it more and more. And it is already justified to speak of half-conscious American imperialism.

Vocational consciousness expresses itself in laws. In these laws both justice and love are actual. The justice of the empires is not only ideology or rationalization. The empires not only subject, they also unite. And in so far as they are able to do this, they are not without love. Therefore those who are subjected acknowledge silently that they have become participants of a superior power of being and meaning. If this acknowledgement vanishes because the uniting power of the empire, its strength, and its vocational idea vanish, the empire comes to an end. Its power of being disintegrates and external attacks only execute what is already decided.

The present decrease in national sovereignty, the rise of embracing power groups, and the split of the world into two all-embracing systems of political power raises naturally the problem of a united mankind. What can be derived from our analysis of power, justice, and love for this question?

There are three answers to this question. The first one does not recognize the inescapable character of the recent developments towards larger organisms of power and expects a return to a number of relatively independent power centres, perhaps not national but continental. The second answer seeks for the solution in a world state, created by a kind of federal union of the present main powers and by their subjection to a central authority in which all groups participate. The third answer expects that one of the great powers will develop into a world centre, ruling the other nations through liberal methods and in democratic forms! The first answer is a matter of foresight. It belongs to the movement of social organisms that the centralizing tendency is always balanced by a decentralizing one. The question is: Which tendency determines the present situation? The technical union of the world favours centralization, but there are other, above all psychological, factors which may prevail. The second answer, the expectation of the world state, contradicts the analysis of power as we have given it. A power centre which unites strength with vocational consciousness cannot subject itself to an artificial authority without both of them. The presupposition for a political world unity is the presence of a spiritual unity expressed in symbols and myths. Nothing like this exists to-day. And before it does exist a world state has no power to create silent acknowledgement. The most probable answer seems to be the third one. It may well be that after the period of world history which is characterized by the rise of *one* power structure to universal power, with a minimum of suppression, the law and the justice and the uniting love which are embodied in this power will become the universal power of mankind. But even then the Kingdom of God has not come upon us. For even then disintegration and revolution are not excluded. New centres of power may appear, first underground, then openly, driving towards separation from or towards radical transformation of the whole. They may develop a vocational consciousness of their own.

Then the power struggle starts again and the period of the fulfilled world empire will be as limited as the Augustan period of peace was. Can uniting love never unite mankind? Can mankind never become as a whole a structure of power and a source of universal justice? With this question we have left the realm of history and approach the question of love, power, and justice in their relation to that which is ultimate.

✧ ✧ ✧ ✧

Justice, power, and love towards oneself is rooted in the justice, power, and love which we receive from that which transcends us and affirms us. The relation to ourselves is a function of our relation to God.

The last question put before us has been asked at the end of the chapter on the relation between social power groups. It was the question of the reunion of mankind in terms of love, power, and justice. No answer could be given on the level of political organization. Is there an answer out of the relation to the ultimate?

It is the merit of pacifism that, in spite of its theological shortcomings, it has kept this question alive in modern Christianity. Without it the Churches probably would have forgotten the torturing seriousness of any religious affirmation of war. On the other hand, pacifism has usually restricted a much larger problem of human existence to the question of war. But there are other questions of equal seriousness in the same sphere. One of them is the question of armed conflicts within a power group, always going on potentially in the use of police and armed forces for the preservation of order, sometimes coming into the open in revolutionary wars. If successful, they are later on called 'glorious revolutions.' Does the union of mankind mean that not only national but also revolutionary wars are excluded? And if so, has the dynamics of life come to an end; and does this mean that life itself has come to an end?

One can ask the same question with respect to the dynamics of the economic life. Even in a static society such as that of the Middle Ages, the economic dynamics were important and had tremendous historical consequences. One should remain aware of the fact that often more destruction and suffering is produced by economic than by military battles. Should the economic dynamics be stopped and a static world system of production and consumption be introduced? If this were so the whole technical process would also have to be stopped, life in most realms would have to be organized in ever-repeated processes. Every disturbance would have to be avoided. Again the dynamics of life and with it life itself would have to come to an end.

Let us assume for a moment that this were possible. Under

an unchangeable central authority all encounters of power with power are regulated. Nothing is risked, everything decided. Life has ceased to transcend itself. Creativity has come to an end. The history of man would be finished, post-history would have started. Mankind would be a flock of blessed animals without dissatisfaction, without drive into the future. The horrors and sufferings of the historical period would be remembered as the dark ages of mankind. And then it might happen that one or the other of these blessed men would feel a longing for these past ages, their misery and their greatness, and would force a new beginning of history upon the rest.

This image will show that a world without the dynamics of power and the tragedy of life and history is not the Kingdom of God, is not the fulfilment of man and his world. Fulfilment is bound to eternity and no imagination can reach the eternal. But fragmentary anticipations are possible. The Church itself is such a fragmentary anticipation. And there are groups and movements, which although they do not belong to the manifest Church, represent something we may call a 'latent Church.' But neither the manifest nor the latent Church is the Kingdom of God.

XXVIII KARL BARTH

Born in Basel, Switzerland, on May 10, 1886, Karl Barth was Professor of Theology in various German universities until forced out by Hitler. He then taught for the remainder of his career in Basel. Influenced by religious socialism he showed deep interest in social and political questions. In the conflict of the German Protestant Church with the Nazis he became one of the main intellectual resources for the opponents of Hitler. After World War II he took a more positive view of the possibility of true Christian life under Communism. While apparently contradictory, the difference in approach is deeply rooted in Barth's theology. Nazism with its anti-Semitic attack against Jesus Christ and thus the triune God is a more substantial threat than Communism with its primitive atheism, denying a God of general revelation—whom Barth denies also.

Because of the sheer bulk of his writings, which might make the choice of a few sections seem arbitrary and capricious, this selection offers a substantial part of one major pamphlet, *The Christian Community and the Civil Community*, which provides a perfect illustration of his influential social-ethical method. What is here only sketched is elaborated in a little more guarded fashion in the more than eight hundred pages of Volume 3, Part 4, of the *Church Dogmatics*.

SELECTION I

The Christian Community and the Civil Community

By the "Christian community" we mean what is usually called "the Church" and by the "civil community" what is usually called "the State."

The use of the concept of the "community" to describe both entities may serve at the very outset to underline the positive relationship and connexion between them. It was probably with some such intention in mind that Augustine spoke of the *civitas coelestis* and *terrena* and Zwingli of divine and human justice. In addition, however, the twofold use of the concept "community" is intended to draw attention to the fact that we are concerned in the "Church" and the "State" not merely and not primarily with institutions and offices but with human beings gathered together in corporate bodies in the service of common tasks. To interpret the "Church" as meaning above all a "community" has rightly become more recognised and normal again in recent years. The Swiss term "civil community"—in Swiss villages the residential, civil, and ecclesiastical communities often confer one after the other in the same inn, and most of the people involved belong to all three groups—the "civil community" as opposed to the "Christian community" may also remind Christians that there are and always have been communities outside their own circle in the form of States, i.e. political communities.

The "Christian community" (the Church) is the commonalty of the people in one place, region, or country who are called apart and gathered together as "Christians" by reason of their knowledge of and belief in Jesus Christ. The meaning and purpose of this "assembly" (*ekklesia*) is the common life of these people in one Spirit, the Holy Spirit, that is, in obedience to the Word of God in Jesus Christ, which they have all heard and are all needing and eager to hear again. They have also come together in order to pass on the Word to others. The inward expression of their life as a Christian community is the one faith, love, and hope by which they are all moved and sustained; its outward expression is the Confession by which they all stand, their jointly acknowledged and exercised responsibility for the preaching of the Name of Jesus Christ to all men and the worship and thanksgiving which they offer together. Since this is its concern, every single Christian community is as such an ecumenical (catholic) fellowship, that is, at one with the Christian communities in all other places, regions, and lands.

The "civil community" (the State) is the commonalty of all the people in one place, region, or country in so far as they belong together under a constitutional system of government that is equally valid for and binding on them all, and which is defended and maintained by force. The meaning and purpose of this mutual association (that is, of the *polis*) is the safeguarding of both the external, relative, and provisional freedom of the individuals and the external and relative peace of their community and to that extent the safeguarding of the external, relative, and provisional humanity of their life both as individuals and as a community. The three essential forms in which this safeguarding takes place are (a) legislation, which has to settle the legal system which is to be binding on all; (b) the government and administration which has to apply the legislation; (c) the administration of justice which has to deal with cases of doubtful or conflicting law and decide on its applicability.

When we compare the Christian community with the civil community the first difference that strikes us is that in the civil community Christians are no longer gathered together as such but are associated with non-Christians (or doubtful Christians). The civil community embraces everyone living within its area. Its members share no common awareness of their relationship to God, and such an awareness cannot be an element in the legal system established by the civil community. No appeal can be made to the Word or Spirit of God in the running of its affairs. The civil community as such is spiritually blind and ignorant. It has neither faith nor love nor hope. It has no creed and no gospel. Prayer is not part of its life, and its members are not brothers and sisters. As members of the civil community they can only ask, as Pilate asked: What is truth? since every answer to the question abolishes the presuppositions of the very existence of the civil community. "Tolerance" is its ultimate wisdom in the "religious" sphere—"religion" being used in this context to describe the purpose of the Christian community. For this reason the civil community can only have external, relative, and provisional tasks and aims, and that is why it is burdened and defaced by something which the Christian community can, characteristically, do without: physical force, the "secular arm" which it can use to enforce its authority. That is why it lacks the ecumenical breadth and freedom that are so essential to Christianity. The *polis* has walls. Up till now, at least, civil communities have always been more or less clearly marked off from one another as local, regional, national, and therefore competing and colliding units of government. And that is why the State has no safeguard or corrective against the danger of either neglecting or absolutising itself and its particular system and thus in one way or the other destroying and annulling itself. One cannot in fact compare the Church with the State without realising how much weaker, poorer, and more exposed to danger the human community is in the State than in the Church.

✧ ✧ ✧ ✧

The Church must remain the Church. It must remain the inner circle of the Kingdom of Christ. The Christian community has a task of which the civil community can never relieve it and which it can never pursue in the forms peculiar to the civil community. It would not redound to the welfare of the civil community if the Christian community were to be absorbed by it (as Rothe has suggested that it should) and were therefore to neglect the special task which it has received a categorical order to undertake. It proclaims the rule of Jesus Christ and the hope of the Kingdom of God. This is not the task of the civil community; it has no message to deliver; it is dependent on a message being delivered to it. It is not in a position to appeal to the authority and grace of God; it is dependent on this happening elsewhere. It does not pray; it depends on others praying for it. It is blind to the whence and whither of human existence; its task is rather to provide for the external and provisional delimitation and protection of human life; it depends on the existence of seeing eyes elsewhere. It cannot call the human *hybris* into question fundamentally, and it knows of no final defence against the chaos which threatens it from that quarter; in this respect, too, it depends on ultimate words and insights existing elsewhere. The thought and speech of the civil community waver necessarily between a much too childlike optimism and a much too peevish pessimism in regard to man—as a matter of course it expects the best of everybody and suspects the worst! It obviously relies on its own view of man being fundamentally superseded elsewhere. Only an act of supreme disobedience on the part of Christians could bring the special existence of the Christian community to an end. Such a cessation is also impossible because then the voice of what is ultimately the only hope and help which all men need to hear would be silent.

✧ ✧ ✧ ✧

In this freedom, however, the Church makes itself responsible for the shape and reality of the civil community in a quite definite sense. We have already said that it is quite impossible for the Christian to adopt an attitude of complete indifference to politics. But neither can the Church be indifferent to particular political patterns and realities. The Church "reminds the world of God's Kingdom, God's commandment and righteousness and thereby of the responsibility of governments and governed" (Barmen Thesis No. 5). This means that the Christian community and the individual Christian can understand and accept many things in the political sphere—and if necessary suffer and endure everything. But the fact that it can understand much and endure everything has nothing to do with the "subordination" which is required of it, that is, with the share of responsibility which it is enjoined to take in the political sphere. That responsibility refers rather to the decisions which it must make before God: "must" make, because, unlike Christian understanding and suffering, Christian intentions and decisions are bound to run in a quite definite direction of their own. There will always be room and need for discussion of the details of Christian intentions and decisions, but the general line on which they are based can never be the subject of accommodation and compromise in the Church's relations with the world. The Christian community "subordinates" itself to the civil community by making its knowledge of the Lord who is Lord of all its criterion, and distinguishing between the just and the unjust State, that is, between the better and the worse political form and reality; between order and caprice; between government and tyranny; between freedom and anarchy; between community and collectivism; between personal rights and individualism; between the State as described in Romans 13 and the State as described in Revelation 13. And it will judge all matters concerned with the establishment, preservation, and enforcement of political order in accordance with these necessary distinctions and according to the merits of the particular case and situation to which they refer. On the basis of the judgment which it has formed it will choose and desire whichever seems to be the better political system in any particular situation, and in accordance with this choice and desire it will offer its support here and its resistance there. It is in the making of such distinctions, judgments, and choices from its own centre, and in the practical decisions which necessarily flow from that centre, that the Christian community expresses its "subordination" to the civil community and fulfils its share of political responsibility.

The Christian decisions which have to be made in the political sphere have no idea, system, or programme to refer to but a direction and a line that must be recognised and adhered to in all circumstances. This line cannot be defined by appealing to the so-called "natural law." To base its policy on "natural law" would mean that the Christian community was adopting the ways of the civil community, which does not take its bearings from the Christian centre and is still living or again living in a state of ignorance. The Christian community would be adopting the methods, in other words, of the pagan State. It would not be acting as a Christian community in the State at all; it would no longer be the salt and the light of the wider circle of which Christ is the centre. It would not only be declaring its solidarity with the civil community: it would be putting itself on a par with it and withholding from it the very things it lacks most. It would certainly not be doing it any service in that way. For the thing the civil community lacks (in its neutrality towards the Word and Spirit of God) is a firmer and clearer motivation for political decisions than the so-called natural law can provide. By "natural law" we mean the embodiment of what man is alleged to regard as universally right and wrong, as necessary, permissible, and forbidden "by nature," that is, on any conceivable premise. It has been connected with a natural revelation of God, that is, with a revelation known to man by natural means. And the civil community as such—the civil community which is not yet or is no longer illuminated from its centre—undoubtedly has no other choice but to think, speak, and act on the basis of this allegedly natural law, or rather of a particular conception of the court of appeal which is passed off as *the* natural law. The civil community is reduced to guessing or to accepting some powerful assertion of this or that interpretation of natural law. All it can do is to grope around and experiment with the convictions which it derives from "natural law," never certain whether it may not in the end be an illusion to rely on it as the final authority and therefore always making vigorous use, openly or secretly, of a more or less refined positivism. The results of the politics based on such considerations were and are just what might be expected. And if they were and are not clearly and generally negative, if in the political sphere the better stands alongside the worse, if there were and still are good as well as bad States—no doubt the reality is always a curious mixture of the two!—then the reason is not that the true "natural law" has been discovered, but simply the fact that even the ignorant, neutral, pagan civil community is still in the Kingdom of Christ, and that all political questions and all political efforts as such are founded on the gracious ordinance of God by which man is preserved and his sin and crime confined.

What we glimpse in the better kind of State is the purpose, meaning, and goal of this divine ordinance. It is operative in any case, even though the citizens of the particular State may lack any certain knowledge of the trustworthy standards of political decision, and the overwhelming threat of mistaking an error for the truth may be close at hand. The divine ordinance may operate with the co-operation of the men and women involved, but certainly without their having deserved it: *Dei providentia hominum confusione*. If the Christian community were to base its political responsibility on the assumption that it was also interested in the problem of natural law and that it was attempting to base its decisions on so-called natural law, this would not alter the power which God has to make good come of evil, as He is in fact always doing in the political order. But it would mean that the Christian community was sharing human illusions and confusions. It is bad enough that, when it does not risk going its own way, the Christian community is widely involved in these illusions and confusions. It should not wantonly attempt to deepen such involvement. And it would be doing no less if it were to seek the criterion of its political decisions in some form of the so-called natural law. The tasks and problems which the Christian community is called to share, in fulfilment of its political responsibility, are "natural," secular, profane tasks and problems. But the norm by which it should be guided is anything but natural: it is the only norm which it can believe in and accept as a spiritual norm, and is derived from the clear law of its own faith, not from the obscure workings of a system outside itself: it is from knowledge of this norm that it will make its decisions in the political sphere.

✧ ✧ ✧ ✧

The direction of Christian judgments, purposes, and ideals in political affairs is based on the analogical capacities and needs of political organisation. Political organisation can be neither a repetition of the Church nor an anticipation of the Kingdom of God. In relation to the Church it is an independent reality; in relation to the Kingdom of God it is (like the Church itself) a human reality bearing the stamp of this fleeting world. An equating of State and Church on the one hand and State and Kingdom of God on the other is therefore out of the question. On the other hand, however, since the State is based on a particular divine ordinance, since it belongs to the Kingdom of God, it has no autonomy, no independence over against the Church and the Kingdom of God. A simple and absolute heterogeneity between State and Church on the one hand and State and Kingdom of God on the other is therefore just as much out of the question as a simple and absolute equating. The only possibility that remains—and it suggests itself compellingly—is to regard the existence of the State as an allegory, as a correspondence and an analogue to the Kingdom of God which the Church preaches and believes in. Since the State forms the outer circle, within which the Church, with the mystery of its faith and gospel, is the inner circle, since it shares a common centre with the Church, it is inevitable that, although its presuppositions and its tasks are its own and different, it is nevertheless capable of reflecting indirectly the truth and reality which constitute the Christian community. Since, however, the peculiarity and difference of its presuppositions and tasks and its existence as an outer circle must remain as they are, its justice and even its very existence as a reflected image of the Christian truth and reality cannot be given once and for all and as a matter of course but are, on the contrary, exposed to the utmost danger; it will always be questionable whether and how far it will fulfil its just purposes. To be saved from degeneration and decay it needs to be reminded of the righteousness which is a reflection of Christian truth. Again and again it needs a historical setting whose goal and content are the moulding of the State into an allegory of the Kingdom of God and the fulfilment of its righteousness. Human initiative in such situations cannot proceed from the State itself. As a purely civil community, the State is ignorant of the mystery of the Kingdom of God, the mystery of its own centre, and it is indifferent to the faith and gospel of the Christian community. As a civil community it can only draw from the porous wells of the so-called natural law. It cannot remind itself of the true criterion of its own righteousness, it cannot move towards the fulfilment of that righteousness in its own strength. It needs the wholesomely disturbing presence, the activity that revolves directly around the common centre, the participation of the Christian community in the execution of political responsibility. The Church is not the Kingdom of God, but it has knowledge of it; it hopes for it; it believes in it; it prays in the name of Jesus Christ, and it preaches His Name as the Name above all others. The Church is not neutral on this ground, and it is therefore not powerless. If it achieves only the great and necessary *metabasis eis allo genos* which is the share of political responsibility which it is enjoined to assume, then it will not be able to be neutral and powerless and deny its Lord in the other *genos*. If the Church takes up its share of political responsibility, it must mean that it is taking that human initiative which the State cannot take: it is giving the State the impulse which it cannot give itself; it is reminding the State of those things of which it is unable to remind itself. The distinctions, judgments, and choices which it makes in the political sphere are always intended to foster the illumination of the State's connexion with the order of divine salvation and grace and to discourage all the attempts to hide this connexion. Among the political possibilities open at any particular moment it will choose those which most suggest a correspondence to, an analogy and a reflection of, the content of its own faith and gospel.

In the decisions of the State, the Church will always support the side which clarifies rather than obscures the Lordship of Jesus Christ over the whole, which includes this political sphere outside the Church. The Church desires that the shape and reality of the State in this fleeting world should point towards the Kingdom of God, not away from it. Its desire is not that human politics should cross the politics of God, but that they should proceed, however distantly, on parallel lines.

It desires that the active grace of God, as revealed from heaven, should be reflected in the earthly material of the external, relative, and provisional actions and modes of action of the political community. It therefore makes itself responsible in the first and last place to God—the one God whose grace is revealed in Jesus Christ—by making itself responsible for the cause of the State. And so, with its political judgments and choices, it bears an implicit, indirect, but none the less real witness to the gospel.

Even its political activity is therefore a profession of its Christian faith. By its political activity it calls the State from neutrality, ignorance, and paganism into co-responsibility before God, thereby remaining faithful to its own particular mission. It sets in motion the historical process whose aim and content are the moulding of the State into the likeness of the Kingdom of God and hence the fulfilment of the State's own righteous purposes.

The Church is based on the knowledge of the one eternal God, who as such became man and thereby proved Himself a neighbor to man, by treating him with compassion (Luke 10: 36 f.). The inevitable consequence is that in the political sphere the Church will always and in all circumstances be interested primarily in human beings and not in some abstract cause or other, whether it be anonymous capital or the State as such (the functioning of its departments!) or the honor of the nation or the progress of civilisation or culture or the idea, however conceived, of the historical development of the human race. It will not be interested in this last idea even if "progress" is interpreted as meaning the welfare of future generations, for the attainment of which man, human dignity, human life in the present age are to be trampled underfoot. Right itself becomes wrong (*summum ius summa iniuria*) when it is allowed to rule as an abstract form, instead of serving the limitation and hence the preservation of man. The Church is at all times and in all circumstances the enemy of the idol Juggernaut. Since God Himself became man, man is the measure of all things, and man can and must only be used and, in certain circumstances, sacrificed, for man. Even the most wretched man—not man's egoism, but man's humanity—must be resolutely defended against the autocracy of every mere "cause." Man has not to serve causes; causes have to serve man.

The Church is witness of the divine justification, that is, of the act in which God in Jesus Christ established and confirmed his original claim to man and hence man's claim against sin and death. The future for which the Church waits is the definitive revelation of this divine justification. This means that the Church will always be found where the order of the State is based on a commonly acknowledged law, from submission to which no one is exempt, and which also provides equal protection for all. The Church will be found where all political activity is in all circumstances regulated by this law. The Church always stands for the constitutional State, for the maximum validity and application of that twofold rule (no exemption from and full protection by the law), and therefore it will always be against any degeneration of the constitutional State into tyranny or anarchy. The Church will never be found on the side of anarchy or tyranny. In its politics it will always be urging the civil community to treat this fundamental purpose of its existence with the utmost seriousness: the limiting and the preserving of man by the quest for and the establishment of law.

The Church is witness of the fact that the Son of man came to seek and to save the lost. And this implies that—casting all false impartiality aside—the Church must concentrate first on the lower and lowest levels of human society. The poor, the socially and economically weak and threatened, will always be the object of its primary and particular concern, and it will always insist on the State's special responsibility for these weaker members of society. That it will bestow its love on them, within the framework of its own task (as part of its service), is one thing and the most important thing; but it must not concentrate on this and neglect the other thing to which it is committed by its political responsibility: the effort to achieve such a fashioning of the law as will make it impossible for "equality before the law" to become a cloak under which strong and weak, independent and dependent, rich and poor, employers and employees, in fact receive different treatment at its hands: the weak being unduly restricted, the strong unduly protected. The Church must stand for social justice in the political sphere. And in choosing between the various socialistic possibilities (social-liberalism? co-operativism? syndicalism? free trade? moderate or radical Marxism?) it will always choose the movement from which it can expect the greatest measure of social justice (leaving all other considerations on one side).

The Church is the fellowship of those who are freely called by the Word of grace and the Spirit and love of God to be the children of God. Translated into political terms, this means that the Church affirms, as the basic right which every citizen must be guaranteed by the State, the freedom to carry out his decisions in the politically lawful sphere, according to his own insight and choice, and therefore independently, and the freedom to live in certain spheres (the family, education, art, science, religion, culture), safeguarded but not regulated by law. The Church will not in all circumstances withdraw from and oppose what may be practically a dictatorship, that is, a partial and temporary limitation of these freedoms, but it will certainly withdraw from and oppose any out-and-out dictatorship such as the totalitarian State. The adult Christian can only wish to be an adult citizen, and he can only want his fellow citizens to live as adult human beings.

The Church is the fellowship of those who, as members of the one Body of the one Head, are bound and committed to this Lord of theirs and therefore to no other. It follows that the Church will never understand and interpret political freedom and the basic law which the State must guarantee to the individual citizen other than in the sense of the basic duty of responsibility which is required of him. (This was never made particularly clear in the classic proclamation of so-called "human rights" in America and France.) The citizen is responsible in the whole sphere of his freedom, political and non-political alike. And the civil community is naturally responsible in the maintenance of its freedom as a whole. Thus the Christian approach surpasses both individualism and collectivism. The Church knows and recognises the "interest" of the individual and of the "whole," but it resists them both when they want to have the last word. It subordinates them to the being of the citizen, the being of the civil community before the law, over which neither the individuals nor the "whole" are to hold sway, but which they are to seek after, to find, and to serve—always with a view to limiting and preserving the life of man.

As the fellowship of those who live in one faith under one Lord on the basis of a Baptism in one Spirit, the Church must and will stand for the equality of the freedom and responsibility of all adult citizens, in spite of its sober insight into the variety of human needs, abilities, and tasks. It will stand for their equality before the law that unites and binds them all, for their equality in working together to establish and carry out the law, and for their equality in the limitation and preservation of human life that it secures. If, in accordance with a specifically Christian insight, it lies in the very nature of the State that this equality must not be restricted by any differences of religious belief or unbelief, it is all the more important for the Church to urge that the restriction of the political freedom and responsibility not only of certain classes and races but, supremely, of that of women is an arbitrary convention which does not deserve to be preserved any longer. If Christians are to be consistent there can be only one possible decision in this matter.

Since the Church is aware of the variety of the gifts and tasks of the one Holy Spirit in its own sphere, it will be alert and open in the political sphere to the need to separate the different functions and "powers"—the legislative, executive, and judicial—inasmuch as those who carry out any one of these functions should not carry out the others simultaneously. No human being is a god able to unite in his own person the functions of the legislator and the ruler, the ruler and the judge, without endangering the sovereignty of the law. The "people" is no more such a god than the Church is its own master and in sole possession of its powers. The fact is that within the community of the one people (by the people and for the people) definite and different services are to be performed by different persons, which, if they were united in one human hand, would disrupt rather than promote the unity of the common enterprise. With its awareness of the necessity that must be observed in this matter, the Church will give a lead to the State.

The Church lives from the disclosure of the true God and His revelation, from Him as the Light that has been lit in Jesus Christ to destroy the works of darkness. It lives in the dawning of the day of the Lord and its task in relation to the world is to rouse it and tell it that this day has dawned. The inevitable political corollary of this is that the Church is the sworn enemy of all secret policies and secret diplomacy. It is just as true of the political sphere as of any other that only evil can want to be kept secret. The distinguishing mark of the good is that it presses forward to the light of day. Where freedom and responsibility in the service of the State are one, whatever is said and done must be said and done before the ears and eyes of all, and the legislator, the ruler, and the judge can and must be ready to answer openly for all their actions—without thereby being necessarily dependent on the public or allowing themselves to be flurried. The statecraft that wraps itself up in darkness is the craft of a State which, because it is anarchic or tyrannical, is forced to hide the bad conscience of its citizens or officials. The Church will not on any account lend its support to that kind of State.

The Church sees itself established and nourished by the free Word of God—the Word which proves its freedom in the Holy Scriptures at all times. And in its own sphere the Church believes that the human word is capable of being the free vehicle and the mouthpiece of this free Word of God. By a process of analogy, it has to risk attributing a positive and constructive meaning to the free human word in the political sphere. If it trusts the word of man in one sphere it cannot mistrust it on principle in the other. It will believe that human words are not bound to be empty or useless or even dangerous, but that the right words can clarify and control great decisions. At the risk of providing opportunities for empty, useless, and dangerous words to be heard, it will therefore do all it can to see that there is at any rate no lack of opportunity for the *right* word to be heard. It will do all it can to see that there are opportunities for mutual discussion in the civil community as the basis of common endeavours. And it will try to see that such discussion takes place openly. With all its strength it will be on the side of those who refuse to have anything to do with the regimentation, controlling, censoring of public opinion. It knows of no pretext which would make that a good thing and no situation in which it could be necessary.

As disciples of Christ, the members of His Church do not rule: they serve. In the political community, therefore, the Church can only regard all ruling that is not primarily a form of service as a diseased and never as a normal condition. No State can exist without the sanction of power. But the power of the good State differs from that of the bad State as *potestas* differs from *potentia*. *Potestas* is the power that follows and serves the law; *potentia* is the power that precedes the law, that masters and bends and breaks the law—it is the naked power which is directly evil. Bismarck—not to mention Hitler—was (in spite of the *Daily Bible Readings* on his bedside table) no model statesman because he wanted to establish and develop his work on naked power. The ultimate result of this all-too-consistently pursued aim was inevitable: "all that draw the sword shall perish by the sword." Christian political theory leads us in the very opposite direction.

Since the Church is ecumenical (catholic) by virtue of its very origin, it resists all abstract local, regional, and national interests in the political sphere. It will always seek to serve the best interests of the particular city or place where it is stationed. But it will never do this without at the same time looking out beyond the city walls. It will be conscious of the superficiality, relativity, and temporariness of the immediate city boundaries, and on principle it will always stand for understanding and cooperation within the wider circle. The Church will be the last to lend its support to mere parochial politics. *Pacta sunt servanda? Pacta sunt concludenda!* All cities of the realm must agree if their common cause is to enjoy stability and not fall to pieces. In the Church we have tasted the air of freedom and must bring others to taste it, too.

The Church knows God's anger and judgment, but it also knows that His anger lasts but for a moment, whereas His mercy is for eternity. The political analogy of this truth is that violent solutions of conflicts in the political community—from police measures to law court decisions, from the armed rising against a regime that is no longer worthy of or equal to its task (in the sense of a revolt undertaken not to undermine but to restore the lawful authority of the State) to the defensive war against an external threat to the lawful State—must be approved, supported, and if necessary even suggested by the Christian community—for how could it possibly contract out in such situations? On the other hand, it can only regard violent solutions of any conflict as an *ultima ratio regis*. It will approve and support them only when they are for the moment the ultimate and only possibility available. It will always do its utmost to postpone such moments as far as possible. It can never stand for absolute peace, for peace at any price. But it must and will do all it can to see that no price is considered too high for the preservation or restoration of peace at home and abroad except the ultimate price which would mean the abolition of the lawful State and the practical denial of the divine ordinance. May the Church show her inventiveness in the search for other solutions before she joins in the call for violence! The perfection of the Father in heaven, who does not cease to be the heavenly Judge, demands the earthly perfection of a peace policy which really does extend to the limits of the humanly possible.

XXIX DIETRICH BONHOEFFER

Born on February 4, 1906, in Breslau, Germany, Dietrich Bonhoeffer was murdered by the Nazis in Flossenbürg on April 9, 1945, as the Third Reich was collapsing.

A young theologian of great promise, he first called attention to the problems of Christian ethics in his book, *The Cost of Discipleship,* of 1937, with his attack on what he called "cheap grace." Soon involved in the struggle against Nazism, he was imprisoned in April, 1943, and never again released.

Because of his long imprisonment and early death, Bonhoeffer's theological work is fragmentary; nevertheless it has proven immensely suggestive and produced even something like a Bonhoeffer "cult" in Europe and America. The cultists tend to ignore his published writings and even his *Ethics* and, seizing some of the more opaque statements in his letters from prison, attempt to develop a "religionless Christianity" for the modern world.

Our selections are taken from his *Ethics,* which is a very significant collection of fragments, and from his *Letters and Papers from Prison,* which illustrate the direction Bonhoeffer's thought might have taken and explain his complex influence on Christian social teaching in our time.

SELECTION I
Ethics

One of the questions Bonhoeffer raised was, "How does the will of God become concrete?" He tried to avoid any "general principles" for Christian Ethics and his mandates are an attempt to safeguard the concrete commandment character of Christian social action.

THE CONCEPT OF THE MANDATE

By the term 'mandate' we understand the concrete divine commission which has its foundation in the revelation of Christ and which is evidenced by Scripture; it is the legitimation and warrant for the execution of a definite divine commandment, the conferment of divine authority on an earthly agent. The term 'mandate' must also be taken to imply the claiming, the seizure and the formation of a definite earthly domain by the divine commandment. The bearer of the mandate acts as a deputy in the place of Him who assigns him his commission. In its proper sense the term 'institution' or 'order' might also be applied here, but this would involve the danger of directing attention rather towards the actual state of the institution than towards its foundation, which lies solely in the divine warrant, legitimation and authorization. The consequence of this can all too easily be the assumption of a divine sanction for all existing orders and institutions in general and a romantic conservatism which is entirely at variance with the Christian doctrine of the four divine mandates. If the concept of the 'institution' could be purged of these misinterpretations it would no doubt be capable of expressing very effectively what is here intended. The concept of the 'estate' also suggests itself in this connexion; it did good service from the time of the Reformation onwards, but in the course of history it has acquired so many new connotations that it is now quite impossible to employ it in its pure original sense. These words now suggest human prerogatives and privileges and no longer convey their original meaning of dignity in humility. Finally, the term 'office' is now so completely secularized, and has come to be so closely associated with institutional bureaucratic thinking, that it cannot possibly render the sublime quality of the divine decree. For lack of a better word, therefore, we will for the time being retain the term 'mandate,' but it is still our purpose, by dint of clarifying the concept itself, to help to renew and to restore the old notion of the institution, the estate and the office.

The divine mandates are dependent solely on the *one* commandment of God as it is revealed in Jesus Christ. They are introduced into the world from above as orders or 'institutions' of the reality of Christ, that is to say, of the reality of the love of

God for the world and for men which is revealed in Jesus Christ. This means that they are not in any sense products of history; they are not earthly powers, but divine commissions. It is only from above, with God as the point of departure, that it is possible to say and to understand what is meant by the Church, by marriage and the family, by culture and by government. The bearers of the mandate do not receive their commission from below; their task is not to expound and execute desires of the human will, but in a strict and unalterable sense they hold their commission from God, they are deputies and representatives of God. This remains true whatever may be the historical origins of a church, a family or a government. In this way, by virtue of the divine warrant, there is established in the sphere of the mandate an unalterable relation of superiority and inferiority.

This means that the commandment of God wishes to find man always in an earthly relation of authority, in a clearly defined order of superiority and inferiority. But at this point it is immediately necessary to define this superiority and inferiority more closely. First of all, it is not identical with an earthly relation of superior and inferior power. The stronger can certainly not without further ado claim for himself the authority of the divine mandate *vis-à-vis* the weaker. On the contrary, it is characteristic of the divine mandate that it corrects and regulates the earthly relations of superior and inferior power in its own way. Secondly, it must be emphasized that the divine mandate establishes not only superiority but also inferiority. Superiority and inferiority pertain to one another in an indissoluble relation of mutual limitation which we shall later have to define more closely. Thirdly, superiority and inferiority here represent a relation not of concepts or of things but of persons; it is a relation between those persons who, whether they be superior or inferior, submit to the commission of God and to it alone. The master, too, has a Master, and this fact alone establishes his right to be master and authorizes and legitimates his relation to the servant. Master and servant owe to one another the honour which arises from any particular act of participation in the mandate of God. There may be abuse of superiority to the detriment of the inferior, but at the same time there may also be abuse of inferiority. Quite apart from personal aberrations, abuse of both superiority and inferiority is inevitable whenever it is no longer recognized that both have their foundation in the mandate of God. In such a case superiority is thought of as a fortuitous favour of fortune; it is seized upon and exploited without compunction, and, in return, inferiority is thought of as an unjust disadvantage, which necessarily gives rise to indignation and rebellion. The whole relation of superiority and inferiority is reversed when the inferior becomes conscious of the forces which are inherent within itself. This is the critical moment at which the inferior suddenly breaks free; it perceives itself to be armed with the dark forces of destruction, denial, doubt and rebellion, and, with these chaotic powers at its disposal, it feels itself to be superior to all established order and to all superiority. There is now no longer any genuine superiority or inferiority; the superior derives its authority and legitimation solely from below, and this superiority, which is superior only on the basis of the inferior, is regarded by the inferior only as the personified claim of the inferior to become superior. Thus in such a case the inferior becomes a permanent and inevitable menace to the superior; in the face of this threat the man who is superior can maintain his 'superior' position only by tormenting and provoking the inferior still more actively while at the same time combating the rebellious forces of the inferior with terror and violence. At this stage, when the relation between superior and inferior is reversed or confused, there arises between them the most intense hostility, mistrust, deceit and envy. And in this atmosphere, too, purely personal abuse of superiority and inferiority flourishes as never before. In the horror which is aroused by the violence of this rebellion the fact that there was ever the possibility of a genuine institutional order established from above can only appear as a miracle, and so, in reality, it is. The genuine order of superior and inferior draws its life from belief in the commission from 'above,' belief in the 'Lord of lords.' This belief alone can exorcize the demonic forces which emerge from below. The collapse of this belief means the total collapse and destruction of the whole structure and order which is established in the world from above. Some will say it was a hoax and a fraud, and others will say it was a miracle, but both sides alike must surely be astonished by the power of belief.

It is only in conjunction, in combination and in opposition with one another that the divine mandates of the Church, of marriage and the family, of culture and of government declare the commandment of God as it is revealed in Jesus Christ. No single one of these mandates is sufficient in itself or can claim to replace all the others. The mandates are *conjoined;* otherwise they are not mandates of God. In their conjunction they are not isolated or separated from one another, but they are directed towards one another. They are 'for' one another; otherwise they are not God's mandates. Moreover, within this relation of conjunction and mutual support, each one is limited by the other; even within the relation of mutual support this limitation is necessarily experienced as a relation of mutual opposition. Wherever this mutual opposition no longer exists there is no longer a mandate of God.

Superiority, therefore, is subject to three limitations which each take effect in a different way; it is limited first by God, who confers the commission, second by the other mandates, and third by the relation of inferiority. Yet these limitations also constitute a protection for superiority. This protection affords encouragement for the observance of the divine mandates, just as the limitation gives warning against the abuse of superiority.

Protection and limitation are two sides of the same thing. God protects by limiting, and He encourages by warning.

✧ ✧ ✧ ✧

On the basis of Holy Scripture, the office of preaching proclaims Christ as the Lord and Saviour of the world. There can be no legitimate proclamation by the Church which is not a proclamation of Christ. The Church does not proclaim two different messages, a message of universal reason and natural law for unbelievers, and a Christian message for believers. Only a pharisaical self-conceit can impel the Church to withhold the proclamation of Christ from one man and not from another. The Church's word derives its sole right and its sole authority from the commission of Christ, and consequently any word which she may utter without reference to this authority will be devoid of all significance. In her encounter with the government, for example, the Church must not simply cease to be the Church; the mandate of the government is certainly not to confess Christ; the government is concerned rather with quite concrete abuses which its divine mandate requires it to remedy. It is only when the Church fulfils what is essentially her own mandate that she can legitimately call for the fulfilment of the mandate of the government. Nor does the Church have two different commandments at her disposal, one for the world and another for the Christian congregation; her commandment, which she proclaims to all mankind, is the one commandment of God which is revealed in Jesus Christ.

The Church proclaims this commandment by testifying to Jesus Christ as the Lord and Saviour of his people and of the whole world, and so by summoning all men to fellowship with Him.

Jesus Christ, the eternal Son with the Father for all eternity: this means that no created thing can be conceived and essentially understood without reference to Christ, the Mediator of creation. All things were created by Him and for Him, and have their existence only in Him (Col. 1:15 ff.). It is vain to seek to know God's will for created things without reference to Christ. Jesus Christ, the incarnate God: this means that God has taken upon himself bodily all human being; it means that henceforward divine being cannot be found otherwise than in human form; it means that in Jesus Christ man is made free to be really man before God. The 'Christian' element is not an end in itself, but it consists in man's being entitled and obliged to live as man before God. In the incarnation God makes Himself known as Him who wishes to exist not for Himself but 'for us.' Consequently, in view of the incarnation of God, to live as man before God can mean only to exist not for oneself but for God and for other men.

Jesus Christ, the crucified Reconciler: this means in the first place that the whole world has become godless by its rejection of Jesus Christ and that no effort of its own can rid it of this curse. The reality of the world has been marked once and for all by the cross of Christ, but the cross of Christ is the cross of the reconciliation of the world with God, and for this reason the godless world bears at the same time the mark of reconciliation as the free ordinance of God. The cross of atonement is the setting free for life before God in the midst of the godless world; it is the setting free for life in genuine worldliness. The proclamation of the cross of the atonement is a setting free because it leaves behind it the vain attempts to deify the world and because it has overcome the disunions, tensions and conflicts between the 'Christian' element and the 'secular' element and calls for simple life and action in the belief that the reconciliation of the world with God has been accomplished. A life in genuine worldliness is possible only through the proclamation of Christ crucified; true worldly living is not possible or real in contradiction to the proclamation or side by side with it, that is to say, in any kind of autonomy of the secular sphere; it is possible and real only 'in, with and under' the proclamation of Christ. Without or against the proclamation of the cross of Christ there can be no recognition of the godlessness and godforsakenness of the world, but the worldly element will rather seek always to satisfy its insatiable longing for its own deification. If, however, the worldly element establishes its own law side by side with the proclamation of Christ, then it falls victim entirely to itself and must in the end set itself in the place of God. In both these cases the worldly element will not and cannot be merely worldly. It strives desperately and convulsively to achieve the deification of the worldly, with the consequence that precisely this emphatically and exclusively worldly life falls victim to a spurious and incomplete worldliness. The freedom and the courage are lacking for genuine and complete worldliness, that is to say, for allowing the world to be what it really is before God, namely, a world which in its godlessness is reconciled with God. We shall have something to say later on about the definition of the contents of 'genuine worldliness.' What is decisive at the present juncture is that a genuine worldliness is possible solely and exclusively on the basis of the proclamation of the cross of Jesus Christ.

Jesus Christ, the risen and ascended Lord: this means that Jesus Christ has overcome sin and death and that He is the living Lord to whom all power is given in heaven and on earth.

All the powers of the world are made subject to Him and must serve Him, each in its own way. The lordship of Jesus Christ is not the rule of a foreign power; it is the lordship of the Creator, Reconciler and Redeemer, the lordship of Him through whom and for whom all created beings exist, of Him in whom indeed all created beings alone find their origin, their goal and their essence. Jesus Christ imposes no alien law upon creation; but at the same time He does not tolerate any 'autonomy' of creation in detachment from His commandments. The commandment of Jesus Christ, the living Lord, sets creation free for the fulfilment of the law which is its own, that is to say, the law which is inherent in it by virtue of its having its origin, its goal and its essence in Jesus Christ. The commandment of Jesus does not provide the basis for any kind of domination of the Church over the government, of the government over the family, or of culture over government or Church, or for any other relation of overlordship which may be thought of in this connexion. The commandment of Jesus Christ does indeed rule over Church, family, culture and government; but it does so while at the same time setting each of these mandates free for the fulfilment of its own allotted functions. Jesus Christ's claim to lordship, which is proclaimed by the Church, means at the same time the emancipation of family, culture and government for the realization of their own essential character which has its foundation in Christ. The liberation which results from the proclamation of the lordship of Christ renders possible that relation of the divine mandates 'with,' 'for' and 'against' one another, of which we shall later have to speak in detail.

We have just said that the dominion of the commandment of Christ over all creation is not to be equated with the dominion of the Church. This raises a crucial problem in connexion with the Church's mandate, a problem which we can now no longer avoid.

The mandate of the Church is to proclaim the revelation of God in Jesus Christ. But the mystery of this name lies in the fact that it does not only designate an individual man but embraces at the same time the whole of human nature. We can testify to Jesus Christ and proclaim Him always only as Him in whom God took manhood upon Himself in the body. In

Jesus Christ is the new humanity, the congregation of God. In Jesus Christ the word of God and the congregation of God are inseparably united. Consequently, wherever Jesus Christ is proclaimed in accordance with the divine mandate, there, too, there is always the congregation. In the first instance this means only that men are there who accept the word concerning Christ, and who believe it and acquiesce in it, unlike others who do not accept it but reject it. It means, then, that men are there who allow that to happen to themselves which properly, as an act of God, should happen to all men; it means that men are there who stand as deputies for the other men, for the whole world. Certainly these are men who at the same time lead their worldly lives in the family, culture and government; they do so as men whom the word of Christ has set free for life in the world, but now they also form a community, a body which is distinct and separate from worldly institutions, for they are assembled together around the word of God and they are men who are chosen and live in this word. It is with this particular 'community' that we must now concern ourselves, and we must first turn our attention to the necessary distinction between this and the divine mandate of proclamation. The word of God, proclaimed by virtue of a divine mandate, dominates and rules the entire world; the 'community' which comes into being around this word does not dominate the world, but it stands entirely in the service of the fulfilment of the divine mandate. The law of this 'community' cannot and must not ever become the law of the worldly order, for by doing so it would be establishing an alien rule; conversely the law of a worldly order cannot and must not ever become the law of this community. Thus the peculiarity of the divine mandate of the Church lies in the fact that the proclamation of the lordship of Christ over the whole world must always be distinguished from the 'law' of the Church as a community, while on the other hand the Church as a community is not to be separated from the office of proclamation.

The Church as a self-contained community serves to fulfil the divine mandate of proclamation. She does this in two ways: first by the adaptation of the whole organization of this community for the effective proclamation of Christ to the whole world, which means that the congregation itself is merely an instrument, merely a means to an end; secondly, by virtue of the fact that, precisely through the congregation's acting on behalf of the world in this way, the purpose is achieved and the divine mandate of proclamation has begun to be fulfilled. This means that, precisely through its willingness to be merely the instrument and the means to the end, the congregation has become the goal and centre of all God's dealing with the world. The concept of deputyship characterizes this twofold relationship most clearly. The Christian congregation stands at the point at which the whole world ought to be standing; to this extent it serves as deputy for the world and exists for the sake of the world. On the other hand, the world achieves its own fulfilment at the point at which the congregation stands in this twofold relation of deputyship entirely in the fellowship and disciplehood of its Lord, who was Christ precisely in this, that He existed not for His own sake but wholly for the sake of the world.

The Church as a self-contained community is subject to a twofold divine ordinance and rule. She must be adapted to the purpose of the world, and precisely in this she must be adapted to her own purpose as the place at which Jesus Christ is present. The peculiar character of the Church as a self-contained community lies in the fact that in the very limitation of her spiritual and material domain she gives expression to the unlimited scope of the message of Christ, and that it is precisely this unlimited scope of the message of Christ which in its turn is a summons into the limited domain of the congregation.

✧ ✧ ✧ ✧

Systematic Considerations Concerning the Assertions Which Christian Ethics May Make With Regard to Secular Institutions

(a) All the possible assertions with regard to secular institutions are founded upon Jesus Christ and must, therefore, be brought into relation with Him as the origin, essence and goal of all created things. It is the dominion of Christ which renders all these assertions possible and significant.

(b) In the proclamation of the dominion of Christ over

secular institutions these institutions are not made subject to an alien rule, for 'he came unto his own' (John 1:11) and 'by him all things consist' (Col. 1:17). They are not made subject to a clerical, humanitarian, rational or Jewish law or to a form of moral natural law. Under the dominion of Christ they attain to their own true character and become subject to their own innate law, which is theirs according to the manner of their creation. Nor, on the other hand, are they made subject to the arbitrary rule of a so-called 'autonomy' which is fundamentally nothing but lawlessness, *anomia,* and sin, but within the world which is created, loved and reconciled by God in Christ they receive the place which is characteristic, proper and right for them. Thus, under the dominion of Christ they receive their own law and their own liberty.

(c) The decalogue is the law of living, revealed by God, for all life which is subject to the dominion of Christ. It signifies liberation from alien rule and from arbitrary autonomy. It discloses itself to believers as the law of the Creator and the Reconciler. The decalogue is the framework within which a free obedience becomes possible in worldly life. It affords liberty for free life under the dominion of Christ.

(d) The dominion of Christ and the decalogue do not mean that the secular institutions are made subservient to a human ideal or 'natural law,' nor yet to the Church (this being a contradiction of the medieval Thomist doctrine), but they mean their emancipation for true worldliness, for the state to *be* a state, etc. The primary implication for secular institutions of the dominion of Christ and of the decalogue is not, therefore, the conversion of the statesman or the economist, nor yet the elimination of the harshness and unmercifulness of the state for the sake of a falsely interpreted christianization of the state and its transformation into a part of the Church. It is precisely in the dispensation of strict justice and in the administration of the office of the sword, in maintaining the unmerciful character of the institutions of the state, that is to say, their genuine worldliness, that the dominion of Christ, *i.e.* the rule of mercy, is given its due. The incarnation of God, that is to say, the incarnation of love, would be misinterpreted if one were to fail to perceive that the worldly institutions of strict justice, of punishment and of the wrath of God are also a fulfilment of this incarnated love and that the commandment of the Sermon on the Mount is also observed in genuine action by the state. The purpose and aim of the dominion of Christ is not to make the worldly order godly or to subordinate it to the Church but to set it free for true worldliness.

(e) The emancipation of the worldly order under the dominion of Christ takes concrete form not through the conversion of Christian statesmen, etc., but through the concrete encounter of the secular institutions with the Church of Jesus Christ, her proclamation and her life. By allowing this Church of Jesus Christ to continue, by making room for her and by enabling her proclamation of the dominion of Christ to take effect, the secular institutions attain to their own true worldliness and law which has its foundation in Christ. Their attitude to the Church of Jesus Christ will always be the measure of the true worldliness which is not impeded by any ideological and alien law or by any arbitrary autonomy. A false attitude to the Church will always have as its consequence a failure to achieve genuine worldliness on the part of the secular institutions, the state, etc., and *vice versa.*

(f) With regard to the relationship of the secular institutions to one another and to the Church, the Lutheran doctrine of the three estates, *oeconomicus, politicus* and *hierarchicus,* has as its decisive characteristic and permanent significance that it is based on coordination rather than any kind of priority and subordination, so that the worldly order is safeguarded against the alien rule of the Church, and *vice versa.* In my opinion this doctrine must be replaced by a doctrine which is drawn from the Bible, the doctrine of four divine mandates, marriage and family, labour, government, and Church. These institutions are divine in that they possess a concrete divine commission and promise which has its foundation and evidence in the revelation. Amid the changes of all historical institutions these divine mandates continue until the end of the world. Their justification is not simply their historical existence; in this they differ from such institutions as the people, the race, the class, the masses, the society, the nation, the country, the Empire, etc. It is a positive divine mandate for the preservation of the world for the sake and purpose of Christ. It is perhaps not by chance that precisely these mandates seem to have their type in the celestial world. Marriage corresponds with Christ and the congregation; the family with God the Father and the Son, and with the brotherhood of men with Christ; labour corresponds with the creative service of God and Christ to the world, and of men to God; government corresponds with the dominion of Christ in eternity; the state corresponds with the *polis* of God.

(g) A word of the Church with regard to the secular institutions will consequently have to place these divine mandates, in whatever may be their concrete form at the time, under the dominion of Christ and under the decalogue. In doing this it will not be subjecting the secular institutions to an alien law, but it will be setting them free for concrete and genuine worldly service. It will speak of the divine mandates of the worldly order in such a way that the dominion of Christ is maintained *over* them and the divine mandate of the Christian Church is maintained *side by side* with them. It cannot deprive the secular institutions of their responsible decision and their service, but it can direct them to the only place at which they can decide and act responsibly.

(h) It may be remarked that the secular institutions are able to perform their service even without the encounter with the word of the Church of Jesus Christ (*cf.* Luther and the Turks). First of all, there is never more than a limited truth in this observation; genuine worldliness is achieved only through emancipation by Christ; without this there is the rule of alien laws, ideologies and idols. Secondly, the very limited correctness of this remark can only afford the Church a thankfully accepted confirmation of the truth which is revealed to her; it cannot lead her to suppose that this is in itself sufficient, but it must lead her to proclaim the dominion of Christ as the full truth in the midst of all partial truths. When the Church perceives that a worldly order is on some few occasions possible without the preaching being heard (but still never without the existence of Jesus Christ), this will not impel her to disregard Christ, but it will elicit from her the full proclamation of the grace of the dominion of Christ. The unknown God will now be preached as the God who is known because He is revealed.

SELECTION 2
Letters and Papers from Prison

These passages are taken from Bonhoeffer's *Letters and Papers from Prison* of June 8, 1944, and July 16, 1944. They express ideas about the autonomy of man in a world come of age. The social-ethical consequences of these insights are being worked out by thinkers of very different basic orientation, yet all stimulated by Bonhoeffer's brief suggestions.

The movement beginning about the thirteenth century (I am not going to get involved in any arguments about the exact date) towards the autonomy of man (under which head I place the discovery of the laws by which the world lives and manages in science, social and political affairs, art, ethics and religion) has in our time reached a certain completion. Man has learned to cope with all questions of importance without recourse to God as a working hypothesis. In questions concerning science, art, and even ethics, this has become an understood thing which one scarcely dares to tilt at any more. But for the last hundred years or so it has been increasingly true of religious questions also: it is becoming evident that everything gets along without 'God,' and just as well as before. As in the scientific field, so in human affairs generally, what we call 'God' is being more and more edged out of life, losing more and more ground.

Catholic and Protestant historians are agreed that it is in this development that the great defection from God, from Christ, is to be discerned, and the more they bring in and make use of God and Christ in opposition to this trend, the more the trend itself considers itself to be anti-Christian. The world which has attained to a realization of itself and of the laws which govern its existence is so sure of itself that we become frightened. False starts and failures do not make the world deviate from the path and development it is following; they are accepted with fortitude and detachment as part of the bargain, and even an event like the present war is no exception. Christian apologetic has taken the most varying forms of opposition to this self-assurance. Efforts are made to prove to a world thus come of age that it cannot live without the tutelage of 'God.' Even though there has been surrender on all secular problems, there still remain the so-called ultimate questions—death, guilt—on which only 'God' can furnish an answer, and which are the reason why God and the Church and the pastor are needed. Thus we live, to some extent, by these ultimate questions of humanity. But what if one day they no longer exist as such, if they too can be answered without 'God'? We have of course the secularized offshoots of Christian theology, the existentialist philosophers and the psychotherapists, who demonstrate to secure, contented, happy mankind that it is really unhappy and desperate, and merely unwilling to realize that it is in severe straits it knows nothing at all about, from which only they can rescue it. Wherever there is health, strength, security, simplicity, they spy luscious fruit to gnaw at or to lay their pernicious eggs in. They make it their object first of all to drive men to inward despair, and then it is all theirs. That is secularized methodism. And whom does it touch? A small number of intellectuals, of degenerates, of people who regard themselves as the most important thing in the world and hence like occupying themselves with themselves. The ordinary man who spends his everyday life at work, and with his family, and of course with all kinds of hobbies and other interests too, is not affected. He has neither time nor inclination for thinking about his intellectual despair and regarding his modest share of happiness as a trial, a trouble or a disaster.

The attack by Christian apologetic upon the adulthood of the world I consider to be in the first place pointless, in the second ignoble, and in the third un-Christian. Pointless, because it looks to me like an attempt to put a grown-up man back into adolescence, i.e. to make him dependent on things on which he is not in fact dependent any more, thrusting him back into the midst of problems which are in fact not problems for him any more. Ignoble, because this amounts to an effort to exploit the weakness of man for purposes alien to him and not freely subscribed to by him. Un-Christian, because for Christ himself is being substituted one particular stage in the religiousness of man, i.e. a human law. Of this more later.

But first a word or two on the historical situation. The question is, Christ and the newly matured world. It was the weak point of liberal theology that it allowed the world the right to assign Christ his place in that world: in the dispute between Christ and the world it accepted the comparatively clement peace dictated by the world. It was its strong point that it did not seek to put back the clock, and genuinely accepted the battle (Troeltsch), even though this came to an end with its overthrow.

Overthrow was succeeded by capitulation and an attempt at a completely fresh start based on consideration of the Bible and Reformation fundamentals of the faith. Heim sought, along pietist and methodist lines, to convince individual man that he was faced with the alternative 'either despair or Jesus.' He gained 'hearts.' Althaus, carrying forward the modern and positive line with a strong confessional emphasis, endeavoured to wring from the world a place for Lutheran teaching (ministry) and Lutheran worship, and otherwise left the world to its own devices. Tillich set out to interpret the evolution of the world itself—against its will—in a religious sense, to give it its whole shape through religion. That was very courageous of him, but the world unseated him and went on by itself: he too sought to understand the world better than it understood itself, but it felt entirely *misunderstood*, and rejected the imputation. (Of course the world does need to be understood better than it understands itself, but not 'religiously,' as the religious socialists desired.) Barth was the first to realize the mistake that all these efforts (which were all unintentionally sailing in the channel of liberal theology) were making in having as their objective the clearing of a space for religion in the world or against the world.

He called the God of Jesus Christ into the lists against religion, '*pneuma* against *sarx*.' That was and is his greatest service (the second edition of his Epistle to the Romans, in spite of all its neo-Kantian shavings). Through his later dogmatics, he enabled the Church to effect this distinction in principle all along the line. It was not that he subsequently, as is often claimed, failed in ethics, for his ethical observations—so far as he has made any—are just as significant as his dogmatic ones; it was that he gave no concrete guidance, either in dogmatics or in ethics, on the non-religious interpretation of theological concepts. There lies his limitation, and because of it his theology of revelation becomes positivist, a 'positivism of revelation,' as I put it.

The Confessing Church has to a great extent forgotten all about the Barthian approach, and lapsed from positivism into conservative restoration. The important thing about that Church is that it carries on the great concepts of Christian theology, but that seems all it will do. There are, certainly, in these concepts the elements of genuine prophetic quality (under which head come both the claim to truth and the mercy you mention) and of genuine worship, and to that extent the message of the Confessing Church meets only with attention, hearing and rejection. But they both remain unexplained and remote, because there is no interpretation of them.

People like, for instance, Schütz, or the Oxford Group, or the Berneucheners, who miss the 'movement' and 'life,' are dangerous reactionaries, retrogressive because they go straight back behind the approach of revelation theology and seek for 'religious' renewal. They simply do not understand the problem at all, and what they say is entirely beside the point. There is no future for them (though the Oxford people would have the biggest chance if they were not so completely devoid of biblical substance).

Bultmann would seem to have felt Barth's limitations in some way, but he misconstrues them in the light of liberal theology, and hence goes off into the typical liberal reduction process (the 'mythological' elements of Christianity are dropped, and Christianity is reduced to its 'essence'). I am of the view that the full content, including the mythological concepts, must be maintained. The New Testament is not a mythological garbing of the universal truth; this mythology (resurrection and so on) is the thing itself—but the concepts must be interpreted in such a way as not to make religion a pre-condition of faith (cf. circumcision in St. Paul). Not until that is achieved will, in my opinion, liberal theology be overcome (and even Barth is still dominated by it, though negatively), and, at the same time, the question it raises be genuinely taken up and answered—which is not the case in the positivism of revelation maintained by the Confessing Church.

The world's coming of age is then no longer an occasion for

polemics and apologetics, but it is really better understood than it understands itself, namely on the basis of the Gospel, and in the light of Christ.

You ask whether this leaves any room for the Church, or has it gone for good? And again, did not Jesus himself use distress as his point of contact with men, whether as a consequence the 'methodism' I have so frowned upon is not right after all? I'm breaking off here, and will write more to-morrow.

✧ ✧ ✧ ✧

Now a few more thoughts on our theme. I find it's very slow going trying to work out a non-religious interpretation of biblical terminology, and it's a far bigger job than I can manage at the moment. On the historical side I should say there is *one* great development which leads to the idea of the autonomy of the world. In theology it is first discernible in Lord Herbert of Cherbury, with his assertion that reason is the sufficient instrument of religious knowledge. In ethics it first appears in Montaigne and Bodin with their substitution of moral principles for the ten commandments. In politics, Machiavelli, who emancipates politics from the tutelage of morality, and founds the doctrine of 'reasons of state.' Later, and very differently, though like Machiavelli tending towards the autonomy of human society, comes Grotius, with his international law as the law of nature, a law which would still be valid, *etsi deus non daretur*. The process is completed in philosophy. On the one hand we have the deism of Descartes, who holds that the world is a mechanism which runs on its own without any intervention of God. On the other hand there is the pantheism of Spinoza, with its identification of God with nature. In the last resort Kant is a deist, Fichte and Hegel pantheists. All along the line there is a growing tendency to assert the autonomy of man and the world.

In natural science the process seems to start with Nicolas of Cusa and Giordano Bruno with their 'heretical' doctrine of the infinity of space. The classical cosmos was finite, like the created world of the Middle Ages. An infinite universe, however it be conceived, is self-subsisting *etsi deus non daretur*. It is true that modern physics is not so sure as it was about the infinity of the universe, but it has not returned to the earlier conceptions of its finitude.

There is no longer any need for God as a working hypothesis, whether in morals, politics or science. Nor is there any need for such a God in religion or philosophy (Feuerbach). In the name of intellectual honesty these working hypotheses should be dropped or dispensed with as far as possible. A scientist or physician who seeks to provide edification is a hybrid.

At this point nervous souls start asking what room there is left for God now. And being ignorant of the answer they condemn the whole development which has brought them to this pass. As I said in an earlier letter, various emergency exits have been devised to deal with this situation. To them must be added the *salto mortale* back to the Middle Ages, the fundamental principle of which however is heteronomy in the form of clericalism. But that is a counsel of despair, which can be purchased only at the cost of intellectual sincerity. It reminds one of the song:

> *It's a long way back to the land of childhood,*
> *But if only I knew the way!*

There isn't any such way, at any rate not at the cost of deliberately abandoning our intellectual sincerity. The only way is that of Matthew 18:3, i.e. through repentance, through *ultimate* honesty. And the only way to be honest is to recognize that we have to live in the world *etsi deus non daretur*. And this is just what we do see—before God! So our coming of age forces us to a true recognition of our situation *vis-à-vis* God. God is teaching us that we must live as men who can get along very well without him. The God who is with us is the God who forsakes us (Mark 15:34). The God who makes us live in this world without using him as a working hypothesis is the God before whom we are ever standing. Before God and with him we live without God. God allows himself to be edged out of the world and on to the cross. God is weak and powerless in the world, and that is exactly the way, the only way, in which he can be with us and help us. Matthew 8:17 makes it crystal clear that it is not by his omnipotence that Christ helps us, but by his weakness and suffering.

This is the decisive difference between Christianity and all religions. Man's religiosity makes him look in his distress to the power of God in the world; he uses God as a *Deus ex machina.* The Bible however directs him to the powerlessness and suffering of God; only a suffering God can help. To this extent we may say that the process we have described by which the world came of age was an abandonment of a false conception of God, and a clearing of the decks for the God of the Bible, who conquers power and space in the world by his weakness. This must be the starting point for our 'worldly' interpretation.

XXX POPE JOHN XXIII

Pope John had the shortest pontificate of any head of the Roman Catholic Church in the last one hundred and fifty years. Nevertheless his influence was tremendous and is still being felt. Born Angelo Giuseppe Roncalli in a village near Bergamo on November 25, 1881, he eventually became Cardinal and Patriarch of Venice. In 1958 he was elected pope. He died, mourned by the entire world, on June 3, 1963.

Not the least of the reasons for Pope John's unprecedented universal popularity among Catholics and non-Catholics alike was the courageous manner in which he addressed himself to the vexing social problems of the time. From his first encyclical *Ad Petri Cathedram* his spirit of charity was apparent: "God created men as brothers, not foes. He gave them the earth to be cultivated by their toil and labor. Each and every man is to enjoy the fruits of the earth and receive from it his sustenance and the necessities of life. The various nations are simply communities of men, that is, of brothers."[12]

In his last encyclical, the famous *Pacem in Terris,* he exclaimed, "May Christ inflame the desires of all men to break through the barriers which divide them, to strengthen the bonds of mutual love, to learn to understand one another, and to pardon those who have done them wrong."[13]

His influence on Christian social teaching is still growing.

SELECTION I
Mater et Magistra

In his encyclical *Mater et Magistra* Pope John reviewed the development of Roman Catholic social teachings and then dealt with some new aspects of the problem, especially the crisis in agriculture.

History shows with ever-increasing clarity that it is not only the relations between workers and managers that need to be re-established on the basis of justice and equity, but also those between the various branches of the economy, between areas of varying productivity within the same political community, and between countries with a different degree of social and economic development.

First, with regard to agriculture, it would not appear that the rural population as a whole is decreasing, but it is an undeniable fact that many people are moving away from their farms into more thickly populated areas as well as into the cities themselves. When we realize that this movement of population is going on in nearly every part of the world, often on a large scale, we begin to appreciate the complexity of the human problems involved and their difficulty of solution.

We know that as an economy develops, the number of people engaged in agriculture decreases, while the percentage employed in industry and the various services rises. Nevertheless, We believe that very often this movement of population from farming to industry has other causes besides those dependent upon economic expansion. Among these there is the desire to escape from confining surroundings which offer little prospect of a more comfortable way of life. There is the lure of novelty and adventure which has taken such a hold on the present generation, the attractive prospect of easy money, of greater freedom and the enjoyment of all the amenities of town and city life. But a contributory cause of this movement away from the country is doubtless the fact that farming has become a depressed occupation. It is inadequate both in productive efficiency and in the standard of living it provides.

Nearly every country, therefore, is faced with this fundamental problem: What can be done to reduce the disproportion in productive efficiency between agriculture on the one hand, and industry and services on the other; and to ensure that agricultural living standards approximate as closely as possible those enjoyed by city-dwellers who draw their resources either from industry or from the services in which they are engaged? What can be done to persuade agricultural workers that, far from being inferior to other people, they have every opportunity of developing their personality through their work, and can look forward to the future with confidence?

It seems to Us opportune to indicate certain directives that can contribute to a solution of this problem: directives which We believe have value whatever may be the historical environment in which one acts—on condition, obviously, that they be applied in the manner and to the degree allowed, suggested, or even demanded by the circumstances.

In the first place, considerable thought must be given, especially by public authorities, to the suitable development of essential facilities in country areas—such as roads; transportation; means of communication; drinking water; housing; health services; elementary, technical and professional education; religious and recreational facilities; and the supply of modern installations and furnishings for the farm residence. Such services as these are necessary nowadays if a becoming standard of living is to be maintained. In those country areas where they are lacking, economic and social progress is either prevented or greatly impeded, with the result that nothing can be done to retard the drift of population away from the land, and it even becomes difficult to make a good appraisal of the numbers involved.

If a country is to develop economically, it must do so gradually, maintaining an even balance between all sectors of the economy. Agriculture, therefore, must be allowed to make use of the same reforms in the method and type of production and in the conduct of the business side of the venture as are permitted or required in the economic system as a whole. All such reforms should correspond as nearly as possible with those introduced in industry and the various services.

In this way, agriculture will absorb a larger amount of industrial goods and require a better system of services. But at the same time it will provide both industry and the services and the country as a whole with the type of products which, in quantity and quality, best meet the needs of the consumer and contribute to the stability of the purchasing power of money—a major consideration in the orderly development of the entire economic system.

One advantage which would result from the adoption of this plan would be that it would be easier to keep track of the movement of the working force set free by the progressive modernization of agriculture. Facilities could then be provided for the training of such people for their new kind of work, and they would not be left without economic aid and the mental and spiritual assistance they need to ensure their proper integration in their new social milieu.

In addition, a sound agricultural program is needed if public authority is to maintain an evenly balanced progress in the various branches of the economy. This must take into account tax policies, credit, social insurance, prices, the fostering of ancillary industries and the adjustment of the structure of farming as a business enterprise.

In a system of taxation based on justice and equity it is fundamental that the burdens be proportioned to the capacity of the people contributing.

But the common good also requires that public authorities, in assessing the amount of tax payable, take cognizance of the peculiar difficulties of farmers. They have to wait longer than most people for their returns, and these are exposed to greater hazards. Consequently, farmers find greater difficulty in obtaining the capital necessary to increase returns.

For this reason, too, investors are more inclined to put their money in industry rather than agriculture. Farmers are unable to pay high rates of interest. Indeed, they cannot as a rule make the trading profit necessary to furnish capital for the conduct and development of their own business. It is therefore necessary, for reasons of the common good, for public authorities to evolve a special credit policy and to form credit banks which will guarantee such capital to farmers at a moderate rate of interest.

In agriculture the existence of two forms of insurance may be necessary: one concerned with agricultural produce, the other with the farm workers and their families. We realize that agricultural workers earn less per capita than workers in industry and the services, but that is no reason why it should be considered socially just and equitable to set up systems of social insurance in which the allowances granted to farm workers and their families are substantially lower than those payable to other classes of workers. Insurance programs that are established for the general public should not differ markedly whatever be the economic sector in which the individuals work or the source of their income.

Systems of social insurance and social security can make a most effective contribution to the overall distribution of national income in accordance with the principles of justice and equity. They can therefore be instrumental in reducing imbalances between the different classes of citizens.

Given the special nature of agricultural produce, modern economists must devise a suitable means of price protection. Ideally, such price protection should be enforced by the interested parties themselves, though supervision by the public authority cannot be altogether dispensed with.

On this subject it must not be forgotten that the price of agricultural produce represents, for the most part, the reward of the farmer's labor rather than a return on invested capital.

✧ ✧ ✧ ✧

While it is true that farm produce is mainly intended for the satisfaction of man's primary needs, and the price should therefore be within the means of all consumers, this cannot be used as an argument for keeping a section of the population—farm workers—in a permanent state of economic and social inferiority, depriving them of the wherewithal for a decent standard of living. This would be diametrically opposed to the common good.

Moreover, the time has come to promote in agricultural regions the establishment of those industries and services which are concerned with the preservation, processing and transportation of farm products. Enterprises relating to other sectors of the economy might also be established there. In this case the rural population would have another means of income at their disposal, a means which they could exploit in the social milieu to which they are accustomed.

It is not possible to determine *a priori* what the structure of farm life should be, since rural conditions vary so much from place to place and from country to country throughout the world. But if we hold to a human and Christian concept of man and the family, we are bound to consider as an ideal that form of enterprise which is modelled on the basis of a community of persons working together for the advancement of their mutual interests in accordance with the principles of justice and Christian teaching. We are bound above all to consider as an ideal the kind of farm which is owned and managed by the family. Every effort must be made in the prevailing circumstances to give effective encouragement to farming enterprises of this nature.

But if the family farm is not to go bankrupt it must make enough money to keep the family in reasonable comfort. To ensure this, farmers must be given up-to-date instruction on the latest methods of cultivation, and the assistance of experts must be put at their disposal. They should also form a flourishing system of co-operative undertakings, and organize themselves professionally to take an effective part in public life, both on the administrative and the political level.

We are convinced that the farming community must take an active part in its own economic advancement, social progress and cultural betterment. Those who live on the land can hardly fail to appreciate the nobility of the work they are called upon to do. They are living in close harmony with Nature—the majestic temple of Creation. Their work has to do with the life of plants and animals, a life that is inexhaustible in its expression, inflexible in its laws, rich in allusions to God the Creator and Provider. They produce food for the support of human life, and the raw materials of industry in ever richer supply.

Theirs is a work which carries with it a dignity all its own. It brings into its service many branches of engineering, chemistry and biology, and is itself a cause of the continued practical development of these sciences in view of the repercussions of scientific and technical progress on the business of farming. It is a work which demands a capacity for orientation and adaptation, patient waiting, a sense of responsibility, and a spirit of perseverance and enterprise.

It is important also to bear in mind that in agriculture, as in other sectors of production, association is a vital need today—especially in the case of family farms. Rural workers should feel a sense of solidarity with one another, and should unite to form co-operatives and professional associations. These are very necessary if farm workers are to benefit from scientific and technical methods of production and protect the prices of their products. They are necessary, too, if they are to attain an equal footing with other professional classes who, in most cases, have joined together in associations. They are necessary, finally, if farm workers are to have their proper voice in political circles and in public administration. The lone voice is not likely to command much of a hearing in times such as ours.

In using their various organizations, agricultural workers—as indeed all other classes of workers—must always be guided by moral principles and respect for the civil law. They must try to reconcile their rights and interests with those of other classes of workers, and even subordinate the one to the other if the common good demands it. If they show themselves alive to the common good and contribute to its realization, they can legitimately demand that their efforts for the improvement of agricultural conditions be seconded and complemented by public authority.

We therefore desire here to express Our satisfaction with those sons of Ours the world over who are actively engaged in co-operatives, in professional groups and in worker movements intent on raising the economic and social standards of the agricultural community.

In the work on the farm the human personality finds every incentive for self-expression, self-development and spiritual growth. It is a work, therefore, which should be thought of as a vocation, a God-given mission, an answer to God's call to actuate His providential, saving plan in history. It should be thought of, finally, as a noble task, undertaken with a view to raising oneself and others to a higher degree of civilization.

Among citizens of the same political community there is often a marked degree of economic and social inequality. The main reason for this is the fact that they are living and working in different areas, some of which are more economically developed than others.

Where this situation obtains, justice and equity demand that public authority try to eliminate or reduce such imbalances. It should ensure that the less developed areas receive such essential public services as their circumstances require, in order to bring the standard of living in these areas into line with the national average. Furthermore, a suitable economic and social policy must be devised which will take into account the supply of labor, the drift of population, wages, taxes, credit, and the investing of money, especially in expanding industries. In short, it should be a policy designed to promote useful employment, enterprising initiative, and the exploitation of local resources.

But the justification of all government action is the common good. Public authority, therefore, must bear in mind the interests of the state as a whole; which means that it must promote all three areas of production—agriculture, industry and services—simultaneously and evenly. Everything must be done to ensure that citizens of the less developed areas are treated as responsible human beings, and are allowed to play the major role in achieving their own economic, social and cultural advancement.

Private enterprise too must contribute to an economic and social balance in the different areas of the same political community. Indeed, in accordance with "the principle of subsidiary function," public authority must encourage and assist private enterprise, entrusting to it, wherever possible, the continuation of economic development.

It is not out of place to remark here on a problem which exists in quite a number of countries, namely, a gross disproportion between land and population. In some countries arable land abounds, but there is a scarcity of population; whereas in other countries the position is reversed: the population is large, arable land scarce.

Again, some countries use primitive methods of agriculture, with the result that, for all their abundance of natural resources, they are not able to produce enough food to feed their population; whereas other countries, using modern methods of agriculture, produce a surplus of food which has an adverse effect on the economy.

It is therefore obvious that the solidarity of the human race and Christian brotherhood demand the elimination as far as possible of these discrepancies. With this object in view, people all over the world must co-operate actively with one another in all sorts of ways, so as to facilitate the movement of goods, capital and men from one country to another. We shall have more to say on this point later on.

Here We would like to express Our sincere appreciation of the work which the F.A.O. has undertaken to establish effective collaboration among nations, to promote the modernization of agriculture especially in less developed countries, and to alleviate the suffering of hunger-stricken peoples.

Probably the most difficult problem today concerns the relationship between political communities that are economically advanced and those in the process of development. Whereas the standard of living is high in the former, the latter are subject to extreme poverty. The solidarity which binds all men together as members of a common family makes it impossible for wealthy nations to look with indifference upon the hunger, misery and poverty of other nations whose citizens are unable to enjoy even elementary human rights. The nations of the world are becoming more and more dependent on one another and it will not be possible to preserve a lasting peace so long as glaring economic and social imbalances persist.

Mindful of Our position as the father of all peoples, We feel constrained to repeat here what We said on another occasion: "We are all equally responsible for the undernourished peoples. [Hence], it is necessary to educate one's conscience to the sense of responsibility which weighs upon each and every one, especially upon those who are more blessed with this world's goods."

✧ ✧ ✧ ✧

Justice and humanity demand that those countries which produce consumer goods, especially farm products, in excess of their own needs should come to the assistance of those other countries where large sections of the population are suffering from want and hunger. It is nothing less than an outrage to justice and humanity to destroy or to squander goods that other people need for their very lives.

We are, of course, well aware that overproduction, especially in agriculture, can cause economic harm to a certain section of the population. But it does not follow that one is thereby exonerated from extending emergency aid to those who need it. On the contrary, everything must be done to minimize the ill effects of overproduction, and to spread the burden equitably over the entire population.

Of itself, however, emergency aid will not go far in relieving want and famine when these are caused—as they so often are—by the primitive state of a nation's economy. The only permanent remedy for this is to make use of every possible means of providing these citizens with the scientific, technical and professional training they need, and to put at their disposal the necessary capital for speeding up their economic development with the help of modern methods.

We are aware how deeply the public conscience has been affected in recent years by the urgent need of supporting the economic development and social progress of those countries which are still struggling against poverty and economic disabilities.

International and regional organizations, national and private societies, all are working towards this goal, increasing day by day the measure of their own technical co-operation in all productive spheres. By their combined efforts thousands of young people are being given facilities for attending the universities of the more advanced countries, and acquiring an up-to-date scientific, technical and professional training. World banking institutes, individual states and private persons are helping to furnish the capital for an ever richer network of economic enterprises in the less wealthy countries. It is a magnificent work that they are doing, and We are most happy to take this occasion of giving it the praise that it deserves. It is a work, however, which needs to be increased, and We hope that the years ahead will see the wealthier nations making even greater effort for the scientific, technical and economic advancement of those political communities whose development is still only in its initial stages.

We consider it Our duty to give further advice on this matter.

In the first place, those nations which are still only at the beginning of their journey along the road to economic development would do well to consider carefully the experiences of the wealthier nations which have traversed this road before them.

Increase in production and productive efficiency is, of course, sound policy, and indeed a vital necessity. However, it is no less necessary—and justice itself demands—that the riches produced be distributed fairly among all members of the political community. This means that everything must be done to ensure that social progress keeps pace with economic progress. Again, every sector of the economy—agriculture, industry and the services—must progress evenly and simultaneously.

The developing nations, obviously, have certain unmistakable characteristics of their own, resulting from the nature of the particular region and the natural dispositions of their citizens, with time-honored traditions and customs.

In helping these nations, therefore, the more advanced communities must recognize and respect this individuality. They must beware of making the assistance they give an excuse for forcing these people into their own national mold.

There is also a further temptation which the economically developed nations must resist: that of giving technical and financial aid with a view to gaining control over the political situation in the poorer countries, and furthering their own plans for world domination.

Let us be quite clear on this point. A nation that acted from these motives would in fact be introducing a new form of colonialism—cleverly disguised, no doubt, but actually reflecting that older, outdated type from which many nations have recently emerged. Such action would, moreover, have a harmful impact on international relations, and constitute a menace to world peace.

Necessity, therefore, and justice demand that all such technical and financial aid be given without thought of domination, but rather for the purpose of helping the less developed nations to achieve their own economic and social growth.

If this can be achieved, then a precious contribution will have been made to the formation of a world community, in which each individual nation, conscious of its rights and duties, can work on terms of equality with the rest for the attainment of universal prosperity.

Scientific and technical progress, economic development and the betterment of living conditions, are certainly valuable elements in a civilization. But we must realize that they are essentially instrumental in character. They are not supreme values in themselves.

It pains Us, therefore, to observe the complete indifference to the true hierarchy of values shown by so many people in the economically developed countries. Spiritual values are ignored, forgotten or denied, while the progress of science, technology and economics is pursued for its own sake, as though material well-being were the be-all and end-all of life. This attitude is contagious, especially when it infects the work that is being done for the less developed countries, which have often preserved in their ancient traditions an acute and vital awareness of the more important human values, on which the moral order rests.

To attempt to undermine this national integrity is clearly immoral. It must be respected and as far as possible clarified and developed, so that it may remain what it is: a foundation of true civilization.

SELECTION 2
Pacem in Terris

Pacem in Terris is probably the most radical statement by a pope on man's responsibility for peace. It found almost universal approval.

Peace on earth—which man throughout the ages has so longed for and sought after—can never be established, never guaranteed, except by the diligent observance of the divinely established order.

That a marvelous order predominates in the world of living beings and in the forces of nature, is the plain lesson which the progress of modern research and the discoveries of technology teach us. And it is part of the greatness of man that he can appreciate that order, and devise the means for harnessing those forces for his own benefit.

But what emerges first and foremost from the progress of scientific knowledge and the inventions of technology is the infinite greatness of God Himself, who created both man and the universe. Yes; out of nothing He made all things, and filled them with the fullness of His own wisdom and goodness.

✧ ✧ ✧ ✧

And yet there is a disunity among individuals and among nations which is in striking contrast to this perfect order in the universe. One would think that the relationships that bind men together could only be governed by force.

But the world's Creator has stamped man's inmost being with an order revealed to man by his conscience; and his conscience insists on his preserving it. Men "show the work of the law written in their hearts. Their conscience bears witness to them." And how could it be otherwise? All created being reflects the infinite wisdom of God. It reflects it all the more clearly, the higher it stands in the scale of perfection.

But the mischief is often caused by erroneous opinions. Many people think that the laws which govern man's relations with the State are the same as those which regulate the blind, elemental forces of the universe. But it is not so; the laws which govern men are quite different. The Father of the universe has inscribed them in man's nature, and that is where we must look for them; there and nowhere else.

These laws clearly indicate how a man must behave toward his fellows in society, and how the mutual relationships between the members of a State and its officials are to be conducted. They show too what principles must govern the relations between States; and finally, what should be the relations between individuals or States on the one hand, and the world-wide community of nations on the other. Men's common interests make it imperative that at long last a world-wide community of nations be established.

We must devote our attention first of all to that order which should prevail among men.

Any well-regulated and productive association of men in society demands the acceptance of one fundamental principle: that each individual man is truly a person. His is a nature, that is, endowed with intelligence and free will. As such he has rights and duties, which together flow as a direct consequence from his nature. These rights and duties are universal and inviolable, and therefore altogether inalienable.

When, furthermore, we consider man's personal dignity from

the standpoint of divine revelation, inevitably our estimate of it is incomparably increased. Men have been ransomed by the blood of Jesus Christ. Grace has made them sons and friends of God, and heirs to eternal glory.

But first We must speak of man's rights. Man has the right to live. He has the right to bodily integrity and to the means necessary for the proper development of life, particularly food, clothing, shelter, medical care, rest, and finally, the necessary social services. In consequence, he has the right to be looked after in the event of ill-health; disability stemming from his work; widowhood; old age; enforced unemployment; or whenever through no fault of his own he is deprived of the means of livelihood.

Moreover, man has a natural right to be respected. He has a right to his good name. He has a right to freedom in investigating the truth, and—within the limits of the moral order and the common good—to freedom of speech and publication, and to freedom to pursue whatever profession he may choose. He has the right, also, to be accurately informed about public events.

He has the natural right to share in the benefits of culture, and hence to receive a good general education, and a technical or professional training consistent with the degree of educational development in his own country. Furthermore, a system must be devised for affording gifted members of society the opportunity of engaging in more advanced studies, with a view to their occupying, as far as possible, positions of responsibility in society in keeping with their natural talent and acquired skill.

Also among man's rights is that of being able to worship God in accordance with the right dictates of his own conscience, and to profess his religion both in private and in public. According to the clear teaching of Lactantius, "this is the very condition of our birth, that we render to the God who made us that just homage which is His due; that we acknowledge Him alone as God, and follow Him. It is from this *ligature* of piety, which binds us and joins us to God, that religion derives its name."

Hence, too, Pope Leo XIII declared that "true freedom, freedom worthy of the sons of God, is that freedom which most truly safeguards the dignity of the human person. It is stronger than any violence or injustice. Such is the freedom which has always been desired by the Church, and which she holds most dear. It is the sort of freedom which the Apostles resolutely claimed for themselves. The apologists defended it in their writings; thousands of martyrs consecrated it with their blood."

Human beings have also the right to choose for themselves the kind of life which appeals to them: whether it is to found a family—in the founding of which both the man and the woman enjoy equal rights and duties—or to embrace the priesthood or the religious life.

The family, founded upon marriage freely contracted, one and indissoluble, must be regarded as the natural, primary cell of human society. The interests of the family, therefore, must be taken very specially into consideration in social and economic affairs, as well as in the spheres of faith and morals. For all of these have to do with strengthening the family and assisting it in the fulfilment of its mission.

Of course, the support and education of children is a right which belongs primarily to the parents.

In the economic sphere, it is evident that a man has the inherent right not only to be given the opportunity to work, but also to be allowed the exercise of personal initiative in the work he does.

The conditions in which a man works form a necessary corollary to these rights. They must not be such as to weaken his physical or moral fibre, or militate against the proper development of adolescents to manhood. Women must be accorded such conditions of work as are consistent with their needs and responsibilities as wives and mothers.

A further consequence of man's personal dignity is his right to engage in economic activities suited to his degree of responsibility. The worker is likewise entitled to a wage that is determined in accordance with the precepts of justice. This needs stressing. The amount a worker receives must be sufficient, in proportion to available funds, to allow him and his family a standard of living consistent with human dignity . . .

As a further consequence of man's nature, he has the right to the private ownership of property, including that of productive goods. This, as We have said elsewhere, is "a right which constitutes so efficacious a means of asserting one's personality and exercising responsibility in every field, and an element of solidity and security for family life, and of greater peace and prosperity in the State."

Finally, it is opportune to point out that the right to own private property entails a social obligation as well.

Men are by nature social, and consequently they have the right to meet together and to form associations with their fellows. They have the right to confer on such associations the type of organization which they consider best calculated to achieve their objectives. They have also the right to exercise their own initiative and act on their own responsibility within these associations for the attainment of the desired results.

✧ ✧ ✧ ✧

Again, every human being has the right to freedom of movement and of residence within the confines of his own State. When there are just reasons in favor of it, he must be permitted to emigrate to other countries and take up residence there. The fact that he is a citizen of a particular State does not deprive him of membership in the human family, nor of citizenship in that universal society, the common, world-wide fellowship of men.

Finally, man's personal dignity involves his right to take an active part in public life, and to make his own contribution to the common welfare of his fellow citizens . . .

As a human person he is entitled to the legal protection of his rights, and such protection must be effective, unbiased, and strictly just. . . .

The natural rights of which We have so far been speaking are inextricably bound up with as many duties, all applying to one and the same person. These rights and duties derive their origin, their sustenance, and their indestructibility from the natural law, which in conferring the one imposes the other.

Thus, for example, the right to live involves the duty to preserve one's life; the right to a decent standard of living, the duty to live in a becoming fashion; the right to be free to seek out the truth, the duty to devote oneself to an ever deeper and wider search for it.

Once this is admitted, it follows that in human society one

man's natural right gives rise to a corresponding duty in other men; the duty, that is, of recognizing and respecting that right. Every basic human right draws its authoritative force from the natural law, which confers it and attaches to it its respective duty. Hence, to claim one's rights and ignore one's duties, or only half fulfill them, is like building a house with one hand and tearing it down with the other.

Since men are social by nature, they must live together and consult each other's interests. That men should recognize and perform their respective rights and duties is imperative to a well ordered society. But the result will be that each individual will make his whole-hearted contribution to the creation of a civic order in which rights and duties are ever more diligently and more effectively observed.

For example, it is useless to admit that a man has a right to the necessities of life, unless we also do all in our power to supply him with means sufficient for his livelihood.

Hence society must not only be well ordered, it must also provide men with abundant resources. This postulates not only the mutual recognition and fulfillment of rights and duties, but also the involvement and collaboration of all men in the many enterprises which our present civilization makes possible, encourages or indeed demands.

Man's personal dignity requires besides that he enjoy freedom and be able to make up his own mind when he acts. In his association with his fellows, therefore, there is every reason why his recognition of rights, observance of duties, and many-sided collaboration with other men, should be primarily a matter of his own personal decision. Each man should act on his own initiative, conviction, and sense of responsibility, not under the constant pressure of external coercion or enticement. There is nothing human about a society that is welded together by force. Far from encouraging, as it should, the attainment of man's progress and perfection, it is merely an obstacle to his freedom.

Hence, before a society can be considered well-ordered, creative, and consonant with human dignity, it must be based on truth. St. Paul expressed this as follows: "putting away lying, speak ye the truth every man with his neighbor, for we are members one of another." And so will it be, if each man acknowledges sincerely his own rights and his own duties toward others.

Human society, as We here picture it, demands that men be guided by justice, respect the rights of others and do their duty. It demands, too, that they be animated by such love as will make them feel the needs of others as their own, and induce them to share their goods with others, and to strive in the world to make all men alike heirs to the noblest of intellectual and spiritual values. Nor is this enough; for human society thrives on freedom, namely, on the use of means which are consistent with the dignity of its individual members, who, being endowed with reason, assume responsibility for their own actions.

And so, dearest sons and brothers, we must think of human society as being primarily a spiritual reality. By its means enlightened men can share their knowledge of the truth, can claim their rights and fulfill their duties, receive encouragement in their aspirations for the goods of the spirit, share their enjoyment of all the wholesome pleasures of the world, and strive continually to pass on to others all that is best in themselves and to make their own the spiritual riches of others. It is these spiritual values which exert a guiding influence on culture, economics, social institutions, political movements and forms, laws, and all the other components which go to make up the external community of men and its continual development.

Now the order which prevails in human society is wholly incorporeal in nature. Its foundation is truth, and it must be brought into effect by justice. It needs to be animated and perfected by men's love for one another, and, while preserving freedom intact, it must make for an equilibrium in society which is increasingly more human in character.

But such an order—universal, absolute and immutable in its principles—finds its source in the true, personal and transcendent God. He is the first truth, the sovereign good, and as such the deepest source from which human society, if it is to be properly constituted, creative, and worthy of man's dignity, draws its genuine vitality. . . .

There are three things which characterize our modern age.

In the first place we notice a progressive improvement in the economic and social condition of working men. They began by claiming their rights principally in the economic and social spheres, and then proceeded to lay claim to their political rights as well. Finally, they have turned their attention to acquiring the more cultural benefits of society.

Today, therefore, working men all over the world are loud in their demands that they shall in no circumstances be subjected to arbitrary treatment, as though devoid of intelligence and freedom. They insist on being treated as human beings, with a share in every sector of human society: in the socio-economic sphere, in government, and in the realm of learning and culture.

Secondly, the part that women are now playing in political life is everywhere evident. This is a development that is perhaps of swifter growth among Christian nations, but it is also happening extensively, if more slowly, among nations that are heirs to different traditions and imbued with a different culture. Women are gaining an increasing awareness of their natural dignity. Far from being content with a purely passive role or allowing themselves to be regarded as a kind of instrument, they are demanding both in domestic and in public life the rights and duties which belong to them as human persons.

Finally, we are confronted in this modern age with a form of society which is evolving on entirely new social and political lines. Since all peoples have either attained political independence or are on the way to attaining it, soon no nation will rule over another and none will be subject to an alien power.

Thus all over the world men are either the citizens of an independent State, or are shortly to become so; nor is any nation nowadays content to submit to foreign domination. The long-standing inferiority complex of certain classes because of their economic and social status, sex, or position in the State, and the corresponding superiority complex of other classes, is rapidly becoming a thing of the past.

Today, on the contrary, the conviction is widespread that all men are equal in natural dignity; and so, on the doctrinal and theoretical level, at least, no form of approval is being given to racial discrimination. All this is of supreme significance for the formation of a human society animated by the principles We have mentioned above, for man's awareness of his rights must inevitably lead him to the recognition of his duties. The possession of rights involves the duty of implementing those rights, for they are the expression of a man's personal dignity. And the possession of rights also involves their recognition and respect by other people.

When society is formed on a basis of rights and duties, men have an immediate grasp of spiritual and intellectual values, and have no difficulty in understanding what is meant by truth, justice, charity and freedom. They become, moreover, conscious of being members of such a society. And that is not all. Inspired by such principles, they attain to a better knowledge of the true God—a personal God transcending human nature. They recognize that their relationship with God forms the very foundation of their life—the interior life of the spirit, and the life which they live in the society of their fellows.

✧ ✧ ✧ ✧

Here once more We exhort Our sons to take an active part in public life, and to work together for the benefit of the whole human race, as well as for their own political communities. It is vitally necessary for them to endeavor, in the light of Christian faith and with love as their guide, to ensure that every institution, whether economic, social, cultural or political, be such as not to obstruct but rather to facilitate man's self-betterment, both in the natural and in the supernatural order.

And yet, if they are to imbue civilization with right ideals and Christian principles, it is not enough for Our sons to be illumined by the heavenly light of faith and to be fired with enthusiasm for a cause; they must involve themselves in the work of these institutions, and strive to influence them effectively from within.

But in a culture and civilization like our own, which is so remarkable for its scientific knowledge and its technical discoveries, clearly no one can insinuate himself into public life unless he be scientifically competent, technically capable, and skilled in the practice of his own profession.

And yet even this must be reckoned insufficient to bring the relationships of daily life into conformity with a more human standard, based, as it must be, on truth, tempered by justice, motivated by mutual love, and holding fast to the practice of freedom.

If these policies are really to become operative, men must first of all take the utmost care to conduct their various temporal activities in accordance with the laws which govern each and every such activity, observing the principles which correspond to their respective natures. Secondly, men's actions must be made to conform with the precepts of the moral order. This means that their behavior must be such as to reflect their consciousness of exercising a personal right or performing a personal duty. Reason has a further demand to make. In obedience to the providential designs and commands of God respecting our salvation and not neglecting the dictates of conscience, men must conduct themselves in their temporal activity in such a way as to effect a thorough integration of the principal spiritual values with those of science, technology and the professions.

In traditionally Christian States at the present time, civil institutions evince a high degree of scientific and technical progress and possess abundant machinery for the attainment of every kind of objective. And yet it must be owned that these institutions are often but slightly affected by Christian motives and a Christian spirit.

One may well ask the reason for this, since the men who have largely contributed—and who are still contributing—to the creation of these institutions are men who are professed Christians, and who live their lives, at least in part, in accordance with the precepts of the gospels. In Our opinion the explanation lies in a certain cleavage between faith and practice. Their inner, spiritual unity must be restored, so that faith may be the light and love the motivating force of all their actions.

We consider too that a further reason for this very frequent divorce between faith and practice in Christians is an inadequate education in Christian teaching and Christian morality. In many places the amount of energy devoted to the study of secular subjects is all too often out of proportion to that devoted to the study of religion. Scientific training reaches a very high level, whereas religious training generally does not advance beyond the elementary stage. It is essential, therefore, that the instruction given to our young people be complete and continuous, and imparted in such a way that moral goodness and the cultivation of religious values may keep pace with scientific knowledge and continually advancing technical progress. Young people must also be taught how to carry out their own particular obligations in a truly fitting manner.

In this connection We think it opportune to point out how difficult it is to understand clearly the relation between the objective requirements of justice and concrete situations; to define, that is, correctly to what degree and in what form doctrinal principles and directives must be applied in the given state of human society.

The definition of these degrees and forms is all the more difficult in an age such as ours, driven forward by a fever of activity. And yet this is the age in which each one of us is required to make his own contribution to the universal common good. Daily is borne in on us the need to make the reality of social life conform better to the requirements of justice. Hence Our sons have every reason for not thinking that they can relax their efforts and be satisfied with what they have already achieved.

What has so far been achieved is insufficient compared with what needs to be done; all men must realize that. Every day provides a more important, a more fitting enterprise to which they must turn their hands—industry, trade unions, professional organizations, insurance, cultural institutions, the law, politics, medical and recreational facilities, and other such activities. The age in which we live needs all these things. It is an age in which men, having discovered the atom and achieved the breakthrough into outer space, are now exploring other avenues, leading to almost limitless horizons.

The principles We have set out in this document take their rise from the very nature of things. They derive, for the most part, from the consideration of man's natural rights. Thus the putting of these principles into effect frequently involves extensive co-operation between Catholics and those Christians who are separated from the Apostolic See. It even involves the cooperation of Catholics with men who may not be Christians but who nevertheless are reasonable men, and men of natural moral integrity. "In such circumstances they must, of course, bear themselves as Catholics, and do nothing to compromise religion and morality. Yet at the same time they should show themselves animated by a spirit of understanding and unselfishness, ready to co-operate loyally in achieving objects which are good in themselves, or conducive to good."

It is always perfectly justifiable to distinguish between error as such and the person who falls into error—even in the case of men who err regarding the truth or are led astray as a result of their inadequate knowledge, in matters either of religion or of the highest ethical standards. A man who has fallen into error does not cease to be a man. He never forfeits his personal dignity; and that is something that must always be taken into account. Besides, there exists in man's very nature an undying capacity to break through the barriers of error and seek the road to truth. God, in His great providence, is ever present with His aid. Today, maybe, a man lacks faith and turns aside into error; tomorrow, perhaps, illumined by God's light, he may indeed embrace the truth.

Catholics who, in order to achieve some external good, collaborate with unbelievers or with those who through error lack the fullness of faith in Christ, may possibly provide the occasion or even the incentive for their conversion to the truth.

Again it is perfectly legitimate to make a clear distinction between a false philosophy of the nature, origin and purpose of men and the world, and economic, social, cultural, and political undertakings, even when such undertakings draw their origin and inspiration from that philosophy. True, the philosophic formula does not change once it has been set down in precise terms, but the undertakings clearly cannot avoid being influenced to a certain extent by the changing conditions in which they have to operate. Besides, who can deny the possible existence of good and commendable elements in these undertakings, elements which do indeed conform to the dictates of right reason, and are an expression of man's lawful aspirations?

It may sometimes happen, therefore, that meetings arranged for some practical end—though hitherto they were thought to be altogether useless—may in fact be fruitful at the present time, or at least offer prospects of success.

But whether or not the moment for such co-operation has arrived, and the manner and degree of such co-operation in the attainment of economic, social, cultural and political advantages —these are matters for prudence to decide; prudence, the queen of all the virtues which rule the lives of men both as individuals and in society.

As far as Catholics are concerned, the decision rests primarily with those who take a leading part in the life of the community, and in these specific fields. They must, however, act in accordance with the principles of the natural law, and observe the Church's social teaching and the directives of ecclesiastical authority. For it must not be forgotten that the Church has the right and duty not only to safeguard her teaching on faith and morals, but also to exercise her authority over her sons by intervening in their external affairs whenever a judgment has to be made concerning the practical application of this teaching.

There are indeed some people who, in their generosity of spirit, burn with a desire to institute wholesale reforms whenever they come across situations which show scant regard for justice or are wholly out of keeping with its claims. They tackle the problem with such impetuosity that one would think they were embarking on some political revolution.

We would remind such people that it is the law of nature that all things must be of gradual growth. If there is to be any improvement in human institutions, the work must be done slowly and deliberately from within. Pope Pius XII expressed it in these terms: "Salvation and justice consist not in the uprooting of an outdated system, but in a well designed policy of development. Hotheadedness was never constructive; it has always destroyed everything. It has inflamed passions, but never assuaged them. It sows no seeds but those of hatred and destruction. Far from bringing about the reconciliation of contending parties, it reduces men and political parties to the necessity of laboriously redoing the work of the past, building on the ruins that disharmony has left in its wake."

Hence among the very serious obligations incumbent upon men of high principles, We must include the task of establishing new relationships in human society, under the mastery and guidance of truth, justice, charity and freedom—relations between individual citizens, between citizens and their respective States, between States, and finally between individuals, families, intermediate associations and States on the one hand, and the world community on the other. There is surely no one who will not consider this a most exalted task, for it is one which is able to bring about true peace in accordance with divinely established order.

Considering the need, the men who are shouldering this responsibility are far too few in number, yet they are deserving of the highest recognition from society, and We rightfully honor them with Our public praise. We call upon them to persevere in their ideals, which are of such tremendous benefit to mankind. At the same time We are encouraged to hope that many more men, Christians especially, will join their cause, spurred on by love and the realization of their duty. Everyone who has joined the ranks of Christ must be a glowing point of light in the world, a nucleus of love, a leaven of the whole mass. He will be so in proportion to his degree of spiritual union with God.

The world will never be the dwelling-place of peace, till peace has found a home in the heart of each and every man, till every man preserves in himself the order ordained by God to be preserved. That is why St. Augustine asks the question: "Does your mind desire the strength to gain the mastery over your passions? Let it submit to a greater power, and it will conquer all beneath it. And peace will be in you—true, sure, most ordered peace. What is that order? God as ruler of the mind; the mind as ruler of the body. Nothing could be more orderly."

Our concern here has been with problems which are causing men extreme anxiety at the present time; problems which are intimately bound up with the progress of human society. Unquestionably, the teaching We have given has been inspired by a longing which We feel most keenly, and which We know is shared by all men of good will: that peace may be assured on earth.

We who, in spite of Our inadequacy, are nevertheless the vicar of Him whom the prophet announced as the *Prince of Peace,* conceive of it as Our duty to devote all Our thoughts and care and energy to further this common good of all mankind. Yet peace is but an empty word, if it does not rest upon that order which Our hope prevailed upon Us to set forth in outline in this encyclical. It is an order that is founded on truth, built up on justice, nurtured and animated by charity, and brought into effect under the auspices of freedom.

So magnificent, so exalted is this aim that human resources alone, even though inspired by the most praiseworthy good will, cannot hope to achieve it. God Himself must come to man's aid with His heavenly assistance, if human society is to bear the closest possible resemblance to the Kingdom of God.

✧ ✧ ✧ ✧

Let us, then, pray with all fervor for this peace which our divine Redeemer came to bring us. May He banish from the souls of men whatever might endanger peace. May He transform all men into witnesses of truth, justice and brotherly love. May He illumine with His light the minds of rulers, so that, besides caring for the proper material welfare of their peoples, they may also guarantee them the fairest gift of Peace.

Finally, may Christ inflame the desires of all men to break through the barriers which divide them, to strengthen the bonds of mutual love, to learn to understand one another, and to pardon those who have done them wrong. Through His power and inspiration may all peoples welcome each other to their hearts as brothers, and may the peace they long for ever flower and ever reign among them.

NOTES

1 Salo Wittmayer Baron, *A Social and Religious History of the Jews* (Philadelphia: Jewish Publication Society of America, 1952), Vol. I, p. 10.

2 *Ibid.*

3 Rudolf Bultmann, *Theology of the New Testament* (New York: Charles Scribner's Sons, 1951), Vol. I, p. 21.

4 *First Apology*, 28.

5 *Epistle of Barnabas* XXI.

6 *The Instructor*, Book II, Ante-Nicene Christian Library, Vol. IV, pp. 194–95.

7 *Ibid.*, Book III, Vol. IV, p. 317.

8 *Ibid.*, p. 328.

9 John Locke, *An Essay Concerning Human Understanding*, Book IV, Chap. 17, No. 23.

10 William K. Frankena in Jonathan Edwards, *The Nature of True Virtue* (Ann Arbor, Mich.: Ann Arbor Paperbacks, 1960), p. viii.

11 The incident referred to by Bushnell was what the historians have dubbed "Dorr's Rebellion." Occurring in 1843, it was an attempt to extend the franchise to all males of the proper age, and in Rhode Island got out of hand to the extent that troops were needed to suppress it. Thomas Wilson Dorr was sentenced to life imprisonment for his part in the rebellion but was pardoned after a year.

12 *The Encyclicals and Other Messages of John XXIII*, edited by the staff of *The Pope Speaks Magazine* (Washington: TPS Press, 1964), p. 29.

13 *Ibid.*, p. 372.

BIBLIOGRAPHY OF ORIGINAL SOURCES CHRISTIAN SOCIAL TEACHINGS

III EARLY CHRISTIAN FATHERS

SELECTION 1 *The Epistle of Barnabas, XVIII–XXI.*
The Apostolic Fathers. Translated by Kirsopp Lake. London: W. Heinemann, 1913–14. Loeb Classical Library, Vol. I, pp. 401, 403, 405, 407, 409.

SELECTION 2 *The First Apology of Justin Martyr.*
Early Christian Fathers. Edited by Cyril C. Richardson. Philadelphia: Westminster Press, 1953. Library of Christian Classics, Vol. I, pp. 249–253, 259–260.

SELECTION 3 *Irenaeus Against Heresies, Chap. XXIV.*
The Ante-Nicene Fathers. American Edition, edited by A. Cleveland Coxe. Grand Rapids, Mich.: Wm. B. Eerdmans, 1950. Vol. I, pp. 552–553.

IV TERTULLIAN

SELECTION 1 *The Apology, Chaps. 39–45.*
Ante-Nicene Christian Library. Edinburgh Edition, edited by Alexander Roberts and James Donaldson. Edinburgh: T. & T. Clark, 1895. Vol. XI (*Writings of Tertullian,* Vol. I), pp. 118–128.

SELECTION 2 *On Pagan Shows, Chaps. 24–30.*
Ibid., pp. 30–35.

V ALEXANDRIAN SCHOOL

SELECTION 1 *Clement: The Instructor, Book I, Chap. XIII.*
Ante-Nicene Christian Lib. (Edinburgh Ed.) Edinburgh: T. & T. Clark, 1884. Vol. IV (*Writings of Clement,* Vol. I), pp. 184–185.

SELECTION 2 *Clement: The Rich Man's Salvation.*
Clement of Alexandria. Translated by G. W. Butterworth. London: W. Heinemann, 1913–14. Loeb Classical Library, pp. 271, 275, 281, 283, 291, 293, 295, 297, 299.

SELECTION 3 *Origen: Against Celsus, Book VIII.*
Ante-Nicene Christian Lib. (Edinburgh Ed.) Edinburgh: T. & T. Clark, 1894. Vol. XXIII (*Writings of Origen,* Vol. II), pp. 556–558.

VI CHRYSOSTOM

SELECTION 1 *Concerning the Statutes, Homily XII, 9 ff.*
Nicene and Post-Nicene Fathers. Edited by Philip Schaff. New York: Charles Scribner's Sons, 1889. Vol. IX, pp. 421–424.

SELECTION 2 *Homilies on Matthew, XIX.*
Ibid., Vol. X, pp. 134–135.

SELECTION 3 *Eutropius and the Vanity of Riches.*
Ibid., Vol. IX, pp. 249–265.

VII AUGUSTINE

SELECTION 1 *Enchiridion, Chaps. 9–11.*
Ibid., Vol. III, pp. 239–240.

SELECTION 2 *Enchiridion.*
Ibid., pp. 245–246.

SELECTION 3 *City of God, V, 13 & 15.*
Ibid., Vol. II, pp. 96–97.

SELECTION 4 *City of God, XIV, 28; XIX, 17.*
Ibid., pp. 282–283, 412–413.

SELECTION 5 *Of the Morals of the Catholic Church, Chaps. XV, XXIV, XXVI, XXVII.*
Ibid., Vol. IV, pp. 48, 54–56.

SELECTION 6 *City of God, XIX, 12; Letter (to Donatus) CLXXIII* (A.D. 416); *Letter (to Count Boniface) CLXXXIX* (A.D. 418).
N and PNF (Schaff) Vol. II, pp. 407–409; Vol. I, pp. 544–547; Vol. I, p. 554.

VIII MONASTICISM

SELECTION 1 *The Sayings of the Fathers.*

Western Asceticism. Edited by Owen Chadwick. Philadelphia: Westminster Press, 1958. Library of Christian Classics, Vol. XII, pp. 181–187. (Part XVII—#'s 1, 2, 7, 12, 14, 18, 19, 22, 23.)

SELECTION 2 *The Rule of Saint Benedict.*

Ibid., pp. 291–337.

SELECTION 3 *The Rule of St. Francis.*

Documents of the Christian Church. Edited by Henry Bettenson. London: Oxford Univ. Press, 1963. pp. 179–184.

IX MYSTICISM

SELECTION 1 *Bernard of Clairvaux: A Letter to Louis, King of France (1142).*

The Works of St. Bernard. Edited by S. J. Eales. London: Burns & Oates Ltd., c. 1890. Vol. II, pp. 635–638.

SELECTION 2 *Bernard: A Letter to Pope Eugenius (1146).*

Ibid., pp. 750–752.

SELECTION 3 *Bernard: A Letter to Henry, Archbishop of Mainz (1146).*

Ibid., pp. 913–915.

SELECTION 4 *Bernard: On Consideration.*

Bernard of Clairvaux. *On Consideration.* Translated by George Lewis. Oxford: Clarendon Press, 1908. pp. 82–91.

SELECTION 5 *Meister Eckhart: The Talks of Instruction.*

Meister Eckhart. Translated by Raymond B. Blakney. New York: Harper Torchbook, 1957. pp. 4, 6–7, 10–11, 25–26.

SELECTION 6 *Meister Eckhart: The Sermons.*

Ibid., pp. 109–117.

X THOMAS AQUINAS

SELECTION 1 *Summa Theologica II/1 Question 90, Articles 1–2.*

Thomas Aquinas. *Summa Theologica,* edited by Fathers of

the English Dominican Province. London: R & T Washbourne, Ltd., 1915. Vol. 8, pp. 1–5.

SELECTION 2 *Summa Theologica II/1 Question 91, Articles 1–4.*
Ibid., Vol. 8, pp. 9–16.

SELECTION 3 *Summa Theologica II/2 Question 58, Articles 1, 11–12.*
Ibid., Vol. 10, pp. 113–116, 132–135.

SELECTION 4 *Summa Theologica II/2 Question 60, Articles 5–6.*
Ibid., Vol. 10, pp. 152–156.

SELECTION 5 *Summa Theologica II/2 Question 64, Articles 2–3.*
Ibid., Vol. 10, pp. 197–201.

SELECTION 6 *Summa Theologica II/2 Question 66, Articles 1–2.*
Ibid., Vol. 10, pp. 221–225.

SELECTION 7 *Summa Theologica II/2 Question 78, Article 1.*
Ibid., Vol. 10, pp. 329–333.

SELECTION 8 *Summa Theologica II/2 Question 40, Article 1.*
Ibid., Vol. 9, pp. 500–503.

SELECTION 9 *Summa Theologica II/2 Question 182, Articles 1–2.*
Ibid., Vol. 14, pp. 134–140.

XI THE MEDIEVAL PAPACY

SELECTION 1 *Sentence of Excommunication Against Henry IV, Feb. 22, 1076.*
Church and State Through the Centuries, edited by Sidney Z. Ehler and John B. Morrall. London: Burns & Oates, 1954. pp. 39–40.

SELECTION 2 *Boniface VIII: Unam Sanctam, Nov. 18, 1302.*
Ibid., pp. 90–92.

XII MARTIN LUTHER

SELECTION 1 *The Ninety-Five Theses.*
Works of Martin Luther. Philadelphia: A. J. Holman Co., 1915. Vol. I, pp. 29–38.

SELECTION 2 *Open Letter to the Christian Nobility.*
Ibid., Vol. II, pp. 158–163.
SELECTION 3 *An Open Letter Concerning the Hard Book Against the Peasants.*
Ibid., Vol. IV, pp. 265–270.
SELECTION 4 *Letter to Count Albert of Mansfeld, Dec. 28, 1541.*
Luther: Letters of Spiritual Counsel. Edited by Theodore Tappert. Philadelphia: Westminster Press, 1955. Library of Christian Classics, Vol. XVIII, pp. 337–339.
SELECTION 5 *Sermon at Marriage of Sigismund von Lindenau, 1545.*
Luther's Works. American Edition. Philadelphia: Muhlenberg Press, 1959. Vol. 51, pp. 357–367.

XIII JOHN CALVIN

SELECTION 1 *Institutes, Book II, Chap. II, #1.*
John Calvin. *Institutes of the Christian Religion,* translated by Henry Beveridge. Grand Rapids, Mich.: Wm. B. Eerdmans, 1957. Vol. I, pp. 222–223.
SELECTION 2 *Institutes, Book II, Chap. II, #13.*
Ibid., Vol. I, pp. 234–235.
SELECTION 3 *Institutes, Book II, Chap. VIII, #39, 41, 45–46.*
Ibid., Vol. I, pp. 346–348, 350–352.
SELECTION 4 *Institutes, Book III, Chap. XXI, #7.*
Ibid., Vol. II, pp. 210–211.
SELECTION 5 *Institutes, Book IV, Chap. XX, #1–3, 8, 24, 31–32.*
Ibid., Vol. II, pp. 651–653, 656–657, 670, 674–675.

XIV THE ANABAPTISTS

SELECTION 1 *The Schleitheim Confession of Faith.*
"The Schleitheim Confession of Faith," translated by Dr. John C. Wenger. *The Mennonite Quarterly Review,* Vol. XIX, No. 4, October 1945. pp. 249–252.
SELECTION 2 *Thomas Münzer: Sermon Before the Princes.*
Spiritual and Anabaptist Writers, edited by George Williams

and Angel Mergal. Philadelphia: Westminster Press, 1957. Library of Christian Classics, Vol. XXV, pp. 64–70.

SELECTION 3 *Menno Simons: On the Ban: Questions and Answers.*

Ibid., pp. 263–271.

XV IGNATIUS LOYOLA AND THE JESUITS

SELECTION 1 *Loyola: Institutum Societatis Jesu, I, 407 ff.*

Bettenson, *Documents of the Christian Church*, p. 367.

SELECTION 2 *Francisco Suárez: A Treatise on Laws and God the Lawgiver, Chap. II.*

Selections from Three Works of Francisco Suárez, S.J. Prepared by Gwladys L. Williams, Ammi Brown and John Waldron. Oxford: Clarendon Press, 1944. pp. 372–375.

SELECTION 3 *Suárez: A Work on the Three Theological Virtues: Faith, Hope and Charity; Disputation XIII: On Charity.*

Ibid., pp. 800–805.

XVI PURITANISM

SELECTION 1 *Milton: Areopagitica (1644).*

Works of John Milton, edited by Frank A. Patterson, *et al.* New York: Columbia Univ. Press, 1931. Vol. IV, pp. 347–352.

SELECTION 2 *Levellers: First Agreement of the People.*

A. S. P. Woodhouse, *Puritanism and Liberty*. Chicago: Univ. of Chicago Press, 1951. pp. 443–445.

SELECTION 3 *Winstanley: The Law of Freedom in a Platform* or *True Magistracy Restored.*

George H. Sabine, ed., *The Works of Gerrard Winstanley.* Ithaca, N. Y.: Cornell Univ. Press, 1941. pp. 591–597.

SELECTION 4 *Baxter: A Holy Commonwealth.*

Richard Schlatter, *Richard Baxter and Puritan Politics*. New Brunswick, N. J.: Rutgers Univ. Press, 1957. pp. 69–75.

SELECTION 5 *Cotton Mather: Miscellaneous Proposals to Gentlemen.*

Cotton Mather, *Essays to Do Good*. Johnstown, Asa Child, 1815. pp. 134–140.

XVII THE QUAKERS

SELECTION 1 *The Rules of Discipline: Advices.*
Rules of Discipline of the Religious Society of Friends. London: Darton and Harvey, 1834. pp. 1–2.
SELECTION 2 *Rules of Discipline: War.*
Ibid., pp. 287–289.
SELECTION 3 *Rules of Discipline: Slave-Trade and Slavery.*
Ibid., pp. 244–246.

XVIII RATIONALISM

SELECTION 1 *John Locke: The Reasonableness of Christianity.*
Works of John Locke. London: W. Otridge & Son, *et al.*, 1812. Vol. VII, pp. 138–147.
SELECTION 2 *Joseph Butler: Upon the Love of Our Neighbor.*
Joseph Butler, *Works*. Oxford: Univ. Press, 1850. Vol. II (*Sermons*), pp. 160–165.
SELECTION 3 *Lessing: The Tale of the Three Rings.*
Gotthold Ephraim Lessing, *Nathan the Wise*, translated by Ernest Bell. Philadelphia: David McKay, 1901. pp. 92–97.
SELECTION 4 *Paine: The Age of Reason.*
Thomas Paine, *The Age of Reason*. Boston: Josiah Mendum, 1852. pp. 71–72.

XIX PIETISM

SELECTION 1 *Pia Desideria* by Philip Jacob Spener, translated by T. G. Tappert. Philadelphia: Fortress Press, 1964. pp. 87–97.
SELECTION 2 *Das Zeitalter des Pietismus* (translated for this collection by George W. Forell). Bremen: Schünemann, 1965. pp. 82–89.
SELECTION 3 *Nine Publick Discourses* by Nicolaus Ludwig Count Zinzendorf. London: James Hutton, 1748. pp. 122–125; and from *Maxims, Theological Ideas and Sen-*

tences out of the Present Ordinary of the Brethren's Churches, extracted by J. Gambold, M.A. London: J. Beecroft, 1751. pp. 309–311.

XX JOHN WESLEY

SELECTION 1 *The Use of Money.*
The Works of John Wesley, edited by John Emory. New York and Cincinnati: The Methodist Book Concern, c. 1895. Vol. I, pp. 440–448.
SELECTION 2 *Thoughts on Slavery.*
Ibid., Vol. VI, pp. 286–288, 290–293.
SELECTION 3 *Thoughts on the Present Scarcity of Provisions.*
Ibid., pp. 274–278.

XXI JONATHAN EDWARDS

SELECTION 1 *Pressing into the Kingdom.*
The Works of President Edwards. New York: G & C & H Carvill, 1830. Vol. V, pp. 461–471.
SELECTION 2 *An Exhortation to Charity.*
The Works of President Edwards, 1809 Edition. Vol. V, pp. 433–437.

XXII ROMANTICISM

SELECTION 1 *Herder: God, Some Conversations.*
Johann Gottfried Herder, *God, Some Conversations,* edited by Frederick H. Burkhardt. New York: Veritas Press, 1940. pp. 169, 171, 190–191.
SELECTION 2 *Schleiermacher: On Religion—Speeches to Its Cultured Despisers.*
Friedrich Schleiermacher, *On Religion—Speeches to Its Cultured Despisers,* translated by John Oman. New York: Harper Torchbook, 1958. pp. 164–176.
SELECTION 3 *Chateaubriand: The Genius of Christianity.*
François August René de Chateaubriand, *The Genius of Christianity,* translated by Charles I. White. Baltimore: John Murphy & Co., 1870. pp. 664–668.

XXIII THE AMERICAN DEVELOPMENT IN THE NINETEENTH CENTURY

SELECTION 1 *Bushnell: Politics Under the Law of God.*
Horace Bushnell, *Politics Under the Law of God.* Hartford, Conn.: Edwin Hunt, 1844. pp. 10–19.

SELECTION 2 *Alexis de Tocqueville: American Institutions and Their Influence.*
Alexis de Tocqueville, *American Institutions and Their Influence.* New York: A. S. Barnes and Co., 1873. pp. 312–316.

SELECTION 3 *Abraham Lincoln: Second Inaugural Address, March 4, 1865.*
Complete Works of Abraham Lincoln, edited by John Nicolay and John Hay. New York: Francis D. Tandy Co., 1905. Vol. XI, pp. 44–47.

SELECTION 4 *Lawrence: The Relation of Wealth to Morals.*
William Lawrence, "The Relation of Wealth to Morals," *The World's Work,* Vol. I, no. 3 (January 1901), pp. 286–292.

XXIV THE SOCIAL ENCYCLICALS

SELECTION 1 *Leo XIII: Diuturnum, June 29, 1881.*
The Church Speaks to the Modern World—The Social Teachings of Leo XIII, edited by Etienne Gilson. Garden City, N. Y.: Doubleday Image Book, 1954. #1, pp. 141–142, #3, p. 142, #11, p. 145.

SELECTION 2 *Leo XIII: Immortale Dei, November 1, 1885.*
Gilson, #13, p. 167, #43, 44, 45, pp. 180–182.

SELECTION 3 *Leo XIII: Rerum Novarum, May 15, 1891.*
Gilson, #1, pp. 205–206, #22–24, pp. 217–219, #36–37, pp. 224–226, #43–46, pp. 229–230.

SELECTION 4 *Pius XI: Mit brennender Sorge, March 14, 1937.*
The Papal Encyclicals in Their Historical Context, edited by Anne Fremantle. New York: Mentor Books, 1956. pp. 250–252.

SELECTION 5 *Pius XI: Divini Redemptoris, March 28, 1937.*
Fremantle, pp. 255–260.

SELECTION 6 *Pius XII: Summi Pontificatus, October 20, 1939.*
Fremantle, pp. 263–269.

XXV THE SOCIAL GOSPEL

SELECTION 1 *Washington Gladden: Social Salvation.*
Washington Gladden, *Social Salvation.* Boston and New York: Houghton, Mifflin and Co., 1902. pp. 26–31.

SELECTION 2 *Peabody: The Approach to the Social Question.*
Francis Greenwood Peabody, *The Approach to the Social Question.* New York: The Macmillan Co., 1909. pp. 190–197.

SELECTION 3 *Rauschenbusch: A Theology for the Social Gospel.*
Walter Rauschenbusch, *A Theology for the Social Gospel.* New York: The Macmillan Co., 1917. pp. 131–145.

XXVI REINHOLD NIEBUHR

SELECTION 1 *An Interpretation of Christian Ethics.*
Reinhold Niebuhr, *An Interpretation of Christian Ethics.* New York and London: Harper & Brothers, 1935. pp. 103–117.

SELECTION 2 *Justice and Love.*
Love and Justice, Selections from the Shorter Writings of Reinhold Niebuhr, edited by D. B. Robertson. Philadelphia: Westminster Press, n.d., pp. 27–29.

SELECTION 3 *Christian Faith and Natural Law.*
Ibid., pp. 46–54.

SELECTION 4 *The Hydrogen Bomb.*
Ibid., pp. 235–237.

XXVII PAUL TILLICH

SELECTION 1 *Love, Power and Justice.*
Paul Tillich, *Love, Power and Justice.* London: Oxford Univ. Press, 1954. pp. 91–106, 122–124.

XXVIII KARL BARTH

SELECTION 1 *The Christian Community and the Civil Community.*

Community, State and Church—Three Essays by Karl Barth. Garden City, N. Y.: Doubleday Anchor Book, 1960. pp. 149–152, 157–158, 161–165, 168–178.

XXIX DIETRICH BONHOEFFER

SELECTION 1 *Ethics.*

Dietrich Bonhoeffer, *Ethics,* edited by Eberhard Bethge. New York: The Macmillan Co., 1955. pp. 254–267, 292–296.

SELECTION 2 *Letters: June 8, 1944 and July 16, 1944.*

Dietrich Bonhoeffer, *Letters and Papers from Prison,* edited by Eberhard Bethge. London: SCM Press Ltd., 1953. pp. 145–149, 162–164.

XXX POPE JOHN XXIII

SELECTION 1 *Mater et Magistra.*

The Encyclicals and Other Messages of John XXIII, edited by *The Pope Speaks Magazine.* Washington: TPS Press, 1964. pp. 281–295.

SELECTION 2 *Pacem in Terris.*

Ibid., pp. 327–338, 365–372.

Professor of Protestant theology at the University of Iowa and Director of the School of Religion, George W. Forell was born in Breslau, Germany. He received his B.D. from the Lutheran Theological Seminary at Philadelphia, his Th.M. from Princeton Theological Seminary, and his Th.D. from Union Theological Seminary, New York. He joined the University of Iowa faculty in 1954 and became associate professor in 1955. In 1957–58 he served as a visiting professor of theology on a Fulbright Scholarship at the University of Hamburg, Germany, and on his return to the United States, became professor of systematic theology at the Lutheran School of Theology, Maywood, Illinois. He returned to the University of Iowa in 1961.

Dr. Forell is the author of numerous books and has contributed to many periodicals, including *The Christian Century, Church History,* and *The Lutheran.*

By the Same Author

THE REALITY OF THE CHURCH
AS THE COMMUNION OF SAINTS

FAITH ACTIVE IN LOVE

ETHICS OF DECISION

THE PROTESTANT FAITH

LUTHER AND CULTURE (CO-AUTHOR)

THE CHRISTIAN YEAR

UNDERSTANDING THE NICENE CREED

THE AUGSBURG CONFESSION:
A CONTEMPORARY COMMENTARY